THE ENIGMA OF
SELF-DETERMINATION

Published by:

Trevor Mercury

Printed in the United Kingdom.

First Printing, 2017

ISBN: 978-1-9998887-0-1

DEDICATION

This book is dedicated to all the people whose life has been and continues to be negatively affected by decisions made by a small group of the elites in government. I feel your pain, frustration, anger of being powerless and manipulated into various actions by decisions made by other people, and the uncertainty of life when your life is affected by other people you are not connected to in any way.

This book is also dedicated to the small group of people in any political party who are 'voted' into power who believes they have the right to make decisions that affect other peoples' life. I hope the discussions in this book will offer insights in governing for the majority of the people in the country and not for the minority of wealthy people to whom you are continually having relations with. I dedicate this book especially for you; to enlighten your hearts and soul and bring to life your consciousness and hopefully make you make a change for the better.

Some of the aspects of the books will be uncomfortable for all to read, but the arguments offer a logical view of governing for the big picture for a better quality of life, and not just for the financial economy that only a few privileged people come to enjoy.

ACKNOWLEDGEMENTS

It has been a difficult path trying to find time to research and publish this book and has involved a great deal of sacrifice and substantial patience from my friends and family. This book is to my two sons who I lost touch with due to family breakdown and I do hope that at some point in time they have the opportunity to read it in order to understand why they grew-up without their biological father and why life is such a struggle. Without the life experience caused by this unfortunate event and my feelings of loss and frustration this book would not have been possible.

Most of all I wish to acknowledge the entire human race in the hope we all can use the discussion within it to become less lost and more closer / friendlier to each other. Without the people I have come into contact with over the years, I do not think any of this book could have been written.

For those, which the book does not shed a shining light on or for those whose conscious receives a wake-up call after reading it; thank-you for making it possible. It has been a privilege but hard work producing it, I hope it has all been worth it as I hope many people read it and become inspired to make a difference not only in their lives but in others too.

CONTENTS

FOREWORD

Here are some of the comments made by people whom have read the book before the official publication date.

"The least PC book to be published in years"

"Controversial and Entertaining"

"A 'slap-in-the-face' for government and society"

"The book highlights what a mess the human world is in right now. The author is right, education is the problem"

"Finally, someone with the courage to tell the truth about societal woes"

"This book gives the far-left and far-right a beat-down, not to mention removes the premise of a middle ground in politics"

"This is a must read book for anyone wishing to know the truth about government and ourselves"

"It just discloses real world problems unblemished and actually gives some palatable solution to solve them"

"Sorry 'smooth talkers' you have just been found out and kicked to the curb – enlightening stuff."

PREFACE

With encountering other people's experiences it is clear people in this country want it to be a great place to live. Furthermore, there are many hopes and dreams along with frustrations of not being able to achieve them for reasons that are seemingly beyond their own control. Throughout my short life it is obvious that the majority of people who live and work hard as they possibly can are still struggling to not only stay afloat with the cost of living but also to pay the bills necessary to keep a roof over their heads with a low quality of life; there are of-course some exceptions to this reality. This problem is now exasperated with the new generation of young people, all of whom have aspiration in life and ambitions in work, but have great anxieties about the future (if people are honest with ourselves who can blame them!) and who are confused about who they are The support services people are all taught throughout our childhoods (e.g. health service, child services, law systems, military, etc.) are slowly degrading to be 'play things' of private companies and wealthy elites who are intent on making a profit at the expense to working family's wellbeing.

This book describes my view on how to assist governing life in the country (for self-determination) to facilitate turning the country around to become a country for the majority and not for the wealthy minority; and can be directly applicable to world governance based on logic, intelligence and peace. The fundamental truth is this all begins with strong communities, where decisions are shared by local people in a 'real' democratic way. It means a country where everyone plays by the same rules; where reasons of religion, race, gender, wealth, nationality and stature does not give an advantage or otherwise in decision making.

The governing party should not be concerning themselves with 'power'; the government should be merely administrators to the will of the people. Where the government responds to the concerns of the people and uses facts, figures and analysis of potential solutions to gain support for tough decisions and not using scare strategies or fear tactics to make people 'invest' into the decisions the government want to make. Moreover, the political system should be equal, fair and unbiased, not 'rigged' as it is now to work for the needs of a few and ignoring the concerns of the many. For too long now people in communities have concentrated their efforts on issues surrounding inconvenience rather than real palatable issues that need to be solved. Furthermore, these small issues are easily solved and used to improve the reputation of councillors/senators or MPs, whilst the large problems continue to degrade to an extent that it expands into adjacent communities before the minimum is actioned to stifle the problem at greater expense to the tax payer.

For me this book is about giving a voice, not a selfish self-serving voice, but a voice for logic and intelligence for sustainability of life in this country for the betterment of all. Writing this book has been a privilege and I'm sure something many people have thought about doing. It is, mostly, about securing the truth not 'spin' and about living within the constraints of the resources available to once again build a country that works for the majority of people not just for the few. This book should be about conscience with a plan to achieve the goal through compromise and trust; working together to fix the problem(s) that are seemingly like a virus spreading throughout not just the West but globally.

Why I wrote the book

Inspiration for writing this book is mainly due to my life being deeply affected (it fell apart) in my early 20s when I met this girl whom I thought was a person I could settle down with and start a family. In my ignorance with relationships, I failed to get to know the real person I was involved with before she became pregnant (by accident). At that time the relationship was going well and so we decided to get married. A year after the first was born, my wife began to pressure me into having another; and this caused lots of friction in the relationship as now I was becoming aware of whom she really was. After nearly a year of 'badgering' and pressure coming from her, her friends and the mother-in-law (with her saying that there is lots of friction because she really wants a second child), we were expecting a second child. After she gave birth to our second son, it was painfully obvious from this point onwards that she has what she wanted and I was just a person who went to work, paid for everything, had zero say with the children and had to do everything that was asked, no told, from both her and her mother. Naturally the relationship did not last long as my 'head' reached breaking point and something had to change; I realised that I had to risk standing-up to both of them as a deep depression and unhappiness was indeed taking control. It was clear to me that there was nothing I could do about it, unless she was willing to give a little rather than take-take-take, the relationship had to come to an end before I was pushed too far over the edge.

I lost a wife, relationship with the children, career, house, car, savings, pretty much everything I had built-up over the years and everything I cared about; and the courts, the child support agency, social services, etc., all but helped; the mother-in-law and my ex-wife decimate everything using stories without anything to back up the claims and all the support services were interested in is getting paid and ensuring money was taken from me and given to the mother of the children. My concerns were ignored and father's rights I had to pay for; I had to save enough for court appearances where I was met with lies and deceit every single time. The last few times I proved to the court she was lying, it was to no avail, they just were not interested even though she broke court orders several times. It was hopeless, I had seen the effect it was having on the children and I was powerless to stop them being in the middle of something I could not control or understand. I had to make the ultimate sacrifice in an attempt to stop them from being used and suffering the mental stress that all three of us was going through.

The situation lasted a number of years, I had no real choice about what was actually happening, other people was making those choices for me and not one of them cared about the real human effects on the children. Do I have ill feeling as to what happened in those times? For a long period of time I became a 'loner' distrusting of everyone and stayed away from relationships all together; the fear was not about me getting hurt, it was about the innocent children that had the potential to be involved in something I could not prevent.

The decade or so after the events I spent a lot of time thinking and debating as to why it happened and what I realised is that not only am I a victim, but, so to my ex-wife (and people like her who do exactly the same thing) and any children involved are also victims of the system that was created shortly after WW2 and is consistently interfered with based on economic ideology. Many people do not understand including people who have lived an entire life and die that actual freedom of choice is directed by decisions made by government and those who work for them; including lobbyists who deface democracy; even down to local level with support services, police and schools, which are the driving forces that affect peoples' behaviour in our capitalist society that drives greed that drives the selfishness that drives the hatred. So when relationships end it becomes second nature to use children as assets or tools to hurt one parent because the other reaps the rewards. It is irrelevant as to how many absent parents commit suicide, it does not matter about choices regarding earning potential for the future and the fact that they do not pursue high earnings because it simply is not worth their while to do so, especially if the 'parent with care' has ruined any form of strong relationship with children. The sad truth is this situation is becoming worse with child support payments being extended until the child(ren) is 21 years old (in the UK) and people being transferred from different assessment criteria meaning that they will pay more for longer; plus, the whole system is still not related to the behaviour of the parent with care nor takes into consideration any other family responsibilities or changes.

From further research looking at all aspects of life to see if any other choices I was forced to make have been directed from a central area, it has become painfully clear that we now live in a world where the government can make decisions without being accountable by the people and force or manipulate the people into choices they do not want to make through being 'cornered' by legislation, incompetence, 'human drone' syndrome (where communication and debate is all but pointless), and bureaucracy. My freedom of choice, my decisions, my life experience has all been influenced and in some way primed by people I do not know nor have met in political circles This type of situation occurs globally in democracies, communisms, religions, dictatorships and authoritarian countries; it is a game – there are a few winners those who control, profit, and establish themselves as leaders; and there are many, many losers who seem to have no choice but to do as they are told, or strongly urged to do things in a certain way set forth by the winners, or through indoctrination of following without question.

One of the main reasons why I decided to write this book is the continual failing of government's prime responsibility/job which is to protect the safety, security and wellbeing of the people in the country. Right now, the nation is facing a funding crisis in the health service, care for the elderly, care for the children but government always has money available for nice to have projects, such as HS2, military projects, Trident project, smart motorways, etc.; and no one seems to taking the government to task. Instead, people set up charities and give the government a 'free-pass' to continue to divert resources away from where it should be and thus, give the impression to the oligarchs (the people behind the government) that they can continue to ignore the prime responsibility. Modern oligarchs are a group with shared self-interests in promotion of capitalism among people where no one benefits apart from those at the top of the pyramid. People in society accept this system because of indoctrination and the false hope given by allowing some working class people to make it rich. (Those with power perpetuate it. The economy, but for a small period of time will benefit those at the top of the pyramid, ultimately will fail.)

The government continues to fail, thus, has ceased to be a useful entity in society by placing concentration in making money for huge corporations besides conceding liberal beliefs and ideologies to maintain a distraction from the real problems plaguing society. The people in the country have continually permitted them to fail by allowing unaccountability to thrive, thus, have promoted the perversion of democracy by not holding the government to account and voting for 'much of the same' for decades. Governments keep giving tax breaks to large corporate businesses and the wealthiest in society, which happen to be one of the issues with lobbying, and asking self-employed people and small businesses to pay more at the same time as cutting benefits for those who are disabled or on low income, which only continues the trend of growing inequality. The question becomes not if the people will eventually rise up against the established elites because of the rapid rise of inequality, the lack of disposable income and reduced quality of life; it become a question of when. This is what the government and the established elites (oligarchs) are fully aware of and it could be one of the reasons why the decision has been made to militarise the police forces all over the West and build these large as yet empty camps throughout Europe and the US. One thing is sure; the oligarchs (corporatocracy) will not stand by and let the little guys take control. Various manipulation techniques of economic sanctions and controls, demonization and assassinations / wars will always ensure control remains with the oligarchs.

People need to have the freedom to make choices that are their own, not to be driven from other's ideologies; it is clear those who have been in power have abused their position and cause devastating effects nationally and around the world. People need to be self-driven to strive for knowledge and with it a growth in intelligence and self-leadership; and power as society currently understand it needs to be divided equally among everyone to stop corruption and abuse in leadership roles. A more fairer society and one that does not neglect those who need help the most in favour of something that will make money for the few. This is why I wrote this book in the hope the discussions will start new movements globally that will bring all human life into equilibrium with nature, wildlife and each other; a better life for all and eventually lead to people leaving / disregarding fairy tales and invisible entities in the past where they belong.

INTRODUCTION

Humans have so much potential but most, in fact the vast majority, waste it with daily distractions and living in their own little life's bubble. Some waste it because their afraid of trying or failing whilst most are not given the chance to achieve their potential due to societies structure and constraint, financial and work pressures. This book is about more than politics and its influence in the world. It is about the state of the human consciousness and how much interest and care people take in themselves, their children, not to mention national and global events. It is true government is the main 'power' which influences people's choices in life and overtime the decisions they make affect everyone in society either in a positive or negative comportment. Some of the decisions government has made decades ago are still affecting people's public, private and working lives right now. They have shaped individual's characteristics and personalities both directly through legislation, regulation or societal rules; and indirectly through indoctrination from parents, schools and other public services.

This book explores the main problems with present day politics, human interactions / control, discrimination, human will (or lack thereof) to fight for change, and how and why society continues to accept instructions from a small group of untrustworthy and poor quality people in government besides looking towards them for help in people's own lives. Moreover, it is hoped the information in the book will, and should, appeal to all levels in society and spark a keen interest to debate and find out what is really happening in our own lives and in the world. Hence, not just accept being distracted from real life problems, likewise, not just believing the context of main stream news bulletins or televised political debates.

For those who have closed-minds or become easily offended and upset by facts and the reality of real life then this book is not for you. Some discussions revolve around political and religious ideologies, which some people take offence to if debates go against their belief system. Furthermore, it is amazing how certain groups of people or individuals are outspoken about stupid little petty stuff that bothers them; things that operate inside their own life's bubble they are concerned about. Yet, be completely blind to the big issues that are really affecting how they live their lives. If I was an egomaniacal, egotistical, greedy glutinous dictator of a leader, I would say that this sort of behaviour is a Christmas present to me that is an everyday occurrence. I think this describes the current state of Western democracy, where government gives in to the little 'pointless' issues (e.g. false narratives of feminism, racism, gender, bus services, etc.) and promotes this as being liberal whilst, concurrently, laughs in the face of same people when they increase the costs of living, taxation, provides poorer public services and send people to die in wars based on a capitalist agenda. In essence, the government is giving people some of what they ask for, but, not what people truly want or require and the outcome will advance the breakdown of society.

People need to 'get a grip' of the truly important issues that affect the quality of life. Thus, this book is for thinkers, those who are struggling to succeed in their hopes and dreams and who do not want to live life inside safe-spaces but are striving to make sense of the issues in the world and want to work to change it for the better.

Most of all, for open minded driven people, enjoy the book for what it is - the start of transparency and some enlightenment in national and global events that you may not even think impacts your own.

The book discusses several areas that impact society and individual's ability for self-determination, however, the chapters are designed to give the reader designated discussions on the problems, some history of how society evolved to be, and how to potentially resolve them giving the reader a break from certain political discussions (politics is very boring subject!) to keep the reader interested in what should be an entertaining book around some dull society subjects. Chapter 1 gives a brief summary of the issues with capitalism and self-determination in modern society. Chapter 2 gives an overview of the main social problems every individual in society faces and should be read as an abstract of the whole book. Chapter 3 delves deeper into how modern history laid the foundation for an unequal system which is causing devastation to society and contributing to environmental problems.

Chapter 4 delves back into politics and how legislation and law is not equally distributed throughout the country. Chapter 5 discusses the fallacies of current Western foreign policy and how the decision made by 'leaders' impact each and every single person and what should be done to remove the obstacles. Chapter 6 touches on the main areas that could cause offence to people who have closed-minds and / or wishes to hide behind politically correct fabrications besides the realities of the world; the chapter debates crime prevention, population governance, discrimination, battle between the sexes and family planning for sustainability of a prosperous society.

Chapter 7 concentrates on the society's responsibility to provide health care for people with concentration given to what once was one of the best health care systems in the world, namely the national health service in the UK; however, the discussion are relevant to all. Chapter 8 debates the issues with the modern day education system, the paradox of academic snobbery and how it relates to central government dictating the needs of the economy and what should be done to improve standards based on common sense logic and the human drive to learn. Chapter 9 introduces the problem of a globalised economy in conjunction with the forthcoming automation with suggestions on what people should do once mathematical algorithms are capable of accomplishing most job tasks (which is sooner that people may think). Chapter 10 touches on the misconception of success and explains that it is highly related to human characteristics than financial acumen.

Chapter 11 introduces the concept of hypocrisy in the human condition and how easy it is for governments to govern based on false premises and promises. Chapter 12 concludes the book, brings all the discussion together and is intended to make the reader philosophise on their own life experience and ask why does the human world continue down a path of chaotic intent. The book closes with a statement from the author of what the intention of the book is and to bring the 'spirit of human enlightenment' to the reader to actively improve themselves and society for enhanced self-determination.

1

SELF-DETERMINATION CONSTRAINTS

Modern politics and subsequent society can be summed up by a political revolution described in a book by Frederick Hayek 'The Constitution of Liberty' that was published in 1960 and marked the transition from honest philosophy or ideology to an outright contrivance; it is more commonly known as neoliberalism. Competition among people for jobs, status and career are the defining characteristics society was and is being shaped to. The intention is to discover the natural hierarchy of winners and losers and thus categorise all 'under' one of these headings. The idea is to create the wealth that would trickle down to everyone. However, intentionally or unintentionally, this created a network of lobbyists and well-funded multimillionaires who saw the ideology as a means for defending and advancing their own interests against 'real' democracy. The problem boils down to value and opportunities that exist with stronger ties with the rich and wealthy and thus promote liberty by spending their money in new ways. But, liberty in this context depends on preventing the majority from exercising choice over the direction that the country and society might take, and instead allow the wealthy to advance society without constraint by public interest or public opinion for economic growth. Thereby, creating a society where the wealthy can experiment with new styles of living meaning progress in society rests entirely on these type of people who have been given the narrative to spend money as they wish to gain as much money as they want. Leading to

Westernised society being as good and useful as it is arising from the promotion and dominant policy of inequality.

Meritocracy, although marketing to the people as the way in which society operates, has no connection to and between merit and reward, no distinction between capability of an individual to job earnings, career prospects or status in society. Thus, has no limits in how much business owners can charge for their services, rents, products etc. - greed is good for the economy and competition means that honesty is being defeated by what is known as 'dirty politics' where the devious and dishonest succeeded. This ideology began in the Reagan and Thatcher years, where policies of massive tax cuts for the rich, the devastation of trade unions, reduction in public housing, deregulation, privatisation, along with outsourcing and competition in public services where actioned, hence, giving more power to the wealthy and less to the majority (or be it less control from government who worked for the interests of the majority). This era marked the dying of 'real' democracy for the West and to the responsibility of governments to change social outcomes for the better, so much so governments can no longer respond to the needs of the people. The rise of charities began and people allowed and continue to allow government to fail in its prime directive: to ensure the safety, security and wellbeing of people in the country.

Real politics became irrelevant to people's lives, debate reduced to a bunch of posh people's 'blah-blah' on television with little value to society. The disenfranchised turned to anti-politics where facts are replaced by slogans, sensations and symbols; and the political elite quickly jumped on the band wagon, funded by the wealthy, and society transformed into a system whereby elections are won and lost on posh slogans and symbols besides demonising and labelling other political parties.

Politics has become a murky world full of 'poshly' dressed smooth talkers who are so intertwined with rich, wealthy corporate interests, that they are so far removed from being a democratic government for the people than at any time in history. 2016, showed that the majority of the elder generation (age 40 and above) who have lived in the country and seen the standard of living, safety and security, and public infrastructure reduce in quality with higher taxation have turned on established politics and the establishment. It began with Brexit and continued with the 'Trump' effect in the US. Both showed a political revolt against elite's complacency, both results contradicted polls and placed a shock to 'politics as usual' strategy of fear and demonization tactics to win elections and referendums. Both the referendum and the election showed record turn-outs with people who had never voted before taking the time to register and place their vote. This story can be echoed throughout Europe and felt within the French and German national elections in 2017.

The stories to be told is successive Western governments have used the identical tactics to win elections for decades, but, due to their continual ignorance (or don't care attitude) towards people in their respective countries, the fear tactics are failing. It used to be enough to vilify, demonise, humorously dismiss, use scare tactics, and labels to turn people off voting for other less established political parties (it worked very well to stop the rise of the BNP in the UK), but, people seeing population increases beyond any control, increase in war efforts that has nothing to do with protecting the people of the country, the reduction in the efficiency of care services and the high cost of living, along with continual bailout of companies who are turning a profit run by the wealthiest in society; people have decided to revolt, although it might only be temporary (hope not, but you never know). It also gives me the glimmer of hope that people will eventually stand-up and be counted, rather than be continually manipulated by the established elite and that it is an end of big business and big politics controlling people's lives.

However, even with the votes going against the establishment, there are still issues. One, the establishment does not go away that easy; and two, the elites see it as a rebellious vote that is just a kink in time. It has become clear that the outcome of the Brexit vote will not be to people's liking, it will not make government close the borders; and the mainstream politicians will and is using it as an excuse for further financial pain that was coming irrespective of the vote outcome; however, it will be used as a convenient 'blame' gate for the decisions made. As for the US election, well lots of labels and demonising was actioned against Donald Trump by the Clinton campaign, by the republican party, by mass media outlets and by Western politicians all over the world before the election in an attempt to persuade voters against voting for him (racist, bigoted, misogynist, sexual predator, etc. and let us not mention his hair style or video evidence from a decade ago (talk about desperate tactics)); overall it did not achieve the outcome that was expected. This notwithstanding, it is clear that the messages rang true for young people above the voting age; a women for president rang true, for most women for that reason alone; but, for most over the age of 40 they decided for something different, for someone who is not a career politician, for someone who spoke more like them, for someone with a silly haircut. A striking resemblance to the people in the

UK with the Brexit vote, people who have lived in the country since birth voted for something different. What made the difference in the US? Could it be that he made no excuses as to who he was or is, people are aware he is a loose cannon and very egocentric, but he is someone who stood up to the establishment and people in his own party – that is different and that meant it was good.

The problem is most of his elected party is part of the establishment and most of the opposition are still the establishment, therefore, he will struggle to achieve any of the objectives he talked about during the run-up to the election. If his rhetoric was honest, the odds are he will have to use the US presidential 'executive order' to pass changes in legislation or to international treaties and the question needs to be asked how many times does he need to do this before calls of being a dictator is used. Voting for Trump was a big risk, but the older generation due to the state of the country believe they have little to lose. A note however, in both elections there were two critical figures, in the UK it is Nigel Farage in the US it was Donald J Trump. Both are rich and wealthy by taking advantage of government rules and are therefore as much part of the establishment as the other politicians. So it is not really a 'change of guard' more an 'I am not going to do what you want me to do, I am doing the exact thing you do not want' type manoeuvre that the over 40s have actioned. It has also to be noted the 180 degree change in Western politicians' opinion of Trump, before the election he was all the names under the sun, a real bad guy and a racist, now the vast majority of them have welcomed the new president and look forward to working with him and wish him well. Another prime example of government 'spin', lack of honour and a backbone to stand by what they previously said, it also illustrates why these politicians cannot be trusted with promises in an election as they are so quick to change their minds when influenced by external parties or events.

An interesting statistic is the difference in voting patterns between the old and the young. The young in both elections bought into the rhetoric of the establishment arguments and without question believed and joined in with the labelling and demonising. In the US, most of the 'facts' they though were true about what Trump said, was factually incorrect; and even when the statement made was played back to them, the youth refused to change their minds. Yet another example of the indoctrination of youth into a false reality was that some were asked by a few reporters whether or not they agreed with policies stated. It came as a surprise that they agreed with all the policies mentioned however, even though they were told afterwards these are policies from Donald Trump, they shrugged off 'this reality check' and continued to protest against him. Western society should all be concerned about this type of behaviour – it is not intelligent behaviour.

The reality is people over a certain age have seen changes in the country that has caused modifications to the behaviour of people through generations, which has led to the detriment of society. These changes have not been felt by the youth of today and therefore do not have the experience of the older people in society. With the younger generation so eager to look for offence, racism and a cause it is very easy to 'jump on the band wagon' when there is even a 'slight sniff'' of anything that resembles these attributes. Young people do not believe that there was a time when people could leave doors unlocked, walk down a dark street and alley without being concerned of being attacked, where people did minor repairs to public footpaths, were people could receive the care they needed quickly and efficiently, were decent interesting jobs were readily available, when there was little paperwork to fill out, were people spent most of their time socially interacting with others, were there was no obesity crisis, were there was little air pollution and were you could drive anywhere without getting stuck in congestion, were you could have fun and entertainment without it costing an 'arm and a leg', a time when you could go for years without being harassed by a stranger, when relationships lasted; and civil unrest was something that rarely happened and when people trusted politicians and politicians repaid that trust by taking care of the people rather than big business. The young people of today do not know and have not experienced this type of life, or seen how things have changed for the worse. This is the difference, the youth have not felt the hopelessness that the elder generation feels now, and until the country's economy reduces to the levels of Spain, Greece, Syria, etc. the younger generation will continually be indoctrinated into believing subliminal messages given out by politicians and mass media outlets, unless something changes.

A recent quote by the newly appointed, not elected, prime minister in 2016 (Theresa May) said "If you believe you-re a citizen of the world, you-re a citizen of nowhere" and was defended by her and interpreted as though she was explaining that everyone has responsibility for the role they play in local communities, to abide by the rules and pay their taxes. Exactly how the first quote is translated to the second is beyond my understanding and I am experienced with semantic logic. It also signifies she has little understanding of why the majority of people are frustrated and choose not to play a social role in society. It is predominantly due to the vast chasm of inequality, long work hours for little pay, high tax rates, and the rich and wealthy running away with all the money.

The quote was a mistake by the UK PM at the time and could be construed as a depiction of the outcome with producing poorly educated people who are not capable of critical thinking and therefore not capable of the realisation that thinking you are part of society by playing by the rules, means that you are a follower hence subjected to being manipulated by those who not only create societal rules but break them at will. The point is the weakest parts of the oligarchs are always the politicians because the dumber people are the more valuable they are to the oligarchs; accordingly, having government populated by these types of people is an advantage to their own selfish aims. Hence, the politicians are trained to read a perfectly prepared transcript with coached hand gestures to appear genuine, but, sometimes let their arrogance and ego get in the way and thus make mistakes and blunders/gaffes. It is these mistakes that people should be educated enough to spot and question 'what is really going on' and 'how on earth did these people acquire such a position'.

Continued Conflict

Remembrance days are for people to learn from the mistakes of the past and pay respect and tribute to those who fought for freedom. The question is why has human civilisation not learned anything from the past? Continued conflict in the world has a strong relationship with the capitalist agenda and spreading political ideologies. The globalised economy has rewritten the rule books for human conflict. Now conflicts in one part of the world spreads to all countries to some degree. In recent times, troubles in the Middle East have caused mass migration of people like never seen before in history. To the extent that terror attacks in the UK and throughout mainland Europe is quickly becoming the norm due to our moral, ethical, stupid and irresponsible manner in which the regions handle immigration whilst conducting military operations in countries involved in the mass movement of people to the West. This is especially poignant in the UK where they have been the US partner on most if not all conflicts, hence, partially responsible for crafting most of the suffering and loss within the conflict zones.

The politicians and diplomats (one and the same in reality) have created another global war with religious connotations, i.e. West (mostly white and Christian) against the Middle East (mostly Muslim). The terrorist acts in the West could be seen as the start of another crusade to ensure one religion is dominant around the world. Looking back in history with respect to wars and invasions with religious contexts, the crusades was either one of two things. One, a religious war to wipe out people of different faiths; or two, to conquer whoever ruled so the invading party's religion or political ideology could control the people. Consider the IRA, they had a political agenda different than the central government of the UK, but they also had strong religious faith. So the question is, did they carry out terrorist explosions and bombings because of religious reasons or did they bomb areas of London, Birmingham and Manchester for a purely political one. Perhaps it was to achieve the goal of removing the resemblance of British rule from Ireland. Irrespective, the UK government had to deal with a group that was being armed by foreign countries, the US for one, and they found it extremely difficult to defeat a group that was continuously being armed by an ally, therefore, the UK government had no choice but to offer positions in the Irish government to the leaders of the IRA. The present day question is, is a similar strategy going to be actioned with Muslim 'Extremist' groups to resolve the problem of terror attacks throughout the West?

The United Nations (UN) is a committee, which is responsible for keeping the peace in the world and ensuring that any nation who 'misbehaves' is punished besides coercing the governments to 'play by the rules' of international law. However, the permanent members of the UN frequently feel free to instigate conflict in foreign countries – the US is the main culprit, but, most countries indirectly cause conflict with arms sales to various regimes and dictators.

Politicians of the member states appear to be laws unto themselves. For example, it seems to be perfectly acceptable for politicians to order assassinations or bomb people in foreign lands; army or police to kill someone; and subsequently, like Hillary Clinton scenario concerning Saddam Hussain, to gloat about it and bask in the glory of ordering the murder of him and his soldiers without any criminal charges sought from the national or international criminal justice system. However, acts such as killing / murdering someone through revenge, due to a moment of madness, or greed, etc., by an ordinary member of the public it is perceived as being heinous with the full force of the law actioned. Yet, the scale of the criminal acts is not comparable with those in positions of leadership and authority being responsible for the most suffering and deaths, but, being punished the least if at all.

Conflict is strongly link to the grandstanding of superpowers on the world stage and the one thing 'poor quality' leaders hate is to share the stage with others they deem inferior. What makes a country evolve into a superpower is the creation of a nuclear deterrent or other such weapons of mass destruction (WMD) – real ones not misguided propaganda for example used for justification of the second Iraq war (How Bush and Blair are still walking free making millions from their destructive war is a testament to the inability of people and what is sold as a law for all to hold leaders to account for their actions).

If countries test nuclear weapons or other WMDs besides those approved by the US or other permanent members of the UN, i.e. they are perceived to be a threat to national security for the world superpowers, they are automatically presented to the majority as hostile and with evil intentions. Presently (2017), the rhetoric used by the US/UK and Europe with North Korea and vice-Versa is putting that region and the entire world at risk. Whether people like it or not the US coalition have only invaded and bombed countries without this capability; and let's be honest the Wests military might is far too strong for other countries to defend against without nuclear weapons. The truth is the US and its allies do not want another superpower in the world, especially one so secretive (the Wests 'poor quality' leaders are so paranoid when they struggle to spy on foreign countries). Nevertheless, if they intentionally start a war with North Korea who would blame the military of the country for striking with the best weapon they have. Justification - once the US coalition begin another invasion, the current leader and military commands will most likely be killed (recent history has proven this to be true), thus, for them there is nothing to lose; therefore, North Korean leaders may as well fire the most advanced weapon they have at their 'enemy' or 'enemies'.

The truth is politicians and military commands of countries that are already a superpower and have substantial military might at their disposal are not keen on attempting to resolve issues diplomatically. Recent history has taught people that the permanent members of the UN bypass the Security Council when the leaders want military conflict with others; and do so without any repercussions. There is also an unnerving inclination that the US ambassadors and diplomats, along with their close allies at the UN, consistently call for sanctions and military interventions in countries that do not fall in-line with US demands.

It would seem the US and its allies are more keen to go to war with other resource rich countries or countries that are developing advanced weapons (not defence technology – this phrase is reserved for Western weapons only), which could be, might possibly be, used to defend themselves (no sorry attack any Western country or armed force), than feed and home their own people, and provide decent health care, including support for war veterans. And how dare any other country develop advanced technology that will be used to discourage any invasion or attack and could be used against US coalition partners (naughty, naughty!), even though the West have the same capabilities and have been more than irresponsible with them. It would appear the US politicians and military leaders still think they are cowboys and everybody else 'Indians', moreover, attempt to force / coerce the 'Indians' to do their will / bidding, including seizing control of more 'Indian' territory whilst killing / murdering those 'Indians' who attempt to remove the invading 'cowboy' force (how dare they!).

The reality is Western powers are testing WMDs, including nuclear weapons frequently and just because another country is doing the same is no reason to panic or spread the fear among people or call for conflict. Paranoid delusion is not a viable reason to kill more people in an international conflict. Irrespective, war is good for the economy and the capitalist agenda concentrates on governing the country for the benefit of the national economy, even though the economy only benefits those with substantial financial resources to begin with.

Modern Capitalism

To operate a modern business today you need more than the knowledge of how to make that business work, you need a drive to make money. To make money requires a business to exploit people at both ends of the business line (suppliers and consumers) and with it the ruthlessness based on business acumen. Unfortunately, making lots of money is something that has caused all the problems in society and endures suffering that is an everyday occurrence for the vast majority of people; and sums up what the modern capitalist society is all about. The truth is business capitalism is all about exploitation of people and having the inhuman ability to 'lock conscience away in a box' and ignore it; if people cannot ignore their conscience they will not be able to run a successful business making large profits. All these big corporations making loads of money year on year at everyone else's expense, including oil companies, banks, technology and construction firms, and some charities, is not because they are good at what they do. It is because they do not seem to have much of an issue in exploiting people of all cultures, causing premature deaths and increasing the likelihood of deceases; their prime motivation and concern is making money above all else.

The corporatocracy uses exploitation of the poor for profit forcing Westernised cultures onto people thus wiping out native ways of life and markets this as helping desperate people out of poverty. The modern day slave traders pay these poor people a negligible salary whilst the business makes millions from the work undertaken, some of whom are paid a measly few dollars a week for long hard hours worked. Are these businesses ethical and moral? It is the same question with regard to people in certain areas of the world who wants more used electronics to strip of precious metals to earn this measly salary whilst at the same time the process used poisons the land and water supply they need to survive. These people look towards the West to supply more waste electronics so they can earn dollars, they do not comprehend the hazards associated with it but the Western governments and businesses that transport these electronics to these regions of the word does. I wonder if Western people realise the suffering caused by consumer electronics or recycling out of date phones, laptops, monitors, etc. some of which is still fully functional, would people still carry on with purchasing the next generation of electronic gadgets?

It is sad to say that the answer is probably yes, as the one thing I am confident on is the human condition of 'out of sight out of mind'. People have become immune to the fact that capitalism is about profiting from the exploitation and suffering of people. Primark only proves that even knowledge of what is happening will not change people's consumerist attitudes and activities. Advertising is everywhere and children more than any other time in history are subjected to consumerist marketing campaigns, everywhere. Just look at the crap bought on eBay to see the problem with consumerism; furthermore, it is being ignored by everybody that people do indeed have an addiction problem with spending money just for the sake of spending it.

People are so easily inculcated into spending money on the thing they do not need or want; the words 'only', 'just' or phrases such as 'incredible prices' makes some people excited to go and purchase the products. The strategy is very effective with marketing companies acquiring a fortune and manufacturing companies spending million upon million advertising their own products, which makes the products more expensive to buy for the end consumer who does not appear to care or notice. All this money is being spent on something, which if people think about it is 'dead money' - it does not do anything useful or perform any function in society (a total of £392 billion spent on advertising globally in 2016 and has increased year-on-year). Furthermore, people have become programmed to buy, buy, and buy products whether they need them or not on a regular basis likewise people have no idea that the money spent on marketing is abhorrent when there is real social, health, and education problems, which need to be solved all requiring money that is wasted on cheaply made but expensive consumer goods.

Additionally, society has big money available for sport events (£millions upon £millions), yet, does have enough to solve societal problems such as homelessness, poor health care, education, etc. People need to ask themselves, what does it say about society if people are more than happy to pay and support sports stars, for instance, boxers being paid £100s of millions for one boxing contest whilst people are living rough on the streets? (I am not going to go into the football, baseball, golf, etc. argument), the amount of money all sports, film, and TV celebrities are paid is obscene at best. If people think about it (not too much) what impact would it have on society if all these sports disappeared tomorrow? The answer is very little, however, those vital services, those that some people have no choice but to depend upon are failing and/or too expensive for some people to use besides not receiving the funding they need in order to fulfil their responsibility to people in society. People are accepting this as the way it is. What level of morals and ethics does everyone have to have in order to deem this type of scenario as acceptable? It is fine for the politicians, business owners and social justice warrior to publically argue or defend the case concerning the state of society. But, from a simplistic point of view an intelligent species would condemn anybody who supports these unjustifiable and obscene amounts of money given to a few sports stars (some of which are average at their sport) / celebrities and conclude it is morally and ethically reprehensible.

It is as if people cannot tear themselves away from their jobs, TV, online gaming, social networking sites and shopping to see what global society they are creating thus leaving their children and future generations. It is why all people are responsible for allowing the problems in the world to continue and contribute to a real active nightmare occurring throughout the world. Is this really a society people should be promoting moving forward into an uncertain future or is it time people took a long hard look at ourselves and the hardships others are living and make a positive change for the better.

Reality of Society

Government continues to spread the message about the lack of money in the national economy and uses it for the justification of raising taxes. Yet, they continue to have surplus funding or unlimited funds for wars and foreign aid projects with the World Bank and the European Monetary Fund (perhaps they find the spare cash under the sofa or perhaps this is where some of the substantial countries debt is created). Concurrently, government endures to give financial incentives to private companies through lobbying strategies, e.g. construction, road works, refineries, technology companies (including speed camera businesses), etc., for nice to have projects, to continue to take money off workers (the majority) and justify job creation whilst at the same time cannot find any money to house the homeless, improve health care, or social services; nor do they wish to discuss the very real problem of human population numbers either nationally or globally. However, the continued conflict in the world, based on a capitalist agenda, combined with all governments spreading the word of fear keeps people looking towards them for protection and in doing so justifies working for less and the poorer quality of life experienced throughout the West.

Strange isn't it the longer I live and the more research I do, the more I bring into question the reality I have been told (indoctrinated) throughout my childhood and adult life. So much so that an internal debate with myself has become the norm where I have to question my continued research into areas that history, even recent history, has already placed a conclusion on because the truth is living life in complete ignorance and accepting the narrative from government is substantially easier than finding out the real truth and having to question the reality that has been sold since childhood.

People are now living in a world full of deception where devious fraudulent truth has become the selling point for all to aspire to succeed financially in the modern world. Most representatives of government and business are trained to be as vague and likeable at the same time to give the impression to people that they share the same values as the majority in society, however, the 'things' said are mere sound-bites. Their concentration is to sell perceived reality rather than true reality; if someone perceives something to be true, it is more important than if it is in fact true. These people are coached to be duplicitous and to take advantage of false assumptions and liberal ideology if it plays to their advantage, although due to the poor quality of politicians and managers their perceived reality 'breaks down' with various individual gaffs especially during interviews. The point is people should be more wary of those who are dishonest (hiding dark intentions) in what they represent through media channels than about those who are more forthcoming about their own viewpoints or outwardly offend certain people; I think these are two of the reasons for the rise of Trump to president in the USA.

It is hard to live in a world full of false truths and realities with the majority of people completely ignorant or disinterested in the real truth but content with consumerist lifestyles and celebrity cultures. It would seem knowing the dark realities of the real world and how it is governed makes you think differently than the majority of people who have not had the strength or the misfortune to be able to break through the indoctrination to see the light through the fog. As such, it makes the world a very lonely place to be where you question were exactly you belong, it also makes the world a lonely place to live in. But once the indoctrination is broken, you can never look at the world the same way again whilst being a 'good little soldier' and work hard for little and accept the 'craziness' of people whom through no fault of their own have become puppets of the oligarchs in a world governed to control people's thoughts and behaviour through clever marketing, schooling, money, boredom and misery of the world.

The sad reality is all who accept the Western way of life, whether below the poverty line or above it, are part of the corporatocracy sucking on the teats of goods made from wars, famine, slavery, starvation and the exploitation of people. All Society places fists in their mouths and think that the next election will bring about change, but, subconsciously people realise that it is our own individual behaviour that has created a greedy monster that if it continues to be ignored will eventually drown all in consumer goods, pollution and starvation. Social health, climate, pollution and quality of life has taken a back seat to greed producing ruthless managers and 'poor quality' leaders that take advantage of cheap labour and poor education to increase corporate gains.

Are any people in society so innocent in the oppression of others from foreign resource rich countries since we all rely and look towards the corporations and government to supply our needs? Suppliers that are exploited enough will eventually rebel and are so called Muslim terrorists today part of that rebellion who believe that no advanced country has the right to exploit those with little power to resist. Is there really no better way for modern human civilisation to live and prosper? Yes, but it will take courage, will and interest; so let's get interested......

2

BUILDING A BETTER FUTURE

There are many problems, both micro and macro in proportion that affects everyone's life; however, the most difficult problems facing the people materialize from decisions made by the current and previous ruling governments under the heading of progress. This chapter attempts to cover most of the macro-related problems, in an abstract manner, which ordinary working people have little involvement of both creating and decision making to solve it; but, nevertheless, have to face the burden of the remedy decided upon. The chapter should be read as an abstract summary of the entire book, to give the reader a taste of the discussion within it.

Politicians promote progress whenever they come to some criticism; it is generally used to redirect the questioning to something more positive. This notwithstanding, progress is an indication of moving forward on something to improve the current state; however, at some point progress has made societal norms worse than what they once were. For issues regarding humans growing as a species, this has become entangled with political ideologies where people have forgotten the differences between fundamental responsibility, nice-to-haves, cultures, genders (sex) and religion, which implies humans have progressed in a negative fashion rather than in a positive way. Seemingly progress, especially to a nation's leaders, means ignoring reality, facts and truths and going ahead with the changes irrespective of consequence. The chapters in the book discuss the area(s) in more detail and give my view of the potential solutions to carry the country forward and bring clarity to real life responsibilities for a fairer, better quality of life for all societies.

Commitments and Consumerism

Across the nation working people know the simple truth; the economy is not working for them. For longer than I can remember, even before I was born, the country's economy has not rewarded everyone. The majority of people have become shackled to a system that falsely promotes working for prosperity for all, when in actuality it is only for the benefit of the corporatocracy (enslavement if you will) and with it the promotion of corruption and bribery in politics and in all government departments. Coincidentally, the people who work the hardest, those who are on low wages putting in long hours including overtime, do not earn enough to make ends meet. In the recession of 2008, too many have been driven from secure, full-time work, into precarious low paid jobs including having no choice but to choose a zero-hour contract position.

There are also issues relating to past and present governments creating jobs, think tanks, and institutions in an attempt to solve the problem of unemployment figures; what I call 'non-job' culture. This has invariably created an open door policy for various people to earn high salaries for doing very little, i.e. Health and Safety Executive – whom seemingly police the lack of common sense in working practices and issue punishment; responsibility for one's own health and safety has now diverged to 'where there is blame, there's a clam' culture. The cost of all this job creation flows down the economic pyramid onto the working class or transfers to the country's debt figures. This sort of creative accounting to solve inconvenient truths in published unemployment figures, quality and pressures of working practices dilute the problem of too many people not enough decent paid work to go around; and has only created a bubble that if not stopped from expanding will eventually burst into a deep recession of the likes never experienced before.

In addition to the stresses and strain of financial support for family and the pressures of stature in society, time to enjoy family and friends is increasingly squeezed due to the high demands of career responsibility, the care of children and elderly relatives. All of which is leading to a societal norm of financially providing to solve such care issues at the expense of real time with people you care about and an ever increasing alienation of personal responsibility to those family members (i.e. work commitments taking higher priority). These problems are now more apparent for the next generation.

Steps have to be taken to look at number of hours worked to productivity, as some research suggests that four hours of intense concentration leads to more productivity than working for eight hours per day. Reducing the number of hours in the working week for individuals will free up time to spend with family and friends and also alleviate the problem of unemployment and the creation of other non-job positions.

The story of non-job creation and pressures of working life began with the large boost to business profits that gave rise to consumerism, especially in the 1950s when people were rebuilding their lives after WW2. Corporate businesses have since taken advantage of peoples wants in society and the marketing campaigns have directly indoctrinated children and adults into a spending culture like never before. Businesses needed people to buy 'things' and they also need a reliable but cheap workforce for manufacturing. Large portions of people on unemployment benefit with little disposable money was not good for the economy, therefore, they needed government to act to ensure that people had to money available to spend on luxurious goods. The government has since ensured large population of people are available for cheap labour, non-jobs have been created (at the expense of the tax payer), loan companies are available to lend, and marketing campaigns are allowed to be directed at young children.

It would seem as though the good times are here, people in the West have all forgot about having the 'needs in life' and have been manipulated into acquiring the 'wants in life'; all without thinking about the ramifications of such a debt ridden society and a disposable way of life. People are no longer concerned about living within their means, people have become greedy (always wanting the next new thing that comes out in the market place) and debt is now a way of life. 'Things' have becoming more expensive, yet, people who have the resources (or credit cards) continue to purchase stuff on a regular basis, furthermore, this addiction has created a cycle of ever increasing prices, which is pricing out poorer families and individuals leading to social segregation and bullying, especially amongst children in schools. Additionally, people have become irresponsible in how they make decisions regarding financial stability for the future; moreover, people are unconcerned with what happens to something once it is disposed of.

Negative effects on social wellbeing, the environment and the pollution factors of living a consumerist lifestyle are not considered; as a species, people have become complacent with a 'do not care' attitude. People aspire to be rich and wealthy at the same time as spending most of their disposable money on what can be classed as 'clutter', it is a cycle of being lost in consumerist ways. There is a trade-off between solving the problem of consumerism and job place availability, which are all directly linked to population numbers for various regions of the country.

Education versus Experience

With the cost of education increasing to uncontrollable levels, young people are now taking on substantial debts to go to university with the hope of obtaining a well-paid job at the end of it, only to realise that the job market is already saturated; and as a result are coerced into low paid work not worthy of their newly gain knowledge or talents. However, it is becoming an increasing concern that graduates leaving university lack in problem solving and management skills due to, in my opinion, a deficiency in understanding of real problems from academics teaching students. The university system is unequivocally producing students who have a large knowledge base on how to use software tools and solve academic problems well founded in academic texts, but not in thinking about real world problems and how to solve them. In 2015, the UK government launched an initiative to give more vocational qualifications and apprenticeships to give younger people a better start in life they deserve and reduce the skills gap left by universities. However, Western society is still promoting academic qualifications over experience within the career market producing an elitist attitude (snobbery) locking more suitable people out of high paid roles, thus, continuing the problem of promoting above 'one's own competence' level.

Goals to success for young people should be through closer ties between parents and schools (at all levels) and a better standard of education with training for the 'front-line' by working closer with industry and technology companies to provide a foundation for decent paid apprenticeships and/or work placements, to give school leavers Knowledge and Skill (K&S) qualifications that are meaningful in the modern technology driven world.

The goal for the country should be to have a highly educated society, but, not to start young people in life having a highly sought after qualification without the necessary 'hand-on' experience needed in todays' global market. In addition, the education budget and teaching standards have to be protected and improved, with reducing class sizes to allow for ease of management and improvement of knowledge levels, especially for 5-11 year olds.

Accountability with Decisions

It is clear, unless you have been distracted by long hours working or living in a virtual environment that successive government are failing in their responsibility to the majority of people. Political parties talk about what they believe people want, the proverbial 'which direction in the wind blowing 'today'', but then ignore the things that really matter once the elections are over. For too long now **power** has been in control of the few without any accountability, concentrating it to the matters of the financial economy, at the expense of individuals and their communities. Democracy should be about people having more say about decisions that will affect their lives, but, for a long time now these decisions have been and are made by a small group of elected (and unelected) officials with individuals and large working class groups being powerless to stop them (if in doubt check out the protest march against the Iraq war in 2005 (and others) if you believe people's voice really matters in state sponsored decisions).

The general consensus in the national media is economic success is down to a few at the top (Bankers, Corporate businesses, Oligarchs, etc.) and intrinsically power of decision making has been in the hands of such elitists lobbying the government for legislation changes to protect the wealth of a few, with little thought of the impacts of the majority. When decisions 'go south', zero accountability is actioned and the real economic powerhouse (the majority) are the ones to take the burden of the choice without having a choice with the few whom have benefitted not suffering any financial burdens. Government should be responsible to make accountable those who have been or are responsible for 'bad decisions' that have negatively impacted the country, especially financially, without forcing the tax payer to 'bear the brunt' of costs.

Ultimately, the quest to be in government should not be about running for 'power'; but should be about hard working people wanting to be in a position to make a difference for the majority. If the decisions they make fail or be detrimental to the majority's quality of life due to incompetence or greed, then the people in government who are responsible for the situation must be made accountable, removed from governing parties and the power of decision; with strategies put in place to dramatically ease the burden on the innocent people (i.e. the tax payer).

Social and Health Care Evolution

People live in a society of distrust and unfairness, which sometimes is confused for racism, discrimination and intolerance.

However, these issues come from successive governments making decisions without involving or ignoring the people; creating advantages (including positive discrimination), benefits (especially for newcomers into the country), and others, for minority groups in the country and the result is a growing society of distrust both of others and of government bolstering the causatum of inequality for everyone in society.

There is also another inconvenient truth in today's society. People are so busy and stressed with everyday occurrences and problems, they feel guilty when creative media advertising on television all asking for help that they do not have the spare time or strength to personally give to charitable causes to help real people who have found themselves in trouble; they give hard earned cash to charities. This has caused the number of charities to explode, with every single charity wanting more and more money; the charities become larger requiring more administrators and require them to be run by 'the best' and 'the best' cost money. This means substantial giving's (money) are redirected to the people running the charities and not to the 'frontline' causes. Charities are there to help social problems, but when the individuals at the top are earning six figures from money given in good faith by people, something has gone drastically wrong with the philosophy and ethics of the said charities, not to mention the government's responsibility to ensure their own prime directive (to protect safety, security and wellbeing of all people in the country).

Stronger regulation is required for charities and salary limitation instigated, along with justification of expenditure of the money given by hard working people by making the accounts published. Alongside this, an investigation of why the charity is needed, what caused the problem, and plans produced that describe how to solve the problem within a certain timescale - how many decades have red nose day been trying to solve their charitable issues – something is definitely wrong when the original problem is far larger now than when the charity first started. For me, charities are morally repugnant besides endorse governments to ignore their prime responsibility and objective. Further, hard questions need to be asked whether the people of the nation should be responsible for funding the charity (if directed at international social problems), as people have a duty to take care at home first!

People see the vulnerable, the sick and the elderly not receiving the social or health care they need, but then money being spent on art, military, rejuvenation and infrastructure projects, along with migrants and refugees being given houses, furniture, and financial benefits; all at the expense of people who have worked all their lives for a better future only to find the future is full of hardships. Can society really blame people who played by the rules and paid into the system for a many years for feeling abandoned and lied to by the system they trusted; whilst at the same time, seeing people who have not paid into the system or newcomers to the country being taken care of without any consequences. Are people really surprised of the result of the UK referendum in 2016 to leave the European Union (EU)? These are hard truths to realise, especially for the new generation of young people, but these issues have to be considered as people grow old thus need to and should know that the system will be there when needed.

In a civilised modern society, the government's only obligation is to ensure the safety, security and wellbeing of the people in the country, but there is strong evidence over the past three decades, especially over the last 10 years, that the decisions being made is of detriment to most in society. The wealthy, however, are benefiting more than ever from privatisation of health care, railways, utilities, worker rights dismantling, and more population to keep salaries low causing 'rapidly growing' profits at the expense of quality of life for the majority.

This simply has to stop.

You cannot protect the areas of education and health care by increasing the population numbers; maximising profit by minimising wages puts more pressure on low paid workers who will do what they have to do to get through the week at a cost to their own (and their children's) physical and mental health.

A maximum number of people for the country, per region, per town and city is required to be sought and stringent controls are necessary to ensure that the country, if necessary, can be fully independent and sustainable irrespective of race, religion, and skills. The providers of health care, transport and energy should return into public ownership along with the producers of ancillary services, e.g. pharmaceutical manufacture, housing, etc. to enable more accountability and control public spending more efficiently; all under control of COMPETENT management with contracts that stipulate efficiency and success targets (there is a considerable weakness both in public and private sectors in these types of strengths, and is germinating rapidly). In essence, more social success than profitability concerns.

Additionally, there is a strong argument that people are now too reliant on the 'state' for hand-outs and to take care of them. My view of the future is people need to take back control of their own destiny and be more independent on ALL aspects of life. This way there is a chance the 'puppet strings' can be cut from those who control the money and society can once more gain a real sense of being in control of our own lives rather than being influenced and manipulated by central government and bank decisions. People need the mind-set of being independent and only look towards the 'state' in all its forms when absolutely necessary. Currently, there is an abuse of the 'state' by people and vice-versa; strategies are needed, through education, to break the 'strings' in both directions or at least loosen them dramatically.

Housing

There is an ever greater call for more 'affordable' housing; without considering the after effects of such a decision. Building more housing invariably means removing land from nature and advancing the concrete jungle, which consequently is detrimental to the air quality that causes various health problems along with other environmental problems that can affect people directly, i.e. flooding. The intention should be to limit the building of new homes, regenerate all the empty 'useable' homes into affordable homes and look at controlling the cost of buying and renting. The number of houses on the market should also give an indication of the number of people that particular region can house and thus serve along with school class sizes and health care availability as an indication of population limitations.

This issue is strongly related to tackling climate change, which is a necessity for the future of all. This country can serve as a blueprint for others into how to manage air quality with economic necessity, but it does require certain constraints that require all to be responsible for their own life decisions (which is something that needs to be taught throughout the education system).

Decision Responsibility

The Government should put strategies in place so opportunities belong to everyone, all discrimination (both positive and negative) should be removed from consideration to help rebuild a country based on fairness to ensure that everyone feels like they have a stake in society's health. Law and order should work to eradicate crime, not control it (as it does now) and jail has to be used to reform criminals and not just be a place to store the problem or increase the potential for reoffending with the release of inmates; otherwise it is a cost to the taxpayer without benefit. All profiteering from law sectors should be removed and be governed as a non-profit sector including, lawyers, solicitors, courts, and parole officers. These should work towards making the justice system available for everyone without worrying about cost.

Government promises should be legal binding documents with the people of the country to come through on the promises in the manifesto of the elected party and criminal charges sought if propaganda (or outright lies) is used to sway the vote. Currently in any democratic country, no elected party comes close to following through on election promises and always finds an excuse as to why. This is an unacceptable cycle that has to be broken. Once elected, any elected party member who fails to fulfil promises they are responsible for should automatically make their position untenable and be prevented from standing in any constitutional elections in the future. Promised or proposed changes to infrastructure, processes, etc., should always be affordable and well-funded with contracts signed with contractors before being awarded in assurance that the public will not be liable for additional cost if project(s) overrun or design flaws are found.

Being a MP/senator is the only job I know that you can attain without a decent CV. All MPs/senators should be time served and experienced especially in decision making under pressure. These experiences should be an overarching concern for those that are given departments to govern; those with an unsuitable CV (like most current career politicians) should be classed as unsuitable candidates. The 'gravy-train' should be derailed and placed on a 'diet' with second homes removed replaced with an apartment block; in addition to various expenses being 'nulled' to ensure value for money for the tax payer. Additional jobs for MPs/senators or entitlement to be on members of boards for other organisations or companies should be against the rules and made illegal. Lobbying or any system which can interfere or perverse the decision making ability of the MPs/senators to act in accordance to the interests of the people of the country should be made unlawful. In addition, tax loopholes for the wealthy, especially those in government, should be eliminated with the punishment of a high percentage of equity to be taken from all guilty parties.

When politicians talk about contributing to society, I have to question their motives. For instance, as a country more people are sat down at a desk working in an office not producing anything of any benefit than actually making or developing something useful. Are these people who produce spreadsheets, presentations and word documents really contributing to society? I do not think so! Instead, they are ensuring money is continuously transferred from the working class through to government and big businesses; how are using electricity and chopping down more trees for paper and not doing anything constructive in society, really benefitting society. The truth is it benefits the few at the expense of the majority with an ever growing national debt.

Bailing out of private companies who run public sector services has to be scrutinised to the 'highest order' and salary payment to higher management to be authorised by government; all companies who have made a profit should not be eligible for a public bailout i.e. rail companies (re: Southern rail bailout September 2016 of £20 million, whilst making £100 million profit in that year). Those who have failed to provide a good service or who have failed in their responsibility should be removed and new short term contracts awarded (if required) or be nationalised to run as 'non-profit', which would be the preferred option for the tax payer.

People used to walk tall in this country and take pride in what they did, everybody was friendly towards everyone else; everybody felt safe and secure; people could leave their houses unlocked with windows open without being concerned about theft. People used to take care of their own land and public land outside their property, even do minor repairs to pavements and public roads. However, due to government taxation, legal interference and the influx of people from different cultures, people do not do this anymore. People have been worn down, been made to distrust others, been made to be miserable; to be stressed. All of society should agree this is not a good path to be going down and it has to change. Greed has taken over everybody's life along with selfishness and being self-centred because of decisions made by government and driven by political ideology.

People surround themselves in a virtual shield to protect themselves from being hurt, which unfortunately means that they themselves stop partaking in society and leave themselves separated from society decisions. This situation simply has to change and government is not the place people should look for guidance and help as they are the ones that have created, over the decades, this type of divided society. The Marxist in me would describe Western society as 'divided we stand, divided we are conquered (divide and conquer)'. People cannot nor never will be able to be masters of their own destiny if a small group of individuals are in charge, in control, are masters of how society works. Only together can society work for the benefit of the majority, a divided society only works for the benefit of those at the top of the financial pyramid.

People live in a situation where those who have paid into the system all of their working lives struggle to receive decent social and health care, and this predominantly concerns the elderly generation. Meanwhile, people can enter the country and receive housing, furniture, carpets, health care, schooling and financial help without putting anything in the system in the first place. People whose family have lived in the country for generations and struggle to receive any benefits from the system, is completely wrong. The irony is whether you loath him or hate him, the Trump slogan of 'putting America (our country) first' is what should happen; priority for the government should be directed to people from families who have lived in the country for generations. Society should not have a government who gives priority to visitors in the country because it is making native people, more and more, pull back and not engage in society.

The plan is to build a better society in a country that all can be proud of with a high quality of life for everyone, were everyone has an opportunity to get on and achieve their own goals in life. Strong effective leadership in all areas of society is the starting point of any positive change, but everyone will need to contribute and play a part, even the elites in society, to change the direction the country seems to be heading in.

Together it should be possible to improve the quality of life, but everyone cannot ignore their own responsibility for the countries wellbeing. The question has to be asked: If we truly love our children and our children's children, why do we continuously ignore the problems in society and turn our backs on our responsibilities to each other. People need to take a step back and look at ourselves in the mirror and determine what is really important in life: just muddle through and accept the way things are or do something about it even if it means inconvenience and/or risk. This book discusses main areas of concern for administering the country, not to preserve our current way of life (which politicians use time and time again to justify their 'hard choices'), but, to open new avenues on the way people think and hopefully question what people think they know about human and political reality.

3

BUILDING A COUNTRY THAT WORKS

People are told from a very young age that hard work pays. However, there is a clear contradiction in term when reflected in the real world. Many people work hard and put in long hours and not reek the rewards as others who do very little; this situation is confounded by the growing issue of a living wage, how should it be calculated, and cannot be confused with the new government strategy surrounding 'just about managing'. The country needs to be governed in the terms of the human cost of hours worked to encourage people to enhance their own ability to secure a more skilled, knowledgeable and more fulfilled society.

Issues Surrounding the Economy

The current state and governing of the economy is not creating a highly skilled, productive and well-paid 'employment system' to raise the living standards for the majority of people. The lack of rewarding careers and opportunities, due to manufacturing and production being diverted internationally, are ensnaring millions of people in a cycle of benefits and low paid insecure jobs. These low-paid jobs produce less tax revenues and higher spending on social security.

In the UK, current statistics (2016) show that over 5 million people are in low-paid jobs, earning less than a living wage (£7.20/hour); 1.3 million people are in part-time jobs finding it difficult to acquire a full-time job. In the US, poverty figures reached 43.1 million and 112.2 million in mainland Europe (governments always feel the need to publish percentage figures to massage the real data and the scale of the problem – it is the problem with manipulation of real data into statistics). Over half of people who live in poverty live in working households and many use the ever increasing number of food banks opening up in all countries.

As a species, we have a history of innovation and enterprise. Unfortunately, with the growth of corporate greed and profit and the evolution of the internet has put real world innovation and invention at risk. Short term, the problems are not painfully apparent, nevertheless, a strong economy with long term benefits for all is predominantly reliant on real world cause and effects. In the current climate, the government is only considering short term benefits and ignoring the potential long term issues with real world innovation concentrating on general consumer goods and gadgets, which is a recipe for disaster for future generations.

In addition to these economic issues, concentration as well as application of government incentives and legislation is focussed on financial impacts to the economy with little or no impact assessments to the human economy. For thousands of years (from slavery to paid work), the majority of people have been used for the benefit of a few and this really has not transformed or evolved:- when the economy is growing, the few acquires profit and more low-paid work is available; when the economy shrinks (and does so quickly), the richest of the elites gains more wealth quickly (generally by short selling on stock markets), and those in low-paid jobs pay the price with unemployment and all the issues and problems that spans from it e.g. repossessions, homelessness and in more severe cases due to depression and hopelessness, suicide.

People accept, without question, that some (most) people's time is worth less than others with no correlation or causation to anyone's ability, knowledge, skill or intelligence. There is an unspoken consensus that 'the less work you do the more you are paid'; 'most managers are promoted way beyond their own competence level'; 'it is about who you know rather than what you know'; 'it is not about ability or meritocracy, it is about how well you can talk, how good you are with being a 'yes' drone'; and 'how good you are at playing office politics and how covertly you can stab your superior or colleagues in the back for promotion'. These frustrations in real working life all add to cost issues of products, services and goods the country provides nationally and internationally, it affects the bottom line and is detrimental to all aspects of the economy, especially to the human cost of experiencing all the above in daily life.

Of course, the financial economy or the health thereto can be broadly separated into three categories: Gross Domestic Product (GDP), national debt, and international debt; with the mass media and Consecutive Governments (CG) separate GDP (for growth or shrinkage in the economy) and debt as two independent statistics with little or no correlation between them. The extent of which means that the country can have a growing GDP along with an increase in debt, which seems counter intuitive - How can the economy be growing at the same time as the country's debt increasing?; Who does the country owe debt to? And why is everyone responsible for it? (The proverbial 'where all in it together' phrase the government continues to use). All these statistics impact on the government decisions that affect all people's living standards. Generally, the people responsible for the issues and debt are the ones who feel the 'pain' the very least and profit from the outcome. This is clearly not fair and nothing has been resolved in regulating (or deregulating with stricter rules/laws for operating) the institutions responsible for negative impacts to the country's economy, however, bailouts and government 'loans' (I use the term loosely) are common place for banks, traders, large corporate businesses and institutions. Whilst the real profit making group, the people who work for a living (the majority), are left out in the cold suffering due to decisions made by the elitists, potentially hundreds of miles away in capital cities or even in foreign countries, and greed of the already wealthy in society (the oligarchs – corporations, banks, governments).

> Then people question why civil unrest, homelessness, poverty, intolerance of others, benefit cheats, charities etc. are increasing in numbers throughout Westernised civilisation.

Society have a system that not only allows for this type of injustice to occur, but in a way promotes this separation of people and responsibility, especially for those at the top of the financial pyramid with contacts in the right places. Why do people accept this? Unfortunately, ordinary working people have a lot to lose, and fighting for change carries with it a high risk of losing all that has been gained (job, house, car, family, etc.) and when you have a family it is generally too big of a risk. Additionally, people have been convinced life is about working long hours to obtain a roof over their head, provide food on the table and to pay ever increasing taxes. This is not what life is about – ask the people who own private jets or luxury cruise ships whether life is about working – these people offer society little benefit other than giving the false message of 'work hard and you can live a lifestyle like me'. When in reality greed, deceit and luck is at play along with taking advantage of people whom have little in their life to feel happy about (i.e. exploitation).

People are also too stressed and lack life skills to do their own research by being indoctrinated into a system that promotes following the people in charge without question, which they have been experiencing since childhood. Leading to people struggling with the task of critical thinking and questioning judgments made by government and therefore just accept the outcomes.

This had led the UK to be known as a nation of 'moaners' rather than a nation of 'fairness and equality', whereas the French are known as a nation of 'protesters and strikers' when the French government attempts to pass legislation that is unfair on the populous. For generations, people in Westernised nations have accepted an ever increasing wealth gap between the poorest in society and the wealthiest with the propaganda that economy figures and interest rates really matter to the majority's wealth status; that hard work actually pays, and you can be who you want to be if you try hard (land of the free, land of opportunity). These are simply not true for various reasons (discrimination, population numbers, devious behaviour, etc.) and I believe the difficulties of real life compared to the messages received from birth are some of the main reasons for the increase in physical and mental health risks people are facing today along with the plain acceptance of worth in society.

Reducing the wealth gap and increasing the standard of living for the lowest paid in society has to be given priority but this need has certain caveats. First, until society grows to the realisation that greed is bad and the financial economy does not have to be linked with a productive economy, these incorrect realisations have to be traded with an improvement in the quality of life. Second, there has to be a consideration that the countries health is highly coupled with people's responsibility; and currently there is a large gap between work ethics, laziness, and accountability of some at the expense of the majority. This necessitates a need for a major restructure of governance and employment/banking laws to match people's skill availability in the local area where the need is required.

Lastly, and probably more importantly, change and an example has to be set for those that are perceived to be at the top of the tree, the people who are voted into government. At the moment, I firmly believe, and there is adequate / sufficient evidence to support the theory, that MPs/senators are voted into government not because of their individual ability to make a positive difference for the areas they represent, but, as in a general election, they are voted for because they are the best of the worst. This perception has to change.

The UK is a small country compared to others in the world, yet, it has the second largest number of people in the House of Lords (831 including lords, ladies and bishops), which are currently unelected, in addition to a large number of elected officials in office. All of whom are personally benefitting from tax payers' contributions with those ever important expenses (the proverbial 'gravy train') and who do not have to worry about the size of their pension funds. Once voted in, they are in the 'chambers of power' for 5 years whether or not they are effective in their positions. Furthermore, their ability and capability to satisfy the requirements of their position, even before standing as a possible MP/senator/councillor for an area, is an incredibly grey area. It would appear the opportunity to be a representative of government is not based on skills and experience, as stated on a Curriculum Vitae (CV) that all people need for any other application or career opportunity; but, by being related to a current or past elected part member, becoming a member of a political party, networking, and being in attendance at party conferences. Being from a wealthy background or from those that are in the group, which are positively discriminated towards, also helps.

Being in government is the most important career path in the country, but does not need a CV that is scrutinised to a high degree by all who is voting. Nor, does experience, skills or aptitude regarded when being appointed to head committees or governmental departments; this seems to be based on networking and having friends in high places within the political circle, not based on suitability. Is it really a surprise when reports are filed showing a massive waste of time, money and effort in various 'failed' projects, especially IT and support services including: the health service and corruption in the Child Support Agency (CSA or CMEC) - I am classing the courts, children's services and the calculations used since the commencement of the CSA as part of the problem here (interestingly, most MPs in the UK who have overseen the CSA have been removed on suspicion of corruption). On the surface this sound ludicrous, but nevertheless this is the situation in a number of Westernised countries. Indeed, when an MP or senator is quizzed, whether it be by a reporter or at an open session, the answers have much to be desired and are tantamount to a redirection of the question to avoid answering it; could it be the politicians are incapable of answering it, unwilling (due to possible fraud, corruption or law-breaking) or too incompetent to give an objectionable response.

However, the key strength of being a mainstream politician is talking, a lot of talking, with trained hand gestures to compel the people to subscribe to topical issues that are being discussed in parliament / senate. These brief accounts are carefully structured by professional writers in collusion with psychologist to be presented, continuously presented, over a period of time (e.g. Russia bashing, election hacking, importance of the benefit of storing money in banks, pensions, etc.) to the people to obtain approval. These verbal and written accounts (if available) lack transparency and in all honesty are carefully configured 'waffle'. If people did not accomplish their own research on the area of concern, what has been presented is very convincing 'waffle', but practically all the time lacks conviction that the 'experts' involved know what they are doing by the consistent 'tangent' or direct avoidance in answering questions. If people did complete research into the area being voted on in parliament/senate, the only conclusion is what has been presented lacks in transparency and depth of knowledge. Keeping track of decisions made by elected officials and ministers regarding various projects, laws and regulations, it is undeniable that they can truly 'talk the talk', but, cannot 'walk the walk' with failures, scandals and farcical outcomes being regular occurrences. Although, is the incompetence and the failed outcomes merely a cover for the success of the real plan? This is the question that needs to be asked as if all projects and plans set forth by the government have failed, why does the wealthy in society always benefit from the outcome? This is an interesting hypothesis for people to research on your own; I would recommend starting at how much money the wealthy made in the 2008 recession.

There is a cyclic event that continues to occur in official capacities, especially when something goes wrong and the political 'poor quality' leaders have to explain to the public why. However, there is a phrase which is used to describe these type of events, and it is 'polishing the turd' to sell something as something else. What this means is to gloss over the incompetent mistake or corruption, change the name of the system, and market it as something improved from the original, but, in reality the system is exactly the same as the old one, possibly even worse. It is a phrase that people in an official capacity hate to hear, but, in recent times is a daily occurrence due to the poor quality of people in all government departments.

To add to this, most front bench politicians are career politicians or are multi-millionaires, which begs the question of the motives of their interest in being in such a position. It is clear, these people have little experience of issues in the real world, lack the knowledge on how 'things' actually work and the problems facing people who are close or on the breadline. At the same time the average back bench MPs/senators have few options open to them: either follow the front bencher's or jeopardize their political career aspects by becoming a 'rebel' and risk becoming de-selected at the next election or being 'stabbed in the back' by others in their own party, re: Jeremy Corbyn leadership contest both in 2015 (which was a joke that accidently backfired on the mainstream labour politicians) and 2016 (to remove Mr. Corbyn from being leader of the labour party after a number of failed internal party manoeuvres). Thus, on a vote in parliament/senate that has strong ethical and moral issues, i.e. going to war; after a study has been conducted in their own constituent regions on how the people are feeling about the subject, an elected official will either vote for (if the majority of people polled in constituency agree, which is a 'double edged sword' because the public never have enough information with which to base decisions on) or abstain against the motion, which is completely useless in a democratic vote and cowardly. For a less critical area the elected officials might vote against the front benchers, at some risk to their position in the party depending on the pressure from the leadership and the likelihood of being elected again the next time. Nonetheless, in such important decisions that will affect all in the country, the majority of people are not eligible to see all the evidence, consulted nor have the opportunity to have their voices truly heard as part of the vote. This is extremely concerning and very anti-democratic i.e. would the majority of people voted to bail the banks out in 2008 knowing that banking regulation and accountability for the recession would be let to slide, despite pledges by politicians on the contrary?

For their trouble, however, there is a good salary compared to most (UK - £74,962) with added benefits in expense claims, (Jan-Aug 2016 – see http://www.parliamentary-standards.org.uk/DataDownloads.aspx) which can account for an additional tens of thousands of pounds, thus the politicians do not have to pay for transport, food, second homes, replacements in their own home, etc., generally known as the 'perks' of the position or for the laymen, the 'gravy train' that sets apart the privileges of being an MP/senator from others in society. As an elected official, the prime objective is to serve the people of the country, however, major weaknesses of being human is greed, arrogance, and ego; so should these officials be treated as privileged people as psychologically speaking they could, after a period of time, see themselves as being more important than others. When or if this happens it would negatively affect their performance and judgement as someone who is working to the betterment or benefit of others, and in extreme cases (maybe common) become self-serving at the expense of others; perhaps this is why certain people become involved in politics, i.e. for selfish reasons.

When watching how politicians behave within the chambers of the house, especially during prime ministers' questions, their behaviour as people who represent our interests is questionable. It is more on par with debates happening in primary school. Is it really that surprising though? During the election period(s) all the debates and the marketing material are more about demonising the opposition parties than what their policies will be once in government. This has led to all parties producing a very professional manifesto that is vacant of any real detail, which is basically a sales pitch. Whilst, the behaviour of the party members is more akin to the 'bitchiness' of the Kardashians. The behaviour is shameful and embarrassing and makes me query how such childish and immature people end up in a position of power. Are these people really the best the country has to offer?

The answer is 'no', however, the approach in which the political parties use to manipulate people into voting one way or the other is due to the technique of using main stream media as stenographers for their cause. There are many different approaches political parties and media outlets coordinate efforts to influence voters' minds, the most general is to demonise the opposition and use 'fear' or 'scare' tactics to sway minds. It is hard to believe that this technique is so affective, but perhaps the key as to why it works is due to the education system teaching people how not to think, just do; not to question everything, just accept what is presented; and probably the reason why the education system isn't working, as producing thinkers doesn't help political sales tactics. This notwithstanding, there are people who will vote for the same party, due to inherited beliefs, irrespective of the current state of society; the main parties in the UK, US and Europe rely on this for control of certain regions of the country.

Thus, for many decades political parties have been able to manipulate choices people make, whilst not being proficient in presenting any details or facts (i.e. not manipulate-able statistics) of any of their decisions into the public sphere because no one has been capable of holding them accountable for their actions. Consequently, it no surprise why manifestos are nothing more than empty promises just so they can achieve power in government; where the ruling party can ignore their own sales pitch and do what they want whilst giving 'feeble' excuses as to why.

This leads nicely to mentioning the 'scandals' of elected officials and ministers. There are substantial defective, immoral, unethical behaviours when politicians are involved that are conveniently always categorised as scandals and nothing else. Illegal wars involving deaths of innocent men, women and children, expense fraud, corruption, lobbying (or more accurately bribery) - payment for favours, which has seen some unfortunate outcomes for innocent people, under age sex, prostitution, forced extradition of people, financial bailouts, failed expensive projects, forced removal of foreign governments, arms deals with dictatorships and rebels, tax avoidance, immigration, non-Dom

P a g e | 48

status of residents and companies who do business in the country … etc. Additionally, due to lobbying, poisonous chemicals, e.g. Carcinogens, are being allowed to be sold in various stores causing health issues in society (i.e. cancer), all while governments secures the scientific data to ensure public release is avoided or delayed for a number of years, or the radioactive impacts of mobile communication technology and its link to various cancers, etc. - (there are more likely additional issues which have not been presented to the public or through leaked documents from whistle-blowers), all of which occurs without any criminal charges being sought. The most that happens, mainly to manipulate public opinion, are commissions or inquiries to investigate why and whether any lessons can be learned (of course this is very expensive and paid for by the tax payer), again this is apparently a waste of time and money as nothing of any substance comes from them (re: Iraq war inquiry, health care commissions, etc.).

Considering all that has occurred within the political field over the past two decades, it would appear that becoming an elected official makes a person immune to prosecution even for the most detestable actions; unless you fall out of favour with the political elite then you're in trouble. Unethical or damn right illegal actions are more and more being labelled as scandals, and clearly there needs to be some clear distinction between unlawful, illegal, incompetent or corrupt acts and most certainly the official(s) whom are responsible should be immediately removed from their positions of authority.

Budget and Spending

Major public budgeted projects organised and overseen by government departments are, for the lack of better words, disgracefully managed and controlled. The evidence is so overwhelming that they do not need to be listed in this book. Most national projects overrun both in cost and time with the tax payer (without being consulted or having a voice in the decision) always tolerating the burden of the issues. The national projects, for example HS2, are more about politicians grandstanding on the world stage than about improving services and the quality of life; and this is the number one reason why money, tax payer's money, is no obstacle in successful completion of it. (Most national projects are 'nice to have' i.e. the 'wants' rather than 'needs' and would benefit the richest in society the most rather than being for a necessity i.e. for solving social issues.) Justification for some of the projects, like HS2 facilitating a 20minute faster rail journey or the most expensive nuclear power plant in Europe if not the world at Hinkley (UK) under a EDF/China contract, are weak at best; but, nevertheless public opinion (cost and environmental concerns) is managed or ignored and the project moves ahead with cost, generally, spiralling out of control. This has detrimental effects on people who pay tax and the ever increasing amounts in shadow tax, i.e. on energy bills, accompanied by the increase in borrowing and national debt.

There is at least a distinct lack of competence and control for authorising project proposals and public purse accounting. If the available budget cannot account for the cost of the national projects or by reduction of spending elsewhere or by private backers, the projects should be further scrutinised as to the benefit(s):cost (trade study) by people who <u>actually</u> know what they are doing in an impartial and objective manner.

Local government spending is also an important area to be concerned about. Just as national projects are badly managed so it would seem the smaller local government led projects are of equal trepidation. I have seen money being spent on refurbishing town and city centres to the detriment of the area and to businesses and traders who operate there; I have seen sculptures, art work, many, many traffic light being installed causing confusion to drivers who are in an unfamiliar area; greenland and woodland given to property moguls for housing estates causing localised flooding; IT projects that come with service contracts because the software package is unreliable; etc. etc. etc. I have also seen and heard of local government leaders and bosses going on 'jollies (holidays or fun events)' or been given football tickets etc. in return for business; not to mention higher management in local government giving themselves six figure salaries and huge bonuses; whilst at the same time raising local taxes and providing less services for the money collected off residents.

What society in the West has is severe incompetence and greed at the national level which has 'trickled' down to the local level and there does not appear to be an end in sight. Costs for everyone in society are increasing and standards and quality of services decreasing, which invariably increases the risk of social disquiet and with it a detriment in social cohesion. In summary, the money that needs to be allocated to solving real problems in society is being diverted into projects for grandstanding both at the local and national stage for the betterment of a few people in society at the expense of those with little available disposable income and in low paid work.

At the minimum, control has to be rejuvenated in public expenditure with critical judgments being made about the benefit to the majority in society and priority given to projects that solve real life and social problems. Grandstanding and high pay packages have to be a mechanism of the past. Costs of projects need to be paid for by savings in other areas, e.g. salary and benefits of higher management, reducing bureaucracies by utilising digital technology mediums, devolving central power and services to local control whilst simultaneously monitoring Key Performance Targets (KPT) stipulated in employment contracts of local government leaders, management, and law commissioners. Further investments in solving social problems are needed, which should reduce the costs of post reactions to such problems and thus the two expenses can be traded off against each other. All of which should assist improving the quality and productivity of public sector services.

Modern History and How We Came To Here

How did Europe, UK and USA culminate to be where it is now? Details discussions on this area is probably left for a follow up book, however, it is important to indicate within this section, in an abstract way, how occupational opportunities, migration and government contracts have affected the state of the country and the decisions people make because of it.

Since the end of the second world war (circa. 1945), when the UK and US gained crucial investments and control over Middle Eastern oil, gas and mineral supplies (more about this later) and the realisation of the business potential of exploiting people for little remuneration; UK, Europe and US business owners along with successive governments have realised the profit potential of moving manufacturing and production out of the country to reduce expenditure costs and maximise profits. The circumstances triggered the end of the great industrial revolution in the UK closely followed by most countries in Europe then the

USA; a by-product of which enabled the air quality, especially around capital cities, to improve significantly. Whilst, the issue of labour exploitation and bad working conditions gradually diminished at home, these problems essentially relocated elsewhere. Short term outcome of this led to huge profits and the expansion of shipyards to cope with the transportation of shipping containers.

Due to productivity observed during the war, the number of women in the workplace began to increase; however, with manufacturing relocating abroad, for the benefit of a few, it became clear a few decades later that a problem of employment availability to suit the number of residence in the country needed a solution. The governments at that time resisted further relocation of manufacturing plants by offering substantial tax incentives and other benefits for them to stay and obviously that situation is still continuing to this day.

Nevertheless, this solution only offered a temporary resolution to employment opportunities. The UK, EU, and US governments needed to create jobs without possessing, what was once a prospering, industrial foundation. This led to successive governments creating a large, now overbearing, public service sector and additional public funded and government sponsored jobs that are not essential to everyday life; most commonly called 'non-jobs' or referred to as 'people who carry clip boards in posh suits looking important' during business hours. As more manufacturing jobs were lost to countries such as, India, China, Asia, etc. more government funded jobs were created, which meant that more tax was/is required to be paid by the people in the country.

As the world became more globalised and governments concluded trade deals with other countries, more jobs needed to be created within the service and 'non-job' sectors to account for those being lost as a consequence of the deals being made. Those who for generations had worked in certain occupations, became disenchanted with most not having those key transferrable skills, and chose not to work in response to the current ruling government casting their voice and concerns aside. Thus, they decided to remain, by choice, on the benefits system (in the UK, the 'iron-lady' Margaret Thatcher years coincided with the change in working ethics of a substantial few in the country), thus began the rise of the benefit state; with some of their relatives still living on benefits.

In former times, working was seen as incurring great pride and dignity; people used to be proud and stimulated to get up in the morning and go to work, even in the most unpleasant environments. This sentiment changed rapidly as more interesting jobs left the country with the manufacturing base all but gone; and the less interesting, damn right boring jobs of the service sector established itself and came into fruition.

Soon, due to high taxes and stress of working life, people stopped taking care of the local area and enthusiasm for taking pride in work diminished. Soon communities began to change for the worse, and local government needed to employ more contractors to repair roads, walls, trim trees and mow lawns, and other general maintenance works that local people had maintained before. This all had to be paid for through taxation, both directly and indirectly, which only supplemented people's disillusionment with government decisions. Those who had enough chose to emigrate for a better life abroad; this however, steered to what is now an overarching problem of migration throughout the West.

Businesses and government needed enough people in the country to work on unskilled, low paid jobs; they needed people who would once again be grateful for the opportunity to earn money and create a better life for themselves; business looked internationally to fill the job and motivation gap. Meanwhile, knowing the current state of manufacturing and occupation opportunities, the native people looked at both apprentices and universities to gain important qualifications so they had a better opportunity to acquire a well-paid job; there was and still is little interest in low paid work.

As the population increased and women became more prominent in the workforce, the government continued to create more jobs at the cost of the tax payer and contributed to the escalation in debt. Meanwhile in the private sector, the competition between employees fostered office politics and with it all the negative aspects of human behaviour to assist in the fight for job security and promotion. With more people living in the country, the need (and demand) for more resources increased, this put pressure on obtaining important natural resources from foreign countries. As a consequence of the increase in service sector jobs, manual labour jobs reduced dramatically and more people became accustomed to working wearing a tidy, smart uniform and/or office wear. Whilst migrants were in a perfect position to accept the jobs that required hard work and/or work in dirty environments.

The technology revolution began (circa. 20 years ago), colour televisions, computers and mobile phones became affordable to the working class, which increased the marketing potential for businesses and became a medium to be used for propaganda. The younger generation experienced images and marketing like never before. The new generation 'wanted' for nothing and would spend like never before to acquire the very latest gadget to keep up with their friends and colleagues; as being left behind led to bullying and being excluded from groups – and so the consumerist era began without any thought of the consequences.

The demand for housing increased as did the acceptance of living with large amounts of debt. Second generation migrants became all too aware of the same opportunities, as such competition in the workforce for decent well paid jobs became increasingly difficult as to was university placements and so did the pressures of infrastructure to cope with the increased population. Fortunately, the technology revolution, which is currently levelling off, created more opportunities for qualified people to move into these areas of work. These new opportunities were/are highly supported by government incentives that further increased pressures on the public purse.

The drive for higher academic qualifications to obtain these new career opportunities meant universities needed to be expanded; and the number of children born in the country was breaking all previous records and placing stress within the schooling system. However, the number of new technology jobs was/is small in comparison to the number of people in the country who need jobs; software programming qualified people reached saturation point (in all honesty the same situation still exists today). The rise of non-important highly paid careers within law, accounting, finance and social science, etc., began to help fill the gap and reduce the problem of the benefit state (well on paper anyway).

With the gap for skilled qualified engineers filled, and the creation of positions whose prime purpose is to increase profit for the few (finance, accounting, traders, etc.), to make money from people's misery (lawyers, solicitors, debt collection agencies, etc.), and instil authority over people, especially parents without having any coherent plan (positions in social sciences), still left the problem of jobs that were needed to help keep business expenditure low by keeping pay low; hence, more migrants were needed than ever before to fill the gap and the EU laws offered the perfect treaty to resolve it.

The rise of the bureaucratic nation began in its fullness, in effect to generate additional jobs and agencies marketed as a method of quality and safety control to reduce the problem of unemployment. 'Tick box' management became common practice in both academia and industry. People responsible for the completion of the paperwork became self-important, but, carried with them respect within higher management. The scheme to increase paperwork is so successful that data completed on paper was to be entered into computer databases, this created more job opportunities as administrators and the proverbial 'non-job middle men'. (However, there is growing concern that the people in these positions are taking work away from higher management; there is a stereotype of management now in the West – 'the higher up the ladder to go, the less work and responsibility you have'.) This is the inevitable problem of creating 'non-jobs' to assist in satisfying negative governmental statistics; this also breeds laziness, complacency and a false sense of importance for the ones who are paid the most.

With software and System on a Chip (SoC) engineering jobs above saturation level, average salaries reducing significantly (in real terms compared to the cost of living) and with most technology manufacturing being completed internationally, the governments needed new opportunities to venture into. Having highly qualified people not being able to find decent paid work could lead to the same societal indifferences that was experience throughout the Thatcher years. New enterprises spanned from the American market, namely the pharmaceutical industry and with it bio-engineering. Then came green energy technology, these offered new incentives for the government and the younger generation to branch into. The growth of research institutions, public and private, funded by government, meant more academics, more degree areas, more qualifications to be had and additional career opportunities to be sought.

Throughout, the few were making real money from the work of the majority, the majorities physical and psychological health began to deteriorate. People had less disposable money at the end of every month and with leisure activities becoming more and more expensive, entertainment at home was the only avenue for large portions of society. The deterioration in society's health was/is marketed to be due to people on benefits causing the countries financial problems and people 'bought' into this message without considering that government and the economy needs unemployed people to further subsidise businesses during normal working hours (9-5). The health issues include the following: - 1) greater pressures in the workplace due to competition; 2) longer working hours without the body moving a great deal; 3) lack of spare time; 4) higher cost of living due to higher taxation; 4) Lack of motivation to 'keep in shape'; 5) diminished thought of worth in society; 6) Lack of any fun activities at an affordable price; etc. People were becoming unhappy with their daily lives and could see the few in society reaping the rewards.

The media outlets used this 'anger' not against the wealthy but to vilify those who claim benefits and live life free of stress and worry with large amounts of freedom. The war against the benefit cheats had begun in earnest, however, the people on benefits grew wise to this and so sought to be signed off with depression from doctors, a system that still works well today.

With more and more competition for few decently paid jobs it became clear that being competent and knowledgeable did not guarantee a career opportunity. An additional attribute was needed, one which in current times takes president over relevant attributes for a job/career. The rise of smooth talkers in all sectors with academic qualifications, all involved in office politics, all in high level positions due to being 'yes' men, not because of ability. *(Smooth talking and money is the answer to 'how can someone so dumb get into positions of power and decision'.)* Consequently, this caused / causes additional layers of management to be employed to correct the lack of competence in doing the job their employed to do; it also meant the price of goods increased dramatically. Whilst those who use a voice that questions decisions, have common sense and intelligence struggle to achieve unless they choose their own course in life (i.e. self-employed) that has high risk associated with it, with the majority failing in the venture.

To tackle the problem of large populations and to increase profit margins, the number of wars increased for control of resources, additional facilities and infrastructure needed by the government to keep pace with the population and maintain a relatively high standard of living on the world stage, all had to be augmented again at the expense of the tax payer and the ever increasing debt level.

The pressures people feel now about keeping their jobs is for some unbearable due to the large pool of people in the country all searching for jobs that they 'drown their sorrows' to forget about the stresses of daily life in whatever works for them. To the advantage of business owners, the marketing strategy used via media outlets has indoctrinated people into purchasing products they do not actually need as a means to feel better and a break from their daily lives and in doing so has created 'consumers' – the consumerist society is something that is good for the economy (for the few), but, has negative impacts on people's wellbeing.

All this has had a detrimental effect of parenting with parents too tired and stressed to spend quality time with their children, meaning that children are now given IPads or tablets as replacement babysitters to keep them distracted whilst being presented will various types of marketing materials. Invariably, this has led to the spoiled and internet generation with an explosion of celebrity worshipping without any decent role models to look up to (I mean it really is very slim pickings); along with the destruction of the English language and young people being involved in joll-ish, potentially dangerous, behaviour whilst being hooked on mobile phone technology and all that comes of it.

But, the pressures to succeed, now more than ever before, far out way the decision to lead a healthy and fulfilling life, whilst simultaneously striving to have the perfect body shape to match the 'photo-shopped' images seen in the media. All of which has a detrimental effect on health, weight acceptance, their status among peers, goals and dreams in life, and gender acceptance.

With competition for career and status in society stronger than ever before between sexes, culture (marketed as race wars), and religion; time with family and the strength to work at relationships to keep the family together is now an all-time low. Children are the ones who suffer the most; images and YouTube videos, along with talk shows like Jerry springer and Jeremy Kyle, and soap operas, has created a generation of people who have some serious relationship and behavioural problems, which have / are being passed down to the next generation of people. It has created a society that is accustomed to 'if you want it, get it; get it now worry about consequences later', 'life is boring let's have a party and don't worry about the consequences', 'having sex without being responsible or care about who it is with', 'incurring gender identification issues', and 'disposing of something once it has served its purpose, or is unfashionable'. For the economy (for the few) it works, but, unfortunately the human consequence means people cannot be bothered to work through difficult issues and protect themselves inside a metaphorical bubble.

People have grown up very 'thin-skinned' and struggle to cope with criticism (in all forms including name calling), failure, and the inability to deal with their own problems to the extent that they are accustomed to ignoring them or undergo plastic surgery to correct a problem that has nothing to do with physical appearance but 'ignorantly' believe the procedure will help, especially with confidence. The outcome of which is experienced everywhere: broken families, absent but 'financially responsible' fathers, and mothers who care for boys and girls without identifying and understanding the differences between genders (sex) (and some who abuse their position by being dominant to the father, sometime being a dictator, at the expense of the children wellbeing whilst the father is forced to be passive). In essence, the modern world has promoted consumerism to the extent that now people have become controlling, emotionally immature and self-involved but equally disposable and replaceable. All without thinking about the underlying mental, physical and social issues associated with these actions. Is this an unfortunate consequence of the dilution of separate cultures into one, consumerist attitudes, competition, greater population numbers and the fall in religious beliefs among native people without a strong family bond?

Competition and the desperation to succeed in the workplace have seen positive discrimination and various other political movements become involved in recruitment. Diversity and feminism are taking centre stage in recruitment efforts after years of complaints about sexism and racism in employment circles. Competition, meritocracy, racism and sexism are now intermingled together that one cannot see where one starts and the other one finishes; there is an argument that now more than any time in history the 'white man' is being discriminating against in all walks of life. In career opportunities it is not a matter of who is best to do the job, but who the smoothest talker is and which person satisfies the diversity and sex policy(s). The age of meritocracy (if it ever was) is now over, the rise of 'the more you complain in public circles - the more you get your own way' has begun.

Diversity as an issue has always puzzled me; society has many groups protesting, lobbying and doing what they can to ensure that commissions, executives and higher level management, football teams, etc., are full of diverse people. But, when examining the current mix in boardrooms and management, there appears to be a healthy mix of people from different skin colours to backgrounds and cultures already part of the team. Turning the tables on the argument, some companies that are owned by people from different backgrounds, religion or culture do not have a diverse range of people in boardrooms or in management; where is the argument to have a more diverse structure here. There simply is not one! Is it possible that diversity is not what some people want as the outcome in this issue? Or is it that some people want more for themselves and less for others? What society have now is a system where government and companies have backed down and given incentives to employ people from various backgrounds, cultures, religions and gender; suggesting society have turned our backs on 'the best person for the job (meritocracy)' in order to satisfy a diversity policy which promotes and is 'in your face' discriminatory to mainly 'white males' (although some white females are also affected) who may be more experienced, skilled and capable of fulfilling the requirements of the role better than the person who has been accepted for the position.

Depending on people's point of view, all this may seem like a good or a bad idea, but the pressures and stresses on people to earn more, to have a good career, to 'stab other people in the back' to succeed, and to behave and work hard to keep a job as there are 'plenty of fish in the sea', is leading to huge increases in depression and people living life unhappy with their own circumstances. But, then there is the other side of the coin, the majority of people are completely distracted all day every day and continue to fight amongst themselves for livelihoods and career success – logically you could argue this type of competition leads to distraction. The statement is true; if a person is working long hours and concentrating on keeping their job at any cost, there is little time or energy left at the end of the day to deeply connect, with interest, and consider what the people who make important decisions that could impact everyone's life are doing i.e. the government.

It is not a big surprise why successive governments have managed to get away with 'scandal' after 'scandal' with only a groan from the majority in society and zero accountability. However, the technological revolution is causing an issue with allowing different viewpoints to be available at the touch of a button; automation is leading towards high unemployment rates and more people will have more time to take an interest in national and global events. More people than in any other time in history are now beginning to take more notice of propaganda or fake news; and it is all too clear that the established elites in government are researching strategies to control the flow of information so that only 'national interests' are available to the majority of the country. A strategy of vilifying and demonising other news networks or internet sites are now common place to the extent that recently RT today (Russian news network) is used in the same context as Islamic terrorists.

It would seem all political talk and propaganda is down to subterfuge to distract and disorient people to make people 'buy' into false realities in order for the government to make these 'hard decisions' that they keep talking about. The reality is all decisions made by the government are based on business and profit reasons, not for human reasons.

Economy Concerns

One area, which demands a detailed mention, is the rise of the banking sector - which is sold as a profit making machine, but, is actually debt making factories with fraud and corruption rampant within the establishment besides placing a huge burden on taxpayers to account for the forever increasing debt ceiling. Governments and banks are intrinsically and uniquely linked along with wars, oil, gas, and natural resources. Whether Western society likes it or not, the people who work in the financial sector are members of the military effort for the corporatocracy whom can and do cause more harm to people's lives than any military technology or bomb can do; and are fully protected and backed up by the oligarchs including those in governments. This institution has spread greed and reduced morals for the masses in society both at home and internationally.

The debt level is more than twice the size of the global economy and unprecedented as a proportion of GDP with a record global debt of over $152tn. The financial economy makes no sense when eye watering values such as this one is being used to instil austerity on people; with no common sense or understanding of how this has happened or what is going to be done about it by any 'expert' in the financial sector. (How about press the delete button on the spreadsheets and databases that concern this amount, then lay the foundations for a society without constraints of money but based on resource availability and let people have freedom as long as their actions benefits to society in some way).

The gap between how business currently operates for maximising profits for owners and shareholders at the expense of paying a living wage and the pollution factors for the environment need to be reduced; in essence, a new type of capitalism and governance is required to be created. This should take the form of regional economies by forming strong relationships with industry, scientists, unions and a new environmental security board (which will look at the impact of running a business, including logistics). These regional economies will help form localised knowledge clusters that is hoped will generate expertise and global technology links that will help the country lead the path for the future of the new environmental and social economy.

Gaps in remuneration between executive pay and front line pay require to be investigated. In a short period of time, the gap has increased and the responsibility and usefulness of the higher paid employees has reduced. The majority of employees in businesses currently have no voice in the decisions regarding executive pay and benefits. This needs to change, the country and businesses can no longer govern with paying 'smooth talkers' a generous pay package without associating it with KPT's that are judged in a democratic manner with all employees. This will assist in creating transparency and help reduce redundancy and therefore help to improve efficiency within the business. Businesses will then operate and be governed on the basis of mutual obligations of all employees within the business and will form partnerships for improving job and human quality (better working life) and promotion of quality people (meritocracy); and place outdated practices, which are currently devoid of any meritocracy process, in the past.

Successive governments have weakened employment 'rights' (there is no such thing as rights at present, only when people lives are not affected by decisions of others, will people have rights i.e.

rights = freedom; for the moment what people think of as 'rights' are merely privileges) and encouraged a hire-and-fire culture helped by the increase in population and thus a greater pool of people to fill gaps in jobs. The regional strategy should help improve the country's route to prosperity and higher living standards through more secure and better occupations with substantially better terms and conditions of employment; competing for profit should no longer be the prime concern; it will be high in the agenda but should no longer be strived for.

For many years there has been copious amount of talk about the setting of the national minimum wage and to bring it closer to the national average earnings. Very recently in the UK there has been a roll-out of the living wage, which in all honesty does not resemble a salary that anyone can have a good quality of life with - there is a big difference between living a quality life and just existing. With the possibility of high profits and further incentives sold by government attracting companies to do business in the country, profit have and probably will (for the short term) take president over giving an actual living wage, which is the main cause of a high percentage of social and health issues mentioned earlier.

The low setting of the minimum wage has caused the rise of payday lenders to take advantage of people's money worries and consumerist / materialistic attitudes. With the poor state of education, especially in financial management, and consumerism people struggle with managing money and with it the true cost of borrowing.

Young adults have grown-up with advertising everywhere and the acceptance of living with debt with the scheme promoted by government. They are only concerned with whether or not they can afford the monthly payments; people have become numb to the real price of products and services. This has caused products to be raised in price well above what it is worth (i.e. Lego), costing people more in the long term with interest payment and/or insurance in order to have the latest gadget, clothing or other technology. People in society have now lost the ability to save before purchasing anything and it has also led people not being fully aware of the true cost of products or services they acquire, they just know how much something is worth to them now, moreover, how it makes them feel. The system has become a self-fulfilling cycle of living in debt and having to deal with the repercussions of this type of gluttony in the future.

Unfortunately, successive governments have been unable or uninterested, due to lobbying, to solve this problem; sadly, debt and money are ways of controlling people. However, better education and more stringent control with the marketing of money lenders along with introducing a high levy on payday lenders should help in the irradiation of this type of scourge. Society need to create a country free of household debt by controlling the cost of living in a better way. The government has the responsibility of setting tax rates for everything people consume, therefore, has data regarding the minimum cost of living, including housing, for different areas of the country and should be capable of setting the minimum living wage based on the most expensive areas in the country to live, which undoubtedly will be near city centre areas. For example, the minimum living wage for a humble quality of life for those on the low pay level is envisaged to be a lot more than the suggested £8/hr by October 2019.

The problem is state benefits outweigh the minimum wage differences between the cost of living and the salary given (i.e. benefits to top-up salary to a minimum earning level) and therefore defeats the object of removing people registered on benefits (i.e. for improved unemployment statistics) and thus drains the public purse. This living wage should be a salary that should comfortably pay bills, food, etc., and provide spare cash for entertainment to improve or maintain quality of life besides enrich the happiness index. The point being there should be no one who works full time (or near to) seeking additional benefits from the government/public-purse. The instant where this becomes reality is the true level of the national living wage, which will increase or decrease with the levels of inflation. The regional strategy should give local authorities a role in enforcing those scrupulous employers who choose to take advantage of workers by paying them less than the legal amount.

For many years, the exploitation of workers in foreign countries has become, sadly, part of normal working practices. Due to greed and the increase in the potential employee pool (due to migration) this practice has seen its way into Western society and is now thought to be more common. It is really hard to improve the quality of peoples' life and secure decent secure occupation for people when successive governments in the country have promoted the ease of hiring and firing people e.g. zero hours contracts, reduction of unions, and high fees (£1,200 in UK) for employment tribunal claimants (in 2017, a court deemed these fees unlawful). There is now a practice of using a loophole that allow companies to undercut permanent staff by using agency workers on lower pay and require less company overheads; generally, these agency workers tend to be foreign migrant workers. All the issues regarding the lack of employee privileges and employment loopholes have to be revoked; affordability should not be a barrier for anyone attempting to gain justice; the loophole has to be abolished and native people who are in need of secure work should be given first choice. There should be government incentives for the re-generation of unions in all employment sectors for added protection against employers who abuse their position; government should force employers to only use agency workers when they have no other choice i.e. when the unemployment figure in the local region or national level is negligible.

There also needs to be a greater incentive offered to people who are unemployed to take these positions; a closer relationship between business, government and unions is needed to generate a strategy to entice people to these positions. Perhaps offer additional training schemes, paid by the employers, to enable people to learn and gain new skills and qualifications to help the employee progress their own interests. It is more than reasonable for employers, especially those who have vacancies available that can be seen as uninteresting, to offer something of interest (i.e. K&S training with qualifications); and thus plan for a large employee throughput. Consequently, these types of jobs should be seen as a step into the working environment to gain experience of a workplace; and government can assist companies who wish to govern the business as such. Consequently, this scheme can be considered and marketed as better work and training, better pay and conditions.

However, there is a problem! The future, the very near future, is leading us to a computer governed world. More automation signifies less manual handling jobs; better intelligent machines (there is no such thing as artificial intelligence until the quantum computer is created i.e. making decisions with other attributes than 0 and 1) denotes qualified people are no longer needed to fill positions that require optimisation algorithms. Driverless cars, buses, lorries etc. will remove logistics from being human oriented; and automated algorithms will dominate the banking and finance sectors. Law can be based on logical reasoning algorithms using the evidence presented to make an automated objective decision.

Nonetheless, it makes perfect business sense to automate as much as possible. It would lead to more reliable results – a computer does not start work tired or grumpy, it is cheaper to run and to maintain, and more efficient than human labour; thus leading to a better profit margin. Robotics can help assist people in their homes and at hospital; they will most definitely make life easier for everyone. But how to manage the economy and the livelihoods of people living in the country with this new technology that will undoubtedly make redundant most non-skilled jobs and greatly affect the current skilled jobs. For example, there is over 71 million people legally living in the UK (June 2017), what are all these people, future generations and more going to do with their daily lives and earn money to live in the future if automation of jobs is the future? There needs to be a strategy in place to manage these changes to prevent mass unemployment in all sectors leading to poverty and civil unrest.

Unless you have been living under a rock current business strategies (some which has been summarised above) are not working; at some point saturation is going to be met (if it has not been reached already), governments cannot keep creating jobs on a whim nor can it rely on 'the next big thing'; the government requires a long term strategy to deal with major 'human' investments needed in the country. The emphasis is on human not on economic investments. This will represent a completely different avenue of investment opportunities. No longer should the economy or hope of economic growth determine the decisions on infrastructure projects, (i.e. empty industrial estates, concrete car parks and airports at the cost of green land or woodland is not progress).

Scientific discovery and technological revolution should be placed at the forefront of advancement for the future. Moreover, advancement of human knowledge and health innovation requires a stabilising force with techniques to concentrate on environmental and human cost : profit margins. The business strategy should, without question, centre on a green economy; moreover, the reduction of poisonous chemicals in the environment. This strategy will endeavour to reduce dependency on oil and gas resources, but, will also require certain living constraints to be met. Investment should consider the impact of continued use of prevalent energy supplies, and whether the cost of continued throughput through the business is worth the long term impacts of such investment.

Young People Support

Currently (2017), there are over 720,000 young people in the UK registered as being unemployed, with the majority not having skills needed to acquire a decent paid job. Nevertheless, total unemployment for UK hit 3.213 million (4.5%), Europe hit 34.56 million (7.8%) and USA hit 14.22 million (4.4%) people as of August 2017 even with government creative accounting. This is both a failing of the education system, the raising of retirement age, financial troubles people are faced with, pension failures, but, also of parenting. The hike in tuition fees has put some young people off going to university, whilst the uptake of the new apprentice scheme set up by the government is disappointing. In the future, student fees are likely to increase with universities governing their own fee structure per unit course similar to the US fee structure. This means that in order to gain those important qualifications, young people will start their careers burdened with over est. £44,000 debt on average excluding additional loans for a two-year course, without a guarantee of a decent career in their chosen subject area.

The reasons given for the conception of university fees is due to the recession in 2008. 'Universities are expensive to run and the burden on the tax payer to provide free education to students can no longer be tolerated'. Unfortunately, the reason given does not satisfy any argument given by the government; and perhaps why the liberal democrats in the election of 2010 promised free education, but, due to a deal with the conservatives repealed that promise, and in the later elections the party lost ground and were almost wiped out. The problem is presented to all working class people as they were paying for other peoples' education and giving them advantages once entering the place of work; therefore, a maximum fee of £9000 was set with a promise that universities would only align some courses to this price. As I expected, however, practically all courses began to charge that maximum fee with an added confidence that fees will continue to increase, just like the university system in the US; and it has! This type of system hasn't worked very well in the US, which is over $21 trillion in debt with >$1.2 trillion accountable to university debt. Why the UK government believed that copying the US system would be good for the economy or the wellbeing of students is frankly a prime example of the poor quality decision making abilities of MPs / politicians, unless of course, they aspire for young people to be in debt for the vast majority of their lives.

Sadly, the reasons given for student fees does not 'hold water' i.e. since its introduction in 2012 has any tax paid by people reduced to account for the decrease in burden from education? – No! The idea of someone obtaining a higher education placement to gain qualifications in the hope of procuring a higher paid job than without is so the additional tax and national insurance (NI) that person will pay, throughout their lifetime, more than offsets the cost of education that particular person undertook and as such is zero burden to any other tax payer. It is a system that worked well for several decades.

But now governments are 'very' comfortable with young people living with debt for many years (several decades) without considering: the national consequences, universities not controlling their own running costs, college and university mismanagement practices and pay structures. Most universities have become businesses that look more like factories to exploit young naïve people for qualifications based on the promise of an I.O.U of a better future in an already saturated society. The likelihood is the debt will eventually be sold to private debt collection agencies thus terms and conditions of paying back the debt will change placing additional stresses to the people involved and/or some will not pay the debt back and thus be in addition to the countries debt ceiling. It is a system that actually works against the countries own financial and society's best interests.

Tuition fees for higher education for the majority has to be free at the point of contact and more efficient and better governance has to be placed on university management and academics. The cost of education is more than offset by the returns in tax and NI of those students. If universities require additional funding or the prospective student is from a wealthy background (found by means testing) then additional contributions should be sought by the individual university involved; consequently, personal contributions for the higher earners and clamping down on tax avoidance will additionally assist any funding gaps within the university system.

Next generation Provision

The Youth of today are very different from the youth of yesterday and it is quite confusing as to how they ended up this way. They are offended and upset by everything and they are under the opinion that the way people live now, the systems society has in place, what is actually happening with respect to open door policies, increased taxes and wars, are OK. There is an increase in rape culture (not really); increase in safe spaces in schools, colleges and universities; increase in people taking drugs; increase in people suffering depression and stress; increase in people self-harming and committing suicide. Yet, these are the people who are voting for more of the same in society. It is really confusing why this is the case and it can only be put under one banner, and that category is insanity.

It is the only way to describe what is going on in how young people think today and is purely caused by the indoctrination given by parents, mass media (including the internet), and schools. Children today when they eventually grow up have very little life skills, they would struggle to survive if energy source were to be removed from daily life, and they seem confused with real life problems; yet they firmly believe voting for the same systems that are in place is the right path to continue along. At present, society has what can only be described as a lost generation and this type of situation cannot be allowed to continue to the next because if the same systems, the same type of people in government are present for too much longer then life will become increasingly more difficult as time goes by. The outcome of which will end up as a human race that is more similar to the one described by the film 'Idiocracy' (terrible film) and it is scary to think that this path people are heading towards.

Young people have/are being let down by the education system failing to give necessary K&S to compete in a global market place with government failing to provide decent paid employment at the end of their studies; whilst at the same time burdening them with substantial education debts. Coincidentally, irrespective of skills or abilities, the elites in society (those with money and connections) are often given paid internships at one of the top 50 companies, which give them a huge advantage over the majority of other young people, some of which have skills and abilities that are more suitable for the internship. Most other internships on offer present little or no pay and those who cannot afford to take the position are often locked out of many professions due to financial constraints. For too long consecutive governments have failed to provide a path which makes best use of young people skills and talents and positively discriminates to those from wealthy backgrounds or with high level connections.

Consequently, there needs to be a scheme to offer incentives for businesses and universities to work more closely together and offer flexible internship study programs to assist young people into the occupation and career they have chosen for themselves. Hence, close the gap on inequality and help remove the advantages the elites, including established political members, have over the majority. There needs to be provisions in every government contract - every employer needs to offer one or more fully paid apprenticeships placing suitability at the forefront of decisions made. These awards should then be monitored and analysed to ensure concurrence with the people chosen for the internship to ensure no discrimination has occurred; if found to be favouring those with connections and money a fine should be issued and a black-mark placed on the employer for future government contracts.

To assist those people who have been brought up in a culture of taking advantage of the benefit system, a compulsory profession scheme has to be initialised, paid for by the bank bonus tax. This scheme will provide provisions to enable people to feel like their life matters to help them overcome the sense of merely existing. There obviously needs to be robust incentives for people to engage in the scheme such as the loss in benefits; and this needs to be a hard line. The scheme ought to offer programs best suited to individual interests (a placement or work which offers little interest is doomed to fail) and offer skills training or apprenticeships with internationally recognised qualifications besides working towards giving the individual a sense of worth with a permanent break from the boredom and reality escaping of sitting around watching TV or playing video games.

Flexible training and likewise apprenticeships are expensive to operate and unless there are provisions for employers to engage in these schemes it is unlikely to be successful. A strict contract of 'quid pro quo' should be actioned in agreement with all three parties involved (employer, individual, government) to ensure there is adequate payback for the employer and government in offering these opportunities. The definition and terms and conditions of the contract has to be in relation to the cost : benefit payback to the employer concerned in consideration of the individual's willingness to stay with the employer for a fixed period of time after the training or apprenticeship is complete. The agreement should be in terms of a fixed term contract with certain clauses that does not favour one party or the other.

Those individuals who choose not to work together to benefit society will not be eligible for benefits payments. With schemes in place which is directed at individuals' interests there should be no excuses why people should be sat at home watching TV and playing video games; depression is not an excuse for nonparticipation, as distraction and doing something of interest assists in coping with the symptoms of depression (A. Orzechowska et., al., Depression and ways of coping with stress, Med Sci. Monitor, Vol. 9, pp. 1050, 1056, 2013).

The people who still resist in being part of a community should be offered support, but not financial – this needs to be the hard line taken to effectively give purpose to people's life; there really should be no excuse - laziness, obesity, depression, 'not in the right frame of mind', stress, low confidence, etc. under this scheme are not reasons for being excused from it. The negative impacts on society spanning from the Thatcher and Reagan years has to be reversed.

Cost of Living Expenses

Energy bills are quickly becoming the greatest of concerns for families. The issue is not helped by the signing with EDF and china for the nuclear power plant at Hinkley point in the UK, nor with the strained relationship with Russia or the continued trouble in the Middle East. This notwithstanding, there is a forthcoming energy crisis that has to be planned for; as a society, people have all come accustomed to 'power on demand' and not so accustomed to the repercussions of our 'lust' for power and the goods that come with it (e.g. charging of our gadgets, heating, cars and bikes, entertainment devices, etc.). In the short term, the government needs to control the rising cost of energy; in the long term produce a strategy to wean people off the mentality that energy can be used lavishly (all of society are guilty of wasting energy or being lazy with the use of).

Tactics used by successive governments have been draconian in nature, i.e. just put prices up to reduce consumption. However, as seen in the panic buying at petrol stations and the statistic of the numbers of elderly people dying over winter periods due to soaring energy bills, there is a limit to which people can and should accept the rising cost of energy. Thus, the rising cost of energy has to be controlled to prevent the burden being on the suffering and premature deaths of elderly people. In the short term, profit margins of the larger energy suppliers have to be monitored and prices governed; the energy market needs to be reformed to allow greater competition and better delivery of fairer prices to the consumer; in essence, the big six energy companies should be separated and electricity and gas will need to be sold through an open exchange were energy tariffs/prices are simplified to make it easier for people to compare and gain the best deal. The ideal scenario would be for all utility companies to become publically owned and operated as non-profit to achieve high value for the public and remove the scourge of running the businesses for the benefit of stakeholders rather than the consumers.

The regulatory requirements for making homes more energy efficient needs to be simplified and made robust to enable knowledge to be transferred to everyone. Access to grants and loans specifically designed for energy home improvements should be made available through local government authorities and community organisations; but with one caveat. The owner(s) are required to prove that they are consuming energy efficiently and cutting down on waste by agreeing to energy usage monitoring data to be used collectively to assess future home improvements with energy saving/efficiency being the prime motivator. Private rented homes will also need to meet a new energy standard to bring warmth and decreased energy usage to millions of other homes.

Water usage in properties has been an issue in recent years with the burden of waste and cost increases being placed on the consumer. The reality, however, is most waste comes from poor maintenance and cheap materials used in the transportation of water from source to destination. The water utility industry is in desperate need of reform; the operational efficiency and management structure is broken and the cost of this system has inevitably made water rates increase to the extent that some people struggle to afford to pay it. The government needs to create a water affordability scheme, which will require all water companies to sign up to helping those who simply cannot afford to pay the water bill. Water usage in every household needs to be reduced and as such the identical monitoring system suggested for electricity and gas should be used, monitored by an independent organisation who will then advice households how best to efficiently use water with regular monitoring to ensure compliance with set targets. Price rises should be accompanied with justifications and be strongly linked to profit margins and salary values of executives in a 'real' transparent manner.

Perhaps, even developing new generation homes, which have fresh clean water piped in from the utility company in conjunction with localised grey water for washing, baths or showers should be considered. It is envisaged the grey water supply will be self-contained and be filtered after each use to ensure adequate cleanliness for washing only with the facility to top-up the tank from the mains supply; then the light-weight cost efficient filter, after a period of time, will need to be replaced by the house-owner. This will considerably reduce water rates for the house owner, but, will preserve far more fresh clean drinking water and reduce the pressure and burden for water availability in certain regions. Then perhaps there will be enough incentive to transport clean water to those regions of the world where people are desperate for it.

Like the health care system, the public transport system is in big trouble with the manner in which it is governed being a complete disaster. Successive governments have privatised many areas of public transport that has led to poor service at greater expense with fare increases but, but greater profits for companies who operate them year on year and an increase in bailouts by governments (why when a company is making profit, does it need bailing out??). This all seems very much like a deal that has been made not with the public in mind, but with the potential to make money for the people who run the public transport links via lobbying techniques. It has to be noted that one new scheme put in place by government to improve the poor service is to enable people to claim back fares due to late arrival trains. Problem being that there are many late trains and if the private run public transport system is not making any profit, services will inevitably reduce in quality and quantity requiring further investment using public funds. Society will then have a public transport system being operated by private companies being paid for by the public twice: one at point of service and one through taxes for the benefit of said companies. This system is a prime example of good idea that has gone wrong due to profiteering and the fact that public transport cannot fail and as such will be continuously bailed out by government.

The public transport system should be the arteries and veins transporting valuable people to their destinations and should be governed and operated as efficiently and professionally as possible; and not for making profit but to provide quality service at an affordable price. Consequently, the public transport system has to come back to being publically run on the basis of non-profit, only then can the people's interest come first and thus have more say in how it is governed. The last time government controlled public transport it was a complete disaster, but, it was due to not acquiring the correct people with adequate skills and abilities to manage their defined area, i.e. the smooth talker syndrome were smooth talkers in posh suits are employed who do not have the ability to do the job at hand. KPT's are required to be placed in the terms and conditions of the employment contract to enable the system to adapt and evolve despite any poor performance of management. This should help in resolving most of the issues that were previously present the last time public transport was publically controlled.

Fares should be governed to enable the system to operate in a non-profit scheme, i.e. to pay for salaries, fuel and maintenance; and should be linked to the inflation rate of the national economy but be set locally by local government. The public transport system, being controlled and governed locally, should be able to decide on availability, routes, drive improvement programs and generate a smart ticketing system for all available public transport systems. A system of feedback should also enable a voice for people to express their views on the services they have paid for.

Prices people pay for fuel has also been a quick way in which government can raise easy cash. With people being addicted to using their cars and with the most efficient manner to deliver goods still being a truck, people are all forced to bear the burden of any price rises that comes with 'filling up the tank'. The amount of tax people and businesses have to pay to be able to use transport has become a contentious subject, as any rise in fuel duty causes a rise in food and consumer goods and places greater burden on families' income. The price people pay has become a weapon government uses to influence oil suppliers or even countries to 'fall in line'. The most recent price drop in fuel was to attempt to bankrupt Russia and to increase control over Middle East oil exporters – however as soon as government realised that the tactic was failing the fuel prices increased again; the excuse used for the drop in prices was an excess of supply, but the excess was still present when prices began to rise. The motorist is also hit by further taxation and prices with 'car tax' and 'MOT' all promoted to keep cars safe and to maintain roads; however, car accidents still occur, some road vehicle are exempt from the MOT, i.e. farm vehicles, and roads are in the worst state ever.

It would seem as though the motorist and transport companies are prime targets for government price manipulation that affects the cost of everything people need or want. To give a small number of untrustworthy people the power to place people into poverty and make smaller companies bankrupt just on the manipulation of the cost of fuel is a lot of power to have in countries that promote democracy where people are supposed to be in charge. Thus, price hikes in the form of taxation needs to be more controlled and managed to give people the opportunity to plan for the change; the current system of immediate price hikes followed by a slow reduction in prices need to be reversed.

Government should not have the power to increase the prices of fuel without justification with evidence, nor should oil companies be allowed for immediate increase in price deviations. Any price drops should be immediate, but any price increases should be phased in slowly and be comparable with the increase in household income. Car taxes should be ring fenced to cope with the cost of maintaining roads, not to pay for projects and certainly not to be used to keep the construction industry working on 'nice to have' road infrastructure projects.

Protecting the environment

The overuses of natural resources such as oil and gas have now raised some important longevity questions. Oil and gas is running out rapidly as 'third world' countries, those who have done cheap labour for decades for the Wests' benefit, are having their own industrial revolution and adding to the problem of climate change by using more fossil fuels. Science has almost proved beyond doubt that humans are contributing to climate change and our addiction to these fuels has come into question. Further exploiting the world's resources may put life on the planet at greater risk, so is burning the rest really the best idea and is there a way to break our addiction to them. In the 1970's, it is arguable that there was too much oil, and this story is still present today with price being controlled by controlling extraction volumes. However, our thirst for fuel along with our drive for greater profit margins has created a relatively new industry called 'Shale Gas Fracking', where high pressure chemicals and water (hydraulic fracturing) is pumped inside shale deposits deep underground to fracture or crack rock formations to release the trapped gas. It is seen as the next great energy revolution, even though the method has been linked to poisoning of land and water supplies, earth quakes; and new research indicates the process could also be linked to the formation of sink holes. Nevertheless, the method is becoming more popular with more countries permitting exploration of possible shale deposits.

Humans' quest for addition fuel resources to keep the economy strong has not slowed even though the effects of climate change and the impact to human health are very real. This notwithstanding, further exploration of the ice caps has revealed substantial gas (and oil) deposits within the Artic peninsula, which ironically is only possible due to the climate change reducing the area of ice making access to huge oil and gas reserves easier. The problem is substantial Carbon Dioxide deposits (~150 billion tonnes) could be vented into the atmosphere in the extraction process. The other issue is these remote areas have not been claimed by one country or another and could set Oil Company against each other, but also superpower against superpower to obtain the untapped resource; besides cause untold damage to the area along with the increase risk to wildlife. These issues alone could make the wars in the Middle East look like a scuffle in a primary school yard as countries fight for control of the resource to allow them to grow economically. The cost and risk of extraction is once again being ignored due to human arrogance and quest for wealth in the belief that fuel can be obtain responsibly even though throughout history and even the current 'responsibility' of oil cartels to both the environment, wildlife, and human life are secondary to making huge profits.

Humans are now releasing poisonous gases into the atmosphere far more than at any other time in history (the release of CO_2 has accelerated rapidly) and much of this change is caused by human activity. There may be enough oil and gas in the ground to keep all in energy security for the next 3-4 decades, but, the impact on the climate will be dramatic with the continual rise in global temperatures, so can people really afford to use it? 80% of the world energy comes from fossil fuels; however, governments are now investing substantial funds in renewable energy. But, for renewables to replace hydrocarbons there needs to be a significant increase in all types of solar, wind, hydro, and tidal energy production. Today only a fraction of energy required by a growing population is generated by renewables and that is after significant investment over more than a decade.

With respect to global warming there is a big push from government, not because of environmental reasons but for economic reasons that benefit the few, for various renewable energy plants such as wind and solar to be built. There are some major drawbacks of using both of these sources with the main one being fluctuations in power energy generation. Others include how the natural wind is disturbed when it flows through the blades of the turbine and its effects of wildlife, especially birds and insects, in how they perceive where they are in flight and premature death caused by the blades depending on how fast they are spinning. Also, the turbines are subjected to environmental decay and high maintenance with chemicals used to ensure correct operation causing localised impact to the surrounding lands/water not to mention the visual pollution they cause; the turbine also uses power in high wind conditions to brake the blades rotation to prevent any damage or dangerous conditions.

The solar solution has seen vast fields, which should be used for grazing animals or growing food, and some woodland chopped down to be converted to solar power generation plants. Isn't this a great idea, remove something that was and could be used for producing clean oxygen and for agricultural purposes for food and dump metal and glass over the land so the land is starved of light, which means after a number of years the land will not be capable of supporting any form of agricultural process as it would have been starved of vital minerals and salts. Why the government has chosen to build these types of plants on fields rather than utilise the roofs of buildings in the concrete jungles of towns and cities i.e. house rooftops, can only be because of who will financially benefit.

The common sense and intelligent decision would be to keep the greenland and woodland as nature intended, as it is better of wildlife and for clean air - utilise something that is already suitable for installation of this power generating technology (although a few properties do have solar installed as part of a green energy introduction). The choice to install all solar on top of housing in towns and cities would invariably mean that energy suppliers would not be able to justify charging households high prices for energy, thus, fields are utilised to ensure money flows in the right direction; for profiteering and greed not to prevent global warming.

It is unlikely renewables alone will be enough to neither supply the demand for energy nor prevent the increase of global warming – energy experts believe nuclear power is the only viable option to provide the nation's energy needs. But, the waste from nuclear generation is a major problem to overcome as it remains radioactive for 100,000s of years and with demand for electricity alone doubling since 1980, civilisation is still left with a situation where energy demand is far outstripping supply and more population equals greater demand. The control of energy is without a doubt unsustainable and there is still no viable solution to the world energy needs to satisfy the ever growing population.

A potential solution has been developed, re: Masdar city in the Arab Emirates (N. Leech, "Masdar City: Role model for a Sustainable Future", The National, United Arab Emirates, November, 2013), at a cost of ~US$20 billion has been hailed as the future of ultra-low carbon city living but requires a 22 hectare field of 87,777 solar plants and a 20MW wind farm external to the city with a 10MW solar plant within to provide the energy needs; and provide homes for 50,000 people and 1,500 businesses. The problem being that the ability to build a city like this requires enough land to install these renewable energy plants, and there simply isn't enough land available in all countries as most land is required for agriculture, rear livestock, and for wildlife; besides being currently used as existing towns and cities and therefore is not a solution to satisfy current needs especially in high densely populated countries.

Another potential solution is to capture current CO2 emissions and pump it back into the ground were the oil deposits were found, however, the emergent behaviour of doing this is far from clear and it still does not solve the current energy demands.

The environment and our energy needs has reached a critical junction and the obsession and addiction to fossil fuels, which is a finite capacity, means extracting the fuel seems to be more of a liability that will eventually end with the last drip being extracted from the ground or our own risk of extinction. So far no viable solution to make this change to steer away from fossil fuels has been found and oil companies are still acquiring huge profits whilst ignoring, as are the majority of people in the world, the lasting impacts of our addiction. People are suffering from escalations in diseases from the increase in poisonous gases in the atmosphere, some all over the world are protesting about global warming whilst at the same time driving around in cars, bikes, planes, etc. This notwithstanding, further exploration for fossil fuels is an ongoing process to continue to feed our addictions and quest for profits.

The prospect for a renewable low carbon future seems to be as far away as possible and our energy future (or lack thereof) seems to be written on the wall already. Oil and gas will probably run out in our children's lifetime (those born from 2030 onwards) and they will live through the impacts of numerous wars, famine, and air pollution. Two main questions need to be asked: - why are all people ignoring our responsibility and continuing to use oil and gas with complete ignorance?; and why is society not taking responsibility to naturally control population numbers to reduce the effects on the climate with our own existence? These are questions that require answering by all and not just the government. Perhaps if humans can somehow overcome our fear of becoming clean from our addiction and accept some lifestyle compromises, conceivably, all in society can build a fossil free energy world/country through careful planning rather than be forced back to medieval times when the resource runs dry.

In the meantime, it is vitally important to protect the areas of nature that through a natural process help to clean the air people breathe and filter out undesirable chemicals and pollutants from the land and water reserves. Everyone should have access to a safe and secure nature environment whoever and wherever they are and for too long these areas of nature have been replaced by concrete or used for dumping human waste. Forests, waterways and areas of ocean need protection and placed in public ownership. A National Capital Committee has to have a more hand-on approach to protect and improve wildlife habitats and green spaces to make them more important and accessible in all communities. There needs to be an improved method for the protection of pets and wildlife with debates about controlling numbers of wildlife to ensure that the most vulnerable among them are protected. Moreover, hunting for sport should be banned and the continued end of the ineffective and cruel badger culls with reinforcement of the laws to be investigated.

The UK used to be a nation proud of its countryside and the quality of farming and there needs to be a long-term strategy to reignite the sector through the national curriculum and prevention of industrial expansion into green lands. The laws that protect nature, waterways and farm land from pollution and construction contracts also needs promoting internationally and effectiveness in this area is about leading by example and ensuring that changes work for the advantage of the people in the country not the shareholders. Developing key international partners whom understand that the rising population means that investment in farming industry has to take priority from 'nice to have' project improvements, moreover, the promotion of the best of national knowledge investment should be endorsed internationally.

To build resilience in international roles concerning the sector implies a full understanding of the impact of not investing in future knowledge and technology for the protection and rejuvenation of both the farming industry and the quality of air and water. Even if the population of the country reduces, protection of these areas must continue and the reclaiming of lands from the concrete jungle should be considered as part of the countries continuous improvement programme.

The truth is humans are not important in the world bio-structure besides the earth and all other life would prosper without us; humans have most definitely abused our position. Plankton, especially marine algae, are the most important species on the planet, they not only provide enough food to make earth's ocean full of life but also contributes to significant oxygen (~50%) production via phytoplankton photosynthesis. They also provide a vital service in the ocean's uptake of CO_2 generated through human activity. However, human activity is also poisoning the population of plankton by polluting waters, blocking the sun's rays with plastics in the oceans and contributing to global warming.

All life which produces oxygen and provides enough food for life on earth to prosper requires protection. The majority of people have to take an interest in protecting the most vital species on the planet, as when they go, we do; and it does denote that nature is a battle human-kind cannot lose. It is not about profits or convenience to remove human generated waste it is about the future of life. The dinosaurs became extinct mainly due to natural disasters, however, humans stand a very real chance of making all life, including our own, extinct by our irresponsible acts of convenience; it has nothing to do with human nature; it is about profits before responsibility.

4

DEMOCRACY FOR THE PEOPLE NOT FOR WEALTHY

For too long now power has been concentrated into too few hands in government and lobbyists with people in the country not having a voice in decisions that affect their own lives. Democracy has been poisoned by the influence of lobbyists, so much so the power of money in politics makes democracy just a nice slogan to be used by politicians to give people the illusion that they matter when in reality the government and politicians in general have just become a face for television; a group of celebrities with carefully prepared speeches to keep the masses at bay whilst big business walks away with all the money at the expense of everyone else. The situation has reached a point where the condition of our political system has been corrupted and no longer fit for purpose. Indeed, those who make decisions on behalf of the people, whether in Westminster, Capital Hill, business, media, the public sector, or the European Union, are too often unaccountable for their 'mistakes'. (Mistakes or purposeful actions; researching decisions made from various legislations to wars, there seems to be 'money' and profit made by the wealthy few at the expense of the majority each and every single time).

The over-centralisation in the country has seen power of decisions be diverted to people with no direct interest in the outcome of projects or budget management. This has led to funds being diverted to local and major national projects at the expense of real problems that require funding to resolve, not managed. These expensive nice-to-have projects are generally mismanaged and only for short term 'pats-on-the-back' for government and local government managers, which then go into disrepair needing more funding to correct.

Elections are ceased rather than being won, captured by money, lobbyists and the media crushing any real choice and thus preventing real political change and transferring power to unaccountable bodies. A perfect setting for disenfranchisement and disillusionment and is the main reason for civil unrest, crime and the increasing mental health issues among people in society. Society have elections based on promises, sold as guarantees, which have seen the national and global rise of a political system based on lies and propaganda that is imploding on itself. Capitalism has caused the rise of greed at any cost and has infiltrated all areas of government and people's lives, which has poisoned democracy and freedom.

The election system is sold as giving the people a voice in the way in which the country is managed and governed. In reality, the election is a similar system as the ones in operation in other reality shows such as, strictly come dancing, X-factor, BGT, etc., were people are merely voting for an individual to be rewarding for competing in the electoral system. The people have little say in anything whatsoever that affects the governing of the country apart from a few choice referendums in the history of the country. These few referendums are the only voice the people have in what direction the country is heading towards, and these are by no means legally binding; the government can override the results and/or manipulate the outcome if the people give the wrong answer (leading to career suicide for the leader of the ruling party). In elections, when members of the government appear with the message about the 'people have spoken', what they mean is 'thank-you for voting for us, we will take it from here'. People must know that the election promises are made just to become elected, as all governments since I have been at working age have never committed to or fulfilled any of their promises as it was sold. People do indeed have poor memories when politics is concerned! (Although Trump within a few weeks after his victory used his executive order stipulation to carry out some of his election promises - much to the shear grin of other politicians, do-gooders, and other activists and still struggles with courts overruling his executive orders).

Businesses, especially those who pollute the environment or poison us, spend billions on politics if they are not to be regulated out of business and this type of corrupt system applies across the board. For example: retail companies exploiting workers, tax avoidance packages for accountancy firms, gambling companies preventing controls or measures to tackle addiction, pharmaceutical companies contract controls and pricing structures, and especially banks preventing financial instruments to prevent outright fraud within the economy, to name but a few; with the political system accommodating their demands (**money brings political change, not the people**). This is leading to a system that works only for them with the real wealth creators those who produce something useful in society, i.e. the majority of public, paying the price multiple times over with less disposable money and a continuing decline in freedom, health care standards and public services. The system of democracy is failing and causing devastation and chaos globally. It simply has to evolve to swing political change back to the majority enabling politics to work for people, just as it did for a short period of time after WW2, and not for the wealthiest in society.

With the results of both Brexit and the US election, it is obvious that the older generation, the ones who have lived in the country the longest, have turned against the political establishment. The result means the political establishment are 'chase their own tails' in an attempt to find out why all their strategies have 'temporarily' failed to achieve the 'correct' outcome; and working towards a solution to help them get back into some form of power and control over the people. But, there is a problem. Every time the people have turned against the establishment there has been a period of instability, thus, it is the majority of people who are hurt the most. The unsurprising factor of these results is that most young people voted for the established politicians whereas the older generation voted for something different….why?…..

In the US presidential election, over 53% of women voted for Trump and that is despite all the demonization, misogynistic and sexist claims being presented by mass media outlets and the scare and fear tactics spread about his relationship with Russia (the bad guys but without any evidence to back up claims). Why is this the case? Is it because all these women's husband or boyfriends have persuaded them to vote for Trump, or is it because women distrust Hillary because both her and Bill Clinton should be in jail for their actions throughout the years (including multiple counts of rape, and lies that could be tantamount treason). A few probable answers are most of these women have a total distaste for the democrats, because in America there are various states which are culturally highly republican or democratic and is some areas Hillary is the 'Devil'; or it may be because people are becoming more savvy in what they hear from career politician especially those who have proven their incompetence and corruption ethics; or perhaps the Russia bashing was just a marketing ploy too far after the Benghazi and Middle East incidents. But, and this is the real issue, the data and statistics can be analysed for years but no definitive answer will be found. Consequently, what happened in the US election has sent shock waves throughout the political establishments worldwide who are struggling to find an answer as to how to stop people voting for something different. People have all seen in 2017 they still have no different strategy to manipulate people into voting for the establishment so they continue with the threats of terrorism and Russia bashing in hope people will be swayed to continue to vote for established political parties.

You can tell when government and the oligarchs are not expecting the outcomes of referendums: Brexit and Trump are prime examples of a system of 'no plan, no hope' politics. If the people of the nation end up giving the 'wrong' answer, there is no plan of how to proceed. As a government, it is their responsibility to generate a viable plan on the way the country is to move forward on both possible outcomes. It was clear the Brexit vote was not foreseen and therefore no relevant information regarding the free movement of people or the specifics of article 50 that require to be addressed were available for discussions. The other and possibly the largest problems with the Brexit referendum is people did not know what they were voting for, nor did the process allow for any government to elicit information on what exactly the people wanted from the Brexit result. Without these specific details, it is very difficult for the government to govern the country and make decisions in the name of the majority. In the UK, the government graciously assumes the manner in which they are proceeding is what the people want, without really knowing what people really want, for example, if people voted to close borders to reduce the population numbers by voting 'leave', where is the information to argue for and against this... there clearly is non available. Thus, society have a game of 'Russian Roulette' where the government is gambling the future of the country based on assumptions from polls which in all likelihood could be wrong. However, one thing is perfectly clear, the public are not involved in any debates or decisions regarding the outcome of Brexit, but, will have to live with the consequences of the outcome – so much for the people being in charge.

This is the main issue with elections and referendums, the manner in which the political establishment behaves, gives and receives information, is abysmal at best. Spreading fear among the people does influence votes (this has been used for centuries and still is the main form of manipulation). Not receiving adequate feedback as to why people voted a certain way leads to a government who guesses and moreover will work in the best interests of the economy balancing the anger of the popular vote. If anger in people boils over blame is not directed at the people who are responsible for issues with incorrect decisions but left at the leader's door. This cyclic event will continue to occur unless government is made, by the people, to work for them not for the financial best interests of the wealthy. People will continue to live a life based on what individuals and minority groups in government want them to do via indirect manipulation of actions based on indoctrination, bad education and nanny state interference in private lives; and direct manipulation via legislation.

When the establishment loses a vote or a substantial group size turns against government, the government are quick to market the blame on un-educated people of the country. The irony is they would know about the poor state of education because they set the standards and curriculum to restrict the native ability and skill set of people in the country; it is also used as an excuse to justify the immigration policy, i.e. lack of home grown talent. Isn't this statement a fitting testament to the governments' ability in educating children for the wellbeing of the country and its economy! They are admitting they have purposely setup a system which fails children and adults in educating to a level suitable enough to understand national issues and admit that the country's performance is below most others in this field; yet they continue to 'play around' with schools and the curriculum without any coherent or sensible plan.

The other viewpoint, which the government is very uncomfortable about admitting, is education contributes to decisions made by people throughout their lives, but, most decisions are made by actually experiencing life and the difficulties associated with it. It is the reason why Trump won the US election and the reason people voted for Brexit – these had nothing to do with education it had a lot to do with people's life experience. Society needs to admit and come to terms with the reason for current rejection of established politics is due to immigration and people can see with their eyes, health service availability and pay packets what is happening to the country. The excuse that the country needs immigrants is simply not true, it is true that immigrants are a reason to keep pay low and profits high. The reality is the country needs immigrants to take care of the growing population where most of the growth is down the problem of immigration throughout the years and to continue to exploit people's desperation to be independent and popular.

In referendums and elections each party contributes to a pantomime game based around dirty politics. Each party demonises the other, vilifies politicians in different camps and in the end when one side wins the people who voted for the other side are naturally angry and paranoid of the effects of the result. Look at how angry the remain campaign voters where at the loss, complaining about lies even though their own side had equally the same amount of propaganda and lies to spread fear into people to manipulate votes. In America, the demonization of Trump has caused extreme protesting and riots in various states. These are prime examples of politicians playing with people's emotions in a badly educated society that has caused hysteria, which sometimes causes more issues than simple protesting.

The first step to improve the voting system is to change the overall election architecture and how votes are counted; the first-past-the-post system is now obsolete as it tends to lead to a minority of people dictating the outcome of elections. Government needs to look closely on how to give individuals in all areas the same power of vote in elections and maybe proportional representation holds the key to ensuring one vote is not worth ten or more votes of someone else. The point is marginal seats and safe seats have to be an arrangement of the past and coincide with removal of most decisional power from Westminster (due to corruption) with the people becoming directly involved in choices. For instance, it is the people who should decide whether funding should be spent on projects like HS2 or Trident etc., whilst the health service is crumbling and failing to provide adequate health care. It is clear the politicians, at present, are unable to prioritise decisions to satisfy their prime directive: **to ensure safety, security and well-being of the people in the country**.

So what are the main factors that are at play and what are the foremost changes which are needed?

Local Government

People in local areas should have more of a say on what aspects of the community require attention and local government managers should be made to ensure funding is directed at solving these problem first. Any changes made or any project undertaken for the betterment of the community is only possible when people of the community take an interest and have a say in how the community if governed. Some MPs/senators and civil servants believe that people have a say in elections and it is then up to the elected officials to make decisions; but, this only promotes unaccountability and the need for department heads to secure budgets for the following year by spending money (their departmental budgets) before their budget in under review (local government departments do this yearly, without considering the after effects on household budgets).

The government trusts people, or be it by media propaganda and the continued spread of the same message on a daily basis, to elect appropriate officials into government; if society is going to solve the nation's problems the people have to have more of a say on how their own money, given by taxes etc., is spent at the expense of politicians whom want their 'claim to fame'. This type of method also promotes motivation for the people to be actively involved in how their local community is managed. Consequently, government has to de-evolve power to deal with real social and economic problems and hand this to local government with strong relationships with the people in the community to innovate local services to drive better quality of life and prosperity.

People require, or should demand, more control and decision making over schools, health care management and structure, policing, housing and transport; and local government need front-line hands-on knowledge into what works and what does not in the community, which is clearly lacking due to continued mistakes made in communities. This does, however, require people to take interest in a model of citizenship based on participation and shared responsibility and in return it is envisaged that local government will be managed by and be accountable by the people to ensure available funds are directed where they need to be and waste is removed. In essence, it is for the drive of the people to transform the relationship between the public and local government. The public have continually and consequently 'sat back' and accepted government spending and decision making without revoke; it is time for this to change and ownership of how local government operates has to be the responsibility of the people in the community where decisions should be managed in a democratic fashion.

With pressures of work and family, time for people to partake in government affairs is limited; it is probably why face-to-face meetings in evenings fail to receive many participants. For this reason, local government and universities should use their close relationship to transform local government into a digital government to enable communications for more collaboration and for sharing data between services and people. This type of facility would enable information to be available online and allow people in the community to voice concerns or approval for various projects or spending plans on a local (regional) network where debate can form the bases of decisions made i.e. taking decisions out of the minorities hands and handing it over to all in the community who are willing and able (with better education standards) to be involved. The more connected society this creates will make local government more inclusive, more transparent, and more accountable. It would also give people an insight into the spending plans and relationships between local government and private businesses to see what taxes really go on and enable the ability to raise questions on something that appears to be mismanaged.

This system relies on people wanting to take part in the scheme and this is a big problem. Families, especially in poorer areas of the country, have for generations been forced into unemployment and seen their own skill set become obsolete, they have seen higher taxes with lower salaries and have generally grown-up with a distrust of government. The other side of the argument relates to people from different cultures (from migrant backgrounds) that have experienced assistance from government with living and expenses; these people are more actively involved in local government and petitioning for change. Unless this difference between 1st, 2nd generation migrants and people from families that has been left behind or failed by government for generations is resolved, the people becoming more involved in the scheme will be the former and thus will cause more segregation and more resentment in the community, which is the exact opposite of what is needed.

Therefore, there needs to a substantial programme to regain confidence in the native public and ensure certain communities do not benefit at the expense of others. It is this problem which will take several years to resolve as building confidence in people is one of the most difficult tasks any government can undertake. There has to be an understanding that not everything or every problem can be resolved immediately, but, for local government it is important that one community is not prioritised over other; currently, there is a perception that certain people from foreign backgrounds are prioritised above nationals.

Some may say why I have mentioned different communities when there should only be one. The reality is integration has failed and every time government pushes for forced integration, substantial money and time is allocated and the results are a disaster. It is clear, people do not wish to integrate at this time, and the probability of people from different communities, cultures, and religion ever coming together, is negligible. People need to be left alone to decide if they wish to integrate into one community; the government's job is to ensure people are treated fairly and justly with decisions made impartially. If management in local governments have their own agenda or bias, then systems are needed to be put in place to prevent any favouritism and the more people in the community become involved, the less likelihood projects will be directed in a biased manner.

National Government

There are many issues between the collaboration of certain local governments and central government, one of which relates to different political parties who are in management at local levels. In recent times, if the local government is controlled by one political party there is a chance the funding will be directed to a local government controlled by the same party who is in control at the national level. This type of arrangement means people in the community do not know who is to blame for taxes being wasted or failed projects as local government will tend to blame national and vice-versa. This is also a reason for de-centralising control of funding and decisions to local government so that blame rests locally and the people responsible can be taken into account. Leading to a reduction of the 'pantomime of blame' that occurs throughout political and media circles all pointing the finger at each other.

One of the issues with national government is people in political parties are assigned to be responsible for certain departments even though the input given in any debates or decisions is minimum. The system is called 'justifying ones' existence'. This type of system has filtered through the hierarchy to academic institutions and industry and is used as a mechanism for self-protection, when in fact there is substantial waste involved.

Being an MP/senator should be a full time career and they should not be allowed to gain money earning positions outside in the public arena i.e. sitting on the board of directors for private companies; and certainly not be given positions in government that are not based on skills or experience but based on 'face-fits' criteria. For example, this type of problem came to unbelievable levels during the ConLib era, in the UK, where an MP who did not even possess 'A' level in mathematics was given a high level position at the treasury. Any normal intelligent person would behold this and think 'this country is being run by idiots' and they would be right; but, the majority of people in the country voted these types of people in, so who is really to blame.

Then society has the problem of expense scandals and corruption charges. There is one area of corruption that springs to mind and it navigates towards the child support agency in the UK. Since 2002, 90% of the MPs who were given the position to oversee the CSA have been removed from the position and investigated for corruption, but, years later still allowed to become an MP; obviously it would depend how much their 'face-fits' – not all were allowed. Can people honestly think that these types of politicians (those that use their position for self-gain at the expense of the people their supposed to serve) have now learned their lessons and are now pristine members of the government and country.

In the UK, the MPs have recently (2016) given themselves a pay rise followed by a further pay rise in 2017 well above inflation; they still have the ability to claim all sorts of items on expenses; they continue to give fellow MPs important and responsible positions far beyond their abilities; they are still allowed to employ members of family; and some firmly believe that the houses of common and house of lords are reserved for those who actually know how the country works i.e. the rich and wealthy, and the thought that common people (those who work but have little wealth) would make running the country difficult. Oh and they still continue to spread the word of separation (etc.) between people using messages such as: benefit cheats, feminism, sexism and racism to justify creating and allocating more positions for their friends and colleagues in the illusion that they are going to do something to resolve issues. In addition, they continue to spread the word of fear to the nation to keep the people looking towards the government for protection.

Even the vote on Brexit has led to MPs spreading the word of racism and anti-migrant sentiment with promotion of the differences between the older generation and the younger one;

thus leaving the young people of the country fearful of the future. So much so that the conservative government can now use the excuse of Brexit for further tax rises and cuts and point the finger to the British public, whilst it is ever so quiet about the condition of the banks who are the root cause of the financial crisis. So no, it is business as usual in Westminster and this has to change.

Observing how governments throughout the West operate, it is clear that the same self-indulging attitude and strategy to deal with the public are prevalent throughout established politics besides the same techniques are used to manipulate the public's voting patterns, which has been used for centuries.

Ostensibly, the education system has failed the public although for many business owners, especially in the service (and banking - not for reasons you think) sector, it has worked out very well. There has always been a problem with governments actively providing an education to give people the key skills needed for them to make independent decisions based on facts. This is why successive governments have always used emotions and feelings to make people 'buy' into what the government wants them to do (i.e. through fear and trepidation); sadly, only when people are pushed to the limit does this type of system fail, i.e. reasons for the Brexit vote. A wise man once said 'The people who own this country (bankers, corporate businesses, arms dealers (defence contractors), etc.) don't want a population of citizens capable of critical thinking. Governments don't want well informed, well educated people capable of critical thinking. That's against their interests. They want obedient workers, people who are just smart enough to run the machines and do the paperwork. And just dumb enough to passively accept increasingly shittier jobs, reduced benefits, lower pay for longer hours, and a vanishing pension pot that disappears when you go to collect it' (George Carlin).

The point is, to give people the ability to be given more power in society needs government to change their mind-sets and become actively involved in producing people who are capable of critical thinking and analysis to provide knowledge and skills necessary to make government and its affiliates/partners accountable; parents play a key role in ensuring their children have these skills. A prime example of the lack of these skills is again based on population numbers (carrying capacity) and limited services, jobs, and sustainable resources. Some in government have blamed uneducated people for voting for Brexit, but, and probably an accidental coincidence, critical analysis of the situation based on facts would conclude that the numbers of people already in the country far outnumber safe population limits for the size of land and resource availability for sustained quality of life. Meaning that all people who voted for remain have ignored this important fact and continue to do so, but, their thought processes are all based on emotional prerequisites given by a clever marketing strategy driven by government and lobbyists.

To counteract the marketing strategy based on emotions political parties use to requisite votes, knowledge and skills have to be given to people through the education system to teach that decisions should be based on facts available and not on emotional mind-sets. Basic research skills should be offered in schools to prepare people for the difficult and responsible task of creating a prosperous country with a high quality of life. Currently, the majority of people lack these types of skills and is probably the reason why many inept and poor quality politicians are voted into government and allowed to 'run amok' for a period of time; sad, but true! Only when given the skills needed and several years of learning how to conduct research and critical thinking will people have the ability to make an unbiased decision based on current available facts. The experience of research methods will also acquire knowledge as to where the possible gaps are in government led information, i.e. is there enough information available to make an intelligent decision or develop a strategy to solve the problem.

Society needs education to produce people to have the ability to question government and bring them to account when information has been doctored to market a 'selfish and/or self-serving' viewpoint. For example, currently, a vast majority of people read simple pamphlets and slogans with 'catch phrases' produced by political parties along with media interviews including trained hand gestures from politicians with which to base decisions (votes) on. There is little incentive or motivation to find out the truth or consider the past performance of respective political parties or legitimacy and skill set of politicians (or potential politicians) due to not experiencing the task of researching facts/truths and identifying conjecture within the education system. Once this critical thinking education system is in place, voting in major elections or referendum can then be given to school leavers (and a similar type of course offered to adults before being allowed to vote) as they will have the necessary skill set to play a full part of society and be actively involved in decision making which affects all.

This will be a major change in how politics works in society and will more than likely be highly contested and opposed by the elites (establishment) because it will not be as easy to gain the positions they once had in society or in political circles (why do you think education is not improving, but heading in reverse). This is the ultimate price of a good education system – power swings to the other side of society, the side that is the majority but individually not a lot of money or wealth.

There is an uneasy relationship between government and private companies, so much so that legislation has been produced / declared for the benefit of said companies. It is not clear when this relationship occurred, but, it began with banks and expanded to other businesses shortly after WW2 and became a mechanism for perverting democracy. There should be no place for politicians to be on the boards of companies, directorships or consultancy firms whilst in government and for a period of time after they leave; their actions whilst in government should be carefully monitored to ensure fair play. If an ex-politician shortly after leaving government lands a high paid role at a company that has had business dealings with the government whilst the said politician was in government then an independent investigation needs to occur for any possible economic advantage the company has been given, or any legislation that has been amended or created, which benefits the respective company; and any financial benefit the politician has received during the time served in the public sphere.

Government and Business

The separation of business and politicians (or at least a relationship at a large distance) has to be actioned; there can be no signs of a true democracy with this close relationship in place. Government is incapable of governing the country for the benefit of all, when politicians are subject to lobbying (bribes) and can influence regulation for the benefit of business at the expense of people in the community. Maybe once this is in place, human-kind will see less conflict, both nationally and internationally, less people homeless and more funding directed to areas where it is needed rather than nice-to-have projects that are only for ego and grandstanding on the world stage.

The lobbying act (how did the public stand-by and let this go through and continue to accept that this is the way it is?) has to be repealed. Government should be required to administer the country for the interests of the majority and not be influenced by rewards from individuals or companies who have money. This act needs to be replaced by legislation that prevents the 'cash for favours' philosophy. This new legislation would break the relationship between big business and government and would hold politicians to the highest standard of integrity and honour. It would also make the individuals or companies who have the audacity and arrogance to attempt to gain favour with members of the government and pervert democracy to take notice of previously acceptable actions. Any company or individual who attempts to, what is essentially 'bribe' a politician, should suffer a high financial fine as a result and be black listed from any future government contracts. Within this new legislation, digital government also needs to take centre stage to allow the people the opportunity to debate with government about various decisions; in essence, to strengthen the public's voice and better hold the individuals or committee members in government to account.

The problem of lobbying has become so severe that police and armed forces are being used to protect certain business (fracking, pipeline, chemical, waste plants, etc.) from protesters who are exercising their democratic right to stop any potential future health hazard from occurring in their communities. Media is then used to present to the rest of the public that these people are not peaceful protesters by selling a certain viewpoint. Another example of this practice was the protests in London and Manchester at the point of the financial crash and the instigation of student fees in the UK and how the police used the technique of kettling (purposely directing people into a small compact area sold as crowd control) refusing to allow people to leave the area whilst they continued to pack more people into it. Ultimately, with the authorities knowing the outcome, people become frustrated, hot and angry that they were being contained hence the peaceful protest became inflamed and trouble ensued. When this happens, main stream media sensationalises the situation using emotions presenting one viewpoint (incentivised by government) to turn the rest of the population against the protesters.

Protesters are a small group of people the government find 'pesky' on numerous issues, and they deal with them in certain ways to vilify them to the people, even though most of the issues protestor are against have an aroma of ethics and morality attached. The method is quite simple and effective: use the police to move protestors, cause certain people in the group to become angry and lash-put at the police, and then sell all the protestors as 'thugs' to turn the majority against the protestors. The strategy to dealing with them has been very affective with most people seeing protesters are a bunch of trouble makers or modern day 'hippies'. This type of scenario occurs on all occasions when government needs to silence public disproval with decisions and is used more and more when big business is being prevented from normal, sometimes unethical and immoral working practices. This is the problem, when only a small proportion of people are actively involved in attempting to drive change government will ignore the requests as when the majority of the population are nearly 100% obedient, governments are not at liberty to care about any complaints and thus not be bothered in changing anything. Ultimately, the real message being sent to people once critical analysis of these situations occurs is matters of the economy and making money will always come first before the financial, health or environmental concerns of local people in the community. That message has to change otherwise democracy and people's freedoms will continue to be an illusion of reality.

Speaking of the association between government and 'big money', it is all too clear in Western civilisation, especially in the UK and US, there is only a choice between two main political parties. Democracy is about the choice between parties with different views on how the country should be governed, however, for several decades the fight to be in government has been based on how much political party funding and donations are available during elections and generally concentrated on the ones with the most money. This type of democracy only works to 'lock-out' other parties' views from mainstream media and gives independents little chance to be heard. A perfect system for those parties with big money donations and an almost certain guarantee of possible election victory i.e. Conservative or Labour / Republicans or Democrats to win. The system needs to change to allow for an even playing field for all those who would like to be in government in an attempt to make a positive difference.

As a result, all private donations to parties have to be banned but donations can be diverted into public projects and rules should be amended to give all potential politicians from all backgrounds an equal chance to succeed. Consequently, this means the main political parties will no longer have the advantage and smaller interests can have the opportunity to have their views equally registering on mainstream media outlets, including those who are deemed by the establishment of having extreme views. The advantage of this type of system is public funding will be diverted to all parties in elections in an equal manner and will hopefully resolve the problem of political safe grounds during elections. The likelihood of one political party holding government will be reduced and it should force elected officials to form a shared government that will have different voices heard in decisions and choices made. Problems such as disagreements in decisions are envisaged to occur, but, digital government should be the deciding factor. Remember, the people should have the final say; the government's secondary job/objective is to provide arguments for and against something besides providing enough facts for the public to debate and decide upon.

It has become clear in recent times, especially in the UK, of the number of unelected public officials, Lords and Ladies for the size of the country is too high. This system needs to change as does the job-for-life philosophy for most politicians. The usefulness of the House of Lords, however, must not be underestimated as sometimes they can cause difficulty for government in passing questionable bills. Therefore, the current system operating in the House of Lords, were the people are elected based on MPs votes, requires to be replaced and the number of officials reduced by a publically voted elected senate which represents the county regions. To improve the democratic legitimacy of the second chamber the needs to be skills and experience constraints in order to stand for office; and should have to be re-elected by the public on a bi-yearly basis. To go hand-in-hand with this change, having an MP which represents every town and village in the country is a substantial drain on public finances; therefore, the number of MPs that represent the people's interests should be reduced to one representative per county or state. The local interests of people in towns and villages should be met with the close relationships with local governments, with the ability to involve the respected MP in disputes that cannot be solved at a local level.

All non-elected officials should be required to partake in the same employment system that majority of people have to go through in order to obtain a career position, i.e. needing a CV to match job description. Politicians and house of lord / senate representatives will no longer be able to automatically hire friends and family, but be required to qualify their assistants (etc.) with relevant skills and experience (moreover family member should be placed under greater scrutiny (due to historic reasons) for the position. This will become a shock to many officials and their families who have permanent job security and availability at present, but, the public deserve to have the right people in these positions and not be reserved for fellow acquaintances.

Part of the job application process should include the public in the local government area being partially involved in the job interview and giving the green light for the appointment - after all they are paying for the employment of the individual. This means the CV of the person requires scrutiny by people in the community and public questions deserve to be answered by the applicant to such posts. It is important for democracy that people have a say on who represents them and who they are forced, at present (by government taxes), to employ. The system will also require transparency of the official's performance outcomes to give the public an opportunity to raise concerns about the individual employed. Digital government will be used to process and present this information to all the people who are interested; although a system which prevents people from other districts obtaining performance measures might be an option.

With devolution in the UK, it has become all too apparent Wales, Scotland and Northern Island have their own elected government where the English MPs have limited power of decision that affects these areas of the union; however, the MPs from these areas can affect the decisions made for England. Clearly, this is anti-democratic for the people living in England, hence, for decisions that affect England only English MPs should be given the right to have scrutiny (along with residents in England) over legislation and vice-versa. Nonetheless, for decisions which affect the union of all countries all MPs should be given the right to have equal say on debates in the commons and thus needs to be considered as part of the Constitutional Convention process.

To go along with these changes, demarcation lines between local government boundary areas require revision. In elections, there are certain areas of the country that can be classed as key swing states (marginal seats) so much so that in the UK the conservatives in 2016 instigated a plan to attempt to redraw the boundaries for their own advantage in national elections. Clearly, changing the boundaries based on election voting habits of people is completely undemocratic and in a small but viable intent can be seen a rigging the election result.

The boundaries are required to be decided upon based on resources in the area, number of people resident, services, unemployment rates, and types of industry in the area. It is unfair for boundary conditions to change based on wealth, countryside areas and voting habits. Moreover, the redraw should provide equal footing in the elected chambers to allow all people's voices heard and not the privilege few who votes for one particular established political party. The shift requires careful planning and agreements from the public and local government regions as the size of boundary will have an impact on project funding, budget amounts and availability.

Sadly, those areas which have enjoyed abundant public funding for many years (those in areas surrounded by green land, mansions, but with a small population) will under this system have to manage with less when public money is transferred to those areas of high population and therefore greater need. However, people in these areas have enough money to compensate for this financial loss without the stress and worry of affording to live thus is an agreeable and intelligent trade-off.

These boundary changes will carry with them the need for accountability in spending plans; no longer will national or local governments be able to spend money on expensive sculptures or unnecessary building refurbishments at the expense of solving the homeless crisis, hospital or social services, etc. It is hoped closer ties between local government and the people will ensure that real social problems and vital critical services (and run down areas of towns and cities) are prioritised above nice-to-haves, which unfortunately over the past two decades, at least, have enjoyed most of the money due to the poor quality of people representing and working in the public sector who do not have the ability or motivation to solve real problems and are highly subjective to 'cash for favours' temptations.

Education vs Banking

The other big issue with having a highly educated society is the impact it will have on the banking system; it currently operates based on fraud (that is ignored by the authorities) and a fractional reserve system creating money (which is counterfeit) out of thin air, which then people have to pay back with interest. I am unsure how people will react if they realise that over 90% of mortgages and loans never physically existed in the first place (i.e. virtual IOU's); and the fact that there will always be a boom and bust and inflation because of the fractional reserve system; and only the people with real wealth benefit in any economic situation (but this is for another discussion). The countries debt figures will continue to increase and one of the main culprits of this is the banking system that are debt factories masquerading as profit making machines. Unless society have 100% reserve banking, the working people in society will always be 'enslaved' by the banking system. Denoting 'slavery' as sold by history has only evolved from people being punished for not doing work without been given a choice of what work to do; to a system whereby without money survival would be extremely difficult (as land and property cannot be owned without money) and people have a choice of what work they do as long as money flows up the pyramid to the top. Thus, people are now 'enslaved' by money and being controlled by the people who control its distribution whom happen to have close ties with ruling governments and heavily influence its function.

Once 100% reserve banking system is in place then the amount of money available in the economy is the actual money that physically exists. Essentially, this means banks will no longer be able to issue IOU's (or virtual money that is created at will just like magic) in replacement of physical money that does not exist as loans or mortgages that people have to pay back. Once this happens the obvious affect will be banks 'profits' (in reality debt) will reduce significantly, but, they will still be able to make real profit based on interest on real loans given out to people. Another added benefit is employing these highly expensive bankers, whom prime purpose is to create money out of thin air for profits of the bank and for themselves using all types of techniques open to them using loopholes in the country's banking charter, will no longer be needed. Neither would stock traders who generates profits out of thin air by manipulation of share prices (if the banks are making all this profit from winning trades, who is losing and where is this newly acquired money coming from?) – The truth is the money is being created from thin air, just like the system used in the fractional reserve banking.

As long as these types of system are in place there will always be a boom/bust economy whereby the banks have to collect physical money back in to compensate for the created money that physically does not exist and why inflation will continue to increase. This notwithstanding, there is a problem looming for the majority of people in society. Banks would like people to cease using physical counterfeit notes and coins, instead, use card payments in replacement of physical money. This follows a trend they have used throughout the years where first they removed any real value from the physical money (i.e. gold and silver) then produced counterfeit money and now they would like people to use virtual money; unbelievably, people are more than embracing the change in complete ignorance of the outcome. Virtual economics is more viable for mass fraud and corruption to occur within the banking system, it is easier for people to lose track of their finances; and it is easier to leave people with nothing than if physical money continued to be used, as all the control will be issued through a keystroke. Thus, any financial control individuals have with regards to money would cease and everyone would be at mercy to behaving and doing as they are told, otherwise, there is a real risk that their card(s) will be cancelled. Try and attempt to protest against government decisions, banks and big business if this comes to fruition; people need to resist this change.

It is clear to anyone who has researched around this area that the banking system is based on corruption and fraud, which is ignored by the authorities besides being promoted by politicians in government. Until society has 100% reserve banking, place some real value back into the hands of the public and remove the people who manipulate the banking act, receive substantial salaries and millions of pounds / dollars bonuses for essentially created debt, the majority of people will continue to be 'enslaved', work long hours for most of their lives for little rewards; pay back loans and mortgages that physically do not exist (only on a database); and freedom will continue to be diminished.

But, powers of decision and people's lives have been in the hands of but a few for far too long. A better education system based on teaching research and critical thinking methods will pivot power back to the people making government more of an administration department than 'being in power' and less relevant in society, which only strengthens what democracy was supposed to be about. The point is the more educated you become the more you question the systems that are in place and with good reason!

Law Consistent for All

The most important and beneficial act to come from the relationship with the European Union is the Human Right Act, which was designed to gain agreement from people in Europe that a joint union would bring good things to all member states. The problem with the act is lawyers use it to protect the guilty and give people who have commit heinous crimes a comfortable life in prison. It is also used for a reason to provide immigrants with benefits over people who already live in the country; and this situation has been exploited by the media to turn people against the act. This notwithstanding, the act does provide protection for some of the most vulnerable in society, including disabled people and victims of crime; and if used correctly can protect people from the greed of banks as such the act has given people an opportunity for a powerful means of redress. Unfortunately, the way the act is written provides equal redress for all including those in society who have violated other people freedom and human rights; this requires to be changed. The UK government should leave the European convention for human rights and abolish the act. Instead, create a new UK Bill of rights (an amended version similar to the magna carte) using the strengths of the human rights act and others from the European court of justice (ECJ), but, be established to protect the innocent and not the guilty. In reality, the EU act may only need minor changes to prevent certain people from abusing it.

People in society have become angry, stressful and impatient and there is a fear of standing-up to certain groups in society due to being outnumbered and less financially able to fight in courts. People feel trapped and helpless and thus pay fines, ignore people who need help, and contribute to the growing greed in society by taking advantage of the ever increasing lawyer numbers for personal gain (the attitude has become: they would do it to me, so I will to others – prime example is claims for whip-lash in car accidents). The new bill needs to work to counteract these negative effects in society and promote a closer individual union in communities. The bill should include and ensure:

- that everyone has access to the legal system irrespective of wealth and each party has the same level and quality of legal representation (to eliminate advantage of personal wealth);
- people should not be subjected to the 'where there is blame, there is a claim' culture (to work towards reducing the scourge of lawyers in the country);
- children should have the right for access to both parents equally and be protected from abuse by a parent for financial gain or as a tool to hurt the other parent; (this needs to carry with it a hard line punishment to prevent, what is mainly mothers, using decisions based on negative emotions to damage the father and child relationship). Exceptions include: a parent addicted to drink or drugs, being involved in violent gangs and/or hard criminal activity. (This is already law, however, people from poor backgrounds have to apply and pay for court to fight for this right (this is unacceptable)). The stipulation, especially the punishment, needs to be included in the bill and educated to both child and parent to ensure compliance. Children should not be a tool for vengeance!
- people should be defended against debt claim companies including banking debt, i.e. additional fines or entry into homes to confiscate property; (being forced to hand over money or other assets (deprivation of property) due to threats written on paper is just using a different tool than a

common thief would use, i.e. paper documents rather than a knife or gun – just a different tool for the same purpose);

- protection of people from being prosecuted if they defend themselves (by any means) against an assailant (even if the assailant works for the Criminal Justice System (CJS));
- that the bill of rights is not available for abuse by people who violate other people's human rights;
- protection of family wealth from the government;
- people can make the government accountable for failing to perform adequately in their prime responsibility; notably the safety, security and well-being of people. i.e. important support services are provided (need before want (or nice to have(s))
- entitlement for people who suffer from a terminal illness or an illness that degrades their body or mind to prematurely end their own life, or to permit a family member or loved one to make that decision if the individual is not able to (with sufficient indication that this aligns to the individuals wishes);
- that government services, social security and career prospects in the country are prioritised towards native people (from generations of family who have paid into the system) first and foremost (those from three – four generations of family who ancestors have lived, fought for and paid into this country);
- that individual(s) from poorer backgrounds have the right to hold government employees, it's various departments and lobbyists, including banks and arms dealers to account if their life has been negatively affected by decisions made (mostly concerns job losses, losing homes, and terror attacks); but, only if the individual(s) (or in the case of death, loved ones) have taken part in democratic decisions

regarding the outcome and/or government has made the decision in an undemocratic way and not involved the public in the debate or the decision making process;

- people have the right to privacy and government shall have no say in how people live their own lives or relationships they choose to have;
- people have the right to choose where and when their property changes hands. No government institution shall arbitrarily have the right to issue fines or confiscate property from people who do not want to relinquish it;
- people have the right to information that affects how the country in managed. Freedom of information shall be guaranteed for people wishing to investigate the power of the executive and private companies operating within home shores; transparency should be guaranteed especially regarding the use of armed forces or 'defence' equipment;
- nature (biological and chemical changes in the body that affects behaviour) not religion should be at the foremost in any justice system. (The understanding of the human condition, attributes and flaws, which are part of nature, should be placed in conditions governing law, thus, no government or justice system shall ignore these characteristics in any issue that may arise).

This bill of rights will place the ownness on the honest and decent people in the country to stand-up to certain groups of people they have been fearful of fighting in the past e.g. the banks, local governments, the police, thieves and other threats/attackers; when decisions made are not based on human consideration but on greed, opportunity and profit. (Through the threat of being prosecuted or an even greater fine causes people to be easily coerced into actions to relieve stress and pressure–

people need to remember as a society a letter threatening further fines or asset removal on non-compliance of demands is the same as being threatened to hand over cash or jewellery by thief; it is just a different tool to take something from someone who does not want to give it). Obviously, education is needed to prevent any potential abuse of the bill of rights and to ensure the support or legal systems does not become swamped with invalid applications.

The slow transition from a culture of fear and greed to a culture of caring and consideration will take time; education is needed for all ages with the bill of right written in a manner that can be understood by everyone and not just lawyers. To be included in the bill shall be a declaration that any lawyer who is been found attempting to use loopholes for advantage or to 'strong-hold' a party by various legal threats shall be struck off the legal register and will have to retrain as a lawyer.

Successive governments for 100s of years have constrained people's life by creating and amending legislation at will, which have the effect of reducing freedoms to a set of allowed privileges. This constraining of freedom is directed to people whom own little with the wealthy seemingly being exempt from certain laws. It is unfair, cruel and oppressive for people to live in a country with little knowledge of all the laws of the land and have a legal system that is seen by many as a 'playground for the rich and famous'. If there are too many laws for people to gain knowledge of easily and to remember, then people are at mercy to specialists in their field and stand a high chance of being harassed by law enforcement for breaking laws they had no knowledge of in the first place. Government has to simplify law and remove any advantage the wealthy has in their interactions with it.

The law has been made too complicated, impossible to memorise and without 'wriggle room' (for the majority anyway) for a number of reasons, with the main ones being: 1) justifying the existence of lawyers, solicitors, judges (all of which need access to the best reference books: the better lawyer knows how to search through the texts for loopholes etc.), police, the number of people in government and affiliated agencies, etc. i.e. job creation; 2) to protect certain people from backlashes over decisions that affect the majority; 3) to protect the wealth and the wealthy; 4) to ensure money flows in the right (depending on your viewpoint) direction up the pyramid to the elites in society; 5) to restrict and control freedoms' of the people; 6) to give the illusion that government are listening to people.

To understand the negative effects of laws I suppose people will have to become an unfortunate victim. Throughout childhood there is indoctrination into believing that law and connected services are there to protect and defend the innocent. However, the law has become a system where the devious (and this includes women who plays the innocent victim) and the greedy among society can manipulate it as they desire - a prime example is law regarding family matters; people need to clear your head and observe from the outside to see the reality that this is indeed the situation.

It is unsurprising when you realise that the police force started hundreds of years ago in the UK as security for rich shop owners to protect their products from being stolen by the poor (mainly to feed themselves) and thus as it was deemed by many as a means of enforcing the new poor law (directed at those who had little wealth). The force evolved over a period of 2-3 decades through clever marketing to a national police force in 1856 and has grown ever since, but, with protection of the wealthy still at it prime core. It is unsurprising that for many who have interacted with the police or CJS, law enforcement has become more of a problem than being attacked or robbed at random by a stranger.

People now live in a civilisation where not only are criminals after stealing your hard earned property (money, jewellery, and other assets) but also people who represent law, i.e. courts, police, local governments, etc. with the only difference being the use of a different tool, i.e. unauthorised criminals (thieves) use knifes or guns to threaten and terrorise, but, people representing law use ink on paper documents to do the same thing with the same outcome to take property / assets away. But, because of the indoctrination given throughout childhood people still rely on the government supported organisations representing the law to protect them, probably because all people know if we protect ourselves, we would be the ones in serious trouble with the law – and that is just plain wrong. There is no argument that the authorities eventually turn up mainly to aid social visibility, but only as an emergent property of legislation, where people are treated not as a victim besides their priority is to ensure they have enough information to complete their red-tape. It is unsurprising many have lost faith and have stopped reporting crimes.

Television programs are now used to show the good work of the CJS including those responsible for debt collection. Watching these programs with sound might convince people that the law and all associated with it are working in the best interests of the people. But, turning the sound off and watching the behaviour of people who wave paper documents in people's faces and seeing the human affect (stress, anxiety, anger, and helplessness) it has on the receiver tells a completely different story. In a free society, no service employed by the public sector should have the power to take away genuine freedom or destroy lives of people for petty reasons.

The police service are the worst culprits; I have never met a police officer who was himself whilst wearing a uniform. Any official uniform transforms a human into an arrogant serious drone with little (or no) sense of humour that have the power to make people dance to their instructions (this is a metaphor): this should be of great concern to the public. They can do this because the public have little knowledge of the law and is fearful of not 'cooperating' (I use the term loosely because that is not what is happening, the reality is being obedient to every command, i.e. subservient) and thus increase the risk of being under arrest if any resistance is met, justified or not.

The reality (looking as an observer) is the majority of people are under the control of people who act as not themselves, who have the ability to abuse their position (and some most definitely do, you do not have to search far to prove this statement), who can mention various letters and numbers to the general public who have little knowledge of what they actually mean to make people obedient to their every command; in addition, they have the power to detain you (remove people's freedom), search through private property, and strip search an individual's person. How long do people need to live to realise that people who do not behave as themselves in an official capacity cannot and should not be trusted; they have chosen to act as someone else for a job – some call it sold their soul.

I am not saying it is all negative, but would you trust someone who changed personalities on the type of dress they wear –

clearly no, you would keep your distance and a close eye due to the distrust in said person - and rightly so. This practice has to stop, no longer must government ask, nay demand, people to change their personality whilst working in an official capacity. Trust and faith needs to strengthen in the law and in the people who represent it; the only way to achieve this is to stop acting like someone they are not, i.e. in the service of the public for the best interests of the public in a human capacity. What this means is an understanding that every human on the planet has a different personality, humans are not the 'borg collective', and it is time the authorities representing the law realised that interacting with a drone, does not produce efficient outcomes, but only strengthens distrust.

(The problem society faces is everyone puts on their best act (face) in working and public life, it is the reason why most work colleagues fail to realise who an individual truly is; with most thinking the people they barely know are nice people when the opposite might be the case. This is not to say that the person people think they know during the day is someone completely different at home, it just to point out that acting is part of daily life for everyone and it is only through personal interactions in the home do people receive a true reflection of the person they thought they knew.)

Concurrently, there are no Gods among men, therefore, the arrogance of power of control has to cease. What this means is the police (and security officials in general) should not be given the automatic power to relinquish or remove freedoms of other people unless they have shown to be a serious danger or threat to others, and this includes ownership of property / assets. The polices' only task should be to protect and defend innocent people, not to enforce financial orders, not to punish minor driving offenses, not to be used as a political tool (and that includes the armed forces) or prioritise the wealthy over the poor in society. The police and security services should be institutions people do not mind interacting with not staying clear of (this is the current situation society has now were people avoid the uniform). They should be friendly, have a personality and have reduced powers that effectively seeks real cooperation with people (not obedience) and only allowed to remove property or freedoms in the most severe cases.

In addition, in any civilised country people would expect that if a minority of people are responsible for the majority of people's suffering and financial loss then there would be a legal system in place for them to claim from the people responsible or be protected from being homeless. But no, as seen in the recession of 2008 the wealthy people responsible where protected by the law, including all who work for the CJS. To add 'salt into the wounds' the people responsible not only made substantial profits but also received additional rewards for it, kept their positions; and then were marketed to public as being the best in the banking sector.

The point here is there was more effort, time, and resource spent protecting the wealthy and debt factories (e.g. banks, corporate institutions) at the expense of the poor some of which still to this day have not recovered their personal or emotional loss. To add to this, if people are all free then any individual's life or prosperity should be protected from others wrong doing, i.e. for freedom, people have to be exempt from external control or interference and for a democracy to work the people need to have a say in what law governs them; and the law for the people has to reflect this. The government has to completely overhaul the law and the CJS to permit people in society to decide on what constraints civilised society should be limited to. This needs to occur to prevent the continuation of a few (wealthy) people constraining the lives of the many; and be permitted for regular votes on as new generations enter adulthood.

I know there will be many lawyers out of a job, but all the legislation requires examining, reducing (dramatically) and simplifying to ensure as much as reasonable practicable that all people understand what laws are being used to govern, and then have a referendum to gain acceptance by the public. The education system needs to ensure the young adults fresh out of school have a full grasp of the laws of the land with which they need to respect or expect reprimand. All new laws, which need to keep up with technology, are required to be accepted by the public before government legislates. There must be no law that gives special privilege to the wealthy and law must promote civilised interaction and be isolated from any financial exchanges (i.e. bribery / lobbying).

Are We Human or Drones?

Does the Government want hard working, obedient drones?

Children are placed in education at such an early age for a number of reasons: indoctrination of children into the working the day and to allow parents to work for the benefit of the economy. There is little evidence to show that this benefits the child as they grow into adulthood, but, there is evidence that shows it hinders the ability of people to cope with life after school and is detrimental to the parent-child relationship. The education system has also been amended over the decades and has removed most life-lessons from the curriculum and concentrated on main subject areas (Science, technology, English and Maths - STEM). Whilst, concurrently, producing badly educated adults, i.e. smart enough to run the machines and fill in paperwork, but, not smart enough to realise real life issues (giving the continuous message of having full faith in government even if it is untrustworthy, and look to government for protection). It is a system which is gradually producing people who do not question but obediently follow; the cause of the growth of the legal sector; and the reduction in union powers that has made people fearful of not only losing their jobs, but, also being drawn into the legal system through not following and practicing the rules and procedure in place for employment.

A sort of unintelligent, uncaring, unconscious, unreasonable, obedient human drone that is impossible to debate, discuss or reason with who shows zero compassion to other human beings; and people who work for government or any related affiliates are the worse culprits, especially where money is concerned. Being a mindless drone brings new meaning to the phrase 'brain-dead' and this does involve people who follow the letter everything written down on pieces of paper without any leeway, human thought or compassion. I am sure we have all met these types of people in our everyday lives and might actually be one during working hours.

If thinking and reasoning is removed from the abilities of people in their interactions, especially to solve issues, democracy has already failed and the country will be controlled and will only work for and benefit the people who have invested in or created the paper document used that people have been told they have no choice (for continued employment) but to follow during working hours. It is the fear of losing possessions and the fear of questioning all the clever marketing presented to people all our lives that makes people follow and treat each other like uncaring, uncivilised drones in our working lives. People all over the Western world must live and realise this as a reality; it is clearly the wrong direction society should be going in.

All rules, procedure, legislation and regulation should always be subject to human considerations. Society needs to produce people who can think and reason, especially with the ability to question, in order to make an ethical and moral decision, even during working hours. Employment law has to allow leeway for employees in order for debate and reason to take place; without this people will become disillusioned and social unrest will continue. The education system has to teach children life skills; moreover, instil the doctrine that ethical and moral decisions always takes priority over rules and procedures written on a piece of paper. Also, the law has to compensate for the human condition rather than to the letter of the law.

Society has to create generations of humans that can be reasoned with, not a race of human drones who operate on the philosophy of 'resistance is futile you shall be assimilated' in a life constrained and ruled by ink on a piece of paper set by wealthy people who you do not know in a central controlling government building (pardon the star trek pun – but it is a valid point). All written text, whether it be legislation or company rules, should be used as guidelines only (an ideal picture of how the system should work), but situations have to be dealt with in a human manner befitting an intelligent human race. Debate and human understanding of life difficulties has to be the forefront of the governing strategy used.

What has nature got to do with it?

One of the main issues that have really bothered me is the lack of understanding of nature and how this relates to human actions. Generally, religion has placed a sort of arrogance and ego on people to think humans have the ability to defy nature. The reality is humans, like all other life on the planet, are controlled by certain rules determined by chemical and biological reactions happening inside people's own bodies and minds, which makes all life less than perfect and subjected to flaws and sometimes acts not becoming of who individuals are. What this means is, humans have a tendency to think we are special on the planet; the most intelligent species on the planet! – well I do not see any other life contributing to global warming or self-destruction or the levels of greed that has no comparison; so probably not the most intelligent species on the planet then, but, probably the most arrogant – sad but true!

The fact nature shows that although humans think ourselves as superior, most other life on the planet, especially mammals, show more caring for children and their own species in general than we do our own. If you have ever watched substantial nature programs you never see any members of a species 'stabbing others in the back' for personal gain, or parents who are determined to wreck the parent-child relationship of the other (let's face it the father is the one that suffers). But, what is observed is the similar sorts of behaviour (i.e. aggression (sometimes leading to death or murder of same species, nurturing, defending loved ones, etc.), the constant fight for land; and some wildlife show the games of affection between the sexes. This is nature - a constant struggle to control ones' own behaviour, the lengths all people goes to for the protection and defence of loved ones, and the constant melee for land and with it resources; with internal bickering that sometimes ends with loss of life. Humans are indeed no different to other forms of life, although people live in a world where our species have developed advanced technology that can end life and cause substantial devastation in the continued battle for the control of resources.

Does this mean that when nature (chemical and biological changes in the body that affects moods, thought patterns and behaviour) gets the best of individuals in society, these people should be punished by the law with the removal of freedom and be locked away in a small building and/or cell or put to death?

It is a tough question to answer, but, as an example is a situation that occurs regularly that every man who has lived with a woman is very familiar with - 25% of the time behaviour and decision making of a woman (age range between 16-45) is erratic and sometimes incurs violent mood swings, i.e. period; people are all aware of this behaviour change, but, society sweeps it under the carpet not to be discussed due to PC reasons (e.g. equality, women in management positions, feminism, etc.).   This behaviour change is part of nature and the chemical changes in the body affecting the normal rational functioning of the mind that makes women do strange and off character things – the same issues happen in men mainly due to testosterone levels causing issues with aggression, rational thinking and sexual urges. (It has to be said copious amounts of drink and drugs can have the same affect in both men and women). It is not just natural chemical changes that make us all act strangely, emotion has a way to override our conscience and do some malicious acts that makes us regret (hopefully) our actions at a later date – it is called being human with all the natural inbuilt flaws.

The point is humans are all slaves to nature and ignoring this reality is not going to bring about peace and a fulfilling life; our arrogance and ego and sense of superiority gets in the way of this realisation that as a species we will never be able to defeat nature. People might be able to manipulate nature and change certain rules of nature, but, will always be slaves to it. But, humans think we are masters of nature, besides, human nature is completely ignored by certain groups who declare that people can behave in certain provocative ways without any repercussions – these people are in denial and on a high ego trip that even makes marijuana say 'were can I get some of what you're on man – what a ride!'. Attitude like this is absolute nonsense and can only lead to confrontations and other unwanted issues. All people need to accept that every part of human behaviour impacts on others and society needs to respect this and behave according to how individuals want to be treated by others. People who do not want anything bad or sexual to happen then do not behave provocatively or push people to the limits; do not antagonise or steal from people; do not prevent a parent from seeing their children; it is very simple: treat people with respect and dignity as you should yourself.

Until this understanding is achieved, there will always be incidents were unwanted or bad acts are (un)intentionally given due to emotional strain or increased chemical mixture, i.e. testosterone, in people's bodies and minds. Society should not be permanently punishing people for this, but, should be helping people control this natural reaction more; maybe a method to reduce certain chemicals in the human body to reduce their affects. Until this does happen, people have to stop fighting reality and realise that for every action there will always be a human reaction; the only thing that differs is the level of the reaction to certain events.

The law and law creators have to come to this reality and not permanently punish someone if nature gets the best of them. Likewise, (and this goes out to all feminists) due to testosterone levels in young men, they are very attracted to women and the less they wear and the more provocative they behave the more difficult it becomes to control the urges brought on by chemical changes in the brain. The other side of the argument is that this 'attraction' also allows women to abuse their position and gain some control over men's actions for their own benefit – again people see this regularly both in private and working life (due to politically correctness reasons this is always swept under the carpet). This is reality, humans are not Gods thus cannot control nature and both sexes have to realise this as both suffer similar afflictions, i.e. nature controlling us, not the opposite; ignoring facts is not the way to move forward.

Therefore, the government, and people in society, have to ensure the law takes natural instincts, urges and behaviour into account to ensure as much as reasonably practicable that the law understands this human (all life in general) affliction and when nature gets the best of someone, those individuals do not pay for it for the rest of their lives. There is a difference between something that happens without a plan, i.e. in the heat of emotion than something that has been carefully planned over a period of time. It is this distinction that holds the key to determining the punishment for crimes – clearly, a planned murder (for some time) or theft has been thought through; whereas, an act of violence in the heat of moment has not; and a mechanism to determine whether the acts of individuals was premeditated or not has to occur.

No-one should be locked away and have a permanent record if they were at mercy to nature; and this does lead to an uncomfortable realisation, but, a necessary balance – people need to understand how their own actions could affect the actions of others via emotional distress affecting the brain. For example, people of both sexes need to be aware and <u>comprehend</u> (are you listening feminists) the effects of biological and chemical changes in the human body to how behaviour and lack of dress (women stop sexualising yourself unless you're looking for attention then do not complain if you receive it) affect actions in each other. By respecting this realisation, it should have positive affects in the interactions between sexes.

5

FOREIGN POLICY TO PROMOTE PEACE

The West's (all Western countries) foreign policy does not promote stabilisation or peace, instead combined with information warfare on the government's own people, it appears to promote the interests of large corporate businesses hence instigate wars and regime changes mainly in countries whose land provides vital resources for the West. The Wests 'poor quality' leaders have been seen gloating when coalition forces end the life of the heads of foreign governments and then seen to oversee and govern democratic elections in said countries with one or more parties having close ties with Western governments. This policy has worked effectively for all those who have strong business interests in these countries, but as all in society have seen the innocent people are the ones on the receiving end of major power struggles and destabilisation, all whilst oil and gas reserves are in full control of Western powers. Countries such as, Afghanistan, Iraq, Libya, Iran, Syria, Ukraine, and due to political interference Venezuela (which had a short pause because of the 2nd Iraq war), have all been subject to Western (mainly US) interventions and some are still suffering with conflicts. The great migration of 2015-ongoing has been caused by Western powers seeking to place 'puppet governments' in these countries.

It is arguable that the 2nd Iraq war occurred because of talks between Saddam (a former CIA operative and puppet of the US) and other countries to trade oil in a different currency than the US dollar. It is arguable that Gaddafi, a former close friend of Tony

Blair (Former UK PM: Teflon Tony – no dirt sticks and is immune to any form of criminal investigation) fell out of favour with the West on the pricing of oil and further opportunities he was seeking from other countries the West did not favour. The point here is the leaders of these countries did not in an instant, overnight, change from being a civilised ruler of their own country to an evil and maniacal dictator who tortures their own people. Most of the leaders of these oil rich countries had previously been helped by the West in order for them to be in power, their nature was fully known and their treatment of people was largely left unreported by mass media for decades because of oil, gas, arms and mineral trade deals made.

Only when it became convenient to get the public buy in for an invasion into these countries, for regime change, did it become important to portray the leaders of the countries as it always has been. Needless to say, none of these countries will stabilise any time soon because of a number of reasons, with one being forcibly attempting to introduce the Western governments' ideology into countries that the people are not accustomed to (sounds familiar to the philosophy of the NAZI party and what they attempted to achieve 'twice' by forcing people in other countries to fall in line with their own political viewpoint) does not and will not work, when it was the ruthlessness of the previous leader that maintained the peace between various sects and groups. Also, a destabilised country is easier for foreign interests to maintain some type of control over the population, as whilst people are fighting amongst themselves, whoever has control of the resources can take it without too much opposition.

Wars in these countries benefit the wealthy corporate interests above the health and wellbeing of the people in these regions. If

Western politicians and armed forces cared about the people they would not have stood by and help place the leaders in power to begin with, nor continued to arrange trading deals with them for their lands resources or to purchase arms. A prime example is Saudi Arabia, who has been found 'red handed' state funding the people responsible for 9-11 (twin towers) and the slaughter of people in numerous countries and other labelled 'terrorists' around the world, including ISIS (allegedly – for legal reasons). Western (mainly US and UK) made bombs, ammunition, planes, and tanks have all been used to further the interests of Saudi princes. Yet, the Western governments still insists on selling arms to them and reflects or ignores Saudi's human right record.

There are many stories about ISIS beheadings and other cruel treatment of people, but Western governments are uneasy, or wish to ignore facts that Saudi Arabia has a worse record than the main terrorist organisation in the world today (ISIS). People should find that disturbing, but, people still stand idly by and allow their government to continue to trade with them. Why? Profits before anything human related; the interests of the wealthy come first for a prosperous economy! Within the globalised economy competition among countries can cause conflict, and as such selling to leaders of countries who torture their own people is a necessary evil for the economic betterment of the home country. This philosophy can be traced back to the ideology of the Reagan and Thatcher years discussed in brief in a previous chapter. Here the chapter shall discuss why these types of arrangements and conflicts are here and why the West continues to interfere with governance in other countries. For this, the book needs to take a trip back in time to the second half of World War 1 where the Wests addiction to power began in its entirety and has led to never ending conflicts, deals with the devil, and multifaceted health and societal problems all people in society are dealing with now (bit of history for readers and a worthwhile tangent from the book).

Oil is one of the greatest obsessions for world leaders and has transformed the way all people live our lives; it has become one of the major reasons why the world is continuously in conflict and has caused a worldwide climate and health risk. The story of oil began in the US in the 1800's in regard to kerosene to provide light, but, the real infusion of oil began in the Middle East when the allied forces faced an opponent (Nazi Germany) whose war machines where powered by oil supplied by Middle Eastern oil. Britain's naval fleet at the time relied entirely on coal power, whilst German ships were faster and could travel further; this gave Germany a critical advantage. As the UK did not have its own oil supply the search for oil began. Winston Churchill instructed British companies to scour the Middle East to obtain Britain's own oil supply with the UK government owning 50% of the shares and profits. Revenues of oil was obtained and Britain's war machine altered to use the new fuel source; it was the turning point of the Great War; the Germans needed to be stopped and now the power was available to move people to strategic locations more quickly than ever before.

With the collapse of the Turkish Empire in 1918, due to their collaboration with the Germans, new opportunities could be sought in the regions rich in oil reserves, the Middle East. Winston Churchill realised the region(s) could keep Britain secured in oil for the future and keep Britain great, and began with his coalition partners sectioning off the regions into a new league of nations that led to a template that is still in place in the

Arab world today. He concentrated on the region of Mesopotamia, now known as Iraq. The problem was he had competition with others searching for oil. In 1928, the plan to create a single oil cartel was created within the Middle East, which concentrated on cooperation and a coalition in the control and pricing of oil.

In 1931, taking advantage of Saudi's poor economic state, the West began negotiations and trade deals with Saudi Arabia a rising oil producer at that time. But, again, competition to control the oil caused a diplomatic headache for the leaders of the UK as one of the UK's diplomats betrayed his own country with a deal from the US company Standard by persuading a finance minister to sign over rights to explore the countries oil potential for just $275,000. The UK missed out due to 'playing politics' with their diplomat abroad among threats of sexual misconduct charges and espionage. Naturally, Standard struck oil, and what an oil reserve, Saudi Arabia was now a major oil player in the world and sat on a large rich deposit of oil under their land. Naturally, the UK and the US continued to present the king with gifts to lobby for oil fields and trade deals for cheap oil supplies. The outcome was the US secured its energy future and the UK missed out on the trade relationship.

Unfortunately, the Second World War was around the corner that began the full use of oil in all types of equipment and the new source of oil for the Germans was in Baku, which was far from the rich resources in the Middle East. By destroying the source of oil for the Germans, Churchill knew Adolf could not continue to run his war machines; and so the war machine quickly ran out of the supply of oil by 1944. This ultimately defeated Nazi Germany; they simply out demanded their own supply of oil, and thus petroleum. It became clear that oil was, and still is, now the driving force in any war effort, in any consumer product, and in transport. Wealth is generated from oil, and the West needed oil in vast quantities. The age of carbon man began and with it the obsession and addiction to oil; and the Middle East was the key supplier.

Others realised this too, including the Americans when President Roosevelt generated a new plan for the Middle East to section off the control of the oil and potential new sources of oil within those countries. He produced a map of the Middle East were various lines were drawn to signify the control of oil, without consideration of the people who lived in these countries, i.e. this began the Western interest in the control of resources in other less developed countries. Within this meeting there were no ambassadors representing the oil rich countries themselves, control indeed was to be shared between allied forces, moreover the US and UK.

However, in 1950, the oil boom created a political shift in Saudi Arabia when profits made by the production and selling of oil shocked the current finance minister in Saudi Arabia; although making profit they were only making a fraction of the profit the oil companies were making in their own countries. Saudi Arabia was being 'ripped off'. They then asked, no insisted ARAMCO, for a fair 50% share of oil profits. Now the nations throughout the region who owned the oil demanded greater concessions or the threat of shutting down the oil fields; the control of oil by private international oil companies from the West was now coming to an end. Middle Eastern countries quickly began to rise; the UK's attention was concentrated on Iran, and the idea of 50% share to the Iranian government was not to the UK's liking.

In 1951, Iran was going through a period of political instability where the people were leading a revolution against the ruling government; a crisis for UKs oil trade with Iran was on its way. The UK refused to renegotiate its deal with the new Iranian government and in the spring of 1951, the Iranian government seized control of all the oil fields and sent the British packing. The UK was now completely frozen out of its own oil supply it was totally reliant upon, the oil security of UK was now in deep crisis; the flow of oil to the UK stopped.

In 1952, the UK ran short of oil and as such coal became the main fuel of choice to burn to satisfy the ever growing need for energy; so much so that it caused thick smog within the London district and people began to choke because of it. Clearly, the thirst for oil was even more sought after, but the era of cheap oil was coming to the end and now oil became a political problem; and the newly formed United Nations was a path to regain the UKs control of oil. But, the diplomatic offensive unfortunately failed and continued the UKs oil fuel poverty; oil was now being used as a political weapon for the first time. Modern living relied, and still relies, on oil and therefore the UK needed oil and this was the start of when politics became fully mingled with interfering with foreign governments and oil cartels within Middle Eastern regions and the fight for control of oil began.

The US and UK signed a treaty 'Clandestine Service History' (how to guide) to action a coup in oil controlled country of Iran and overthrow the reigning government and place at the head a leader who would work for the interests of both countries. The beginning of a foreign policy to overthrow a ruling government began with operation AJAX, approved by both Churchill and Eisenhower. The US saw this as a strategic operation to prevent other world powers, such as the Soviet Union, from gaining control of oil rich territories. Tactics such as, demonising the current leader, labelling and other dirty tricks was used; money was no object to achieve the objective. This way Iranian people would do most of the work, driven by propaganda from the Western governments, and overthrow their own government by encouraging civil unrest. By August 1953, the Western handpicked leader was in power and the previous leader arrested and spent the rest of his life in jail. The UK achieved it objective and acquired back its oil, but at a 50% share; it turned out that the war, the lives lost and the money spent due to UK government's arrogance and greed, was for nothing.

Among the growing cry for Arab nations to control their own oil, more trouble began for the West in their quest for oil that they so desperately needed. Far from placing the Middle East in its place, the situation in Iran merely ignited the calls for nationalisation and more control of oil in all countries in the region. In 1956, Egypt's leader came the latest executive to realise how much potential profit his country was losing with the agreement of letting oil tankers through the Sewers canal. The president ordered the canal to be blockaded until the Western leaders renegotiated the terms of access; UK supply was completely shut-down again; a stark similarity to the Iran crisis suffered earlier. By the end of 1956, the UK was again running dry. A coalition force overseen by the British and French government led military action and took control of the area around the Suez Canal, unfortunately, with eyes on the canal the Soviets gained a foothold in the Middle East. The US was upset with the UK for not informing them of their intentions and threatened sanctions if they persisted; the coalition finally bowed to pressure in March 1957. In the aftermath, UK and France found their influence as world powers weakened thanks to the situation surrounding the Suez crisis.

By the 1960s, the drive for oil meant the world was producing too much and led to the creation of OPEC (Organisation of the Petroleum Exporting Countries) in an attempt to control the nationalisation, price and supply of oil. The leaders of oil rich countries were acutely aware that the same type of interference from the West could mean the end of their reign. But, the creation of OPEC shifted power and reduced the fear of the threat of foreign intervention. The status of oil as a commodity changed to permit oil to be 'drip fed' by the nations that had oil connections to countries who could afford to pay for it. Good news for Arab nations, bad news for countries who did not have their own oil.

By 1970, the US was acquiring most of its oil from Saudi Arabia and drove the US boom and built the very fabric of their lives, they were more secure in oil than the UK. However, in 1973, the US backed Israel in a war in Syria (Soviets' supplied weapons to Egypt and Syria) and it was a decision that affected the US supply of oil, OPEC angry about the support for Israel in the conflict cut-off the US supply. Within a month, the US was running short of oil and by late 1973, all products inflated in price and people would defend their own supply of oil with weapons; it also led to the downfall of the US auto industry. Along with the Watergate scandal this resulted in major changes in the American political system that put more power in the hands of lobbyists and generally the wealthy in society. Both the US and the UK was in deep trouble regarding oil supply; both economies had been crushed by the lack of a stable oil supply (even in the 70s, majority of products for sale from food to toys to electronics through to transport needed oil).

The situation meant exploring new ways of acquiring oil, and as a result the start of drilling for oil within the oceans began. The success of the exploration was not so transparent as communication between oil contractors and government occurred in coded, encrypted messages. The UK for the first time struck oil, good times ahead for the UK; they had now become an oil exporter. However, the good times still meant high energy prices that put at risk the UK manufacturing base. The gradual demise of the British car industry hastened by the extra cost of production, and encouraged the switch to smaller vehicles; consequently, Japanese cars came dominant in the UK.

The Middle East, once seen as friends of the West, had become hostile with terms of the embargo; however, now the US and the UK had struck oil and new hydrocarbons, OPEC's oil power in the world had been disrupted. No longer could they alone control the price and supply quantity of oil. A new period of global control of oil began and this time Western powers had influence. With new oil deposits being found all over the world it helped countries out of recession, but, with so much oil around the prices fell below the cost of bottled water and had a drastic impact on countries who were large exporters, so much so that the low price of the oil assisted in the downfall of Soviet Russia.

After the 1973 oil embargo, the relationship between the corporatocracy, banks and governments (the oligarchs) was strengthened like never before with the purpose of never to be blackmailed or held for ransom by smaller countries ever again. The oil embargo was probably one of the worst decisions and actions ever to plague the public as this strengthened the further decline of democracy and increased the problem of an elected government making decisions in the interests of the oligarchs to endure the flow of money (the hijacking of democracy began in its earnest).

Due to the increased profits made by Saudis with the embargo, the West enticed the wealthy to study at Western universities. This led to the dilution of strong religious following and introduced consumerism into a rising economy. A strong relationship between the West and Saudi Arabia began to flourish and is still strong today with Westernised culture being promoted and Western companies involved in expanding cities, all the while ensuring petro-dollars flowed to the Western oligarchs.

By 1991, the Soviet economy collapsed and the rationing of food became part of life. A state of national emergency in Russia was declared and shortly after the empire was dissolved and land was up for grabs, some of which had oil deposits. Western oil companies flocked into these regions to take advantage of the soviet downfall and trade deals were made for Caspian oil deposits and new underground pipelines installed to transport oil to Europe.

Saudi and the Middle East became a gold spot for the construction and engineering businesses of mainly US companies. In return there were trade deals and a promise to defend Saudi interests. (The relationship between the Bush family and the Saudi royal family (and Iraq) goes on for more than 20 years. Bush is an investor of US Saudi Oil Company. Could this be the reason why suddenly after 911 wealthy Saudi people boarded planes out of the US, with no one coming forward to admit clearing the flights - Allegedly!) The West assisted taking a desert dwelling society into a modern civilisation with projects that built new cities from petrodollars in partnership with US. Perhaps this is why there is indiscriminate (little restraints) air strikes from coalition forces: because there are business opportunities for the engineering and construction businesses to rebuild what has been destroyed. Western foreign policy, in exchange for corporate interests in foreign lands, offer technology, infrastructure projects, schools and work to indigenous people, which are marketed as assisting the people out of such societal ailments as poverty without the understanding that enforcing Western ways of life on people is something that people may not want in the long term. It is clear in some areas of the world these new facilities only benefitted the wealthy few and promoted an ever increasing gap between rich and poor and the 'slow death' of native culture.

Meanwhile, developing nation's governments were looking at the West and demanding the same progress and standards; the burgeoning economies of Asia were demanding more fuel (oil and gas), more products, bigger cities, better electronics, meaning more energy demands needed to be catered for. Global consumption escalated, oil is now the driving factor of the world's economy and to control the use of oil the price of oil needed to increase. However, with more countries in the world now addicted to oil, demand for oil continued to grow and led to the sharp rise in consumption within a short period of time; many experts issued sharp warnings that the demand for oil was unsustainable.

The rising price of oil did not affect the demand for oil, meaning the demand had outstripped the supply. In 2014 the price of oil dropped. The reasons given was due to large oil reserves; however, shortly before the price drop Russia gained back control of Crimea due to trouble in Ukraine (perhaps to prevent further NATO expansion) caused by international interference in their political affairs (some say US interference). This led to additional economic sanctions for Russia in the hope that Russia would retreat from Crimea - the West was hoping for a repeat of 1991 economic crash. Unfortunately, OPEC disagreed to reduce production of the oil to assist in this type of political warfare and with Europe reliant of Russian gas and new trade deals with China and other Asian nations, the sanctions hurt Europe as much as Russia and the 1991 affect did not occur. Instead, it caused stronger ties between Russia and China possibly at the expense of Europe and the US.

To control energy supplies, the Western governments had three main strategies that worked successfully to assist in maintaining some control, at least through third parties (puppet leaders), of the oil production countries. Interference from the West in oil rich countries had begun in its earnest in the 1950s and continues to this day, where manipulation of the price of oil and additional sanctions are used to influence the leaders of the country to fall 'in line' or the identical tactics used on Iran in 1953 is generally the first strategy undertaken. If this fails, the one used by the British and the French in 1956 is actioned and then all-out war; sometimes a combination as per the removal of former CIA operative Saddam Hussein again in Iraq (invasion ordered by Bush and Blair in 2003 in which ~1/2 million people died).

Unless people have been hiding under a rock over the last two decades there is stark similarities with what is happening at present in resource rich countries: look at Egypt (start of the Arab

Spring), Iran, Iraq (twice), Syria, Afghanistan, Egypt, Libya, Ukraine, Lebanon, Venezuela, etc. All these countries have within their boundaries a supply of oil or gas or are important in the transportation of oil or gas to Western countries as modern society is fully dependent on oil and it defines modern living. As always Russia has separate national interests to the US and Europe and probably the main reason why there is resentment between the US and Russia – are people are now living in the 2nd cold war? (2015 - ????).

In the 1980s and 1990s, the emphasis on business shifted from entrepreneurship to deregulation, which saw most small independent companies swallowed up by large corporations or by public utility companies. These companies then found legal loopholes to create holding companies that could own both the regulated utility companies and the unregulated independent energy producing corporations. Many of them launched aggressive programmes to drive new businesses, which had the nerve to trespass onto their domain, into bankruptcy and then purchase them. This time also invited politicians own interests in the oil, engineering and construction companies so much so that it is now increasingly difficult to identify were the separation is between government and these types of corporate interests. Moreover, especially in the US, the administrations were either part of the oil industry or were part of the engineering or construction companies. Consequently, this was also the time when social welfare, environment, and other quality of life issues came second to greed and an irresistible emphasis was placed of promoting private businesses. Eventually, it was seen as socially and culturally acceptable that projects owned by wealthy investors rather than government was (and is) seen as the appropriate way forward; and the world bank bought into this notion, advocating for deregulation and privatisation.

As a result, large companies sought cheap labour, the most accessible resources and the largest markets; and the larger the company the more ruthless in their approach. They promised a way for third world countries to use the private sector to relieve them of debt; they also built schools and highways. In the end, if the companies found cheaper workers and more accessible resources elsewhere, they abandoned the communities they previously interfered with and the consequences where often devastating to both the indigenous people and to the reputation of the company's own country, but they did this without hesitation in the search for greater profits.

Towards the end of the 1990's and in the early 2000s many people, especially in isolated communities living in tribes, saw little difference or independence between oil companies and military forces, as they both seemed to have the same interest in hand and both worked together to achieve the same outcome. Many tribes and large areas of natural wonder, i.e. jungles and rain forests, have been devastated leaving behind polluted lands and rivers; and military action in the area in support of the companies killing or completely wiping out entire tribes and cultures for oil deposits specifically exporting to Western countries.

There are many regions of the world where countries was promised affluence and prosperity in exchange for oil companies permissions to work there, only to end up in financial debt that they will never be able to pay off. But, it was not just about the money; the destruction of indigenous cultures, human lives, and the thousands of species of animals, reptiles, insects and plants that have been lost because of the addiction to oil, some of which might have contained undiscovered cures to any number of diseases. The search for oil and with it profit goes beyond the calls of ecologists for saving such places, it goes beyond the world of slavery that all in society thought had been left behind in the times of the romans.

The exploitation of land and people has now built a global empire that not only ignores the impacts of its operations on all life, but enslaves more people than any other colonial powers before us. People are all told how our government is the epitome of civilised behaviour. Meanwhile, recent history has taught people, along with their continued behaviour of forcing people from their native homes, killing those whom fight for their land and the destruction of nature for resources, people in government are far from civilised nor do they care or respect other people's rights of freedom when profits are to be made.

Each region of the world that possesses precious fossil resources is now a battleground for life's soul. However, governments decree that they are doing a good job in governing in a global world, but the rich continue to get richer and the poor poorer and suffer ill health as a result. Yet, the World Bank, international development agencies, the IMF, corporations and governments involved continue to inform society of the great job they are doing and that progress is being made. It is the same old malady, profits for the oligarchs above all else, even human life. Yet, people carry on working living in a fog of ignorance or not even caring about the effects they are allowing their own government to authorise on behalf of the corporatocracy.

There are currently (2016-2017) two main areas of interest in mainstream media being talked about: Iraq and Syria. One country, Aleppo in Syria, is being bombed by Russia and Assad mainly and their actions have to be condemned because innocent people in both East and West Aleppo are being killed by being caught in the crossfire. The excuse Russia is using is the fight against terrorists or rebels, who are supported with weapons and intelligence by the Western governments, so obviously Russia and Assad are 'bad people'. On the other hand, is the battle of Mosul, which is in Iraq, was/is led by the US coalition and the message given to people using mainstream media is the US is good and great, and all in society should offer support to the coalition as they are defending people from oppression. But, apart from how these two circumstances are sold there is very little difference between them: images of suffering in Aleppo are widespread in Western main stream media, whereas similar images in Mosul are only accessible in other media outlets, i.e. being hidden from the main news sources the public generally watch. The point is in both circumstances innocent people are dying in a political war for corporate gain of resources, and the people in the West are made to believe that the situation is black and white, where US, UK, France, Germany, etc. are the good guys and Russia is demonised. Yet, the outcomes of the airstrikes are towns and cities that require to be rebuilt - I wonder who will benefit from these contracts? Corporate interests in the West will, as they have done in the past; war and destruction in foreign countries, places puppet governments in power and allow Western companies to win contracts. It should make people question if all the unnecessary destruction and loss of human life, is to achieve this purpose!

To further their issues between Russia and the West, it is my understanding that part of the Lisbon treaty signed by all relevant parties after the 'cold war (that never was)' is an agreement that NATO forces would not expand the territories further into Europe. Slowly but surely in the decades that followed, NATO bases have been expanding into many countries and the current state is a situation where NATO bases are strategically located in neighbouring countries of both Russia and China. The problem with NATO is the prime benefactor is the US and at least 2% of national GDP of every member state is directed at further procurement of military technology and personnel and is highly associated with the UN; with both incurring diplomatic immunity for any actions they wish to do in any country. (One example of how this immunity can be abused is what happened in Haiti in 2015-16 where NATO along with the UN knowingly failed to dispose of their own waste appropriately and created an outbreak of cholera which killed many people; but, no accountability can be sought due to the immunity clause).

Overall, the build-up of technology, large bases and personnel means that NATO and the UN are now overbearing corporations or power that people cannot bring to account or have any democratic right to vote against any of their actions. Looking back at Germany's history, moreover the NAZI movement, something of great concern comes to light. The NAZI movement, unlike what people are all taught at schools, got permission to expand their bases into Europe from the ruling governments, much similar to NATO. However, history remembers NAZI bases as an invasion and therefore horrific, but NATO is being marketed to the public not as an invasion, but, a force for good.

People who question the government about their narrative, for example David Irving and his questioning of the holocaust and whether Hitler was indeed anti-Semitic using actual documented evidence; have their reputation completely and totally destroyed because governments cannot have an individual or small groups issuing actual facts on top of government led propaganda. Indeed, there is an unnerving trend that the more politicians ridicule an idea or a person, the more viable the ideas or truths there seems to be.

Hitler annexed Germany out of international financial debt and started to print their own money along with moving his people out of destitution and drowning in debt. He loosened the German economy from the world trade system and built an independent financial exchange system and bought the nation into a power house soon after the world war. The problem was Jews controlled most of the world's banking system, (and still do), took exception to this isolationist approach; so who was responsible for the war(s)? History is written by the winners and presents one viewpoint only, thus, the main point people need to be aware of is all history presented by government should be taken at face value only, as government to all residents have to be seen as a force for good in the world otherwise government will struggle to maintain power and civil unrest will occur.

The government needs to send a message to the people that they are in danger, in order for the people to look towards the government for protection and give the 'green light' to actions. It is why facts are not easy to come by and why government hides behind national security in some claims because evidence to justify claims and judgments is hard to find. It is also why governments create man-hunts for whistle-blowers and demonises them to the public as they do not want real transparent truth about how leaders and some corporate businesses operate, for now what should be obvious reasons, e.g. fraud, corruption, illegal and unlawful activity, destruction of environment and cultural life, etc.

It is very confusing and does not make any sense as to the determination of the differences between the two military purposes and the more research done, the more hypocrisy is the rhetoric of the leaders of the countries who agree with the ever expanding NATO bases, which is a provocation to countries that are against the Western government's ideology and philosophy.

One aspect is clear, the Western powers are 'nervous' about displeasing Saudi Arabia, so society have a situation where this country is both supported (by large weapons export trade deals) and ignored for its own crimes against humanity. With the arms trade, wars and various other trade deals with countries that are well known to have a bad human rights policy, the decisions made by government to partner with these countries is purely all about greed and whoever dies because of these sales is just a victim of circumstance. The Western powers do not care about the outcome of the trade; it is all about the quest for profit. Whether people like to admit it or not, all in Western countries who know that these deals are being made are fully implicit in the devastation caused by the use of such arms by not making their own government accountable for the suffering and misery caused. The world of foreign policy politics concentrates on acquiring resource for profit no matter what cost (human life included), it has created a constant spiral of world conflict and regime changes that first began over six decades ago.

Remembrance Sunday or any other event that is supposed to remember all the sacrifices people made fighting for people's freedom and country is not only about honouring the people who made the ultimate sacrifice (lets' be honest about this there were people who volunteered, but most was forced to fight in the wars otherwise they would be arrested and tried for treason) the other is to try and remember the lessons learned before, during and post war eras. The problem is humans have not learned anything from the mistakes are ancestors' made. The people of the country are still allowing the government to order our armed forces to rage wars and invasion internationally; this process is certainly not defending the country or its borders although it is marketing as such by using the possible threats of terrorism.

The other point to make on this issue is the people in the army are used as a political hard shoulder. What this means is the army is used for political grandstanding on the international stage and for corporate interests. People see this in the numerous wars that are still going strong, even though mass media does not report many stories in these regions anymore, e.g. Libya, Iraq, Iran, Syria, Ukraine, etc. The leaders of these countries have been targeted and most assassinated plunging the respected country in chaos because the leaders refused to be a puppet of Western governments; and it concerns the price structure of resources (mainly oil and gas) and what currency these resources are to be traded in (it would have been bad for the US banking system if oil was traded not in dollars but something different). The evidence to 'connect the dots' for the real reason Western powers decided to intervene in these countries is presented throughout media outlets, especially on the internet, and in some cases politicians, always post intervention, even admit that these were the real reasons for the wars; after all who is going to make them accountable to breaking international law when they themselves draft it.

Speaking of how morally good the US and the UN is, consider just one of their acts in war torn Syria, where the pentagon has always refuted the use of depleted Uranium missiles and bullets. However, in 2017 they admitted to have used 5265 rounds of depleted uranium rounds in Syria; and these are the good guys, apparently?! What happens with these types of rounds is they poison the air and land besides being highly linked to various cancer and birth defects; the UK, French and all the members of coalition forces are all implicit in using these types of ammunition rounds knowing the damage to health they cause. Why do people still question why the world is suffering with the rise of all these terrorist groups hell bent of destroying Western civilisation or who exactly are the real culprits who have caused the problem (i.e. root cause analysis)?

At the end of the day there is no black and white answer. All sides are morally and ethically unsound, but you can be sure that the West are the ones who instigated the trouble in the first place in the quest for resources and profits by interfering in foreign countries for decades. It is a hard realisation to find out that people's voted in government and armed forces has been partially responsible in purposely interfering in foreign affairs, wiping out innocent civilians lives; and knowingly causing hatred for the West. The question is where is the justice for war crimes, where is the tribunals. Well that is the thing isn't it, the Western powers set the international laws, there not accountable to follow them and the government leaders are protected by people in the oligarchs.

People, globally, can now see the effects of Western politicians interfering in the affairs of Middle Eastern Countries. The countries in South East Asia are now looking towards the Eastern bloc (China, Russia, etc.) for trade deals and closer ties. Another reason for this is the US 'hard ball' bullying tactics, especially regarding the missile defence programme, which the US politicians don't even comprehend that people in various countries have any right to oppose a US base to be placed there. In South Korea, with the recently elected president, there are issues when the people to whom have been presented with evidence of the close ties with US protest asking her to resign because of possible NATO expansion base in the country nor are comfortable with how she got elected; and similar scenarios are playing out in places like Malaysia, Laos, Cambodia, etc.. It would seem like the bullying tactics of the US military and political system have now worked against their national interests; perhaps that is why there is substantial Russia bashing continuing in political circles – to manipulate people's emotions and play on fear.

What exactly are National Interests?

Greed and control of resources have led to many Western countries interference with other countries elections and governing systems, which invariably means, due to globalisation, all humans live in turbulent times. The propaganda given by governments and mainstream media have turned people against people from other cultures and religions, leaving the indigenous population with false knowledge as to how the trouble started, who are the terrorists, and with little real intelligence of how to solve the problem. It is true, the UK is a small collection of islands compared to the larger countries and continents of the world, but, nevertheless is one of the most advanced countries competing on the world stage. Consequently, continuing working with other countries to tackle terrorism, climate change, and poverty should be a priority for the government.

Currently, the UK is a member of the UN Security Council, NATO, the G#, G##, the commonwealth, and a (outside) member of the EU. Although some of these groups have lost their way or produce propaganda to justify their existence and some have been responsible for causing problems they are sold as attempting to solve; it is important that the UK government play a continuing role to ensure that these groups re-evaluate their roles and incur a mechanism of accountability, i.e. abolishment of diplomatic immunity for UN if they cause issues in foreign countries (e.g. cholera outbreak in Haiti). It should be the UK governments responsibility to stand-up to business ventures and concentrate on human factor issues to remove, as much as reasonably practicable, home interventions in foreign affairs. Even if it means control of resources are relinquished to lands it is gathered from to stop a reoccurrence of the growth of terrorist cells from uncivilised actions from Western governments to control important resources.

It maybe once the government is transparent in the actions abroad and informs the people about the costs of relinquishing some control or not selling arms to countries that the government has oil or gas trade deals with, the people will permit the government to continue interference in foreign governments or supplying arms to dictators (who will use them to oppress not only their own people but people in foreign countries) (F.Y.I. Saudi Arabia now has twice as many UK made warplanes than the Royal Air Force). But, the people also need to recognise the after effects of such a decision e.g. revenge attacks (terrorism), mass migration, starvation and poverty; and have the choice of whether or not they wish the government to continue in their efforts. It will be questions of do acts of terrorism caused by a coalition of Western powers (sold as protecting our national interests) to people in foreign lands really benefit the majority in the West.

Who can say that ISIL, ISIS or DIESH (which ever) are the terrorists who have just appeared due to religious reasons (as mainstream media want you to believe); if foreign countries were robbing and pillaging our country at the expense of everyone who lives there and killed members of your family with air strikes to remove your government heads of state, would you want to seek bloody revenge? Reality in these matters is more confusing once research in the area is completed. The UK government has to work to keep the UK out of international conflicts even if it means sacrificing good deals. Human rights, freedom from oppression and true real democracy (where the people are in charge) needs to be at the heart of the UK foreign policy.

The armed forces have always been used to defend our country, but recently and ever since WW2, what exactly have the armed forces been doing? Invading foreign lands is not defending our country, antagonising a world super power (Russia) is not defending our country, seeking control of foreign oil deposits or oil and gas pipelines in foreign lands is not defending our country; all this is achieving is moving a stage closer to WW3. It is true, the UK government should ensure the armed forces are ready and capable to defend the country and only used in foreign countries when there is a justifiable humanitarian crisis where diplomatic means have failed, but, also that they are not used for economic reasons nor for illegal forced regime change. That is the problem with Western civilisation, the countries armed forces are used as a strangle-hold to other countries governments for economic gains (just ask Iraq, Libya, Syria, etc., leaders who 'overnight' went from being a friends of the West to evil, cruel dictators who need to be removed due to talk of trading oil in a different currency than dollars and not keeping prices down), but governments never inform society of the real reason even though most people probably realise it anyway (it is called being hard-faced). Hence, the government must place diplomacy and moral and ethical considerations at the foremost in any global challenge – at the end of the day oil and gas will become a scarce commodity soon and people will have to live without it; prolonging the agony by further wars and oppression works opposite to achieving peace in the world.

The trouble caused by successive government in Middle-Eastern countries has been a disaster for all countries in the world and instigated the rise of terrorism like never before; hence, Western governments cannot just pack-up tools and walk away. It is clear, once control of resources has been handed back to the governing country, there needs to be a diplomatic solution to bring peace to the various regimes, cells and groups who are consistently fighting for power using weapons supplied by Western governments. Politicians are delusional to think that enforcing our current system of democracy to these countries will work as most of these countries have a strong religious culture and most have a dictator at the helm (whether or not they have been voted in, due to the fear of not voting the correct way). Nor can continued activity in foreign countries, both covert (via NGOs – re: George Soros (who utilises the method of using poor education to play on people's emotion to pressurise political change; he is also responsible for most of the trouble and protesting caused globally because of the election of Trump in the US) and others who use propaganda and money to make the people or armed forces attempt a regime change through political unrest, protests, riots, etc.) and military (via invasion, or through providing arms to rebel fighters directly or indirectly through third parties— both are a disaster look at ISIS and Yemen). Instead, the UK needs to step back in terms of military force and look at a way to help bring peace and stability in these areas through diplomacy by being mediators.

Countries in conflict, however, sometimes refuse to talk through their problems and compromise on each other's demands (Israel and Palestine are a typical example). At some point a decision has to be taken to pull away from further discussions and hope the people of that country will band together and make all sides come to the table. Otherwise, Western politicians just need to wait for the outcome of the civil war whilst concurrently working with other countries towards preventing any further armaments entering the fold – once all sides cannot fire any guns etc. perhaps they will be keener to talk. This will be hard technique to action because of our moral and ethical standing not to mention bad for the economy due to lack of arm sales, but, history has taught people one thing interfering like the West have for many years in resource rich countries does more to cause trouble, chaos and loss of life both in said country and at home than if Western politicians just left it alone; although most people in society continue to ignore it.

Apart from working to prevent any supply of weapons in the country, this technique of watching and waiting for the outcome of internal conflict is nothing new, especially in countries with little resources in their land, just look at some African states. (Many people have little knowledge of what is really going on in the world if they do not hear it on the mainstream media outlets, people need to remember news is edited and generally does not present the whole truth in its true context, more time is needed to research the area to obtain a true reflection of reality.) The problem becomes how to obtain partnerships with other countries to stop the flow of weapons and thus remove profiteering from civil wars. Well, sanctions do not work - it only hurts the poorest people in the country; perhaps if the governments of said countries refused to cooperate then a method (or threat) of releasing information to the people of that country about the activities of their own government might be enough to achieve cooperation or at the very least restrict activity along with some other incentives to cooperate in a truly globalised world.

Europe as an entity is suffering a huge problem. Not only are some countries held in financial intimidation (Greece, Spain, etc.), but the influx of migrants means salaries will not rise any time soon and so people will have no choice but to work for less in real terms as taxation rises to cope with benefit additions. A perfect storm for those with little money, nonetheless, a perfect profit making mechanism for those rich business owners (people wonder why they have instigated an open door policy, it has very little to do with human rights and ethics, it is good business sense).

The immediate problem is the threat of terrorism and radical ideology which is both within and external to our borders. The unilateral decision to continue to bomb leaders of groups such as, Al Qaeda, ISIS, Al-Shabaab, etc., is inflicting many innocent civilian deaths, which increases the risk of further people seeking revenge; this tactic needs to change. There should be a long-term multi-national political strategy starting with banning the selling of arms abroad including removal of any private sector companies involved in defence contracts. This will be a major blow to the defence industry with losses of many jobs, but, nonetheless defence means defence and all arms developed to defend this country needs to remain in this country and be controlled within the borders under tight regulations. It is in UK's interests to ensure people remain healthy, thus, the nuclear trident project which invariably means poisoning of the environment if it is ever used, needs to be cancelled and the budget transferred over to provide much needed services to the public.

The problem of religion and how it relates to radicalisation and terrorism cannot be ignored, nor can the possibility of the damage one in ten thousand people can cause given the right knowledge and tools. Therefore, strong border controls have to be in place with stringent security checks before anyone should be allowed to enter the country from a number of foreign lands that are experiencing turmoil. Then emanates the question of how to deal with problems internal to the country's borders? The country's interests have to concentrate on the indigenous people first that is people whose close ancestors lived, fought and paid for this country. It is clear, successive governments have failed these people and led to a life of low paid careers and resentment, while certain policies created by government has led to advantages being open more to migrant families. The diversity policy for religion, culture and sex is a total disaster and only adds to discrimination and the continued welcoming of people who protest and promote a different governing system (i.e. Sharia Law) adds to the problem.

A fair society is what everyone should want, therefore, no favouritism should be shown and those groups who continue to protest are clearly not happy and should be provided with assistance to migrate to other countries. There should be zero-tolerance for any religious hate crime and any person of foreign descendent committing crimes should be deported after being convicted and/or completing any jail time. The message needs to be sent out to people in any foreign country: you are welcome to apply to live here, but do not expect any special treatment and be sure you respect native culture (do not try and change it), if you commit any major offence you shall be deported and charged for the privilege.

Many government officials continue to explain that people coming to the country to look for work will benefit the economy and society; and they contribute to the public purse. Whilst this statement is true, it is not the whole truth. The problem is native people are missing out on decent paid careers, university places, and suffer due to poorer strained services. The reality is the immigration policy is not working in the manner sold. A simple stipulation to the policy to read, "As long as there is near-zero 'real' unemployment, the benefit bill is below £1million/year and population numbers are below x million then....., otherwise, the country is full and cannot accept anybody at this time"- would ensure opportunities are available for current residences first and would go a long way to making the country more sustainable for the future.

Speaking of the growing number of migrant populations in the country, it has become clear that one culture or religion in particular has issues with respecting native culture, whether or not people like to talk about it. Some Muslims, actually all followers with strong faith to be honest, who genuinely believe the writings of the biblical texts are the revelations of God, show themselves as a superior race and all others are infidels and should be slaughtered. Western society really should show more of a concern in this issue. (The Muslims today are a victim of circumstances of what happened in Middle East regions 1000s of years ago when an advanced Mesopotamia society (most innovative, progressive and knowledgeable in the world) was forced to turn their backs on mathematics and science and worship a mythological God – the region was, and still is, split based on false religious beliefs.)

Governments are very uncomfortable to talk about the Muslim faith and the issues related to having strong faith in Islam (regarding the interpretations of the biblical texts) or debate that strong followers of the faith (extremists / terrorists) are carrying out rules and instructions set forth in the biblical texts of the Quran. Government would rather spread the message that these people are perverting the rules / laws of Islam (it is a political ideology intermingled with a God) or following misinterpretations of the biblical texts due to mental health issues (there are many interpretation of the Quran).

The problem is people, especially in political and religious circles, do not want to discuss the fact that there is something inherently wrong with the Muslim religion that causes people, rightly or wrongly (depending of your viewpoint), to conduct acts of terror in the name of Mohammed or Allah. The problem is exasperated due to differences in political ideology within the same religion causing different sects of the Muslim religion to be constantly fighting with each other.

The problem for the West is there are two methods to bring about religious rule in society, one is by invasion (for quick change), and the other is by peaceful coexistence over time (Da'wa – spread of religious message over time to invite people into the religious political ideology). Who is to say the recent migrant movement in Western countries and the high birth-rates among Islamic families is not setting forth the Da'wa of Western society. After all, there is now a Muslim mayor of London and Sharia courts throughout USA, UK and Europe working alongside government systems. So are these people at some point going to be offered a power share in government just like the IRA was to bring peace to the region? I think it is something for all people of all faiths should be concerned about besides being resisted at all costs.

Western society is based on certain premises with the main one being an elitist class system, which is far different from Muslim beliefs of a faith in the justice of a higher power and a rule of law based on interpretations of religious texts. Hence, both types of society are always going to be drastically different and at fighting odd with each other. So much so that in present times certain sects of the Muslim religion are fighting for their rights to live the Islamic way free from Western interference and exploitation. The Western governments are classifying such actions as terrorism as they have done for decades whenever any trouble arises from corporate exploitation in the Middle East. (I wonder what the world would be like if we in the West lived in lands rich in resources and the people in the Middle East went through the industrial revolution first?)

Concentrating on national interests, do people honestly think that once the Muslim community outnumbers all other faiths or cultures in the country and they exercise their rightful democratic right to stand for and vote in elections leading to a majority in government, which is a very real possibility in the near future (10-20years): can people in society be sure that they will not action sharia law. (FYI - there is already thought to be around 100 Sharia Law Courts operating throughout the UK outside our own legal system). What this would mean is white women would not get the support or defence they require even if they were raped, it would be the victim herself who would be put on trial and punished (look at what happens in other Muslim controlled countries to come to this realisation); any other religions will be outlawed and persecuted (look again at Middle East countries); can people really be confident that this type of Islamisation would not happen here. Whether people like it or not with the excessive birth rates in the Muslim community, due to religious reasons, this possibility is looking more like reality.

Lots of do-gooders, protesters, and government officials, though not wanting to anger the Muslim community will dismiss this as fear tactics and paranoia – words of a racist etc. (and other labels to demonise). However, research into other Muslim countries shows this to be an unfailing trait of that faith. The constant political rhetoric of 'facts that are too inconvenient to mention because it will divide communities and thus should not be spoken', has to be consigned to the past and people need to face reality no matter how this reality goes against our current moral and ethical standing (as it does mine, but logic has to be the deciding factor).

As a result, the separation of religion and state should be obligatory and legislation written to ensure that no religious texts or religious interference with government action is permitted. To coincide with this, all Sharia Law courts should to be abolished and all Sharia Law councils terminated; as a country, people must not tolerate any 'peaceful' but unauthorised and unelected additions to legal systems working outside the nation's best interests. Again, people who strongly object should be offered relocation to a Sharia Law country with their passport removed and re-entry back to the country denied (I firmly believe the government allows these courts to continue as they are afraid of what will happen if they crack down on them, but government needs to).

Those Muslims who have taken ownership of various streets in communities and self-proclaimed them a sharia Law area thus coerce people of different cultures to stay away or respect Muslim rules, should be nicely asked to cease all activity once and then deported to a Muslim country thereafter. This is a strong message both nationally and internationally: the country is a very tolerant society and you are welcome, but, there is a line and people who cross it shall be removed from the country permanently.

Exclusion of faith schools in the country should also be deeply looked into. There is a contention that this is indoctrination of children into a false reality and a religion that they are too young to understand or make judgement upon. All schools in all communities should teach all religions, but placed in the context of mythological based beliefs; this should be compulsory for all children of all cultures – there should be no room for opting out. It is the governments job, moreover parent's responsibility, to ensure children are well-educated in actual knowledge based on facts (as we currently know) not beliefs to prevent any indoctrination into various factions.

Thus, when the child is old enough (early-mid teens) to make an informed decision based on knowledge gathered from all religious based stories, they can decide what path to take in a spiritual context with help and support offered if this contradicts their own family's belief structure. The likelihood is this system might deter people from other countries migrating here, hence, assist in reducing the population numbers of the country. It would seem as though people who a very religious have real issues when it comes to giving knowledge about broad range of religious texts for instance: knowledge that Christianity and Islam was created from two step brothers, one in wedlock one born from an affair; it is unsurprising that both the original texts are very similar. At least Cristian's had the good sense to rewrite it to market a more forgiving God whereas the Quran was amended and is now vastly more about the word of Mohammed (a paedophile, child trafficker, war lord, etc. (I mean no offence, these are facts!)) than Allah - 'Mohammed-ism if you will'), i.e. both created by humans not Gods.

Religion has been and is used to control the minds of primitive people; knowledge is needed to give children the answers to questions such as how many religions (myths) have there been and why did humans stop worshiping these other 'Gods (invisible make-believe entities)'? It is in everyone's interest to ensure all children are given truths and facts to help counteract being indoctrinated into a religion due to being born into a religious culture (i.e. accident of birth). The UK has always been a multi-cultural, multi-faith country and it is government's responsibility to ensure FREEDOM of choice for people when it comes to religion or any other path people wish to take, but, also to ensure people are not forced into religion or cultural norms especially if it promotes oppression.

With the vote on Brexit, it has become clear that the continuing shift of power from West to East has to be stifled, and government has to put policies in place to attract more useful knowledge based businesses into the UK and remove the affliction with being subservient to trade deals with international partners. That is to say the government should maintain a strong relationship with Asia, but, plan to be more sustainable and offer international partners more of an opportunity than service sector business. This means concentrating on more home grown talent for the future and a redirection of priorities from services to knowledge sectors; this should also assist in transferring from a low wage service economy to an international Hub with the knowledge and skills for solving real world problems. The UK is small, but, has a lot to offer as a Hub for international trade in many areas. These real world problems should include the promotion of freedoms around the world, including in the Middle East, real gender equality (not bitterness and selfishness), eradication of starvation and poverty by promoting education and family planning techniques linked to resource availability (i.e. carrying capacity).

UK businesses are going to take a short term 'hit' due to the single market and product prices will purposely increase with the excuse of Brexit (even those that are fully produced and manufactured in the UK, strangely?), but, some businesses will boom due to exports from the UK being cheaper. The government continually argue that the single market encourages the inflow of capital and investment from European countries and helps government focus on job and growth creation. This notwithstanding, look what has happened since joining the EU –

population boom; services reduced and of poorer quality; wealth gap drastically increasing; low wages in real terms; and despite all the efforts to price people off the road air pollution continues to increase, etc. In a way, the government is correct, the single market has created substantial gains for the rich and wealthy, but not much benefit for the majority of people living in the UK – and it is a similar situation for the US and all individual European countries on the whole; it has been one massive pyramid scheme! So, it is a good decision to come out of the EU and it is important to keep all the good rules (and possibly legislation that benefit the majority) from Brussels and eliminate those that are a waste of money and place a burden on each and every working person or family.

Nevertheless, there is a matter of the common agricultural policy that needs to be addressed. Due to the number of people currently living in the UK, it is important not to lose trade-deals with certain EU countries and that may mean, for the short term, having a strong relationship with Brussels is key to ensure supply = demand in this area. The likelihood is in the next decade or so the EU parliament will implode on itself due to election results in individual countries swaying to the anti-EU parties, thus, the UK government should work towards trade deals with individual countries themselves and attempt to bypass EU red-tape and much as practicable to reduce waste and inefficiency. Concurrently, the government has to increase and emphasise the importance of agricultural education in schools and ensure that suitable land is fully protected from being built upon. There needs to be at least a two-fold increase in the agricultural market in the UK to cope with demand and this increase will take some time to come to fruition thus government needs to offer incentives for younger people to become more actively involved in this industry.

Note: In all likelihood, nothing will change with respect to the single market or immigration rules from Europe. Thus, officially the UK will not be part of the EU, but, unofficially most of what deals and treaties the UK has with Europe will remain. Only items which the government can use to reduce people's freedoms or ability to fight government or business wrong doings will change for the disadvantage of the majority of people.

Relationship to UN and NATO

The UK has a proud history of providing support and assistance for those fleeing prosecution and wars by upholding international obligations, including working with the United Nations and NATO to support vulnerable refugees. These agencies are marketed as a vital necessity for post-war order and prosperity that are needed to ensure global peace – Hmm?! Unfortunately, the global agencies of the UN and NATO have over the years lost their way and become these overly complicated bureaucratic institutions that all society is told defeated fascism but instead created global organisations whose ambition is to continue to extend their wartime commitments, work in the interests of multinational defence contractors, promote Western culture and way of life; and whom are fully immune to legal prosecution. It could be described as an alternative face of dictatorship but is in fact a way to promote a different type of fascism.

The UN Security Council is one of the most powerful 'bureaucratic' bodies in the world with the authority to issue legally binding resolutions that can be backed up with peacekeepers, force of arms or sanctions; and works closely with its partner NATO. Consequently, it is sometimes difficult to determine any separation between these two organisations. Every invasion, every natural disaster, all recent wars, these two agencies work side by side in foreign lands, whether they are welcomed or not, whether they have been authorised by the government of the land or not, in the name of helping people. Whilst at the same time extending their own bases and working in Western governments and corporatocracy best interests. The Western media consistently markets these agencies as peace keepers (gooder than good) and the UN is sold as a means to maintain the peace globally and a forum for countries leaders to resolve their differences whilst keeping other non-permanent members in control.

Moreover, the UN routinely permits its main five permanent members of the council (US, UK, France, China, Russia) to pursue their own interests globally and use military might to seek control of foreign resources completely unchecked. For example, using the powers of veto; and without any real accountability for their actions as there are no consequences for violating a security council resolution (something the US, UK, and European countries have done consistently for the past two decades). It is clear, members of the UN address the strategic interests and political motives of the richest member states and this now extends to Saudi Arabia, even though they have a worse human right record than the terrorist group ISIS. Additionally, the UN who prides itself on being a democratic organisation only represents the interests of the governments of member states and not the individuals in those countries. The UN it seems has become a place where political 'poor quality' leaders can play the game of 'one upmanship' without any consideration to majority in any of those countries the UN is supposed to represent.

No other organisation in the West would and could have survived all the allegation of mismanagement, scandals, and corruption that has plagued the UN for decades. I mean what sort of organisation only helps starving people by forcing a country to agree to the terms and conditions of the oil-for-food programme; or data that shows a rapid rise in child prostitution and rape upon the arrival of peacekeeping troops; or the cholera outbreak in Haiti; and the list continues. As a result, the UN has long since been irrelevant in maintaining the peace or working in the best interests of people. Thus, have become an expensive waste of time, money and energy whilst concurrently only appears to be efficient in acquiring wealth for the corporatocracy – is this a mere emergent behaviour of the UN or is it because that is what the UN is primarily for, i.e. the further generation of wealth, no matter the cost, for the privileged few in society.

NATO has been in trouble since the end of the cold war, it has lacked a threat to fight and as such a purpose for existing so much so that routinely it has to create a 'big bad' to fight; and now it has come full circle and refocused back onto Russia. The truth is NATO is still functioning on its founding principles – build up conventional forces as to be able to fight, and win, a conventional war against the Soviet Union (Russia), while at the same time possessing a second-strike tactical and strategic nuclear capability. At some point promotional messages to people in countries that are members of the union became less about the nuclear threat and more about acquiring sufficient forces in size and strength to inflict military defeat upon an aggressor to defend people of the country. The clever marketing meant that one of the stipulations of joining the UN is to agree for NATO expansion into the country. NATO has become so entrenched with membership of the UN that the number of bases and the percentage GDP each member state has to contribute continues to increase without any justification. The only one who benefits is the defence industries whom happen to be the main lobbyists in most countries, especially the US, UK, France and Germany. However, cracks in the argument for the existence for NATO keep appearing and questions arise about the bureaucratic alliance that has been in existence for more than three decades with the nuclear umbrella argument becoming less consistent and more or less irrelevant.

To add to the crumbling mess of NATO is the reality that the ending of the cold war meant the signing of the Lisbon treaty in which one of the terms and conditions was that NATO would not extend its bases and thus reach further into Europe and closer to the Russian border. However, it became clear NATO and the UN broke the agreement a number of times and coerced governments of various countries to permit NATO base expansion, even though the people in said countries where not involved and/or disagreed with it. The Ukraine crisis of 2014 saw Russia make a decision to counteract the aggressive actions of NATO and ceased control of Crimea (without any deaths, or bombing and with the approval of people in Crimea – a complete breath of fresh air compared to recent Western involvements in the Middle East) and ensured some instability within Ukraine to prevent another country from being puppets of Western led governments to further their own interests. NATO's enlargement remains a talking point with Russian leaders, yet something that has been ignored by Western media; to add to the problem China is also deeply concerned about NATO expansion near its borders. However, the punt by Putin to prevent a strategic location been overrun with NATO forces appears to have backfired with more NATO involvement in all surrounding countries since the cold war. This notwithstanding, there appears to be a standoff between the three main superpowers of the world when it concerns NATO involvement in some of the most recent troubles in multiple countries worldwide.

The question is should all people in all countries be concerned about the lack of accountability and the further expansion of a global military force that causes so much devastation worldwide and appears to be surrounding and showing aggression to the two other world superpowers (Russia and China) whilst consistently interfering with countries in the Middle East and Africa. The last time someone decided it was a good idea to expand their bases across foreign lands with and without permission, two world wars occurred in which millions of innocent people, those not responsible for decisions being made, suffered the worst while those who conveyed orders largely came away in good health (not Hitler of-course).

There is even a secondary concern - the US is the prime member of NATO and the country that injects most GDP into funding the organisation even though most of the NATO bases are within the European Union. This could just be because of the genius of defence contractor lobbying the US government or could it be a destabilised Europe (one that has years of infighting (migrant crisis included), wars, and financial hardships) work towards the US national interests in the region? It must be clear to everyone that the American philosophy and dream is to be the one and only world power (even in films the US is the only country in the world that saves everyone consistently and the only one who leads whilst the world follows). In order to do this, it has to make all other countries subservient to their will and give themselves a prime opportunity to shape a world order and civilisation that is congruent with US interests and US ideals. A prime example of this happening in a short period of time in is countries such as Japan, Saudi Arabia, Dubai, South Korea, Vietnam, etc. etc.; again when evidence is available for all to see, it is not a conspiracy.

The question for all European leaders is 'who exactly is using whom'; there is a reason why the US is key contributor to NATO, even though the country itself does not need NATO for defence purposes as the US budget for its own military far exceeds that of any other country. So what is the reason? Could it be NATO and the technology required to arm all the bases has a strong connection to US defence contractors. As a result, the US can coerce NATO members to become involved in conflicts that suit US interests or/and is it because of International Traffic in Arms Regulations (ITAR) restrictions give countries have no choice but to cooperate with the US for continued supports of military technology or could it be something else. Either way it would seem that the US military power has substantial influence over European military forces within NATO itself.

By far the biggest problem for NATO is the rising concern that the elected governments of Europe are so entrenched with US interests they are becoming nothing more than warmongers who are only concerned with resource grab and arms-control negotiation for the sake of profiteering from the deals and the promotion that Europe have superiority over bordering countries, whilst being puppets for the US. To counteract this concern, governments have for some time now engaged in misleading and miseducation of the public with publishing fake news and propaganda to spread fear and paranoia of a forth coming invasion into Europe from terrorists, Russia, etc. for justification of the continued expense of NATO funding. I mean how is invading countries and bombing their towns and cities killing thousands of innocent people and forcing leadership change, defending Europe? It clearly is not!

NATO has always been the strong arm of the UN, but, in some cases when countries ignore or completely bypass the UN, NATO has been used to force political ideology in foreign countries. What happens to the member countries involved in such acts – nothing! The UN is supposed to be about discussion, debate and then produce and authorise recommended actions to global issues, including when to use forces such as NATO worldwide. If the council is unable to make accountable countries that abuse their military might and use the name of NATO for nefarious means, then the council is all but pointless and has become a media front to give the illusion that the Security Council is ensuring global peace. Who would have thought that a council made up of 'poor quality' politicians would not be effective in ensuring global peace? This is again the problem; the UN is constructed of people whose job it is to 'talk a lot without saying much'; to ignore human rights abuses of its members for possible future trade deals for one or more of the permanent member states; to play politics with civilian lives mainly in areas of resource rich lands; etc.

The real predicament is European politicians are attempting to sell NATO and the UN as something they are not and more people as time goes by are questioning the roles these organisations play in global events. It is all too clear the UN is under the direct influence of the US government; unfortunately, over the last two decades the US government has become more nationalistic that is more concerned about its own interests and more willing to act unilaterally to pursue its interest abroad and call on its NATO partners to back up US military might. European governments themselves have a huge problem; more people are becoming impatient with their country becoming involved in wars abroad and less susceptible to the fake news in main stream media, i.e. promoting NATO as peacekeepers whilst being involved in many atrocities.

The idea of a fully functioning UN and a NATO defence (key word defence) force is one that should be carried forward to fruition, but the current manner in which they are governed will eventually make both organisation fall apart. These two organisations cannot be used as 'play things' for politicians to grandstand on the world stage or be used to further the corporatocracy interests. NATO membership should not be inclusive of purchasing technology from certain countries or be required to have a permanent NATO base within the member country. Nor should NATO be fully dependent upon the United States. People have all seen over the past two decades European leaders have been corrupted and political individuality has diminished along with the human considerations of possible conflict.

The US has become a global 'bully' and therefore membership of NATO should be revoked, but, should still remain an ally until the US becomes more global than nationalistic. The technology used within NATO should be completely clear of any ITAR restrictions and countries should be allowed to acquire from contractors within Europe. Moreover, there should be checks and balances in place that prevents NATO, which is a Western military and political organisation, from using its forces for regime change and for any profiteering for the corporatocracy.

As a result, NATO leadership should consist of political and industrial neutral experts with diplomats whose background consists of strong human right activists, environmentalists, political critics and those who have a high degree of critical thinking and analysis skills whose express purpose is to ensure the might of NATO is not used for nefarious means, furthermore, not for any countries national interests. In essence, no politician or anyone with military connection should form part of the leadership and the procedure used should ensure all sides of a situation are fully heard, including civilians on the frontline, with results from real evidence used as the basis for decisions. Only then should military or political debates/solutions be investigated using experts from respective fields.

Additionally, the number of NATO bases needs to be reduced to prevent provocation of those superpowers that are becoming increasingly concerned about military expansion on their surrounding borders. NATO should be used for defence and peacekeeping missions only, not as provocateurs to give false justification for further invasions to coerce a certain political philosophy onto countries. NATO needs to regain its self-respect, a feeling of control over its own destiny and that is in full concordance with human rights thus be fully protected from powerful (wealthy) people with less palatable aspirations. Moreover, the actions of NATO representatives should not be protected under diplomatic immunity; if they have caused suffering, the people responsible should and must be taken to account. These changes will send shockwaves through all aspects and areas of NATO as well as the UN, where most of this work in rebuilding NATO from the ground up needs to occur.

For the UN to be affective there must be accountability for each and every member country. If a member country pursues its own interest by using political or military coercion or force in foreign lands, it should risk possible isolation from the global market (if this ever happened the US, especially the UK, are in serious trouble, but perhaps this will be enough of a deterrent to prevent illegal wars and deaths of innocent people for corporate gains). As a result, any country who wishes to trade on the global market must sign up to the terms of condition of the UN and in that way be subject to the same rules and governance as all member states or risk isolation; and with oil reserves running out, isolation could send countries back to the middle ages. Therefore, it is in all people's best interests to ensure their own government behaves in a civilised manner.

Overall, the UN should be the council who watches the watchers (those whom ensures political ideology or corporate greed are not the deciding factors in interfering in foreign affairs). Carefully considered representatives of all countries are required to be chosen to fill the places within the UN. These are to be politically neutral, have no relationship with the corporatocracy and most of all not liable to be bought. Consequently, politicians, millionaires, business owners, academics, lawyers and accountants, need not apply. A complete overhaul of both organisations is needed for them to be effective and useful and it is up to all the people in all countries to ensure that enough pressure is placed upon politicians to rewrite the rules and procedures that govern both organisations.

Society needs to remember all people pay for these organisations and currently have no say in how they are operated but have to deal with the repercussions of their abuse (NATO military force) and lack of action (UN) with issues such as rises in taxation, threats of terrorism, the migrant crisis, spread of diseases, illegal wars, etc. Otherwise, what people are expressing is a small group of people have the right to express and force their ideology onto the majority of people in foreign lands using political and military might and the majority of people will sit back and accept any repercussions that those people (who have suffered at the hands of these organisations/governments) decide to take on Western people.

The UN and NATO should be forces for good and to genuinely defend the majority in member countries from invading forces; and to ensure that profiteering and grandstanding using military might are not an acceptable term of practice or governance, therefore, be subject to punishment with the potential use of NATO in defence to any hostile act; thus, encompassing these two negative aspects of current human society. Moreover, the system should be used to keep military superpowers from expressing their will onto others for their own nationalistic interests. People throughout all member countries need to work to change these organisations so they actually do 'what it says on the tin' and not continue to be another front to bamboozle the public into another false reality, whilst being used for the corporatocracy's best interests.

6

A BETTER LIFE FOR THE MAJORITY

Crime Prevention

The crime rate in Western countries has risen sharply since the end of WW2 with a large increase in prison population from 1994-present.   In the last few years (2013-2016) the prison population in the UK as hovered around the 85-86,000 with a large portion (37%) being reoffenders, (G. Allen & N Dempsey, "Prison Population Statistics", House of Commons Briefing Paper, No. SN/SG/04334, July, 2016).   The statistics show the greatest proportion of offenders in prison were there due to violent crimes, second greatest was for theft, third for drug offences and fourth for sexual offences.   The latest trend also shows that the number of adolescent females in prison for three of the four top crimes outnumbered their male counterparts.   The average age of prisoners making up the majority of the population is between the ages of 25-34 with the numbers reducing dramatically past the age of 40. The problem of prison population has been growing with some prisons over 150% of normal accommodation levels which has led to judges to consider this in their sentencing of offenders.

Throughout the criminal justice system there is a lack of human consideration as to why these people are here and how to help them rehabilitate seems to be a completely separate consideration that successive governments have failed to deal with. Instead, governments throughout Europe have followed the US system and privatised the prison system signifying that now the prisons are being operated to make profit.   In essence, the justice system is now set-up to make a profit for private contractors, but at the same time is very expensive for government to budget for and the human cost both to the offender and victim is placed behind 'business as usual' politics. Prisons should work to not only punish criminals (so they do not reoffend), but also to find out the real reasons why they offend besides rehabilitate or support the offender to assist with life outside prison – the system fails on both these accounts. To prevent crime, the UK government introduced ASBOS, which were a complete and total failure with young offenders seeing it as a badge of honour; and there is strong public opinion against suspended sentences for anything more than a 'mister meaner'. Again, fire-fighting the problem does not solve it and only ignites further resentment, anger and disillusionment in both the justice system and the government.

With the advent of new technology, e.g. online purchasing, payment cards (inc. wireless), and additional cultural crime (forced marriage, religious courts, etc.), there needs to be a more intelligent crime prevention method that not only tackles these new types of crimes but does not neglect the more traditional crimes such as, burglary, street violence, sex abuse, rape and domestic violence. Successive governments have talked about various agencies and people in society working together to deliver significant cuts in certain crimes and although in recent years the number of reported crimes have fell, the statistics have to be questioned in relation to the number of people who do not report the crimes to the police. There are issues regarding the victims view of the crime and/or of the offender, but, subjectively the main instigator for this non-reporting is the lack of response and faith of the police force.

This notwithstanding, reporting a crime can often be a stressful ordeal with the victim being left with the feeling of being interrogated by the people who they believe are there to support them in their time of need. The number of sexual assault victims being 'dragged' through a long legal process to no avail, the trust in (alleged) victims being questioned, the fear of not obtaining protection from the police if the offender seeks revenge and issues with crime involving people of different race, religion or culture have caused faith in the police to waver; not to mention far too many victims of child sex abuse are being let down by the services that should keep them safe (oh dear I have just mentioned it – oh well!).

Clearly, the current statistics presented to the public could wrongly show that the government strategy is working to reduce the impact of criminal behaviour nationwide and be used to promote political party ideology. The statistics, if they are to be believed, suggest there are six key drivers of crime:

Opportunity – This is when offenders choose targets that offer high rewards with little effort and risk such as: cold calling to obtain bank details, online hacking, taking advantage of the elderly or those who are not able to understand or physically defend themselves.

There are major issues here especially in cybercrime as the internet permits offenders to be based in other countries firmly outside the reach of national police. Also, one of the major failings regard the speed of technology refresh that government and law enforcement officials are slow to adapt to, and therefore opens vulnerabilities. The support for the elderly regarding safety and security arrangements in modern transaction have for the large part been ignored by the police and by loved ones leading to greater risk of being swindled out of assets.

Character – This concerns factors offenders are exposed to within their environment from an early age that might lead to a high probability to commit crimes. It also concentrates on those individuals who are previously known to the legal system; this information (i.e. number of reoffenders) can be used to expose weaknesses in any crime prevention strategy).

There is an unhealthy reasoning that people who willingly break or question societal norms give strong predictors of being a possible criminal offender. Questioning how things are in society is a predictor of critical thinking only and all people should be encouraged to continually question legislation or believe it is cruel and unjust, what is deemed normal in society or why people are willing to fall in line even when they are not happy.

This notwithstanding, there is a strong relationship between the development of criminal character traits and peoples' upbringing, e.g. being in company of delinquents, experiencing social depravation, abuse, or being in an environment of drink and drugs. Parents and teachers play and important role in identifying children at risk and identification of someone who has low self-control. The early years is the point where character traits are formed and is fundamental to encouraging the injection of positive character traits. However, strategies such as 'Prevent' in the UK, which is to tackle the problem of extremism (opposition to national government values (sold as British values)?), radicalisation (support for extremism?) and terrorism (use of violence in the pursuit of political aims in opposition of ruling government) *(more on these later)* places too much burden on teachers and other support workers besides operates by the promotion of paranoia among peers and demonization of children. This strategy simply must be repealed and a more intelligent one concentrating on prevention of indoctrination into ideologies (especially religion) and compulsory education revolving around religious (mythologies), political and cultural distinctions.

Child sexual abuse is a more complex crime to prevent and although an inconvenient truth, sex with children has been continuing since the dawn of civilisation and is very predominant in some cultures and religion(s) even today and sadly due to open borders these very same cultures have been introduced into Western civilisation i.e. child grooming gangs. As a society, including parents at large, have accepted the over sexualisation of young children and adolescent teens through mediums such as music videos, watching soap operas, and the use of mobile devices to send photos to others. Children who have been exposed to such material have grown up with an unhealthy account on how to behave and have shaped their own character and values as such. These children then grow up to be adults who are confused about the appropriate way to behave and take advantage of the next generation to satisfy their needs (this is an oversimplification of the issue but the point still stands).

People in society then hunt down any potential offender and punish them with jail (mass paranoia then ensues with innocent people labelled and reputations ruined, much like the witch hunts of the 15-18 century) without the understanding that this is the inevitable outcome of allowing explicit images, magazines, and videos (including what is now termed as attractive fashion, which very much sexualises young girls (mainly)) to be readily available to children and adults alike.

It is all well listening to politicians promise new child protection laws and prevention of child abuse programmes, but all are doomed to fail. The reality is all people need to protect children from sexually explicit material in all forms; parents need to know where their children are at all times and to prevent access to any form of medium that could teach the wrong lessons on how to behave and dress (or lack thereof). Government need to prevent any soap opera airing before 9pm or music video from including any sexual content, including raunchy dancing, dress or words that children are able to gain access too. In essence, society have to prevent the over sexualisation of children to avert anyone from sexually experimenting with children. Moreover, as with the footballer revelations on child sex abuse in 2016 reveals, young children now are debating with themselves about the pros and cons of allowing an adult to perform sexual acts on them based on very limited knowledge and life experience. If a child is making a decision like this, it denotes that they have been exposed to material for limited understanding; meaning they know it is wrong, but, will let it happen for potential future benefits. People have to understand where a child obtains this type of belief system and eradicate it at the source and media outlets are the prime target (soap opera stories are full of people using sex to get what they want, whether it be for promotion, a baby, to break up a relationship, or to hurt the person they had sex with – the comparison to real life events is unnerving at best).

It is not just children who are involved in these types of decisions for possible future career and financial benefits. Young adults also make a choice of how far they are willing to go.

Celebrity revelations in 2017, moreover stars of movie and cinema (re: Harvey Weinstein), reveal some have regretted decisions they made in the past to become rich and famous; including stripping for line-ups, allowing themselves to be seduced by people in power or partaking in sexual relationships with producers and film makers. The law has been used as a means for vengeful discourse / reprisal, justified or not, for regret of the choices these now famous and rich celebrities made in the past for their 'big break' in show business. There needs to be an intelligent debate about personal responsibility and the position of the law with taking action based on future regret of personal irresponsibility of the past.

People may have an unnerving feeling towards the people in position of power who have taken advantage of people willing to do whatever it takes to make it 'big', but, the 'victim' in cases such as these made a choice and some have made a very good living out of that choice that they now regret later in life. It is very unlikely they did not know what they were getting themselves involved in as people's reputation is generally known 'through the grape-vine'. I am sure if people had a time machine there are plenty of decisions people made in the past that they now regret and would like to change by travelling back in time, but, that is not possible. People need to understand the decisions they make that they were uncomfortable with might have personal consequences when they reflect on the past in the future when the brain matures. It should not be the responsibility of the law to attempt to bring some type of justice on previous bad life choices made; people need the strength to deal with any repercussion with their own life choices when they thought they knew what they were doing when they were younger.

How to deal with offenders is also complex, labelling them and demonising them will inherently mean that the individual, due to external forces, will never be allowed to rehabilitate; unless their identity is protected from the media. This would mean that police, victims and their families will need to be persuaded not to sell their story to journalists – but, who does this actually help? There is of course a medical treatment to add to a rehabilitation programme run in prisons that could help ensure the offender does not commit further sex crimes, but it means altering their natural chemical balances. It should affect their decision making but also inhibit their sexual impulses, and perhaps even for a temporary basis (until the offender reaches a certain age whereby they can control better their sexual tendencies), could be a solution in preventing any further issues. Although this will violate human right laws it is to the victim and potential victims that have to be considered above the individual who has violated the human rights of others. The victim's needs to be given a voice to the type of humane punishment and rehabilitation programme offered under court judgement even if it means a rewrite of national law on treatment of criminals or removal of the country from any international human right laws.

There is a real issue with de-indoctrinating people from different cultures about how to treat young women and adolescents. To the extent all people in society have to understand why, but, predominantly information is gathered from academics that place assumptions at the forefront to decision making, which sadly, is a continuous mistake to make in all circles - academics tend to lack real world experience and thus their conclusions lack real world rigour. The fact is offenders of this kind are driven by their own nature/character that has been moulded by their own life experiences including being indoctrinated into cultural and religious belief systems since birth. A term in jail is unlikely to rehabilitate these types of offenders. Consideration needs to be given on removal of any religious texts and abolishment of any religious worship for these types of criminals, and instead real cultural and scientific knowledge in the form of an up to date library system offered to <u>all</u> inmates to promote self-learning and possible de-programming of their current belief system.

Failure to actively gain real knowledge by using library facilities should be seen as a sign of a disinterest for rehabilitating and may affect potential release dates as prisons need to have a high degree of confidence that the individual will not reoffend. Removal of religious rights will be a difficult step to take for the offenders, the government and religious leaders at large, but, if the offenders behaviour is found to be part of cultural and religious ideology and given the fact that they themselves showed no compassion for their victim's human rights to their own body, then this type of programme should be commissioned. Also, if any gangs are found guilty of sex crimes, then they should not be allowed to interact with each other, and no member of the gang should be present in the same prison.

The main problem, although it could be seen as being generational in nature, is how to rehabilitate adult offenders once their character traits are formed. Fortunately, as people age their character traits formed before and during adolescence change as their chemical biology alters and the realisation of their own responsibility for family and friends 'hit' them. Also, it takes plenty of physical and mental effort to commit crimes and stamina falls as people age. This is not to say that people between the ages of ~16-40 should be abandoned, but a realistic rehabilitation success should be considered and perhaps placing offenders within this age group on a programme, with a tag, can be successful in controlling their possible criminal acts.

Effectiveness of the Justice System – The justice system should act as a deterrent to offenders. However, with jail population at saturation / breaking point; with judges making rulings that simply do not fit the crime, and with people reoffending; it is fundamental that there should be no weaknesses in this system. However, various statistics (freely available from government websites) can be used to show there are numerous incompetence(s) within this system that are not only letting down victims, but also failing to re-educate and rehabilitate past offenders.

The criminal justice system (CJS) is made up from the police, the courts, prisons and probation services. There needs to be a coherent and concurrent strategy between such organisations with partnerships from schools and parents in working to prevent crime and ensuring that offenders learn valuable life lessons that serve them and promote not reoffending. The CJS has always marketed itself on fairness and equality, unfortunately, the CJS is integrated with all other law systems which the rich and wealthy use to their own benefit and in some way spreads the message of bias towards people with money – the message is reinforced with the recent changes to legal aid in the UK.

Also, the lack of punishment available to the CJS for youth offenders is an issue, with children under a certain age unlikely to be punished for criminal behaviour, nor is there any real punishment for parents of said children to promote more affective parenting. Rehabilitation efforts are concentrated on easy to tackle causes such as treatment for drug addiction and anger management courses with limited success. There needs to be a more grown-up discussion on how and why individuals offend (obtain a background story of their particular life experiences) because every person will have a unique story and it is up to the CJS to ensure as much as practical that the causes are reduced dramatically to prevent future generations falling into similar criminal behaviour. Even if the cause leads back to irresponsible government decisions, these need to be discussed and resolved for the future. This type of process could also hold the key to helping offenders work through their criminal behaviour and be shown a better way to live.

Successive governments have implemented a wide-ranging program of justice reforms to focus on measures to make the CJS a more effective deterrent. Generating strong local partnerships to bring together police, medical staff and local authorities are used to amend routes and times of police patrols, to reposition CCTV cameras, and introduce strategic points of contact for the general public. Moreover, this type of partnership has been used to gather more data on criminal activity, i.e. money and time concentrated on data gathering and firefighting after a crime has been committed. Prisons and criminal records have been used as a deterrent for would be criminals, whilst on the surface this serves as a warning, young people do not understand the consequences of their name appearing on a database and the support services are seemingly powerless to assist children who are having difficulties integrating peacefully into society – it is this area which needs to be concentrated on.

In most cases, giving offenders a criminal and prison record has a detrimental effect on the rest of their lives, their earning potential and career prospects are, generally, permanently damaged. No matter how difficult it is to realise the situation does not help rehabilitation, but, it also does not help the victims of crime nor the perception from law abiding people. Nevertheless, if rehabilitation of people is the goal of the CJS, it is something that has to be considered as sometimes the CJS, with all of its resources, get it wrong and as such condemn further an innocent party or someone who had a moment of 'madness'. If rehabilitation is to be taken seriously, then society should not punish most offenders for the rest of their lives and therefore criminal records should not be a permanent mark on the offender to give them an opportunity to make something of their life once rehabilitated.

Prisons do need to be setup with rehabilitation as their top priority. All games consoles, TV privileges, fitness rooms need to be removed and replaced with libraries and workshops concentrating on increasing the knowledge and (hopefully) intelligence of inmates. Prisons need to be a place where people do not want to be because of the lack of entertainment facilities, but, also double as a place to help inmates obtain new skills and thought processes that may help them once their term is up and hopefully change their mind-sets.

Those criminals who are guilty of severe crimes should be treated accordingly: for sexual crimes: a treatment to alter chemistry (e.g. testosterone) levels to reduce overwhelming natural instincts along with psychotherapy to cope with urges; for violent crime: a deeper understanding as to the reasons why, a life history, has to be sought under complete privacy to understand the inmates thought patterns. Moreover, the human rights of the victim of severe crimes are put above and beyond the offenders, i.e. the European human rights act should be considered for the victim, but, used as background knowledge when dealing with the offenders of such crimes.

Greed – This factor has been passed down from the elites in society where everyone believes they have the right to live the lifestyle of the rich and famous; using some of the strategies that have a remarkable similarity with legal business trades and deals, only not approved by the government. As a result, criminals have become all too aware that organised crime pays.

Profit, profit, profit, this is the driving force for all living in modern Western civilisation, only sometimes certain people take it too far. Profit is most certainly the driving force of most types of high-volume theft. All items that are worth something in this capitalist society are the targets, which mean that our consumerist society has made targets of each and every single one of us. Greed can be linked to every single crime that occurs all over the world from the killing of one individual to the murder of thousands in politically motivated wars. All people learn lessons from those in leadership, but, some take the lessons to literately. Taking advantage or the exploitation of people is the number one reason why this type of crime is one of the most popular. The reality is that whilst there is abject inequality in the world, certain groups of people will always try to take advantage of certain situations to make profit. People have learned from banks and traders that greed is good; it is also the reason why more people are miserable and depressed because competition for the best positions in work never stops; and better positions mean more money to buy more expensive 'stuff'.

Drugs – All governments in all countries are attempting to pursue a lost cause in the 'war against drugs' (why has everything the government does got be a war against something?), it costs the UK ~10.7 billion every year and the US ~$50 billion. There isn't a clear strategy to tackle to problem, and believe ruling governments are disingenuous in stopping the drug trade at the source. This money could be diverted to services to help people remain healthy, however, for some yet unjustified reason it is not. The issue is how to stop people taking drug, and how to prevent people who are addicted from partaking in crime to feed their addiction.

Organised crime groups supply the market of drugs and the psychoactive effects of drug use pose challenges for social cohesion. An estimated £6 billion is attributed to the social and economic cost of drug-related crime in the UK; acquisition offences (including fraud) are committed by drug users. However, drugs do not necessarily cause people to start committing crime, but, it has been found that drug use can accelerate and extend criminal careers creating a group of prolific offenders. Treatment evidence suggests that recovery from drug use is more likely to be achieved through continued support and recovery capital investment, particularly around meaningful employment and housing. However, rewarding people for personal damage to themselves and others through drug use does not necessarily promote social cohesion. People who have not gone down the path of drug use misconstrued it as a 'reward for failure' and incurring some form of jealously and favouritism especially when additional support is being diverted away from people who need it but are not addicted to drugs. Support needs to be available to people who are serious about rejecting drug use, but not at the expense of others; individuals need to provide sufficient evidence and signs of mental effort before financial support is given.

Prevention is again the path money should be concentrated on through various education programmes; however, drugs are seen as a necessary social construct to fit in with various groups especially in teenage years – most politicians are guilty of taking drugs through college and university years and some still use i.e. the Keith Vaz effect. The problem is drugs are seen as cool, the same as cigarettes where in the 1950-60s, and social pressure to not be the outcast could cause individuals down a downward spiral – the doing something the authorities don't want you to do scenario. With certain drugs being classed as illegal it makes the subject taboo, which invariably makes it cool. A program of legalising drugs along with education programmes, starting at age 11, illustrating the negative effects of drug use on the body and mind; and association with drug crime groups should be commissioned. The positive effects of social drug use should be avoided and instead concentrate on how drugs alter the chemical makeup inducing bad decision making involving real life stories on drug induced sex, pregnancy, suicide, violent crime, homelessness, alienation from family and friends, damage to one's own body and mind, etc. This type of education programme needs to part of the fixed curriculum.

Enforcement of drugs has had a negligible effect in solving drug related crime, although punishing someone who is 'not in their right mind' is something that needs to be questioned. Clearly, whether someone is under the influence of drugs or is desperate for the next 'fix' the individual's decision making ability has been compromised, thus, punishing someone for their actions when there is clear scientific evidence that they are 'acting not as themselves' is uncivilised. Support has to be given and ideas from treatment of psychiatric disorders can be used to help the individuals recover and offer them a different path than jail to personally see the impacts of their actions on any possible victims. Enforcement of dealers can be affective at suppressing emerging drug markets of dependence-inducing drugs before they become well established. Working with international partners and border controls can reduce the supply of drugs and a combined support and education programme should show a reduction in demand. It is really a matter of the relationship between supply and demand - if there is little demand, there will be little supply; it is a matter of economics

Alcohol – Alcohol related crime involves street fights, unwanted sexual advances, morning after regrets that turn into possible rape accusations, damage to property, drink driving and a noise pest for others. These problems have been around ever since public houses opened and the modern working class came into existence. With all other activities being expensive, drink is a good relatively cheap way to enjoy a night out with friends. The only solution is to solve the questions: How to stop people from drinking excessively; and is there anything government can do to enable people to have a good time without relying on a chemical additive?

Although perfectly legal, around 50% of violent incidents are believed to be caused by an offender under the influence of alcohol and the proportion increases in the evening and at weekends and is common in public places. Alcohol misuse places incredible strain on support services, especially medical, and incurs a significant burden on society; latest estimates show that the cost of alcohol-related crime is £11 billion, which is offset by the ~£14 billion alcohol duty collected by the UK government, meaning that there is a surplus affect in budgetary concerns and this relationship is prevalent throughout the West. It is probably why there is no significant education programme targeting over consumption. There is a striking similarity between the negative effects of drugs and for alcohol, but, there is sufficient justification for collection of tax on drink than on hard core drugs, plus, pubs have and are a significant part of community life. Hence, people should be able to socialise, eat and enjoy entertainment without the fear of becoming a victim of crime by someone who has drunk excessively.

(A note about morning after regrets and rape accusations: because of the feminist movement and the coerced movement of the ideology into girl's minds from a young age, Western society is quickly becoming a place where a man should ask a woman to sign a legal waiver before they have intimate relations, especially if they have recently met, just in-case there are any issues afterwards, especially the morning after when regret might occur. It is a sad reality that men are no longer innocent in any accusations of sexual assault or rape; the paranoia and fear spread from central government and feminist groups are creating an atmosphere of disrespect for men and an environment where women can do anything without recourse. It is causing a lot of men to have their reputation tarnished, whereas women are treated as a victim even if they have been found to be deceitful. Men who are guilty of such crimes should be punished, but, the increase is false accusations reduce the likelihood of guilty judgements in future. It is quickly becoming a self-destructing cycle that works against the feminist agenda, which prescribes equality and respect to women (well as it describes in the abstract).

Strong community partnerships are required to ensure people are educated to know their own limits and town centre public establishments should restrict the sale of alcohol to people of correct age and mind set. It should not be the governments' direct responsibility to manage local effects of alcohol consumption. Individuals have to carry the burden of their own responsibility when it comes to drinking decisions and subsequent acts. Equally those selling alcohol need to consider societal impacts. Both selling establishments and individuals are responsible for any alcohol related crime; currently only the offender is punished, however, a system where the selling establishment(s) will also be held accountable needs to be actioned and a share of any criminal damage should be allocated between the two parties. Purchasing of alcohol at licenced establishments, including supermarkets, individuals should need proof of ID that is electronically connected to the purchase of alcohol. Using a simple computer database, the licenced establishment will have access to how much alcohol an individual has purchased within the day and the past week and so can make a valid decision on whether to sell the alcohol to the individual. Strong local partnerships offering support and education programmes will be the heart of the successful management of sales and the night time economy.

Another important factor is giving people a reason not to take excess drink or drugs, by reducing daily stressors and pressures and giving people affordable activities and entertainment that can bring fun into people's life. Giving people an opportunity to have an interesting yet challenging daily life is an important factor that consistently is ignored; with people being highly stressed and bored in daily life it festers major social issues that causes the use of drugs and excessive drinking. The manner in which the economy is managed and balanced has to change for any positive impact in prevention of social crime. The prevention methods summarized above will only allow for a marginal impact on the problem, bringing fairness and interest in people's life are the key to eliminating the vast majority of crime.

It should be clear to everyone that when there are more opportunities to offend, crime increases and it does so by taking advantage of weaknesses of individuals but also in the countries own legal system. Opportunities to make profit is and always will be the driving force of all adult crimes, including all the wars (those that are deemed to be religious wars always have a hint of profiteering at the foundation). Even some crimes caused by under 12's have profits at the forefront of their actions, with the other types of crimes committed from the age group being about status in a group.

To reduce the prospect of crime the only method is to decrease the likelihood of crime by making it harder for criminals to benefit from perpetrating the crime in the first place. There has been a strong argument for the installation of Closed Circuit Television (CCTV) cameras throughout the country and it is true the overall use of cameras has reduced crime but not in significant numbers and has been most effective in car parks. The impact to budgets has been significant with the cost of operating and monitoring the CCTV system costing ~£320 million a year in the UK; the control of how the data is being used by local councils is questionable and has unfortunately created a surveillance society at the expense of freedom and privacy (this type of surveillance has become endemic across Western countries).

To add to the issue of the general public being 'spied upon', especially in the UK, the new 'snoopers charter' (internet surveillance) has been approved (November 2016) meaning that every aspect of everyone's life is now being monitored. People are now living in a period of time where the book '1984' written by George Orwell has become a reality people are still not fully aware of the magnitude and possible consequences of or completely ignorant in. This is most definitely not the path society should be willing to accept to prevent crime and there is no evidence that any of this monitoring will prevent criminal activity. With CCTV, if someone wishes to commit a crime he/she will wear a hoody and cover their face rendering the cameras useless; and the authorities already have the technology to ban various websites, but choose not to and the only reason is to justify their existence and for job security.

It is so easy to say that "crime can be prevented by removing opportunity to commit it", but to do so the financial system, greed, competition, inequality, religion and others will have to be removed from everyday living with all people working in a combined effort to grow knowledge and intelligence. Short term this 'quote' is an impossible suggestion and can be dismissed as rhetoric and a pointless semantically null statement; as financial (economy) systems and population numbers inherently mean that people are scrambling for opportunities to make their life better.

If there is anything that celebrity culture has taught is that you do not have to be a genius to make lots of money, you just need the drive to take advantage of people and situations. Whether it be legally, politically or illegally that is what people all over the world are doing; even those who are born into status and wealth are 'playing the game' i.e. British royal family. It is hard to take an honest look at who we are and what we have turned into! However, it is also true that some people will never commit a crime, regardless of their situation; lots of experts have linked this to religion though there is no evidence to back up this claim but overwhelming evidence to show that severe crimes are linked to religious ideologies and differences between various sects of the same religion.

Cooperation with Authorities

The police force has seemingly evolved into an agency, moreover has similarities to a gang of 'thugs' in uniform that the majority try to avoid for a number of different reasons, which concentrates on filling out forms with the victim of crime rather than pursuing a human interaction and understanding of the level of offence and human impact that has been caused. The police force, which now has to concentrate on KPIs with instruction from government, does not prioritise the majority of 'nuisance' crimes that affect the majority of victims the most.

Whenever people come into contact with the police force, people wish to be treated with dignity and respect, and with their freedom intact; the police can see this as resisting and use the excuse of 'not cooperating' to escalate the situation(s). This type of scenario plays out whenever a government or debt collection agency wishes to enforce some type of control over people's actions. The reality is if people wish to communicate, debate and discuss the issue with them a hard line is taken and is usually driven by text on paper which they follow exactly without wavering, sometimes the first strategy used even in court is to demonise you in front of the judges and accuse the defence of not cooperating.

Unfortunately, what is being asked for is for people to be subservient to their every command whereas cooperation requires mutual discussion between parties, i.e. give and take. The authorities are not interested in cooperating with people; they are interested in enforcing their legal right given to them by a piece of paper to make people subservient; and with it fearful of any further actions if people resist their orders or physical restraints, i.e. the full pressure of the authorities is actioned to make individuals subservient. The authorities have the power, given to them by government legislation, to reduce or remove people's freedom and to confiscate privately owned property/assets. The truth is the authorities do not need to cooperate with people; they are only interested in fulfilling their job role; thus, reducing people's freedoms and giving the message that people have no choice. The sad thing is people who work for these types of authorities (e.g. police, council/state government, debt collection companies, etc.) know that there is not a level playing field and do not hesitate to use and express the power they have over people to spread the fear ensuring people 'fall inline' with what government wants them to do.

For some time now police have been given authorisation by government (not voted for by the people in the country) to indiscriminately stop people in the street and forcibly search their person for any drugs or weapons; there is a strong argument that the process disproportionately targets more ethnic people than whites (based on current statistics and does include issues relating to cultural differences) and has only increased under recent counter-terrorism legislation changes. To attempt to keep people safe, allowing the police stop and search powers to be used on people suspected to be involved in criminal activity should be seen as having a positive impact on crime prevention, however, present activity of the police does show an abuse of these powers. This notwithstanding, government have been all too keen on publishing statistics to justify this activity and continues to market legal, fair and proportionality in the police stop and search activities. Nevertheless, the policy does infringe on people's freedom and privacy giving individuals no choice but to comply with the police searching their person in a public space and thus contributes to the increased distrust in the police service.

In January 2010, the European court of Human Rights deemed that stop and searches under section 44 of the Terrorism Act were unlawful as police were not required to demonstrate reasonable grounds for suspicion and thus were in breach of Article 8 of the human rights act; however, stop and searches still continues in the UK. The manner in which the UK government is tackling the problem involves concentration on reducing the gap between disproportionally stop and searching black and Asian people compared to white and thus concentrated on the race equality in statistic reporting and not on whether the people were suspected of planning any criminal acts just prior to the stop and search activity. The larger argument is if people are going about their daily activity they should not be unjustifiably interfered with from the police service. Stopping someone and forcing subservience on them to undergo searching of themselves, their personal possessions or vehicle represents a deprivation of their liberty and an intrusion into their private lives without justification. To add to the problem, people who resist could be arrested and be searched anyway, so if targeted by the police with stop and search powers means people have no choice but to comply with having a stranger touch them and then continue to live with the thought that you had no power or rights to prevent or defend yourself from this personal intrusion.

This nicely leads onto discussions regarding strip searches. I think there is nothing more terrifying than the possibility of being forced to strip in front of strangers and having the possibility of someone placing their finger up the anus. However, the government along with supreme courts have authorised the police and some other law enforcement services to strip search the public even on minor offences and this includes children as young as 12. Let us think about this – during a strip search suspects are required to remove some or all of their clothing, can be <u>compelled</u> to bend over and spread their legs; but, this is not restricted to people that are arrested, they can be used where a person is detained as part of a stop and search procedure. Compelled is underlined for a good reason, within the legalised police procedure this word is 'asked', but the truth is there is not really a choice; people are made to do it through coercion or force. If people attempt to defend themselves from having their clothes removed or their anus searched, further legal action will occur and include assault on a police officer; so there is no choice.

The reality is strip searches are an unhuman and degrading experience that some people who have been subjected to never fully recover from and further increases the distrust in the police and the legal system; and what about the mental issues caused if the process is used on young people/adolescents. It is rather odd that if someone, a stranger not in uniform, stopped you and patted around your person then forced you to strip then bend over and subsequently put their fingers up your backside for a 'rummage around', all of these individual acts would be classed as a sexual assault, maybe worse. However, when if a stranger is placed in an official uniform does this become an acceptable legal process? In both stop and search and strip searches people in the country have accepted that authorities have overwhelming power of coercion and control over people and have allowed sexual assault to occur in the name of 'keeping the country safe', probably because most people firmly believe they will not become a victim of such actions as they are law abiding citizens. I would strongly advice people to research the real data on this area as most people who are stopped and experience the police treatment summarised above are innocent of any crime, so yes this could be you next.

There should be no confusion what the police and affiliates are in the country for, it is to keep people safe and not to restrict the freedoms of people or commit sexual assault on the general public. There needs to be strict control on stop and search powers and only used if backed up with sufficient intelligence that the person targeted has weapons about their person; control has to be maintained with authorisation given by multiple signatures from police and human rights leaders. Strip searches should only be undertaken with permission from the suspect, if the suspect has drugs placed within their person it might be better to use radiography technology to identify such foreign bodies not to have a stranger place their fingers up their anus.

Political Intervention

Ultimately, there needs to be legislation to prevent police authorities from purposely sexually assaulting or humiliating a person; freedom above all else needs to be maintained within the institute whose prime purpose is to protect freedoms of people. This should go without being said, but current systems in place are more and more removing any resemblance of privacy, freedom, choice and self-determination. People need to be aware that governments are becoming less concerned about people's right to privacy and freedom, besides trust in the authorities are quite rightly diminishing and with good reason. This trend needs to be reversed and human freedom of choice placed at the forefront of governing the country and the police are in the frontline when dealing with keeping the country safe besides they should be more concerned about preserving the freedom of people not giving people no choice but to be subservient - this does not produce strong community bonds between people and the authorities and only aids in separation and anger towards the state.

Reducing privacy of people in society is a reduction in freedom (or moreover the illusion of freedom, it is a privilege in reality to choose what we do rather than a freedom; only the wealthy has the ability to do what they want when they want to do it, the majority of people have to trade freedom for working life). Unfortunately, there is a theory that this is the main reason why people commit crime, i.e. they do not want to give up their freedom and get up early and spend all day doing what they do not want to do for very little, whilst the owner(s) and shareholders are the only ones who really benefits; and then give most of what they take home to other businesses who gain substantial profits for the privilege of keeping them warm, dry, in clothes and actually having some fun and entertainment in life. Sound familiar? And majority of people do this and accept this as a way of life from when they leave school till they retire.

Successive politicians, when justifying invasions of other countries or expenditure for the 'war on terrorism', use the quote 'we need to do this to protect our way of life from groups that are working to destroy it' to mean that our way of life is worth preserving. Clearly, there is something very wrong with 'our way of life', if our way of life is 'good' then why are people willing to risk arrest for committing a crime; when if the setup of our society benefits all people, all individuals should be more than happy to live within societies accepted constructs.

Naturally, the excuse given by authorities is that people are lazy and are looking to make profits the easy way, others argue over mental health issues, others say some people are living in poverty and steal out of a sense of need'; others direct the problem to badly educated people feeling hopelessness about finding work; others steal or harm people because of jealousy or envy; others say some people steal for pure thrills or status among peers. Although some of the most heinous 'profiteering' crimes are perpetrated by people that are already 'well off / wealthy', the continued drive for greed and power seems to be worth the risk, especially if their well-connected in political circles.

Violent crimes may result from pent-up anger causing an individual to eventually let out frustration all at once. Children, if exposed to violence throughout their childhood, may grow-up with subconscious thought that compel them into angry reactions; causing the possibility of crimes following a family of different generations. Other violent crimes are planned out for personal gain or vengeance, even in the business arena. The truth is violent crimes are on the increase, but fewer violent criminals are being caught. Do-gooders in society blame this on video games without any evidence to back-up these claims; could this be a distraction as to the real cause of the problem – the method in which society and the economy is managed!

To distract and disorient people in society regarding crime, government in the UK has seen it upon themselves to employ a high level police monitor in local areas – the police and crime commissioners. These people do not need any experience in policing and are predominantly members of a political party. So, what use if any are these people to improving policing in the local area? The answer is no use at all! These positions are voted for by people in the local community which again has nothing to do with the individual's ability to do the job. The job itself is another government created 'non-job' that only benefits a political party's role in the community so policing in the community further becomes another political strategy to use at election time. There are already high level police officials in positions that can reorganise and restructure policing in the local area; therefore, these commissioners are not needed and require abolishing so the money can be spent wisely to improve policing not provide a party member with yet another 'cushy' job.

The state of policing has reached a level were 'vigilante' groups with very limited resources are more successful in bringing offenders to justice, especially sexual predators, than the entire resources of the police force. This is an abhorrent assessment of the system the police have been forced to use by the government with concentrating on KPIs. There is clearly something rotten to the core about how the police and support services operate, because it has not gone unnoticed that the wealthy or celebrities are well protected and incur police presence before and after any possible threat. People only need to look at how police resources are used wisely to 'guard' WikiLeaks founder Julian Assange at a cost of £10 million (and counting) for 24hour guards at the Ecuadorian embassy; there clearly not protecting or defending anyone in the community and the decision for this is highly politically motivated as governments do not like whistle-blowers.

There has been substantial media attention on whistle-blowers and how governments are hunting them down (labelling their acts as treason) along with presenting to society that companies/military are intolerant to whistle-blowers and they do not hesitate to 'fire/dishonourably discharged' them from their positions in the company/military. The message is whistle-blowers are somehow in the wrong; but, if these people have the ethical and moral grounds/standpoints along with the conscious and the guts to let the people of the country know what is really going on in government and private sectors. They actually should be looked upon as heroes who are letting people know the devious or illegal activities of leaders who should be brought to account. The depressing issue here is that I am confident many people are not surprised that politicians and mass media market these people as enemies of the state because of the poor quality of people society have in governments and belief that corruption is rife. The politicians do not want the real truth to be released to the majority in the country, they do not want people to know how untrustworthy the government is or what war crimes or mass murder they have authorised, private companies do not want people to know about their questionable waste disposal acts that poison the land and water supply (fracking included), etc.

Whistle-blowers are vilified throughout the media for one main reason – to make people fearful of actually blowing the whistle on various ethical and moral misconducts of their employers, government and armed forces. But, whistle-blowers are people who should be promoted in society, the true heroes of the people for the people; not what society currently has which is: celebrity worshiping. All countries should be rewarding whistle-blowers, not hunting them down and attempting to stop true transparency; they are trying to force accountability to various government and corporatocracy officials for wrong doings.

Unfortunately, the plight of whistle-blowers is falling, for the majority, on deaf ears; it would seem the majority of people are not that interested in knowing the details of actions that have been/are covered up. It is amazing the amount of information available on sites such as, WikiLeaks, which would make even the most hardened person question how and why have governments authorised such acts knowing the human devastation it would cause. The reality is these actions are based on a business model for profit. For instance, Mr. Boris Johnson who made available £23 million to a group known as 'The White Helmets'; they are marketed in the West as a group which saves people in the aftermath of bombings in the Middle East – but on other news networks the same group is seen working with terror groups such as Al-Shabaab, Al-Qaeda, and even ISIS, yet the UK government is funding them probably to buy more weapons from our defence contractors (or be it through third party intervention). Whistle-blowers should indeed be protected and promoted throughout society if only to keep an eye on those who keeps an eye on us. There should be no man-hunts for whistle-blowers, instead the country should become a nation that embraces whilst-blowers and protects them from prosecution from other nations.

The UK government has authorised spending more on surveillance and detaining an uncharged political refugee than on investigating the issues surrounding the 2nd Iraq war, which killed hundreds and thousands of innocent people; even though in the

Assange case Swedish legal aids have been invited to the embassy and offered interviews through video conferencing. The Western allied governments and other coalition partners declared a war and an invasion of Iraq, which was/is illegal and no one has been made accountable; indeed, most senators and MPs responsible are still in government to some degree today. What happened is equivalent to heads of criminal gangs ordering the assassination of someone and others nearby and walking away 'scot free' unrestricted to go about their daily business. The people responsible for the Iraq war have made millions since the invasion (most notably ex-PM Mr Tony Blair), caused the rise in rebels and so called 'terrorists' groups; and arms dealers (or PC speak - defence contractors) salivating with the ability to sell weapons into various regions in the Middle East.

Government has to be taken to account, for too long government has been allowed to make decisions without providing to the public any evidence with the excuse of national security. It has to be made illegal and unlawful for any government to authorise any military action or arms sales without the real facts made available to the public and for the public to have their say on the decision. Any politician or affiliate who is implicit in withholding evidence to ensure a bill passes should be dismissed and their financial account examined for any potential conflict of interest.

People in the community need to become more involved in keeping their community safe; for too long the threats of legal action has made people fearful of not only defending themselves but others too. The legal system needs to be re-evaluated and people have to be given the confidence and backing of authorities to take action to defend themselves or others without the fear of prosecution. The law has to take a stance of 'it is not your fault you found yourself in this situation, and it is not your fault that the offender got hurt or worse, you were merely defending yourself or others and providing a service to the community'. Nowhere else is the natural world where if life defended themselves the victims would get punished. But, the law has been stretched, manipulated and distorted to a degree that criminals now have the power within the legal system to get their victim a criminal record. This has to stop! If an individual makes a choice to attack, steal off someone, or worse and the victim defends themselves which leads to the offender becoming injured or worse, then the victim, who never asked for this situation, has to be protected from prosecution and not be treated as though they are guilty of something. Whereas, the offender(s) should be charged for any medical treatment needed and be fined or punished to a degree that they will feel it for a certain amount of time.

This will of course reduce the dependency of lawyers and solicitors in the legal system, and hopefully reduce the scourge of them benefiting for others misery, which will only benefit society and make more efficient the judgment and punishment of offenders. Whilst, giving the people in the community the confidence to protect themselves if needed without the fear of prosecution. Unfortunately, in the short term this system has to extend to those offenders who are under a certain age - victims must have the right to defend themselves and their property against any assailant no matter how old they are.

It is crystal clear that the police and justice system are not independent of government and this is a major problem which needs to be resolved as no individual or group of people should be able to manipulate an organisation employed to maintain the peace and protect the public for their own or others benefit. Nor to should pieces of paper be enough to dissolve responsibility for decisions made by heads of government that bring atrocities to all human life for political and corporate gains both at home and internationally. There should be no possibility of wealthiest in society or those with strong connections to people who control the flow of money in the economy being exempt from the same type of justice given to the majority of people living in the country. Unfortunately, as history consistently reminds people, law and justice does discriminate and is used to control the majority with the people in power who amend the laws being immune to it; unless individuals in political parties 'fall out of favour'. Confidence in the police and justice system that they will bring all criminals and offenders to justice even in the government, arms dealers and multi-national corporations has to be improved and the only way to do this is to separate government from the police force in every day operating tasks.

Is extremism really a problem?

Over recent years there has been a shift in threats to the public. In the past these threats came from standard and routine criminals and associated gangs, but now the rise of extremism has become the major threat. The government has made the link between extremism and terrorism and has continued to produce propaganda based on the threats and consequently passed various bills to tackle both. However, the link between extremism and terrorism is weak at best; you can be extremist and not be a threat to anyone's life. Definitions of extremism vary from the belief in and support for ideas that are very far from what most people consider correct or reasonable; or people who advocate or resorts to measures beyond the norm, especially in politics; or someone having the beliefs that most people think are unreasonable and unacceptable. But, Western governments have drawn a hard line about extremism and changed the definition to: activities or ideology that is considered to be far outside the acceptable mainstream attitudes of the ruling government that are a threat to the status quo and peace in society, i.e. Donald Trump was (when he was running for office in the states) or is (now that he has claimed office and depending on which way the wind is blowing in the UK and EU governments) an extremist, or at least the propaganda presented by the established elite has released that message. This has caused so many protests in many states – protest based on the message given through mainstream media outlets that plays on people's emotions and not on facts. The governments fight against extremism has got to the stage that they have now placed media outlets such as RT (Russia television news network) in the same government documents as ISIS meaning that they see both as the same type of threat to the ruling elites.

This is going to be a surprise to many, but extremist views should be welcomed, especially ones that are critical about government decisions. For too long people have been far too quiet whilst ruling governments go about their business both nationally and internationally, which have caused resentment, poverty (including economic slavery i.e. Greece), radicalisation and the threats of terrorism. Notice how this explanation of real threats to people has nothing to do with extremism, but due to the business and conscious acumen of the people in government and associated partners (big corporate businesses and banks – the oligarchs). Extremist views are needed to be available for people to read, watch and listen, but above all Western governments, no all governments and all people throughout the world, need to listen to views of people who offer a different narrative than that being pushed by the ruling elites. It is my experience that governments provide little evidence for questionable decisions i.e. WMDs in Iraq, hacking, supply of weapons; whereas people with alternative viewpoints, 'the extremists', generally provide a more viable alternative to the decisions being made and offer more evidence than the government to back-up their explanations.

Under the threats of extremism certain bills have been passed to allow government agencies to 'spy' on people, especially over the internet. This is a clear violation of privacy and what people do over the internet in their own private homes is their business only. However, the GCHQ (government communication headquarters) and other equivalent 'spy' agencies prime job should be reallocated to the removal of child pornography images and videos from the internet with addresses of people who have looked at these images passed to local authorities for them to deal with. The 'spy' agencies should not issue warnings to people who are researching conspiracy theories around various areas, if people do unearth facts about certain areas that have been covered up by previous governments or by the intelligence agencies then people involved have to be made accountable.

Through the global action over the past two decades, trust in government is low and governments throughout the Western world know it, thus, the fight against extremism has become the fight for information dominance i.e. to ensure the correct message (based on the ruling established elite's narrative) is being sold to the people. This is why the fight against extremism has become such an issue. The establishment has to regain the power to control minds of people to prevent issues such as Brexit and Trumpism and the only way to this is to control as much as possible the information people have access to – it does sound somewhat like the thought police in George Orwell's book '1984'.

People should not just accept the omnipotence of any ruling government for the period of time they are in office and government should not be allowed to control information in a way to sell a message/propaganda to the public. Democracies are about the people being in control, not the government. For too long the country has been managed for the benefit of the few at the expense of the many and there is one particular message given by government and mainstream media which for me outlines the evidence of this. Benefit cheats –people who refuse to work are taking advantage of the benefits system and this is why the government has no money to put into various schemes and is the excuse for raising of taxes; this is true but also an outright lie. There are people who take advantage of the benefit system (cost of est. £166.98billion per year in the UK - sounds a lot), but the reality and actual fact is this amount pales to insignificance to the amount of money the rich/wealthy and corporate businesses are taking from the government purse every year and it does not include the fraudulent activity of banks and its effect on the public purse. This is not the message the government wants to expose to the masses and therefore is classed as an extremist view and is hidden from mainstream outlets.

The message presented through main stream media outlets is clear: - fight amongst yourselves. However, in reality something is missing at the end of this statement: - whilst we and our partners run away with all the money/wealth. This is the unfortunate and sad reality. Why do you think over the many decades when every political party promises to reduce the gap between rich and poor – the gap continues to increase? In the defence of government part of their job is to protect the wealth and prosperity of the country and it is unfortunate that the majority of the people in the country do not have any real wealth, so this contributes to the problem as they will protect the people who have the wealth, for many different reasons.

In an attempt to remove propaganda and 'fake news', information needs to be freely available, as a result any government sponsored media channel needs to be 'set free' to compete with others and therefore television licence laws have to be revoked. Coinciding with this, news channels need to be made to publish alternative viewpoints on real news stories especially the more serious ones i.e. war. There needs to be a method of issuing fines for broadcasters for sensationalising news reports to prevent the spread of fear and paranoia within communities.

Many political parties market zero-tolerance approach to hate crime, however, it is clear 'hate crime' needs to be redefined. The problem is hate crime is subjective and can be used for the benefit of others. People's viewpoints and beliefs are not hate crimes and the reality is some people will never understand or integrate with people from different cultures or religions or identity, it is something all people in society have to get used to. Just because people become offended by someone's views does not make it a hate crime; the nanny approach used to amend legislation in these cases have used the delusion of hate crime as the basis for debate (and this includes online posts being construed as hate speech). All people need to be 'grown-up' about life and accept that some people just are not going to like you or the decisions you have made or make and certain people will be hostile towards you due to indifference. These are similar problems that everyone faces and have to be dealt with in the same way with communities, moreover schools and parents, concentrating on hardening children's minds to make them more mature and grown up enough to accept and/or be strong enough to dismiss other people's views without it affecting personal views on one's self.

To add to the problem of hate crime there is the culture and religious government being promoted by mainly Muslim communities that have led to various religious sects in countries within the Middle East to be constantly at war besides promoting martyrdom and caliphates to force change. People from this type of background and culture are now living in the US, UK and Europe – who thought this was a good idea? Radical extremism, moreover some Islamic religious groups, have to have a privileged place when it comes to prevention of any hostility. People have seen throughout Western civilisation a rise in religious groups chanting for sharia law and calling for Muslims to take over the governments, which have caused considerable unrest in local areas; and in Europe the rise of anti-Semitism causing the same type of problem. It is clear that profound revolutionary methods of dealing with the problem are needed. Clearly, people who have the audacity to publically call for revolution against the current countries law and culture, which is what it is, cannot be left to spread the message of aversion against people from a culture or religion that has been set in the country for a long period of time.

Although by protesting, these types of people have not broken any law, they are clearly not happy with the countries culture and they clearly have a problem with native people; hence, government needs to help these people move to a more favourable country that follows their own belief system. So let society do them and native people of Western countries a favour and offer them a free trip to one of the homes of Islam so they can live in peace (sorry constant civil war) with people of the same mind set, whilst simultaneously compelling government and the armed forces to pull out of any political, corporate or otherwise interests in these regions and let people solve their differences by themselves. The public, in the West, have enough problems to deal with without being 'dragged' into a religious revolution of hatred against people not of the Muslim faith. In essence, the message needs to be sent is 'you will not promote religious laws or radicalisation in our culture, if you do so you will be helped to be moved to a country more in-line with your belief system'.

This notwithstanding, the West should be open to people from different faiths and backgrounds who do not spread the message of a religious takeover or think they can create areas of the country where the law is governed by a religious ideology that overrules the country's own law. The hard line has to be drawn which says 'anyone who partakes in these types of activities will be immediately deported to an area of the world matching their ideology, citizenship removed and re-entry to the country denied' - and this rule needs to be valid for anyone of any faith or ideology spreading the word of 'hate'.

Population Governance with Immigration Controls

The Zoological Society of London generated the living planet assessment (which is produced every two years) that states global wildlife populations have fallen by 58% since 1970 and if the trend continues two-thirds among vertebrates could be wiped out by 2020. The data suggests that animals living in lakes, rivers and wetlands are being affected the most; with human activity causing pollution and climate change, habitat loss and wildlife trade contributing to this decline (with the way water is used, the fragmentation of freshwater systems through dam building, etc.). The indication is that other species are also in trouble because of poaching and overfishing.

Briefly think about the impact of Westernised civilisation. As the population grows the amount of forest areas and grass lands reduces to make way for the urban jungle which reduces the amount of land available for agriculture and wildlife (farmlands replaced by villages, towns and cities; rivers, lakes and oceans polluted with toxic waste and plastics). Land and nature is being mismanaged on a global scale to satisfy human population numbers that is having a negative effect of both other species of life but coupled with the levels of consumption of humans has led to degradation in human health and wellbeing; and especially the environment.

Overpopulation is a controversial subject that people like to ignore and bury their heads into the sand rather than debate as it brings up tough issues about ethics, religion and governments control of family size. Currently, humans see ourselves as masters of the universe and delude ourselves that the planet will provide for all our needs no matter how many people there are. But, there is the biggest elephant in the room and it has something to do with the term 'carrying capacity'. This term concerns the number of people, animals, and crops that a region can support without environmental degradation. For example, consider Ethiopia and similar regions that have been helped by major charities for decades. The population numbers in certain poor dense regions have increased, but so too has the suffering and the low mortality rates of young children – the land cannot provide enough food and the climate is not providing enough water to feed all and so disease and starvation spreads causing more suffering. Whilst concurrently, the people are having more children, mainly due to religious reasons. It is a losing battle as without population control, these people are and will need continual assistance from external sources to live a life of misery and suffering. Whereas, common sense and intelligence reveals a reduction in population will enable the land to recover and the water supply to be ample to feed and quench the thirst of the people.

What in fact people in the West are doing is making life easy for a few whilst increasing the suffering on the majority by ignoring the carrying capacity of the land and environment all whilst following religious doctrines. All the hundreds of millions of pounds spent in these regions have not improved the quality of life; it has just increased the suffering with the increase in population. Carrying capacity is a variable attribute that depends on how much resource each human need to survive, how fast food can grow on the land (including freshwater) and how the natural systems in the region can handle the waste – sustainability is about finding the equilibrium between population, consumption and waste assimilation.

Population growth is one of the biggest problems facing the world, as an example Indonesia's population has doubled within 40 years from 119.2 million in 1971 to 237.6 million in 2010. It is estimated that in another 40 years the population in this region alone will exceed 450 million, resulting in increased usage of natural resources and with it an increase in pollution levels. Population numbers should be an issue that all people should be concerned about.

Unfortunately, humans also invented religion (yes folks, it is all make believe, from sun gods to Zeus to Xemu to the tooth fairy; all from the mind of humans) and religion teaches people that God will provide; meaning that people can continue to procreate and God will provide enough food, shelter, air, and water. However, in the real world science and reality inform that this path will inevitably lead to extinction with forever dwindling resources. Therefore, with no proof of Gods existence it is human intelligence that has to take the lead in population number governance and the effects of real life circumstances on children's wellbeing.

But, some religious people, usually from the densest populated regions on earth, are not concerned with science or knowledge as their belief in God overrules any intelligent or common sense reasoning, thus, God will provide every creature with the necessary resources in which to live. Unfortunately, it is not just these regions which are of concern with globalisation and migration, cultures are mixing (not integrating) and having the same ideology of conceiving many children, which is contributing to mass population growths in Westernised countries including US, Europe, and the UK. The fundamental cause of wildlife population reduction, increased pollution, strain on public services and civil unrest is because of the mass increase in human population causing multifaceted environmental, infrastructure and social problems.

Climate change and decreasing biodiversity has received quite a bit of attention in the media of late, but is still not a priority for the governments except in regions of the world on low lying coastal areas (i.e. Bangladesh). Instead, local environmental problems, which are not widely reported on in main stream media require attention, including shortages of fresh clean water, arable land and water, air and soil pollution, and flash flooding, etc.; these stressors have been building up over time and are now increasing in severity as population and economies are rapidly expanding to account for births and migrants.

Additional problems regarding economic stagnation leading to poverty and an increase in birth rates (poverty and an increase in population numbers go hand-in-hand) necessitates industries, housing, schools, health clinics and infrastructure to be built to accommodate and maintain the standard of living. With population numbers increasing faster than ever before in Western countries, such as the UK, many areas struggle to meet the additional demand as evident from high unemployment rates (innovative accounting aside), overcrowded schools and health facilities, and decaying infrastructure (e.g. roads, utilities, public transport, etc.). The ability of government to provide jobs for the people has never been under the pressures it has now; the economy is struggling to provide reasonably paid jobs for the rapidly growing number of people seeking to enter the labour force; and vigorous competition for limited number of jobs leads to low wages, which contribute to poverty. The presence of these stressors frustrates and angers the population and contributes to socio-economic tensions, high crime rates and political unrest. It does not matter which country you live in at this moment in time, all these issues are being felt by everyone everywhere (well not the wealthy in the West and not Japan with their strict immigration policies), and it is a sign of the irresponsibility of humans to control population numbers.

The issue here is that people (humans) are sensible and intelligent when it comes to culling other species of life to protect local environments or other life in the region, but totally ignorant (blinding ourselves), probably due to religion and ego, to our own numbers. People need to be mature enough to understand that nature has a balance and humans consistently fight against this balance and are arrogant with it. It has to be clear to everyone that no population can grow indefinitely, it would cause immense competition among the population for resources, ultimately lead to shortage of resources then human suffering and death. (Competition among humans leads to devastation of areas through increase in wars and haven't people had enough of pointless political wars based on religious, ideological and ethnic differences throughout the centuries.) Nature relies of the 'circle of life' principles: an increase in one species causes an increase in predators and vice-versa, but with the ingenuity of humans (development of technology) only microscopic predators are a real threat. Consequently, the increase in population density will also increase the risk of disease.

The real factor which enabled human population growth have been innovation in science and technology over the last two centuries that has assisted in overcoming most threats of bacteria, viruses and natural disasters. With concentration being put into scientific advancements will this help control the population numbers or further place additional stressors on resources and the environment? Intertwined in this argument is the belief that human population numbers will eventually top out and cease growing, but, current trends show that despite all the natural disasters and wars numbers are exponentially increasing and every attempt to control numbers has failed. So the decision to be made is: can people voluntarily control their own family numbers or will the population be eventually controlled via loss of life through wars, environmental disasters (caused by humans), diseases or malnutrition?

There are recommendations to voluntarily control human numbers and was first put forward by Robert Engleman in his book 'State of the World 2012: Moving Toward Sustainable Prosperity"; that has been amended as follows:

- Provide universal, fast acting and free easy to use contraception for both sexes (preferably in pill form to make it easy to take).
- Reform education to concentrate on family and relationship education – concentration needs to be about the financial cost, responsibility, and ensuring both parties truly 'get on' and know one another including other issues in giving birth: the loss of financial and personal freedom, issues with affordable housing, the effects on carrying capacity, the effects on the child if parents separate and for the men detailed discussions about Child Support. Additional discussions need to be had on the lack of financial support the government will provide in future.
- End all policies of rewarding parents financially based on the number of children they have – government needs to promote the reduction in population numbers by restricting benefits and making this a hard line decision despite any ethical or religious arguments; parents should ensure they are financially secure before conception.
- The environmental cost of adding to the population need to be made clear to all including the social cost of schools, health care, public transport, housing etc. to reinforce that the decision to have children is purely a rational decision

based on feelings rather than financial and housing benefits.

- The social services have to consider the well-being of children when the parent(s) have issues with alcohol, drugs, violence, laziness or ideologies. Children need to be in the care of adults who puts the knowledge growth of the child(ren) first. Indoctrination of children in a religion at an age before they are capable of critical thinking (age of reason) and into false realities should be of great concern. These children should be considered and discussed as a high priority to be removed from parental care and placed with approved carers.
- Coaching programmes should be debated and then commissioned for potential parents along with parental IQ tests to ensure suitability in fulfilling responsibilities of being a parent. This is a controversial measure that will target possible indoctrination and those lazy parents who have children for financial or selfish reasons. Those who are deemed unsuitable to be parents will be advised not to conceive until their mind-set has evolved and support will be offered; those who do conceive whilst being judged unsuitable to be parents should not receive financial support and will be subject to regular visits by support services with a higher possibility that the child or children will be removed from their care.

Although these strategies may on the surface look drastic and it may be argued that one or more targets certain cultures. No rational argument can and will be made against the logic of these strategies to ensure that new generations are born for the right reasons into a loving family with parents who care; and that the numbers of children should be controlled based on the financial and maternal instincts of both parents. These strategies can be used to successfully control population numbers in individual countries, but what about population numbers worldwide as without international cooperation in controlling numbers resources will continue to deplete and wars increase. Thus, individual countries working in splendid isolation to control population numbers will have limited success in achieving what should be a worldwide objective.

The foreign aid budget is defended by politicians as helping people in other countries out of poverty and starvation. However, foreign aid has without question assisted in the raid growth of population in what Western leaders describe as underdeveloped countries, subsequently, multiplying the problems and suffering and adding a new dimension to the question of foreign aid ethics. The Western leaders are deluding themselves on the success of giving financial support to be able to lift other nations out of hopelessness, poverty and suffering when the people continue to increase the pressure on resources with rapidly expanding population numbers (it is the same scenario with giving to charities who help in these regions). Unfortunately, the growing population numbers in these areas along with the lowered mortality rates contributes to the immigration crisis that Western countries are now feeling the pressure to cope with besides the strain of health services, infrastructure and education facilities, etc. So far no academic or think tank have devised a different method of helping people in underdeveloped countries other than providing foreign aid (and with it construction, technology, and education programmes) and higher population numbers has been ignored up until recently.

Intelligence has to take centre stage when thinking of helping people in underdeveloped and poorly educated countries as the current method is increasing the problem at an exponential rate. Sadly, there is no magic solution to the problem and any change to people's habit have to occur within a long time frame as public attitudes are likely to determine success or failure of efforts to reduce birth rates. Thus, foreign aid should be directed not to improving living standards in an area but to measures directed at human nature and the human need to understand the real world. This presents a drastic shift in how resources are allocated and how education programmes are delivered, which will cause substantial criticism from those who are looking for an immediate solution without considering long term outcomes. What needs to be prevented is people in these countries becoming their own worst enemy and abusing the help given by the obliviousness of their situation.

Education programmes should concentrate on working towards changing mind-sets from a community driven by religious connotations and human sexual needs to giving the people knowledge with respect to carrying capacity and climate change. It is futile to concentrate on STEM subjects if the mortality rate is low and birth rate high as the problem of resource availability and living standards means that the problem expands from their area onto others (re: immigration crisis); and common sense and intelligence state that solving a problem in a small region is easier than the same problem in large numbers of areas. Indeed, religion and culture are the biggest problems when it concerns controlling population numbers and why there is no silver bullet, nor does firing one (as the West have been doing for decades) solve the problems but rather makes them worse. To coincide with the education programme, a strategy of de-indoctrination of the community is needed to work towards giving knowledge of various mythologies regarding religion, moreover, concentrating on the contradictions of their own religion and how science has overtaken religion in human's quest for facts and the workings of the real world.

Despite people in the West ignoring the natural male human need to reproduce and therefore have a drive to fulfil their sexual need; this ignorance cannot be helpful for people in underdeveloped countries that have a culture driven by the women being subservient to the male needs and wants. Therefore, there needs to be alternative method to satisfy the human sexual needs in regions where carrying capacity and mortality rates are low. This is where technology based on sexual pleasure can be used to coincide with other strategies to reduce birth rates. This may not sit well with politicians or those feminists who seem to think that nature can be controlled and all men are primitive, but, nature should be respected and human ingenuity and adaptability have developed a manner to satisfy these needs without the need for a sexual partner. This is probably one of the most important, yet missed, realities when intervening in these areas and why the problem(s) are intensifying to an extent that all countries in the West are struggling to cope with mass increases in population.

To coincide with the introduction of sex technology to these areas, women rights have to be inclusive in the education strategies used in these regions; in fact society should offer all feminists a free trip to help the people gain equity between the sexes – it is areas such as these that feminists can do some good rather than just be a group of whinging women (and some feminine men) who have equality with advantages and privileges besides no intelligent argument backed up with facts thus have no cause in the West. In all seriousness the worth of women in these regions have to be promoted and males have to be educated to respect them and treat them as equals rather than someone that is at their 'beck and call'. Working with the education programme there needs to be political solution to arranged marriages and parents selling their own children to men. Currently, in many third world regions these types of exploitation are deemed culturally acceptable and many children have been born for the specific purpose of a financial exchange later in life. Unfortunately, the ruling government these regions should be given external pressure, via the 'carrot and stick' strategy, to change the law to prosecute anyone involved in these types of transactions. Charities and other groups in the West have to understand that, again, there is no silver bullet and it will take a number of generations before the culture is changed and this venture will cease, although it is unlikely to change in anyone current life time.

At the most extreme level where carrying capacity and mortality rates are extremely low there has to be a programme offered to people to prevent them from conceiving another baby. This should be offered to both sexes and before anyone is permitted to undertake the procedure the education programme should provide the people with enough knowledge for them to make a responsible decision based on basic scientific and environmental reasons. Furthermore, only the person involved can ask for the procedure to be done, i.e. no man should influence a woman to have a hysterectomy; a procedure needs to be actioned to ensure as much as possible that it is the individual's choice and not the choice of others.

Foreign aid should only be used to provide education programmes and the promotion of human rights in all regions where support is welcomed. It should not be spent on infrastructure development without ensuring that people in the region have the knowledge and common sense to control population numbers. There is however one exception. Any land that is healthy enough to grow agricultural crops should be vegetated and infrastructure developed to ensure enough water supplies to keep the land maintained allowing it to continue to produce food and to give people fresh clean water to drink. Investment in pipeline infrastructure, suitable farming equipment (based on people's ability to maintain the equipment) and plants are required to provide enough food for the population of people, but this does not mean that the population can grow or that current desalination numbers are sustainable with the increased food supply. There also needs to be a debate of whether regular water shipments from countries with excess rainfall to the area is a possibility and more financially equitable for the area.

Water is a far more valuable asset / commodity then oil ever was or will be to human existence, so if governments can transport oil over vast distances why not fresh clean water from those regions of the world that have substantial rainfall to regions of little or no (drought) water for sustainability of both wildlife and human civilisation. Perhaps new forms of capturing and storing water is needed, thus, governments can utilise universities to research water capture techniques that could also have the emergent property of preventing floods.

Humans are the most adaptable species on the planet thanks to technology; so why do people in society lack the will and drive to resolve environmental sustainability problems when the capacity and capability is already here? The simple answer is the majority lack the will and courage to care (out of sight out of mind) and the people with substantial money (the elites in society), as they are not affected by the outcome of flooding, drought, etc., have no benefits to be made by potential solutions, even if elements of the solution is the same as the one used for transporting 'profit making' oil around the world.

Waste is one of the factors that is ignored when foreign aid projects are commissioned. Waste is one of the prime causes of low mortality rates due to diseases, viruses and insect numbers. If waste can be recycled efficiently in these areas then technology should be installed to ensure this process occurs and the people educated to maintain them, if however, waste has to be buried then enough land or waste water is required away from densely populated areas for waste to naturally degrade with minimal impact to human health.

If funding is low, then managing waste should be given priority above all else; if waste is removed, human ailments caused by contamination will reduce. It may not prevent people suffering from starvation due to population numbers being incongruent with land available for providing food; but, if education is provided surrounding carrying capacity, people in the West need to have confidence that the people in these regions will eventually realise that this type of suffering can be prevented by controlling birth rates. It is not other people's responsibility to continue to support groups of people who choose to ignore the constraints of their environment or who refuse to believe that a mythical God will not provide even with all the evidence of death and suffering surrounding them.

Immigration

This type of ignorance (God will provide) is also prevalent in Western nations and so is birth rates of certain cultures who have made their home in the US, Europe and the UK. So much so that it has taken 30 years of the immigration policy and the irresponsibility of people in controlling population numbers to place pressure and strains on infrastructure and public services to the breaking point.

Here in the UK, the four regions that makeup the UK has been declared one of the most crowded regions in the world, and according to the ONS estimator the UK population numbers reached 71.4 million in figures released in 2017 (an increase of 1.16 million in two years), compared to ~<25million in Australia, which is ~50 times larger than the UK, besides having their own issues regarding population numbers and migration. The UK has some major issues regarding sustainability of population and resources with the numbers of people and the amount of land available to provide for ecological need and to absorb the waste products of consumption decreasing to nearly a tenth of that available in 1750.

For a country to maintain or increase the quality of life, everyone in the country needs to feel safe and government needs to ensure that there is strength in controlling the country's border, the communities, and security in the workplace. The UK has seen high levels of immigration in the last 30 years including low-skilled migration that has increased since the Brexit vote, which has given rise to increasing public anxiety about the impacts on salaries, public services, and longevity of the British way of life. Feeble attempts amounting to no attempt by any government has been aimed at stabilising or gradually reducing the current environmentally unsustainable population increases; instead, concentration is given to economic growth and profits at the expense of long term survivability and prosperity.

There is also great concern, especially in middle classes, that controlling borders will mean that the UK will become isolated from the rest of the world and this concern is only strengthened from the rhetoric heard by politicians in the EU. People continue to hear commentators, politicians and other 'economic experts' (using the term very loosely) on most mass media networks selling the message that the country needs immigrants. A thorough analysis of the situation using population data as a source reveals the realisation for the justification of migrants is due to population growth and because the education system is not adequate enough to produce well educated young adults with relevant skills, i.e. to fill the places that native people lack the skills necessary to fill or not willing to do due to poor working conditions and pay.

Allowing migrants from a culture who are naturally accustomed to having a high birth rate into the country causes the population of the country to grow without any control and thus government is forced to provide additional school places, additional health care services, additional transport links, etc. which all costs money and everyone pays the price (apart from those near the top of the pyramid). The point is massive growth in population numbers (keeping salaries low) means more jobs are required to be created, which has a negative impact on the quality of life of native people in the country, i.e. more tax, less disposable money.

In essence, government has forced native people not only to pay for migrants throughout the many years, but has also forced poorer services and poorer quality of life on them whilst allowing businesses to obtain higher profits from exploiting the worker availability pool. The sad realisation is the immigration policy has created a national system where it needs migrants to take care of (previous and current) migrants and have made native working class people worse off in all areas of life. It has little to do with racism or populism; it has a lot to do with worsening national services and poorer prospects for the future.

This notwithstanding, there are two main factors that are the cause of this: natural increase (more births than deaths) and net migration meaning that annual population has quadrupled since the 1970s. Some people have begun to 'wake-up' to the issue of human numbers albeit with regards to the number of migrants presently in the country and the strain on public services with increases in taxation because of it. With obvious conjecture, most population density is concentrated in Capital cities (i.e. London and the South-East in the UK), with people who have lived in these areas for many years moving out into the suburbs and the countryside to make way for others, but finding these areas too under growing population pressures. This situation has continued for so long that it has become clear that redistributing population provides no real long-term solution to environmental sustainability.

The integration project managed via successive governments is a complete failure with more segregated communities 'popping' up throughout the West with most communities lacking the will to integrate. Leading to various migrant cultures living in isolated communities where original inhabitants have vacated elsewhere not wanting to live next to people from different cultures or religions for various reasons. The issue is creating distrust between segregated communities and in some cases loss of native people i.e. east-end of London which is now described not as cockney but as something depicting a scene from a stereotypical Bagdad.

The media coverage concentrates on the story from the migrant's point of view, whereas the other point of view is always demonised as racism and hatred to people from other backgrounds. Like most stories from main stream media there is always a propaganda message being presented whereas the real reasons could be, for instance: some people do not want to live next to people who parade around a garden chanting and whipping themselves in the back; some people do not want to live next to someone who lives on spicy food because of the smell the food makes when cooking, some people do not want to live next to people who leave small carcasses out for birds because it attracts all sorts of pests; some people do not want to live near a large family which increases on a regular basis because of all the noise coming from the property at all hours of the day and night; some people find it unnerving to live next to someone speaking a foreign language consistently; some people find it difficult to understand why women have to wear veils or burkas all the time; some people do not want to live next to a property that has someone smoking outside it a lot of the time; etc., etc. etc. These reasons have nothing to do with racism, but, a lot to do with migrants not respecting native people's feelings and the native community or culture.

Integration will always fail if migrant families ignore native culture and carry on living the same way as they did in their own home country with complete ignorance of the people around them; this is where the distrust grows from. A programme of native cultural education should be taken before any visitor is allowed entry to the country and be expanded to those isolated communities currently in the country, in an attempt to strengthen social cohesion and integration to ensure migrants play their part in native society. Concurrently, cultural differences need to be educated in schools to help avoid any misconceptions between people from different backgrounds. People who live or apply for entry to come to the country need to speak a decent level of the native language and people who work in the public sector should be required to be fluent in the native language of the country.

The benefits system, moreover in the UK, has long since been blamed for the rise of immigrants coming to the country; this needs to be curtailed and benefits restricted to those who have contributed in society. Along with a grading system similar to Australia, those that come to the country should not be able to claim any sort of benefits for the first five years; this of course means that low skilled workers will be required to take an approved skills tests and be sponsored by a company or university before entry to the country is considered; those with qualifications will need a job offer before entry.

Benefits for migrant families currently in the country will need to be assessed and any child benefit being sent abroad stopped; in addition, any member of family living in the country should not automatically qualify other members of that family currently living abroad entry – there should be no special entry system to bypass border control systems. This system should be easy to manage and govern to restrict the lure of benefits for people abroad. Concurrently, expensive hotels, hostels and detention centres for migrant entering or being deported need to be avoided; the cost of operated them and the issues with contractors and alleged abuses needs to end; delays in the system need to be removed - if individuals are not authorised to be in the country immediate deportation should be actioned meaning that overnight stays restricted to a minimum and most certainly not in a (5 or more star) hotel.

The country needs to immediately introduce strong border governance controls and prevent those that have committed crimes coming to the country, in addition, to deporting those who commit crimes while in the country possibly after they have served a hard sentence over here or in their home country. To avoid further jealousy, which currently is sold as racism, native people should have the first opportunity for any job vacancy before being offered to new visitors or foreign workers. The law has to be tightened and tough penalties or sentences offered to those scrupulous business owners who exploit migrant workers to undercut local wages to promote a culture of acquiring low-skilled migrants to maximise profit margins. Recruitment agencies need to be stopped from hiring low-skilled labour from overseas and concentrate their efforts on the home labour market. Student visas have also been abused over the years and needs to be tightened up to ensure that after their course, the student(s) will have to leave the country.

In essence, the drastic changes in the numbers of people in Western nations besides the effects on wages and public services, has changed countries that had a high quality of life in the post-war era to countries of low wages and an ever decreasing quality of life. There is deep concern on the pressures regarding infrastructure and the disposal of waste besides the desperate attempts by politicians to keep the population in order with propaganda and the promotion of diversity in all walks of life. Ostensibly, the Western leaders are following the same path as the people in underdeveloped regions of the world who have 'thrown caution to the wind' and ignorantly carry on without a care to the long term repercussions of irresponsible behaviour besides ignoring carrying capacity of the country.

Relationship amid Migration & Destabilising Countries

The government has let in migrants, meaning that the chances of letting one or two terrorists into the country that could cause devastation, destruction and acts of terror that causes deaths and suffering to people, families and friends, is high and simply not worth the risk. What 'do-gooders' who protest on behalf of migrants do not understand or choose to ignore is one terrorist in the mix of thousands refugees / migrants can actually cause more deaths of innocent people in the country and these deaths are the responsibility of government and the people who promote this type of migration reform.

The sad realisation is, unless the 'do-gooders' are on the receiving end of such acts, they will never understand the after effects of an open door policy. Even if there is a minor risk of this happening, no country should allow the mass movement of people from certain areas of the world into the country; each individual's background should be known first. Emotion wise, it is easy to become drawn into wanting to help ease the plight of people who have been forced out of their native lands, but, intelligence and risk awareness should always overrule any news story that is intended to pull at those emotion strings. Letting people into the country when there is a risk of terrorists within the group is a risk not worth taking and needs to be resisted. Look what is happening to Europe since the mass migration movement of 2015/16, terrorist attack after terrorist attack and governments continue to look dumbfounded as to how to deal with the problem.

It is very easy to exploit compassion with regards to economic migrants or refugees to urge people to support or help them. But the problem is, especially in the UK, the country is already too full for the country to be sustainable besides presently facing a crisis in health care, infrastructure and a growing deficit. The situation becomes an issue of: when our compassion gets in the way of our ethical and moral duty to the people in our own country, society have a situation where our compassion will be our own undoing. Humans need to control our compassionate urge to help people seen throughout main stream media and think of the problem on a more higher plane of thought. Society cannot allow compassion and caring of others damage the nation's quality of life and potentially drag the home country down the same path that some of the countries which these migrants/refugees have fled from has gone down.

The WikiLeaks posting on the Libya 'tick-tock' document, which describes a close relationship between Hilary Clinton and Saudi-Arabia describe a plan in 2010-11 to overthrow the Libyan government and plunge the country in complete chaos. Obviously, this would work in favour of Saudi-Arabia due to oil interests. But, with the destabilising of Libya and the arm shipments to all other African countries, it started the migrant and refugee crisis that moved toward Europe. Looking closely at the leaks, it would appear that this refugee crisis was foreseen (and possibly planned) by the close relationship between the two parties to effectively weaken, destabilise and bankrupt Europe. Before the coalition forces started to bomb the country, Kaddafi warned against forced leadership change as it would in fact lead to mass migration of people to Europe. What is sold to the people is foreign tyrants are responsible for the migration crisis, when it is / was in fact (reading between the lines of the leaked documents) planned by the Obama administration to cease some control over resources and to move Europe closer to bankruptcy to make the system subservient to other richer countries; look what has happened to Greece and Italy where the people are in financial slavery to the EMF.

The crisis is highly linked to the <u>Pedesta</u> emails, where they describe the shady deals with government officials, charities and other countries that are oppressing their own people. The governments of the UK and US (and some European countries) continue to sell arms to countries like Saudi-Arabia knowing that they are being used against innocent people, especially in African nations. Yet, the rhetoric used by the very people in government authorising these arms sales is that the country has a responsibility to help and support these people who are being oppressed and bombed at will, it is the humane thing to do. These politicians are hypocritical; they knowingly approve the sales of arms that are being use for oppression / murder / devastation whilst at the same time giving the impression that they care about the people who are suffering because of it. It is an insane cycle of politicians behaving as warlords at the same time as a moral and ethical people to the electorate. This cycle has to be broken and any politician involved in such shady deals brought to account.

The irony is, if the 'do-gooders' really cared about these people, then they would work hard to show the government that selling arms to despot dictators and Muslim countries should stop; along with the invasion of foreign countries for the profit of a few. People, both in the public and private sectors, should combine their actions until this is achieved; ignoring the reality and allowing ourselves to be emotionally 'blackmailed' by edited news reports only makes situations worse. Society should be 'grown-up' enough to target the problem, not deliberately allow ourselves to be manipulated by oligarchs who contribute to the problem(s). Sadly, most people in the West continue with their daily activities in blissful ignorance or sheer foolhardiness of the eventual outcome of population numbers. The people in the UK should be deeply concerned what the impacts will be in a decade or so as unless something drastic changes with respect to population numbers in the country, it will be the first Western country to fall back into a third world country status with the services to match.

On the bright side, perhaps the UK will become a country where others will learn valuable lesson from and work not to repeat the same mistakes, thus, place preventative measures based on intelligence and common sense not on human emotions and feeling. Human feelings and emotions urge people to help, but when too much help causes the helper to fall too, all that has been accomplished was for nothing. Not that government is helping based on unselfish emotions, but on greed as all the programmes produced by foreign aid or the World Bank involves someone profiting from it. The World Bank and the European Monetary Fund (EMF) make loans to countries which they know will not be able to payback, but, it does allow for manipulation or influence within those countries governments and gives the people who print the money their pound of flesh to further the interests of modern corporatocracy. It is why the end never justifies the means and why the problems are never resolved; there is no money to be made in solving problems and global issues.

Problems with Negative and Positive Discrimination

Discrimination in all forms is bad for everyone in society although some people benefit from the differences in wealth thus power and status; and capitalism is fundamentally about people benefiting at someone else's expense because the system only has limited opportunities available. Some groups have higher status, a better chance of a greater quality of life and greater privileges than others. The best positions are always acquired by those who have strong family or political connections at the expense of others. In this unequal system there is often unfair treatment directed against groups of people. Discrimination comes in a variety of categories: racism, sexism and prejudice. In today's modern society certain groups work towards addressing two of the three types of discrimination related to race and sexual equality, due to historic reasons, whilst the main part of discrimination (prejudice) is often ignored, but, is more wide spread than the other two.

Ten years ago there was an argument that bosses would not hire people from certain ethnic backgrounds or certain gender / sex types; but, this was done 'through the back door' as an unofficial covert and unspoken system based on personal dislike of certain people. Now the country has seen, through wanting to be more welcoming, a system where there is blatant 'in your face' positive discrimination where job adverts are specifically specifying a certain type of applicant to fill the position, for example there are job adverts which describe – we would like to encourage female applicants to the role or after the advert in small print; or as a company we are interested in increasing the diversity among our workforce. Or, as in a research position advertised at a leading UK university – 'The applicant should satisfy eligibility criteria for early stage researchers as defined by the EC. In short, they should still be within the first four years of their scientific career and must be nationals of a country other than that of the host organisation, where they will carry out their project, i.e. UK. Researchers must not have resided or carried out their main activity (work, studies, etc.,) in the UK for more than 12 months, in the 3 years immediately prior to the date of selection'. Meaning the UK tax payer or UK citizen who has lived in the country since birth is automatically denied access to this position at a UK tax payer funded university. Unfortunately, this type of scenario is live throughout Western society where promotion of foreign students for diversity is prioritised; inconveniently, these positions are usually higher paid too. Whether the do-gooders of the world like it or not this is direct discrimination against people who could be better qualified to fill the roles on offer.

Admittedly, it is not the discrimination that various groups have been fighting for, but the best way to describe the situation is using an analogy of 'a coin has been flipped', it is now positive discrimination towards people from certain ethnic backgrounds or gender / sex types. In adverts such as the snippets described above is sending the message if an individual happens to be white, lived in the country all their life and their male, do not waste time applying for these positions as there is no real incentives from government to employ individuals in this category due to political ideological reasons.

What these groups and government have allowed to happen is to create a system where it is seen as being fine to discriminate against white males (and some white females) to achieve an objective for a more diverse and gender neutral workforce. By fighting covert discrimination, society has allowed official documented discrimination to be of normal working practice, but not only this, there are financial incentives to discriminate against native white males. It would seem that these groups intention is not to fight discrimination but to reverse the trend of discrimination on the type of people and gender that for historic reasons has dominated the workforce for centuries.

There are always certain advantages for those who 'play dirty' in the workplace. To ignore this fact and debate about race or sex is diverting attention away from what drives inequality in Western countries and places the discussions around groups who gain attention and government funding to drive forward ideologies that promotes further separation from society and allows the continuation of discrimination. It should be clear that discrimination begins at school age and continues through into adult life - in schools, discrimination is strongly linked to bullying and isolation from certain groups e.g. from groups following the popular students, being chosen for sports teams, and to maintain status by bullying those who aren't physically 'fit', etc.

In adult life, discrimination manifests itself by some of the same reasons. Also due to some people who generally know what they are doing and refuse to be a veritable 'yes' person who are continuously excluded from possible promotion in favour of those who are smooth talkers but at the same time untrustworthy and incompetent whom 'own comfy knee pads' in return for possible promotion in future.

It is almost impossible to rationally argue that people make a country a bigoted country, as recent data suggests non-whites are now more likely to hold top jobs than whites; so why does the media and government place great emphasis on race? Racism is generally misunderstood as jealously and frustration, nonetheless, the government is responsible for allowing this feeling to manifest in society. If people see migrants enter the country and given housing, furniture, free health care, whilst the white working class people are struggling to make 'hens meat'. Whilst, concurrently struggling to receive basic health care quickly and efficiently, then the feeling of being put second to visitors in the country grows. To add to this feeling when members of native families whom have lived in the country for generations struggle to get a decent paid job with wages being kept low, due to the pool of people available to do the job; and then believe due to life experience that jobs are purposely being given to people from migrant backgrounds, further ill feeling occurs.

The problem of integration and cultural differences enters proceedings. Migrants bring their own culture and religion whilst it is perceived they do not respect native culture (whatever this is) and as a result integration does not happen. Instead, native people leave areas and migrants enter in force and create isolated communities thus in some cases entire streets are of an isolated culture (just look at what is happening to the East end of London (land of cockney, well used to be!)). Due to wealth of some migrants from Iran, Iraq (oil rich countries) and the connection to certain foreign banks with much better interest rates than the ones available to native people, more businesses and franchises become controlled by migrants (whether it be 1st, 2nd, or 3rd generation). Native people become frustrated due to the feeling of being discriminated against by their own government believing migrants have more advantages and privileges than those who have paid into the system for generations. This is what is referred to in modern society as racism, but is in-fact a failure of government in listening to native people's concerns about how society is changing and making it harder to acquire well paid jobs, good health care, and issues such as higher taxation, long term unemployment, and unequal treatment by support services, law, finance and education.

When being concerned with people's differences, government along with local government have a responsibility to help remove these differences by ensuring all people from all walks of life get treated the same. Yet, both seem to work not only to maintain these differences but to increasing the tensions between people from different backgrounds. This scenario goes down to levels such as market stall rents, where recently in my home town white British market owners are paying twice the rental fees than those that are classed as being from diverse backgrounds and have been for a period of five – six years. This type of division enhances racism issues throughout many different communities and only contributes to the growing tensions nationally.

People coming to the country for a better life should be promoted, but, once it begins to affect native families that have been living here for generations, then looking at more stringent border controls should (have) become a priority of government and successive governments have failed to listen to the people. As a result, countries throughout the West are split on the issue of migrants and refugees. Racism as a propaganda message exists because of certain migrants and groups wanting to use it for certain advantages (the 'R' card is sometimes used to a favourable outcome, it is extremely affective in employment and law); otherwise, actual racism is intertwined with jealousy. However, the problem is subtly different in the US where black culture and white American culture is and has been at odds since the country's Independence Day with the Democrats relying on this separation and racism culture for votes.

Sexism has been created to solve some historic societal norms i.e. man is hunter gatherer, women nurturers. It spans back to the formation of Christianity in the dark ages with the creation of the Roman Catholic Church when men controlled the limited opportunities in society and educated people to believe that women are inferior to men. To a certain extent in some areas of the world this still hold true and religion is one of the prime reasons as to why. As the industrial revolution began women began to politically fight for more rights and ownership of private property; and women's rise to gain respect came to fruition in the 1960's when women gained better jobs, more earning potential and political say (the work women did during WWII helped the cause). However, men historically monopolized the highest status and earning potential throughout the West and as a result progress of women in these positions have been slow and opportunities, which were/are limited anyway, have become less available and even more sought after. Even in today's society were more women attend university than men, were women have reached the highest status in society, there is still a belief in Western countries that female members of the working class still do not see their interests as being the same as that of their male counterparts.

The feminist movement has done a lot of good to improve the standing and status of women in society, but, now appears to be redundant and refuses to gain momentum in the Middle East where movements like this can do a lot of good (wonder why?

you decide!). Instead, the West have a situation where feminist organisations receive funding by government and constantly 'shout and complain' about discrimination and 'rape culture', how there is not enough women in government or at boardroom level in companies and about the unequal pay gap; all without any adequate real data to prove any of their claims; in its place various manipulated statistics are used that cloud reality. I wish the argument was about equal share in opportunities; it would be a breath of fresh air to see more women in the construction industry, road working, drain cleaning, gardening, being a car mechanic, etc., but it isn't; the 'S' card is used to gain similar advantages as the 'R' card does when convenient.

In modern Western society, women are as free as men to seek opportunities, the problem is most women and these middle class feminists do not want the hard work low paid jobs, they want the high paid, low physical work careers; they want a monopoly on the highest paid jobs in society. Whilst concurrently, women want a family life and seemingly more free time and favouritism from employers than their male counterparts. It is already illegal to pay men less than women (purposely written in this way), however, when it comes to management levels, it is salaried and this is where the problem occurs, (so sorry for those who aren't in management, the feminist movement doesn't care about you! It is probably why the movement is gaining substantial criticism in the West, but, still being pushed by those liberal elites). If a woman wants a have free time or a family life and requires spending more time at home (i.e. personal choices), whilst a male counterpart does more hours at work and has greater work related availability and may gain more deals for the company, then it is a simple question of which <u>person</u> is worth more to the company. As a result, any pay gap is an 'inconvenient way (or convenient depending on your point of view) to distinguish the difference. The gender pay gap has been an issue that has been ongoing since the early 1970's and has been 'debunked' every single time, but, the issue refuses to 'go away'. Unfortunately, sexism and gender pay gap is used by politicians (and feminists) as a means of receiving the female vote, but, is in-fact a false belief or ideology that clouds reality.

There does exist sexism, but mainly involving family matters and the worth and rights of the father compared to the mother, and certain employment advantages involving quotas. Otherwise, feminism in the West is all but dead, and the question as why the movement has not progressed to other areas of the world where it can do some good remains, but it may have something to do with a religious context. However, Western politicians can take advantage of false beliefs in people to manipulate voting habits; and racism and sexism are areas that can be taken advantage of to secure votes and obtain various political posts.

Incidentally, when has anyone experienced a man use his physical appearance to get or obtain promotion in a company?; whereas, there have been a number of incidents were a woman uses her femininity for her own advantage i.e. to 'manipulate' rational decision making tasks and take advantage of an inherent male weakness for female beauty. One of several experiences that springs to mind involves a poorly performing tele-sales operative (blonde, skinny hour glass figure, symmetrical face, etc.) who at a works Christmas party made her move on a fairy new but single logistics director; shortly after she gained a promotion to sales supervisor and within a few months became a sales manager; with all colleagues standing back in shear amazement but the full understanding of how someone who was frankly bad at her job acquired such a position. Sadly, for the logistics director after she gained enough experience as a manager he became single again, with a distinct distrust of women. Similar experiences are felt throughout the Western world and are probably an inherent impact of a capitalist system where people take advantage of others to gain opportunities. But, where does feminism stand in this type of behaviour or the behaviour of women who appear on programmes such as 'Babestation' whose task it to take money away from mainly men by using their body assets?

Positive discrimination or diversity in the workplace / alternative or positive action (as some PC correct people know it) is targeted at perceived disadvantaged groups of people in society. Unfortunately, positive discrimination leads to negative discrimination for all others. For instance, there is a greater drive for companies to acquire more female board members and more ethnic 'minorities' (I use the term loosely) employed, but, this does not necessarily mean they are the right qualified person for the position. There are greater incentives from government for companies to use positive discrimination to 'create a more level playing field'. But, allocating a default number of spaces from a specified group means not hiring the best candidate or risk putting the less capable in these positions, and it is this type of discriminating and self-destructive system that is all common practice today even in governmental positions.

Positive discrimination is generally unlawful in the UK as an employer would be committing discrimination under the Equality

Act 2010, however it does not prevent some employers using reasons of diversity to attempt to circumvent the fair competition grounds where the best candidate should be offered the position. Diversity in the workplace is often talked about within political debates throughout the West with some politicians leading the calls for circumventing equality and competition for career opportunities in favour of a more mixed workplace; this is especially dominant when it comes to acquiring more women in positions.   The issue is protected characteristics (e.g. age, disability, gender, race, religion, sex, marriage and civil partnerships, pregnancy and maternity) are fully intertwined with diversity in the workplace and giving advantages or discrimination because of someone's characteristics, even if it is to obtain a more mixed workplace, is unlawful in the UK and many other Western countries.   This is not to say that an employer cannot encourage people from certain protected backgrounds from applying for job positions, but it would be illegal for the employer to employ a person from one of the protected characteristics if another person is better qualified for the role – the employer must still appoint the best person for the job.

However, in the UK, especially in academic environments, positive action is used to satisfy diversity numbers and there is a strong argument that the British white male is being discriminated against in applying for academic positions; unfortunately, this type of scenario is infecting industry and it is all driven by government incentives.   There have been greater calls from 'do-gooders' who represent various groups ranging from feminist to religious organisations to the LGBT community to put pressure on businesses to hire people from certain backgrounds (the trend is: 'minority' groups complain consistently in public mediums and what they want costs little, then eventually the government will cave). So throughout the West, people now have a situation in businesses and all academic institutions where not only do people in society have the problem of incompetent smooth talking 'yes' people in management roles, but, they have embarked on ignoring the more qualified candidates giving the position to someone based on their sex, colour of their skin, disability, religion or sexual gender to fulfil a quota.

It was hard before positive discrimination / positive action became a reality to figure out how certain people acquire the roles there in due to their shocking decision making skills and performance, now the reality is completely blurred. This has led to a level of unease among current workforce or resentment from people not in the 'special' advantage/privilege list. Additionally, there are issue regarding toilet and person designations, prayer breaks, and respect for the people employed in the position due to been given the position not due to their knowledge or skill applicability to the role. It is exactly like saying to a candidate and the rest of the employees that 'congratulations, the person has the job not because of merit, but because of race/gender, etc.'; this is not good for efficiency of the economy in general.

In this new idea to bring equality to the country people have seemingly forgotten about the majority of the people currently employed in companies or institutions, the number of applicants who are better qualified but not in the special 'advantage' list, and the fact that positively discriminating toward people means you are in fact negatively discriminating against all others. In the West, this is now mainly white males (although white females are being affected also) who are the ones losing out on positions not due to suitability or ability reasons.

This notwithstanding, it is also extremely difficult to remove someone who clearly struggles to fulfil their job responsibilities if they are on the same list. I have even come across the problem myself with Human Resources when procedure and dismissal of someone who is not white and/or male becomes very difficult to do, whereas it does not cause the same problem if the employee is a white male; it has become a disturbing work practice. Positive discrimination does more to divide people than integrate various cultures together into a seamless whole. The ideology of providing equal representation for all religious, cultural, sex within government, boardroom and management levels goes against ensuring the right person is placed in the right position for efficacy of governance; and it needs to be resisted in favour of intelligent decision making regarding skills, knowledge and ability to do the job.

Just as a tangent to the discussion – there a growing tendency to rewrite history (both non-fiction and fiction) to match present day social justice trends to suit diversity; and present these alterations to children, which invariably indoctrinates them in further false realities. For example, changing various characters from history from white or pale skin actors to non-white; it is the same with some comic book characters. Other examples includes the fictional superhero superman who in recent times has been overshadowed and beaten in a fight against supergirl (girl power) destroying what was once a comic book legend to be weaker than the female equivalent, i.e. spreading the false narrative to children that women are the stronger sex/gender when biologically (most) men are naturally stronger than (most) women (I'm, not even going to mention the changing of the ghostbusters male team to an all women team with a dumb male receptionist – oh dear!). The point it, history should not be rewritten to suit various present day ideologies, nor should children's books or film characters be changed to suit diversity principles – it is not that difficult to create new characters.

Hate crimes have become a major issue for Western governments in recent times, especially, because of the issues with migration, religion, sex, and issues with propaganda. Hate crime is described as acts of violence or hostility directed at people because of whom they are or who someone thinks they are. Basically, for some unknown reason, most common minor crimes or even harmless banter have been classed under this category meaning that most crimes or incidents that individuals do not like or take offence to are classed as a hate crime; and most news reports are targeted on incidents involving non-white, eastern European and women.

The message being sent from media outlets is that there have been many 'racist' attacks on non-white people, but only gang attacks on white people, which are not related to racism, i.e. double standard reporting. Because the law and the media are frightened of being accused of race discrimination this type of double standard has caused lots of underage girls to be used for sex by child grooming gangs for a considerable amount of time even though the police where aware of the issue for years before the gang were taken to task by the law. There was even an incident of underage white girls being used for sex by non-white gangs in my home town and the only act the police chose to do was to send out letters to residents known to have had sex with them, no criminal charges have been sought yet.

The issue is a white gang or an un-famous individual will not be given that sort of privilege treatment and nor should they. These situations can only be described as positive discrimination towards people of certain culture, religion and colour; or a strategy to prevent social anger among the non-white religious residence at the expense of underage girls and the direct ignorance of the countries justice system. Whenever someone in a political part points this out, i.e. Sarah Champion of Labour in the UK when she mentioned the problem of Pakistani men exploiting and raping British white girls, they are quickly dismissed from the party, with some, but little interest from main stream media.

Nobody in public circles is allowed to discuss reality in these types of events. Some might even go as far as saying that the government has purposely given leeway and special privileges to people from certain religious and cultural backgrounds due to ongoing trade deals with countries such as Saudi Arabia. Then society have individuals who are protected by money, status, and popularity (e.g. Jimmy Saville, MPs, football trainers who have been implicated in sex crimes); it gives the impression that the law does not apply equally to all in society nor does it give the confidence that the people at the top in society care about the people of lower status.

Other questions that are conveniently ignored are: where are the parents of these underage girls and why do they not care about where they are or doing?; and why are the authorities not asking some poignant questions of the parents and/or placing any other children in their care into somewhere where they are safe and monitored because clearly their parents are unable to satisfy this responsibility. The only act the authorities appear to do is offer support to both the victim and their parents. The reality is, the child or children are victims (even if they do not think they are) of this sort of exploitation because of the lack of parents' interest in their own children and they are the ones who should be 'named and shamed' throughout all media outlets to spread the message: society does not accept this sort of 'don't care' attitude with respect to parents taking care of their own children. The nanny state society has a lot to answer for in this type of disgusting trend spreading throughout the West; and the problem is only increasing as population numbers increase due to immigration from countries where it is culturally acceptable to use girls and women to satisfy men's sexual desires.

However, these are changing times or so some people think, a new 'witch hunt' has started and paranoia is heightened amongst people. With people more than in recent past quickly jumping to incorrect conclusions and accusations and by using the internet reputations are wrongly ruined to the extent of causing the suicide of innocent people. It would appear by the law neglecting to investigate incidents at the time of being reported because of the threat of discrimination or racism; it has allowed further suffering and now a high injection of news stories that has people more distrusting of others than ever before.

The governments' solution is to place greater emphasis on hatred and separation forcing people to 'walk on eggshells' to avoid offence. The circumstance has even gone to the depths of justifying 'wolf whistling' as a hate crime. Oh and thank you to whoever in government gave the feminists the power to spread the message to men that they need to watch what they say or do to the opposite sex; as now if a woman does not like the look of a man in a night club and the man attempts to 'chat her up', he might be accused of a hate crime - further bad luck to those guys who have not been blessed with good lucks. In essence, a hate crime can be classed as a subjective crime based on whether or not a woman is attracted to a man or whether someone of colour (non-white or from a migrant background) wishes to make an official complaint to the police.

For an incident to be classed as a hate crime the perception of the victim, or witnesses, is the defining factor; no evidence is needed for justification, just a feeling is required. The law is supposed to be delivered impartially and objectively and with fairness, however, recent changes have damaged the ability to function in this way. With the incompetent actions of the law in the past due to threats of discrimination and racism, the law has now lost its way and some respect; and with it people in society have become more divided. It is all being driven directly by a deceptive agenda through government.

It is clear this has to change. The law should not be politically motivated to ignore crimes, such as child grooming, due to potential threats of racism and anger among segregated communities or religious groups. Nor should anyone who is protecting someone because of status be immune to prosecution. The law cannot be allowed to positively discriminate through fear nor should it be apprehensive of being accused of targeting people from certain backgrounds if adequate evidence is available to act. There needs to be a strengthening within the CJS and government of 'one law for all people in the country, without exceptions'; and anyone walking on 'eggshells' to prevent possible trouble in the community should be motivated or obligated to step down from their position in favour of someone who will not discriminate or offer favouritism to certain groups of people.

This notwithstanding, the close relationship between government officials and the CJS is concerning. There are many news reports over recent years that have not shined a shining light on the police force especially when investigations are directed at official offices of government. The police should operate in complete separation and be immune to government influence; yes, the government and the people of the country should be the ones who decide on the law, but the police should be the organisation who upholds it without being forced to act or not based on political pressures.

Family Planning

The natural world controls population numbers with the relationship between predator and prey, unfortunately with the adaptability and invention of humans we are now at the top of the food chain with no identifiable predator (with the exception of a few incurable viruses and diseases). There is a strong argument that humans, to a certain degree, are defying nature in that evolution is all about survival of the fittest, but, with our medical knowledge even the weakest of the species survives and has the opportunity to procreate. Society have also invented a system where the strong do not lead, but, the wealthiest and the devious are in positions of power; and where technology replaces physical strength - we have become the most un-natural species living on earth. This invariably means that controlling our population numbers is our own responsibility.

When speaking about the large families' people have you cannot help thinking this is because of the financial help the government provides via the benefits system and has been one of the main reasons why the country has a large migration issue leading to huge population increases. The situation is no longer sustainable with the large population already adding to the decrease in the quality of life and services the country provides. Only providing public financial support for the first child until population numbers fall to a sustainable level is one workable solution but will be a massive cultural change and what this means is there will be many people still having more than one child firmly believing that government will provide in relation to money, schooling and other services. It is this type of mind-set that has to change as the country cannot afford to support large families anymore besides sustain or improve the quality of life.

Society needs to reduce the numbers and this does mean people have to sacrifice what they want for the greater need of one child rather than struggle financially with more. This will be a tough pill to swallow, but nevertheless it is medicine that as a country society needs to take. What this means is there is a high probability people from certain cultures will be put-off from moving over here and some with already large families will migrate to other countries more financially favourable to their mind-sets. This situation is probably a good scenario for the country but nonetheless the transitional period from people realising the government will only support up to a certain point and are not there to help support if people choose to not follow advice, i.e. one child; and then as a family unit the financial responsibility for other children is purely with the parents. This sort of change will take a number of years for people to get a firm grasp on and will be a difficult cultural change, but, there should be no leeway on only providing support for one child until a sustainable level is reached.

The ownness has to be with the parent(s); if they want more than one child, then the support for the additional child has to be provided for by them and this includes school places and health care. This breaks away from the benefit culture where the government provides for the family choices of individuals or couples; thus, if people want to have large families then there is a financial burden to think about before this decision is made. Breaking this culture means parents will have to take responsibility for their own actions and not blame government for the potential hardships that will occur. For too long government has been the sole entity responsible for the growing poverty level, this responsibility has to be shared. It is not the governments job, nor everybody else's responsibility, to provide for children couples have decided to conceive; if the choice is made to have a large family leading to financial hardships; then who is really to blame? Not the government, not other people, but the couple who chose to live in a situation where they know bringing up children costs a lot of money and have not planned for it.

People from certain cultures and religious backgrounds will find this uncomfortable, but, you (not God or government) have the responsibility for your children and conceiving them without thinking of what future they will have is irresponsible and you need an understanding that more people equals more hardships for them and others, it is this fact which needs to be educated. More people thus less resources equals more civil unrest and more wars, therefore, more suffering, this is what uncontrolled population numbers results in. God does not enter the equation and faith, in this case, will lead to a disastrous outcome; just look at highly religious areas of the world that are plagued by disease, starvation and lack of clean drinking water. It cannot all be because they worship the wrong God as people from all faiths are suffering; it is because there is more human life in the region that the land cannot support. The sad realisation is that the more charities help, the worse the problem is because of lack of responsible family planning.

At present in most countries in the world, people are having children without a second thought of the life they will live in the future. It is the most irresponsible life decision and gives justification to argue that parents do not actually love their own children enough to prevent suffering in future. Deciding not to have a large family and work towards reducing the numbers of people in the world in a natural way will help prevent future suffering of children, will give greater opportunities to those new children as they enter school and adulthood and help reduce the strain on natural resources and health services. It is simple logic based on scientific data, human compassion and responsibility.

Correct family planning has the potential to reduce poverty, starvation and disease whilst concurrently improve quality of schools and long-term environmental sustainability. However, responsible family planning globally remains an issue with most resistance coming from a religious agenda followed by an economic necessity to continue to make high profits for the few. Little progress over the decades has seen little reversal of this omission and migration has contributed to further hardships in various parts of the world. It would seem people, especially in government, cannot see (or choose to stupidly ignore) the strong relationship between population growth and increased poverty.

The question of childcare is a difficult one and as a nation a greater question needs to be investigated; as such, why does society need childcare and why is it so expensive? The financial pressures of everyday life have forced both parents to work giving rise to full time nannies, breakfast and after school clubs for their children whilst concurrently being too tired and stressed to spend any quality of time with them once collected; this cannot be healthy for strong family bonds. There needs to be a greater push for family friendly careers giving both parents the flexibility to spend time with children and family with possible introduction of a job sharing scheme so multiple fathers and mothers can benefit. Additional government support is needed to account to the reduction of work hours to go to the cost of living, but, be controlled to not support the idea of financial and work security.

Family planning proponents should reassert greater recognition of the difficulties encountered with population growth and pursue a series of education stimulus throughout schooling, especially high (secondary) school (ages 11-16), to teach children the effects (including costs) of large family commitments on parents, public services and society in general. It should also be emphasised that family planning should be taken more seriously than any religious ideology about Gods providing by advocating logic about resource requirements and limitations of acquiring such resources.

Human beings should value compassion, tolerance and a sense of decency, but with the growing population and the greater pressures of support services on family life, growing inequality, anxieties about anti-social behaviour and a wide spread loss of trust in established politics and politicians, are creating insecurity to many communities. The binding factor on how communities work is about relationships and family, but, various life pressures (low pay, work commitments, poor health, etc.) has placed strains on the very fabric that binds people together. For decades the government has concentrated on placing profit (the economy) before family, which has filtered through to individuals who concentrate on what benefits themselves, what entitlements can they receive and completely ignore the impact of their actions on others closest to them.

The government should understand the importance of a good quality of family life and grasp the importance of placing family before any other life commitments to build on the fabric of basic human consciousness – love, care, and resilience. A whole-family approach to policy making needs to be introduced looking at the long term impacts of a countries economy with concentrating on people before profit and supporting relationships. Eventually, once parents are being responsible for the number of children being born by considering available resources, health service size, number of career opportunities available and school placements, there should be a guaranteed well-paid job for all young people that are not government created 'non-jobs', but real jobs in a technology and knowledge driven world that suits their respective interest(s).

A situation regarding gender identity has reached an extreme level whereby even social networking sites have a number of option with which to identify yourself as, i.e. Facebook has at least 74 definitions of gender; this comes as a surprise to many people, especially religious people; but, comes of no surprise to me. This is a consequence of bringing children up the way society has deemed acceptable, i.e. broken families, where boys are being bought up by the mother who treats them as girls and feminises them whilst masculating the girls (girl power to be more like men); the endorsement from society institutions that children/adults can be who they want to be based on their own mind-sets; and a society that promotes 'wrapping children up in cotton wool', not letting them go to school in snow in case they hurt themselves (there is also a legal twist here), mothering them, etc..

Questioning who and what an individual is based on an ill-founded belief system, potentially caused by two separate words meaning the same thing (gender and sex), is a psychological disorder based on the 'illusion of reality' inside people's own heads; and they are deluded enough to think they can change who and what they are without considering any scientific facts. It is why gender identity has become a new religion, i.e. a belief that has no scientific foundation and cannot be justified given the knowledge and reality of nature. Unfortunately, young children are now being looked after by people with this mind-set and treating them in manner not established on sexual organs / gender and science or even nature, but, passing this delusional mind-set onto them causing great confusion and long term mental health problems. The situation has gone to the extent society now have organisations who experiment on children, mainly boys, in an attempt to emasculate and feminise them. Then people wonder why society has a depression epidemic and a gender confusion issue.

By normalising single parent families, removing the father figure from the family unit and then promoting feminising new fathers, society will experience more issues with gender identification. Science defines two types of gender, male and female, and due to a mutation sometimes people are born with both genitals, but personality will still favour one over the other;

gender is not separate from sex. People and society have to stop this type of movement from increasing and present it as a mental disorder caused by their upbringing with parents wanting to be more of a friend to their children rather than a parent and government liberalists giving in on the issue so they can carry on with nefarious acts elsewhere. This liberal ideology is driving society down a path that has the potential to be more devastating to the human population than religion.

More fathers need to be involved in family life and decisions, moreover, in modern times when divorce and Child Support have caused many fathers to lose any form of relationships with their own children to the financial benefit of the mothers. The law has to be tightened to prevent any parent from taking advantage of their position, sex and wealth to manipulate outcomes if a relationship does 'break down'. Furthermore, family law has to be adapted to ensure that sexism against the father and the notion that the mother is the best parent for the child is removed to allow a level playing field (i.e. equality) where the children's needs are the priority. The law has to be strong enough to punish a parent who is found to 'lie' and wittingly use their own children as assets and tools to hurt the other parent with a mandatory sentence at a boot camp to teach the importance of being a parent whose prime task is the wellbeing of the children.

In circumstances where a family is found to be unsocial or consistently causing trouble in the community there needs to be a new approach to dealing with them. Currently, when a household is causing trouble within a local community, huge amounts of police, social service and local government's time and money is spent attempting to work with the family to resolve the anti-social issues, with little support directed at the victims. Generally, once the issues escalate, the authorities have no other choice but to move the family out of the area and place them in another house in a different area, but, the cycle continues.

The problem is worse when the offender is under the age of responsibility then the authorities have little solutions available to them. Ostensibly, the support services are allowing children to 'grow-up' with the knowledge that there is little punishment if they are under a certain age. This needs to end as it is the children in this category that will most likely commit greater offences and end up in jail in the future. There needs to be greater support for the front line and an innovative approach for social working involving a stronger attitude to supplementary, and in some cases mandatory, provisions for these troubled families.

The priority is to prevent further victimisation within local communities, but, support services must not abandon individuals in these troubled families. Instead, promotion of a hard line approach has to be delivered. The root cause of why the problem exists has to be investigated, with military style boot camps for both the children and parents; with possible psychological advice given if needed. Additional financial restrictions must also be actioned with reduction in benefits and support given for any drug, drink or other such addiction that plagues the family. Furthermore, depending on the severity of the circumstances, removal of the children from the parents should be considered until authorities are confident that the parents fully understand their responsibility and the children are educated that for every action there is a reaction and bad actions receive punishment. It may also be beneficial to offer or order suitable community service to the family (including the children) to deter any possible slide back into trouble. The more society 'stamp-out' the scourge of these lesser crimes the more community bonds will tighten which can only lead to a more prosperous society.

Schools need to teach children and young adults more about relationships, moreover, the negative impacts of the wrong type of relationship with the wrong person. In the short term, this needs to be more prevalent in the education system because at present people are becoming involved in relationships, having children and they are completely ignorant to the negative effects when the relationship breaks down. It hits people like 'brick-walls' and sometimes, especially for men, it causes them to lose control and sometimes inflict harm or commit suicide because of the strains with the father:child relationships that come with relationship breakdown. These men then have all kinds of problems in trusting women and in some cases can lead to assault and using women just for sex with no intention of becoming emotionally involved.

In the woman's case, it can promote greed and with the law being soft with the female of the species courts can sway towards believing a mother's stories in most cases and leads to a culture where mother's use the children for financial stability and to hurt the father; and intern make the father struggle to have a decent financial life for a long period of time (most of their working life). These negative effects are often ignored by the education system and condemned by religious leaders with further do-gooder insisting that children should be protected from the reality of the real world for as long as possible. But, not giving children the knowledge in which to cope with the negative effects of adult life would invariably lead to the same social problems society are dealing with today - a spiralling fall in social health. With children living in broken families, the support services need to provide children the knowledge in the hope that future children will not have to deal with the current problem (level) of relationship breakdowns, help to reinforce that problems should be worked through, and better cope with the emotional impacts of relationships.

Looking at the youth today people should realise there is something wrong; people over the age of 40 who took the old O-levels or GCSE grading, cannot believe how easy the examinations are now at schools. Even though the country has a high percentage of high achievers at school, internationally the UK is one of the worst educated countries in Western civilised world. With children being spoiled with IPad, games consoles, phones etc., they grow up spending all their spare time with these electronics that they end up as adults being satisfied with these types of distraction, thus, are not too concerned with learning new things or being interested in national or world events. The electronics and all that is associated with them, i.e. social networking sites, pacifies them into being 'not that bothered' with what they do in daily live or what value they are worth, which all leads to further mental health issues when their subconscious questions their own actions and further increases the use of drugs to cope with depression, anxiety and stress.

It is a perfect, brilliant outcome for the oligarchs because it is producing good obedient workers who question nothing. But, now there are lots of different issues, such as assault being reported, which is not actually assault, but just a misunderstanding of signals given due to the lack of social interaction experienced as children with the addiction of electronics given to them by their parents. This has caused incidents for example in night clubs when a guy goes up to a girl who is not attracted to him, touches her on the arm; she can actually report the man to the police as a hate crime. This type of scenario simply has to stop.

The lack of social skills and social interaction given to the youth of today, along with the distinct lack of patience or understanding caused by the experience of being spoiled with electronics and gifts throughout childhood has meant that parents are no longer preparing their children for life. All they are doing is providing the children with these types of gifts as a distraction from parent's responsibility of spending time and looking after the children; so the device babysits the children rather than them. This happens for a number of reasons including: the parents are too tired and stressed from work, parents are more interested in watching TV or interacting with people via social networking sites, etc. A child(ren) to a parent these days are nice things to have, but are a pain to look after properly (hard work) and they do not want to spend quality time with them when there is something more enjoyable to do. It is a sad and harsh reality that parents who love their children are abandoning them to the distraction of electronic devices and cannot see the lasting impacts caused by this type of abandonment.

Governments and universities throughout the world have already conducted research on this area and come up with the same conclusion, the child's mental wellbeing is being detrimentally affected by overuse of electronic devices and the lack of time spent with interacting with parents and children of their own age. Parents also know this, but choose to ignore the warning over convenience. Young adults of today are the first to live a childhood with electronic devices, the first of a generation to be 'hooked' on anti-depressants and the first to go through an ever increasing obesity crisis. People see the signs everywhere and still choose to continue down a path of increasing social and individual health problems.

For big business the path is a lucrative path to take, but for social health the trend needs to be reversed. There needs to be limitations to the time spent using electronic devices and more time spent interacting with real people and experiencing real life. There needs to be education given from early age about the detrimental impacts of playing computer games and promotion of outdoor activities with local government doing more to provide necessary suitable outdoor play areas with varying activities to keep the interests of children. A systematic training course should be given to new parents and soon to be parents to encompass the responsible way to look after children; and marketing in main stream media outlets about the negative effects of using electronics to babysit children; hence correct not lazy, parenting. Moreover, there needs to be a debate on whether the social services can hold parents to account if it is found that the child is spending most of his/her time on electronic devices; and there should be discussions on recuperating costs if the child 'grows-up' suffering from depression caused by lack of social skills, drive, or laziness that can be associated by lack of parenting when they were younger.

Speaking of family, modern day society has destroyed the natural social construct that has made the human race thrive. Boys who have grown into adult men have been parented by the mother (with the father passive or absent for many different reasons) have been emasculated and the girls who have grown into women have been told through many mediums that they are in control and have become more violent than men in such a short period of time (and why wouldn't this happen when everyone is told men cannot hit women (they will get into legal problems), but, not the other way around). Then society has the problem of child worshipping, created from academic work surround the psychology of children, where children must not be punished for misbehaving as this could cause psychological problems for them in the future; and hitting children creates an atmosphere of fear – even though fear of pain is, generally, what keeps people from doing the same act in the future.

Unfortunately, some children need more discipline and punishment than others, furthermore, are simply not receiving it. Some badly behaved children, especially those with some form of 'Jekyll and Hyde' personality, need both at the age of 6 or at the very latest at age 8 when they receive the burst of hormones before personality traits are more or less set to prevent any bad decisions or actions later in life. New modern day parenting and the nanny state society, however, does not permit this due to fear of social services and parents not willing to discipline their children for numerous reasons, instead the children are spoilt and infrequently learn that there are consequences to their actions.

At some point with this new nanny system respect for adults and authority has been lost with children gaining knowledge that they can shout abuse without any real repercussions, report parents and other adults to the authorities. This is causing a large percentage of children and young adults who struggle to cope with their negative emotions (i.e. anger) without lashing out because they do not have a firm grasp of repercussions due to over-protectionism given to them when they were younger. The outcome is there are many people wandering around who have lost sense of what makes them human and different with the false belief that they can be someone else other that who they actually are. For example, in areas of the world where feminism is taking centre stage in political decisions society have men who have been indoctrinated to suppress what makes them men, mainly due to legal threats and single parent influence, and women who are attempting to surpass men in all areas of work (be dominant) and simultaneously becoming more miserable and depressed which has cause an increase in suicide rates.

Society then ponders why there are issues with drug addiction, depression and questions why prisons are overpopulated – all I can say is well duh! This has diminished the chances of the next stages in intelligent human evolution using science and knowledge to help people grow and unfortunately humans are becoming more lost as a species.

Control Distinction between the Sexes (Genders)

Relationships have become ever more complicated in recent times with more women taking over household decisions and men backing down on decisions or disagreements to have a peaceful life. For example, in a relationship where both parties are equal you would expect to see in shared home items what the woman likes (ornaments, photos, scatter cushions, i.e. clutter) being on display as well as the man's 'clutter', but the man's belongings (tools, sports memorabilia, workout gear, etc.) have all but been relegated to the shed or garage. Very rarely do you come across a family house where the man's belongings are out on display. It is this type of control that a man gives over for a peaceful life. The problem is, has this decision (men being passive) caused serious ramification outside the home? Society now have a system were the woman is accustomed to being in control at home and men are inured to backing-off; the problem is this sort of mentality is now more than ever before edging its way in working life. Society has friction, favouritism and discrimination all being used in work as a means of maintaining control and seeking promotion; where men are motivated to 'walk on egg shells' to avoid any possible offence taking place and therefore remove themselves from questioning directives from women and avoid any harmless male banter in case it is heard and offence taken.

Western women have lost respect for men and men have lost self-respect for themselves because changes in the law, feminist movements and the rise of single parent (mother) families have made men somewhat passive in all areas of life through fear of offending, upsetting or even defending themselves against a woman onslaught because of the cost to family relationships and the risk of a criminal record due to the biased manner the law is executed. For men, modern relationships with women is incredibly difficult and interactions with them can become very frustrating and confusing.

People live in a world where Western women, due to change in political correctness and being influenced by, pampered and spoilt by their mothers (you do not need a man you are independent and you have the control of your own decisions) have a psychological problem of 'control freakiness' (coercive control) that women far from being fair in relationships, delude themselves due to be so self-involved, that they do 'give' and 'take' in decisions. To contribute to the problem, Western women have an unrealistic and unhealthy impression of what men should be and behave like through media outlets and movies detailing that men should be the ones who would sacrifice everything for his beloved. Modern women want this type of submission and commitment in their relationship, i.e. they want a human male puppy dog that behaves and does not disagree, but, is always there and will put up with the female hormone behaviour swings without any recompense (there's a good boy!). Unfortunately, men are becoming more like well-trained dogs as time goes by in their relationship life, not wanting to offend, upset or make the woman angry in anyway; those that do might end up with a broken family with children being the unfortunate victims.

Modern Western women are more and more primarily concerned with their own happiness and feelings in their personal life so much so they live in their own bubble and ignore the effects of their behaviour on others and blame all their woes on their male partner for making them feel negative emotions. However, some men (a few) do suffer the same affliction but it is certainly not as wide spread yet. Sadly, with mothers (and some new modern dads) feminising and emasculating boys, spoiling them (so they grow up only caring about what they want and what they want to do and having tantrums when something or someone disturbs them) and over nurturing them beyond what they require or need all supported from nanny state ideology driven from government; and with the lack of a disciplined father figure, this sort of self-centredness, selfishness and ignorance is quickly spreading throughout the male of the species. Unfortunately, nobody takes the time to notice or chooses to ignore reality and those who do cannot be bothered to care; or it could be that people are too distracted filling their spare time with something to divert attention away from the mystery and dullness of societal and working life.

Society has to accept that new modern women are more irrational to the extent men struggle to understand some of what they say or do leaving men with the thoughts of bewilderment and confusion. The irony is most men (boyfriends and husbands) do not want to upset the one they love, in fact most men attempt to interact with zero intention of offending or upsetting. (Ladies if you don't believe this, just ask your boyfriend or husband, making it clear they won't upset you no matter what, for an honest answer.) The future of relationship interactions should not be about the man walking on egg shells besides trying their best to be noticeably over sensitive to a woman's feelings to avoid upsetting the one they love. This simply does not and will not work as the more men give way and question their actions the more controlling and more easily upset women become. It transpires into a cycle of passive behaviour for men and more take, less give with women, which men's psych cannot maintain plus women's rational behaviour in in their personal life's diminishes.

Coinciding with this irrational behaviour, modern Western women are becoming more short tempered, angry, foul mouthed and violent, and have little consideration of the repercussion of their actions, which generally ends in crying due to emotional overload. They do not forget the bad times and hold a grudge, sometimes for an entire lifetime; and will ignore their conscience if it means paying back someone for their woes, especially men. The modern woman debating their case with a man will turn the debate into an all-out argument where they will refuse to accept that there is a happy medium, it is either her way (what she wants) or an unfounded extreme and she will not be persuaded otherwise.

A prime example is when a disagreement occurs the women never backs down and continues until the man surrenders – he has no choice; most Western women will escalate the issue until she secures her own way or the man lashes out to quieten her then she can use this to control him or hurt him more. It is especially true when it involves children. 99% of fathers would never think about removing children from the mother, but, sadly upon a relationship breakdown a significant proportion of mothers would not give it a second thought because of the financial implications and the advantage of hurting, followed by controlling, the father. For some men having children means their life, personality and future outlook is negatively affected when family life breaks down; and government has put systems in place not to prevent this type of repression, but, to promote it. Apparently society has deemed this type of practice amicable and acceptable; likewise continue to demonise the father if he is not in a good mental state due to conditions surrounding contact and actually wanting to be a parent then makes rash decisions in an attempt to be financially secure and away from the control of the mother.

Men have become somewhat disposable to women and mothers in today's modern society. The law has given too much power of control to the female sex that now they use their power to make men passive; if the man refuses to be passive there is an 'or else' accompanied with the control freakiness that concludes with single parent families. It is the reason why most men are miserable later in life and more children grow-up without a male role model in theirs. Women use emotional and sexual blackmail, sometimes accompanied with crocodile tears for manipulation and control; this is more prevalent in family life where the wife or girlfriend wants her man to be subservient and obedient to their needs. (Every woman I have had the privilege of knowing consistently say 'not all women are the same'; yet, somehow they always find a way to prove themselves wrong and I endeavour to point it out on occasions, just as a reality check. But, the problem is also affecting the way women interact with each other; there appears to be a time limit in which women can mutually coexist without trouble ensuing and this is equally applicable to female family members. A woman desires to be in control and be the centre of attention, more than one woman interacting with each other or in a group for long periods of time means both are fighting for control with each other).

Most fathers or step-fathers are overruled and controlled by their female counterparts, so much so that the male voice is relatively unheard (in real terms) in children's lives thus boys grow up believing that women are in charge and girls grow up with a controlling and materialistic mind-set. This contributes to the current social problems people see today where young adults struggle to cope with life's problems; they have been over mothered by the controlling parent who has provided and spoilt them since birth. This mothering continues through into adult life where mothers continue to offer too much support that true independence and the courage to handle life issues has all but gone.

I think it is true to say that most men have enough hassle at home without bringing it into the workplace. More men are pulling away from workplaces that have high potential of having a superior that could be from the opposite sex. Not only this, businesses that do have a female manager are creating a working culture where the men are becoming 'whiners'. This is a contributor to men turning away from office and manufacturing jobs and looking towards driving jobs, i.e. due to the same type of attitude, emotion and control women have at home and bringing it into the workplace. This means that reason and common sense is leaving workplaces and blame culture, like never before, is being initiated by women (and certain ethnic people) in the workplace to keep control. It is a sad realisation that men are being pushed out of certain jobs due to decisions made with the feminist movement forcing men to 'walk on egg shells' so as not to offend or upset the female of the species. It is not sexist to look at what is going on and state facts, just like it is not racist to state facts; these are real issues that are happening in the world and people need to come to terms as to the reasons why.

Controlling women is a reason why many men are pulling out of relationships or not getting married throughout the West, especially in the US and the UK – it simply is not worth their while to be involved in this way. People need to admit that this is a problem and ask why men are feeling more like this, otherwise the gradual shift in dominance between men and women in the workplace will continue to occur and probably start a cyclic pattern of women movements followed by men movements; and the world has had enough of various movements already causing major disruptions and social chaos.

In public life, women are too keen and eager, just like people of colour, to use labels (e.g. sexist, misogynist, etc.) in order to gain preferential treatment leading to men walking on 'egg shells' when interacting with the opposite sex   The problem with the feminist movement is women already have more than equality, they have privileges (some of the main ones listed below) that now there is no basis for continued campaign on the issue; the same scenario goes for diversity in the workplace. However, now that people have equality some do not know what to do with it, so now they want favours such a positive discrimination or fake truths to keep causes going. They would like special privileges whilst at the same time continuing with the rhetoric of the 'white man is oppressing me'.

The main list of women privilege and advantage in family, legal and public life, which goes beyond any and all calls for equality, includes the following that some might argue is from the alt-right, but, facts of real life prove them to be relevant:

- Women have the privilege of having standards lowered to suit them if and when they choose to join the military voluntarily.
- Women have the privilege of having Female Genital Mutilation be illegal but Male Genital Mutilation not to be.
- Women have the privilege of being sentenced to far less time served or a lesser punishment than a man for the same crime.
- Women have the privilege of not being described or treated as rapists by the mainstream media when they commit statutory rape against young boys.
- Women have the privilege of being deemed the more suitable parent in child custody court cases 95% of the time (even if they are a deadbeat parent with addictions)
- Women have the privilege of being more likely to be excused of crimes due to 'mental' issues.
- Women have the privilege of being more likely to be helped when assaulting their partner, or indeed anyone, despite who started the assault, or if they are in the right.

- Women have the privilege of being seen as a victim in any confrontation with a man and this includes in a court of law.
- Women have the privilege of being able to murder their partner and blame him for her actions, thus ridding themselves of guilt and proving their innocence.
- Women have the privilege of blaming all of her woes, faults and negative actions on her male partner (it is his fault; he made me do it; I am like this way because of hum) whilst all of her achievements have been accomplished despite her having a male partner. Whereas most male accomplishments is due to having a good women beside him and supporting him.
- Women have the privilege of blaming an affair on their partner, whereas if a man has an affair he cannot.
- Women have the privilege of the violence against women act.
- Women have the privilege of being given sympathy even if they murder their children.
- Women have the privilege of being innocent until proven guilty after a sexual assault allegation.
- Women have the privilege of domestic violence being considered a male crime against women.
- Women have the privilege of declaring rape the day after a drunken mistake with a man, whereas a man does not.
- Women have the privilege of paying lower auto insurance rates.
- Women have the privilege of holding feminist meetings and rallies without fear of men protesting and disrupting them or outcries of sexism.

- Women have the privilege of having their case taken more seriously by law officials by virtue of the alleged victim being female.
- Women have the privilege of blaming inappropriate and violent behaviour on hormones.
- Women have the privilege of having society ignore the effect of hormones on their mental ability for decision making and capability to do their job.
- Women have the privilege of government and private funding to set-up charities and institutions specifically to emasculate boys (child abuse), whereas there are no institutions looking to defy nature for girls.
- Women have the privilege of be chosen for a job position, even if a man is more qualified.
- Women have the privilege of using a child for financial gain and not being demonised in society.
- Women are hailed as heroes in society it they bring-up a child by themselves after they have purposely ruined any sort of parental relationship between the child and the father.
- Women have the right to decide on the outcome of a pregnancy; and murder of a new life not being seen as revolting and sickening in society.
- Women have the privilege of accusing men of having privileges, and for that accusation to go unchallenged.
- Women have the privilege of declaring false claims with society, including government, taking these claims seriously without any evidence to justify them.
- Women have the privilege of having female only media content and songs that promote women being in control and having the power in relationships without men being outraged (i.e.: Little Mix: Power - you're the man; But I got the, I got the, I got the power; You make rain; .. I make it shower;

You should know, I'm the one who's in control; I'll let you come take the wheel, long as you don't forget. This type of 'stuff' is being presented to children)

- Women have the privilege of never being labelled as "creepy" because they are attracted to a person who does not reciprocate.
- Women have the privilege of touching a colleague of the opposite sex without the risk of being accused of sexual assault.
- Women have the privilege of being consistently represented in a positive manner on television, and cannot be shown as the dummy spouse in advertising commercials.
- Women have the privilege of being the secondary breadwinner in a household, or the choice of a stay at home spouse, and still be respected by society.
- Women have the privilege of the definition of equality having a pro-women bias.
- Women have the privilege of the definition of sexism applying only to women.
- Women have the privilege of refusing a male physician to examine them, without their request being seen as sexist.
- Women have the privilege of Female only short-lists when applying for political office or other career opportunities.
- Women have the privilege of Female only short-lists when applying for promotions within certain companies.
- Women have the privilege of companies being offered government incentives to employ women for a more diverse workforce.
- Women have the privilege of the existence of the U.N. Ambassador for Women.

- Women have the privilege of mainstream media spouting lies and hogwash statistics which portray all women as perpetual victims and all men as perpetual villains.
- Women have the privilege of mainstream media spouting lies and deceit about the mythical wage gap between men and women without any account for lifestyle choices being part of the debate.
- Women have the privilege of being paid the same as a man for less work at the same job.
- Women have the privilege of sexualisation of men and boys being excused while sexualisation of women and girls is demonized.
- Women have the privilege of not being reprimanded as children for acting in their nature.
- Women have the privilege of not being reprimanded for acting in their nature, whereas men are demonised and their reputation ruined.
- Women have the privilege of not being coerced at universities into taking anti-rape courses.
- Women have the privilege of free entry into many nightclubs and bars, where men have to pay.
- Women have the privilege of not having their motives questioned when they play with children in public or private spaces.
- Women have the privilege of being far less likely to become homeless and far less likely to stay homeless.
- Women have the privilege of being given free stuff because someone finds them attractive.
- Women have the privilege of being considered the most valuable gender -. (when a ship is sinking it's women and children first in the lifeboats).

- Women have the privilege of having their sensitive feelings considered at all times, and their emotional needs and depth being considered greater than that of men.
- Women have the privilege of their voice or claims being taken more seriously than those of men.
- Women have the privilege of never being expected to do hard manual labour.
- Women have the privilege of it being socially acceptable to be deceptive about their level of attractiveness.
- Women have the privilege of positive body image standards (fat acceptance) allowing them to now compare themselves to plus sized female models, so that they do not have to feel intimidated by having to live up to Hollywood's ideal standards.
- Women have the privilege of objectifying men without men being offended.
- etc...etc...etc.

It would seem as though these privileges have to be removed and government should work towards abolishing these cultural abnormalities so equality can become a true reality. It is true that some if these privileges are truly sickening and sexist to the male of the species, especially those that are experimenting on boys to emasculate them because of some delusional belief system; I cannot believe this is being allowed to happen in an 'alleged' civilised society – it is most definitely child abuse and those responsible need to be held accountable.

More than any time in history the man is becoming the victim of domestic violence (verbal more than physical) because of the distasteful approach used to unfairly judge the man as being the aggressor and the women as being the nurturer. People still live in a culture where the woman can justify her actions and point the finger of blame to the male using 'crocodile victim tears' to influence third parties. It is why more men than in history are not settling in relationships and choosing to live the single life and more women are feeling lonely and depressed. The data also reveals men are put-off by the intimidation of Western women, supported and sponsored by political correctness gone mad giving men little benefit of the doubt or fairness in legal or work circles, that they are looking towards Asia and the East to find love and happiness where their voice and opinion matters in family life. Many women say these men are looking for a woman to be subservient, but, the truth is men do not mind discussion and debate plus have no problem with equality in the home and work; but, that is not what has happened in the West.

The balance has shifted to give superiority to the women is all walks of life that makes men apprehensive about Western women. Unfortunately, most men and women do not realise the problem until a relationship that they have put everything into goes sour. It is especially poignant when children are involved and the father realises that he is little more than financial support with the mother holding all the cards besides the legal system and government promoting such culture. And many mothers eventually realise the problem later in life when they account for the decisions they have made.

With the balance shifting so quickly, Western women are struggling to control their own negative attributes and are completely ignorant of their own actions; a realisation has to be made that men have had thousands of years to gain some control of their negative attributes. In the last 30 years, women are not on par with men in society, but have advantages over them in private and working life; women and men need to realise that so much change in such a short period of time leads to complacency over the correct and reasonable ways to behave. Some women who are honest with themselves know the power they have in society to control other men and ruin their lives. Systems need to be amended to ensure that advantages and privileges for women are removed from all areas of society and ensure that women are treated on par with men so that 'crocodile tears' or 'crying the victim' or 'thought that the mother is the best parent for children' does not favour the gender. Controls have to be in place to prevent any further dilution of family values, emasculation of boys and men; and the removal of discipline for children by their mothers due to society condoning the absence of real father figures.

Men need to have to courage and self-respect to tell their wives or girlfriends that equality is all about mutual respect and debate not about control and men should demand equal say in home, work and family life. This should also be made clear before the start of any serious relationship, preferably before any children are conceived, to ensure their other-half understands that control is shared not given. Men need to make it perfectly clear that if society and women in working life ignores (does not consider) female hormone imbalances as an issue that affects attitude, personality or performance, then it should take no part in private or family life. Thus, the wife / girlfriend need to reign in 'the craziness' (sorry hard-core feminists, but you admit it to each other, but, never to a man); and those delightful few days every month were moods and anger take over female actions should disappear from proceedings besides being an unacceptable form of interaction in the future. To coincide with this, government, health services, authorities and other political ideological movements should concede that the advantages and status of women has been given too higher priority in society based on unproven and unsound rationale. Hence, the laws/rules of society need to change to balance the inequitable manner in which legislation and rules have favoured the female of the species over the last 30 years (or more). These should be voted for by the majority in the country not just people in the government.

This notwithstanding, there needs to be an acceptance that there are fundamental differences between males and females of the species just like all others in the animal kingdom. Thus, equality means taking all things into consideration and putting systems in place to suit these differences. It does denote the understanding that there are certain needs and infirmities females have that males do not and society has to depart from confining to liberal ideologies where science and biology is ignored and only one side of the story can be told. Likewise, there are various character behaviours caused by testosterone that males are at mercy to – this thing we know as nature. Unfortunately, the human race completely dismisses nature when it is not in their advantage to accept the constraints about their own person or the biological effects on behaviour.

To coincide with the problems of emasculating men and over nurturing them by mother (and modern day new age fathers), society has to realise that men are just as vulnerable to their mental health being affected by influences beyond their control. More so, are more vulnerable than women of doing something out of character when something affects their "heart" (so to speak). Emasculating boys and masculating girls at a young age does not stop nature from lashing out later in life, and perhaps this new age thinking (by mostly feminist women in political positions) is causing more problems than what it is intended to solve. Just look at the overpopulated prison systems and the number of severe crimes being committed by both genders/sexes; something is definitely wrong with this new age thinking and continuing down the same path is a mark of insanity.

There is one phenomenon that is abundantly clear, all those fighting the feminist cause in the West, please take a look at all the advantages and privilege you currently have and realise that these have to be removed for 'true' equality to become reality and stop presenting false claims. Understand the ideological cause being fought for simply does not exist anymore in the West, so 'stop with the whining and grow-up thus act more mature and intelligent; and stop perpetrating child abuse to confuse who children are to suit your outlandish ideological cause' or better relocate to Asia, African or the Middle East where you can actually do some good!

'The real culprit is modern day men and women. We are simply not suited to playing games with one another anymore, and there is good reason for this. In the past, we were allowed to verbally abuse the post office worker (etc.) without fear of prosecution; and people were allowed to defend themselves and property from anyone, including children, without the police coming to arrest you. We were allowed to shout at and punish our children without being followed home and persecuted by social services; men were allowed to have a voice at home and within relationships; and we were allowed to hate whatever country we were at war with. Today of course none of this is possible. We must welcome our foes into our midst with open arms and big signs insist that we remain calm when presented with gross stupidity and incompetence from those in charge. And if our children misbehave we must give them money, gadgets and a few sweets so they do not tell the authorities that we have 'told them off'.

It all sounds like utopia, but, of course the human being has a temper; it has an aggressive streak. It likes to put a cloak over whom and what it is and disregard common sense and intelligence at will; and ignore nature because it thinks it is better than all else. Nevertheless, when nature catches up, when systems put in place that people blindly follows fail, very bad thing happen because we ignore the things that is most obvious. We are just another species of life on earth and have all the same faults and flaws as all the others. Furthermore, if we do not allow nature to flourish in our own bodies and minds in a natural way and not consented to live in a civilised society that allows natural tendencies to be satisfied in a controlled way with constraints and discipline put in place from being young, then disaster is around the corner for all.' – Author

Financial Security and Responsibility

It has been long known that due to poor education attainment, many people choose to have children for the addition social security and housing that the government provides; to the extent that large families equals better financial benefits, especially for single mothers. This unfortunately leads to large communities which have 'grown-up' used to being unemployed and having a very comfortable life living off benefits along with attracting people from foreign lands to take advantage of the benefits system. Granted the system has very recently changed with the introduction of the universal credit, but, there is still a perception that there is a comfortable life for those who do not benefit society in general at the expense for those who work hard in society (obviously those who are wealthy and business owners generate their own wealth at the expense of all tax payers).

Financial security needs to be provided for those who lose their jobs or fall sick; including those on retirement who need a decent income. This type of financial security is provided to people who have themselves contributed for a large period of time to the benefits in society, or who for a short period of time need financial help in times of need. To guarantee this type of security for the future, costs need to be controlled and those who have abused the benefits system taken to task; this does include employers, landlords and utility companies who takes advantage of their position for their own financial gain and the wealthiest in society who take advantage of lobbying techniques, tax breaks and non-Dom status; thus, pushes up the social security bills. This is a total and complete failure of the current system with not taking to account the greed of others, and allowing third parties to take advantage of what is a disorganised and inept system, but, also a system that politicians of all parties are comfortable with due to their and their parties own gains and benefits.

Rent costs have to be controlled and reduced on behalf of tenants who need to claim housing benefit to retain some elements of savings. Government agreement with utility companies and minimum wage levels have to be more in line with the cost of living levels and therefore reduce the strain on benefits budgets; this needs to be completed within regions of the country as cost of living varies between regions.

In essence, the social security system should reward those who contribute. Therefore, for those who are not in work there needs to be an easier method to prove they deserve the additional financial help, moreover, giving benefits without the individual giving back to society has to be a system and a way of life left in the past. There needs to be tailored training programmes for long term unemployed in partnership with local and national businesses, not paid for by the tax payer, but issued as an I.O.U. directed at the individual and reimbursed to partners once a career opportunity has been offered and accepted. This will enable individuals to obtain the necessary knowledge and skills they lack to serve them in the future when they obtain work in an industry that interests them. The identified lack of knowledge and skills should then be used to improve future education systems to ensure that young adults and children are given a diverse range of learning to find their own niche in life.

If, however, an individual does not follow through on the opportunities given, then a constructive placement to match current known aspirations will be offered as a last resort before benefits are removed – this needs to be a hard line given to all claimants. Obviously continued support will be given, but, financial support will only be re-introduced if the individual is shown to give value to themselves and thus society. Above all else this system, which will take a number of years to action, should give a better deal for the unemployed, individuals which the education system have failed, and for working people who currently begrudge people who do not benefit society receiving financial support from taxpayers on a long term basis.

A difficult area to discuss surrounds disability and the social security system has to continue to support many disabled people who live independently, and ensure the system continues to treat sick and disabled people with dignity. But, there needs to be a 'grown-up' debate within the country about what life will be had by taking to term babies with severe disabilities. It is clear that termination of life to many people is repugnant, and quite right. But, people being responsible and intelligent should consider the impact a severe disability has not only on the individual themselves for their entire life but on the people who support them. Like most people I have come into contact with, if I had an accident which led me to be trapped inside my own body or mind, much like a severely disabled person, I would want someone to end the suffering even being fully aware of the continued medical advances which might ease the symptoms in the future. Part of the decision is because it is hard enough life when fully abled and independent, but, most because being alive in that condition is no life at all and the burden and mental strain placed on people around me is suffering that I have no wish to cause.

Whether anyone likes it or not, ending a lifetime of suffering before a foetus gains consciousness has to be considered as the most humane path for all parties involved. This type of decision also has religious connotations, where belief in God causes additional suffering, stress and pain, Any parent who wishes their child to live helpless and trapped clearly has no love or compassion (bravery and courage to love a child no matter what, is considering 'your' feelings only, not the feelings or life of the child) and has forced suffering on the child for purely selfish and ideological reasons, which all people would not put any other species of life through no matter how emotionally attached they are to them.

It is clear that established government with the continued raising of the retirement age has little interest in the older generation enjoying a secure retirement, moreover, a 'work-till-you-drop' scheme appears to be operating in the hope that the majority of the workforce will die before claiming a pension. But, older people have contributed all their lives to society and thus help build a country for future generations besides people deserve to enjoy life after giving up most of it working; in essence, the government needs to respect the contribution made by the older generation. So it is justified and fair to provide a sustainable pension which should be eligible for claiming at a reasonable age. Pension values need to increase in-line with inflation levels and transparency is needed to enable people to have time to plan for changes in circumstances. Moreover, the justification of raising the retirement age to keep the pension system affordable is for accountancy reasons valid; however, the decisions regarding the population numbers have been made by the few in government with continued promises of controlling population numbers falling short, it should not be the majority of people and the elderly who faces the burden of such decisions. Therefore, the retirement age needs to be reduced from present levels to ~55-60 for both men and women and any shortfall in pension funds to be strengthened by higher taxation on the wealthiest in society, including defence contractors and large corporate businesses, which have benefitted from the high numbers of people in the country.

In addition, pension schemes for politicians need to be reassessed so only long term officials have the ability to claim full state pension, second homes for politicians need to be scrapped, and expenses rules tightened all of which should assist in providing a decent pension settlement for all. Private pension schemes are a major issue and many in the 2008 recession fell victim to retirement rip-offs. There needs to be greater support and proper guidance for people to avoid mis-selling, hence, private pension schemes need to provide constraint limits on what people will receive irrespective on how the markets behave.

Davos Meeting

I have to cringe and question how people accepts / puts-up with inequality in the world when I see important leaders and the super wealthy meeting in Davos to discuss the problem of the global economy. If the richest 1% of the people are in attendance and there is no one from any working class background or from a poorer background, what interest do these wealthy people, who rely on money flowing up the pyramid and taking money from the majority through government legislation, have in changing their own habits to make the economies of the world work for everybody. The sad truth is they do not want the change their status in the world or share any of their wealth; history has taught society that the richest 1% in the world will never change in their greed and never wish to use their wealth to bring a massive difference in the quality of life for all. These decisions made a Davos are concerned with ensuring the wealth of the people in attendance, whilst keeping the poorest in society pacified and in acceptance of their status; it is the main reason why government leaders are in attendance – to discuss how the 1% are going to continue using the pyramid scheme (flow of money to them) in light of current world events.

People should not respect any government leaders who attend this annual event. People need a government who respects democracy and uses the strengths of a societal system, i.e. capitalism, to ensure everyone fairly benefits from it and not just a privileged few, i.e. the pyramid should be 'knocked down' and the people at the top should be forced to earn their status and respect and not be given it by default.

Issues Surrounding Housing

The country is facing its biggest housing crisis, with the lowest levels of house building in peacetime since the 1920s. It has been clear for some time that housing supply is not keeping up with demand and the migrant crisis only adds to the problem of providing homes for people. There are substantial amounts of poor housing available that research has shown has a direct impact of resident's health, educational attainment and the ability to find decent interesting work. As the demand for good housing is high, the real estate business has seen it fit to increase the prices of housing beyond most people's affordability bracket. Young adults have been the hardest hit with most being priced out of home ownership. With house building now belonging to a few private businesses, fewer affordable homes are being built and people are facing poor standards in renting sector. Everyone should be able to live an independent life in a secure home and the current plan is to build more homes to give young people the aspiration for home ownership in the future.

But there is a problem with this plan, with more housing denotes more estates, more estates comes less green land and wooded areas, less green land means more air pollution and greater levels of flooding, more pollution means more health issues, more health issue means more human suffering and greater pressures on support services, more pressures on support services means higher taxation and privatisation, higher taxes means more poverty, more poverty means more human suffering, and so on and so forth. People have to understand that land and resources are limited and have to grasp the notion of living within our means. The housing crisis has been born out of population numbers spiralling out of control and building more homes is only a 'sticky-plaster' which invariably will make the problems in society worse as the real problem is ignored. The problem is the lack of responsibility for the future wellbeing of children. People ignore the problems of population increases on resources, standard of living, salary expectations and health resources, without even considering the impacts on nature and wildlife. Building more homes is not the solution to a problem that our children and their children will have to deal with.

Instead a programme of house improvement needs to be actioned to replace those homes that are not environmentally friendly and produce high quality homes which are energy efficient. Greater powers need to be given to local government to identify those industrial units and empty housing that have been unused for a period of time and give permission to develop them into new housing, if appropriate. Moreover, instead of building new housing on green land, green land needs to be protected and expanded to counteract the impacts of air pollution and help bring back the natural environment. Existing and new cities need a program of being 'in tune' with nature (Garden cities) using the example of Singapore as the foundation of the works needed to be accomplished. Furthermore, there needs to be stringent and strict education and family planning laws to assist in population control to ensure the population numbers does not exceed the housing availability. At present, parents and government are completely ignoring the independence of young adults and not considering the future housing opportunities for their children to start a family, with both sides pointing the finger at each other. This cannot be allowed to continue. How about people being responsible for their own choices/actions and decisions and cease being ignorant as to the long term impacts on the environment and quality of life that their children will have.

Homelessness

The value of society can be assessed by the amount of people living rough through homelessness, which is also a symptom of a strained housing system. The cost of housing and the pressures of home life have forced many people to move out of their family home and onto the streets with little support availability to help those in need. How in a society where there is so much wealth, so many 'nice to have' projects being completed by local governments and national government alike, does society have homeless people? It is unfortunately a result of people not caring about others, and is directly driven by government and their wealthy associates! This is a cold harsh reality; homelessness is a prime example of how the wealthy in society has no interest in the poor; and how governments are not really working for the best interests of the people who live here.

This notwithstanding, homelessness is not just economic in nature; the problem has social ramifications too that are sometimes outside the control of the individual or family concerned. The solution, due to society functioning on economic values, does require financial support and political acumen. The problem is confounded by other policies that require government to provide homes for migrants and refugees whilst no responsibility is sought to house people for whom life has found themselves on the street. Even royalty has the resources, facilities and the ability to remove homelessness from the streets on London, but, chooses not to; apparently the homeless are used by the royals for publicity only. Thus, the root cause of homelessness and rough sleeping is multifaceted and known to social services, but, the will of the people in the country is not directed at 'stamping' out the problem. People do not trust others, and there is a stigma attached to people who beg on the street. Until people begin to hold the authorities to account, homelessness will continue and with the current housing crisis the problem will increase. These are human beings who think they have no other option but to live like 'rats' on the street. All people should all be ashamed of ourselves, especially those who have the resources and financial acumen to do something about it without affecting lifestyle choices.

Every local government needs to have a department specifically designed to direct resources to solving homelessness in their area. Part of the responsibilities should be the ability and authority to redirect funds from 'nice to have' projects (which there are always many) to providing homes and additional support to people who have found themselves homeless to help them 'out of the gutter'. Greater transparency of accounts in local government are needed to reduce the problem of 'fat cats' in higher management and 'jollies' private companies offer management staff in return for business deals, to ensure money is available for much needed programmes to solve real societal problems, such as homelessness.

$$\bigcirc \quad 7 \quad \bigcirc$$

RESPONSIBLE HEALTH CARE

One of the greatest and most useful social programmes and organisations setup anywhere in the world is in the UK; the National Health Service (NHS) together with care services and other public services make up the essential fabric of UK society. Before the NHS, poor people often lived without medical treatment and relied on dubious remedies or the charity of doctors; this often led to people not being able to work for long periods of time, long term suffering and early death. These types of symptoms are still in existence today not only in third world countries but also in well developed countries; where the health care system is seen as a business to maximise profit for owners and shareholders at the expense of individuals' debt where the poorest or the ones with prevalent medical conditions are denied health insurance and left to suffer.

The conception of the NHS appeared at a time when the UK saw health care as crucial to the reconstruction of the country after the Great War and was seen as the corner stone of a civilised society. It began in it fullness in 1948 when people were hardened and disciplined by war. The NHS's organisation was so successful it became one of the greatest national institutions. So much so that people rely on these types of health care facilities to be able to live secure and fulfilling lives and businesses could now cope better with employees taking only short term absences due to illness or injuries.

However, since the end of World War 2 people have become less accustomed to austerity and less disciplined in taking care of their own health that what was once a well organised system is now befalling to the point of saturation because of its own success. The plan for the NHS was to expand or contract in size to account for population variables; what was not seen was the irresponsible nature of people in the future or how the culture of the country would begin the change in such a short period of time. The extent of the problem is now affecting the NHS's ability to manage patient numbers, its huge budget constraints, and patients are finding it increasingly difficult to get the care they need. The NHS is now so inefficient that some patients who could have been treated so as to lead fuller lives are now being diagnosed with life threatening diseases further down the line due to waiting lists or even die before they are seen by a medical expert.

The strain on the health care system throughout the West is woefully apparent. The number of prescription drugs people are taking, all issued by doctors, to cope with everyday life is incredible, which has now led to antibiotic resistant bacteria that could plunge humans back into the 17th century (medically speaking); and with the power of influence pharmaceutical companies have over the government, they do not have any incentive to research new antibiotics unless the government gives them what they want. It would seem as though, like the arms dealers (those which are marketed as defence contractors) and petrochemical companies, the government and the majority of people are being held hostage to private companies with maximising profit as their bottom line / priority above all else, including human life.

This notwithstanding, there is another problem with the NHS other than those who interact with the system externally; it comes under a shared heading of management and leadership for governance. It is clear that without competent managers there is nobody to lead an organisation or set priorities. With weak 'poor quality' leadership emanates an increase in management hierarchy and bureaucracy. The same errors in judgement, which led to incompetent managers being in charge in the first place, more additional managers are employed with more bureaucracy added, etc. etc., all with smooth talkers in suits attempting to manage various departments knowing that the problem is beyond their abilities to solve. At the point where the management structure became too heavy for the organisation to support on current budgetary constraints, the politicians became involved and with them numerous monitoring organisations and think tanks befell prominent. However, with the poor quality politicians and a management structure, which is too complicated to fully understand how the NHS functions, and introducing KPI's without understanding the problem inevitably increases the risk of medical experts missing patient symptoms. Thus, increasing the possibility of greater health risks to individuals who could have made a full recovery if a competent well organised and structured NHS were still in existence.

Due to the misunderstanding of the management structure of the NHS and a lack of knowledge as to how the system functions, NHS managers are paid significant amounts of money to entice the best into these roles in an attempt to solve some of the functional problems. Unfortunately, living in a time were ability and skills come second or third to smooth talking; what happens is someone who looks good in a suit and can talk in a 'professional manner' (those who are 'yes' people and who follow to the letter written documents) are employed who can then hide in the complexity of the structure and continue to employ people below them in an attempt to take care of their responsibilities. The outcome leads to overblown employment with costs caused by internal bad decisions spiralling out of control. These cost are then added to the costs from external interactions, e.g. patients who don't take care of their own health, issues with inbreeding due to cultural differences, drugs (alcohol, cigarettes, class drugs, etc.), dramatic increase in population numbers, etc.; which create a health care system that is about ready to implode on itself due to consecutive and sequential bad decisions by successive governments.

It very similar to a balloon, there is an optimal pressure to which to inflate, at this pressure the balloon reaches a state of optimal quality and robustness; further pressure places strain on the balloon's external walls and becomes a weaker boundary to the pressures from within. At some internal pressure the boundary becomes too weak that it explodes and is no longer useful with shards of the balloon's wall on the floor and walls. The NHS has now been at critical pressure for several years.

The growing number of managers, foreign and agency staff, and non-executive directors are reaching on for three times the rate for doctors over the last decade, and five times the rate of increase for nurses in the recent years. The NHS is funded by over a £100 billion a year and if the NHS was a country, it would be the thirtieth largest in the world and is current lead by est. 45,000 managers. It produced a 28% rise in manager numbers between 1997 and 2010. The numbers are still rising and some argue that it is still undermanaged (ONS, 2010); with substantial time being spent by medical professionals (doctors and nurses) completing bureaucracy created by managers to resolve efficiency issues. From the last available reports on the area bureaucracy accounts for ~£80 billion of NHS spending as 'pen-pushers' (Hansard (House of commons) 2010-11); (what? More time spent filling in forms than taking care of patients; this is meant to improve efficiency? I think the bureaucracy is there to protect the NHS from being sewed in the legal system rather than improve health care!).

The burden of regulation is another major instance where concentration of medical professionals are redirected to focussing on satisfying regulation from numerous different regulators, auditors, inspectorates and accreditation agencies whose numbers have grown over the past decade with some large additions e.g. Care Quality Commission, the foundation trust regulator monitor, and the National Institute for Health and Clinical Excellence. These are in essence highly expensive 'quangos' that are financed by government but are supposedly independent of it. It is really hard to argue that significant parts of the NHS are bureaucratic 'nightmares' that feeds the regulatory machine to be transparent on performance data, drive accountability and improve quality – which all comes at a cost that the NHS now can no longer support. The question is why when successive governments introduce ever more regulatory bodies, do they criticise the NHS for bureaucracy? Could it be because of the incompetence of MPs not understanding the problems associated with the NHS that they themselves are responsible for the increase in inefficiency and poor patient care due to form filling.

The interesting statistic throughout the entire data gathering within the NHS is there is no accurate data on administration and management costs within general practice. Although plenty of data about front line costs, including mental health and ambulance services, exist even though management cost should be one of the easiest data sets to collect as they should not vary with daily demand – so why is this data not readily available or merely estimated? One of the unfortunate truths to come from numerous reports from the national audit office is comparable to what has been said earlier that savings and efficacy of practice can be achieved by improving procurement of management, back-office estates and functions by concentrating on the skills and abilities needed for the positions. Justification for these conclusions come from numerous accounts of remarkable management failures in recent years involving paediatric surgery deaths, outbreaks of hospital acquired infections and awful patient care across all disciplines. The increase in these reports is the possible reason why government has increased the number of regulatory bodies in attempt to present to the public a strategy to improve care. However, the result has been a redirection of resources away from patient care to form filling, costing the NHS more and incurring negative effects on resolving some of the issues with even more 'smooth talkers' being employed within the management culture of the NHS.

There have been two major government initiatives to improve the efficiency and quality of care; these have been an IT project and a restructuring strategy, which have both been a complete disaster. The investment in IT infrastructure was orchestrated by a past labour government (2002), which was sold as the biggest civilian IT project of its kind in the world and had already cost the tax payer well over £12.7billion before the following coalition government (Conservatives and LibDems) dismantled it and replaced it with cheaper regional initiatives with control being in local hospital hands. The cost of this would have paid for an additional 60,000 fully trained nurses for a decade and is commonly remembered by those who took notice as the most egregious example of incompetence and waste ever seen throughout the globalised world.

The conservatives generated the 2012 Health and Social Care Act, which saw a major restructure of how the NHS is funded and paved the way for private firms to take over much of the running of the health services or even its privatisation. The cost of the restructure cost over est. £3billion and has caused profound damage to the NHS (details of which is beyond the scope of this book). The Act as far as I am concerned appears to be 'unintelligible gobbledygook' that somehow and in some way got approved (which just goes to illustrate how politicians 'stick together' for possible promotion; or due to benefiting from lobbyists or private interests; or through fear of being deselected at the next election); with all politicians involved seemingly crawling back under a rock and remained silent ever since. Although, all private businesses involved in both disasters made lots of money out of something that most intelligent people with common sense could have seen to be a failure before any money was spent; it would be very interesting to see whether there is any association between contracts awarded to businesses and MPs personal interests.

This notwithstanding, this gave a massive boost to private health care interests to the extent that the only method to acquire good, decent health care is to go through the private sector, with some NHS funding being redirected, as with patients, to private clinics as per government recommendations.

Whilst the rise in failures of management transpired; through the back-door private sector health care services increased that began a disturbing trend which as of today is comparable to the American system. Most NHS senior doctors and surgeons are working both within the private sector as well as within the NHS, as they delegate their NHS patients to junior doctors – there is more money to be made working for the private sector. Front line leadership has in effect been reduced due to better 'carrots' being taken advantage of by senior frontline leadership. Although politicians are aware of and condone the practice it has been largely ignored even though priorities are redirected from primary care to making more money; there is in essence no real strong frontline leadership and thus public care within the NHS is negatively affected.

Concurrently, due to lack of UK born medical professionals and to save money, agency staff is employed throughout all sectors of the NHS some of whom cannot speak a good level of English and lack social interaction skills; and some who are paid more than their NHS employed counterparts. Imagine working with someone on the same level who has a better contract and paid more than you along with senior leadership handing down their responsibilities so they themselves can earn more money in the private sector; would it really persuade you to be 'gung-ho' working in a high pressure environment or would it indeed breed resentment and a view to 'just come in, do work and go home', which in patient care is the exact opposite of what is needed. The problem has best been summed up by Turnbull James:

'However enticing in a pressured environment, the fantasy that getting the right leader in place will be enough to change the system, is

untenable. The healthcare context requires people who do not identify with being a leader to engage in leadership.

Leadership must be exercised across shifts 24/7 and reach to every individual: good practice can be destroyed by one person who fails to see themselves as able to exercise leadership, as required to promote organisational change, or who leaves something undone or unsaid because someone else in supposed to be in charge. The NHS needs people to think of themselves as leaders not because that are personally exceptional, senior or inspirational to others, but because they can see what needs doing and can work with others to do it' (Turnbull James, 2011).

To add to the internal issues, the government have enforced a junior doctors contract (October 2016), which will force junior doctors to work exceptionally long hours and some weekends for a seven day NHS. Meaning that patients will be seen by an over tired, over worked, over stressed doctor(s) that will inevitably make mistakes in diagnosis and treatment; who feels they are taking the strain of work whilst the leadership are taking home the 'cream' from secondments in the private sector. In addition to no government official considering the cost of the change, costs of operating the NHS will increase over annual budgetary increases.

Looking at the general practitioners' level, there is now a disturbing and inefficient practice being undertaken. Not only is it next to impossible to acquire an appointment in the same day or within a few days of initial contact, which unfortunately has the negative affect of people taking upon themselves to go to the nearest clinic or hospital to be seen, but the IT system takes priority for doctors when diagnosing symptoms from patients. Instead of talking to patients and conducting a preliminary examination, concentration is on ensuring the form on the computer is completed during the consultation process. Additionally, I know this is a taboo subject, but more and more GPs are difficult to communicate with and understand besides possess below than average English language skills; and there is in some regional areas a general consensus that people from certain cultures, migrant or religious backgrounds take priority in waiting times – why is this opinion there? To add to these issues there are discussions to charge people to see GPs even though people already pay for the services through wages at best two times over throughout their lifetime.

The NHS is struggling with staffing issues; the overreliance on foreign workers is a direct indication of an institute that for one reason or another is not attracting British people in what should be a very admirable profession. Accident and emergency (A&E) is in serious trouble, with more people facing long waits for tests and treatments, and the public are confused about what the A&E department should actually be used for, i.e. not to be used to bypass waiting lists of GPs.

Increasing the tax revenues and the amount of funding available to the NHS is only a good idea if the targets are to make the richest in society pay more for the benefit of everyone in conjunction with additional funding from those companies and businesses who sell unhealthy products or who are responsible for above average pollution factors; obviously, without affecting the price of their goods to the public. However, additional taxation for all will only increase the pressures on the public and further damage peoples own health state and thought processes. As a result, the improvement to services will only hold for a very short period of time before the quality of service reduces again due to the increase of people who further damages their own body in their attempt to forget about the misery of life.

Most politicians to get elected will promise a GP appointment within 48hours and on the same day for those who need it. This notwithstanding, the current population numbers and the number of GPs along with people who are not using common sense or not taking care of themselves, the harsh reality is this is not possible. The simple solution would be to employ more GPs, but this does not resolve the root causes of the problem and will surely make the budget more difficult to manage if not impossible and therefore will increase taxation on all. Instead, government should set in place strict guidelines and rules regarding personal health care and advice for people to follow on decisions regarding possible GP visits. For <u>convenience</u> basic diagnosis for illness or injury should be educated as part of the fixed curriculum at schools and colleges.

Next, society has an uneasy relationship between pharmaceutical companies, doctors, GPs, and patients. Every time a visit to the GP, every time a new prescription, it is the same for a trip to the hospital were one of the first items on offer is some form of 'pill'. People often say, "I'll just go to the doctors and get some painkillers or antibiotics or blood thinners etc. and it'll be fine". The situation has become so ingrained that many people in society believe that they can continue to abuse their bodies because medicine can alleviate the effects (people know now the overuse of antibiotics is on the verge of creating bacteria that are immune; if this transpires, all people are in big trouble). This creates a false sense of feeling and false sense of mind/body connection that not only feeds the greed of pharmaceutical companies but makes taking medicine a normal part of life with little or no consideration of what the long term effects of the behaviour or the medicine will have. The problem is similar to energy, people have become addicted to easy fixes on demand without thinking about the repercussions until the damage has been done and it is too late to change.

Additionally, there is a problem with political correctness within the health services, with substantial patients suffering ill health because medical professionals are urged not to be honest with people about their lifestyles in case they offend or upset anyone and increase the risk of legal action. Substantial time and funds are spent tackling the effects of obesity, drink and drugs without any preventative actions, as being truthful and firm with the patients can, and most likely will in the modern day of being offended by everything and anything, cause problems for the doctor when complaints are raised and investigation is pursued by the quangos. Medicine and substantial visits to NHS services is not a permanent solution to problems caused by people ignoring their own responsibility for their own health.

This is why society has a problem: for example, when people visit a doctor, the doctor cannot be frankly honest, instead they have to sugar coat the problem to ensure the patient does not become offended or upset. The doctor cannot say for instance, you have a massive problem with having too much fatty content in your body, you weight too much, you do very little exercise therefore your joints are not being lubricated properly and is the reason why your heart muscle is weak. If a doctor said something similar to this today, not only would the patient take offence, but the odds are the doctor would be suspended from practice due to complaints and chances are they will be removed from practicing altogether.

The sad reality is, the human body is design to be moving most of the active day; however, modern Western society and working practice is structured for people to work in offices, which promotes people sitting down barely moving for the majority of the day, consequently, this contributes to health issues facing people. Parents also put their children at risk of health problems when they are older by letting them become addicted to games consoles and spending money on expensive brand names for 'sweet stuff', e.g. Biscuits, crisps, sweets, etc.; but, choose not to buy real healthy food, including vegetables, because their children refuse to eat it besides use the excuse that healthy food is expensive to buy. It would seem like the new age parenting does not allow for real parenting to enter proceedings due to parents wanting to be their child's best friend, wanting gadgets to babysit and the fear of being reported to social services by their own children. The modern children's diet and lack of exercise (due to being addicted to games consoles) tends to lead to health problems when the children are older.

Moreover, medical academics and/or 'experts' need to stop creating new conditions or disorders for their 5 minutes of fame. Every time a new medical 'buzz-word' is created, flocks of people immediately begin to suffer with the symptoms described. This is especially poignant when debating potential solutions to long standing societal problem. It causes substantial distractions to solving real social problems, such as drug addiction, and promotes unhealthy directives, such as fat acceptance, or excuses such as slow metabolisms (good grief!) to avoid people facing their problems 'head on'. Truth should not be something people should shy away from; nor should people be offended by someone who uses all or some of their senses to observe and state facts; nor should society promote a unhealthy lifestyle because people are too lazy to keep themselves in shape; nor should people use racism or sexism as an excuse when someone states the obvious that is in fact based on truth. If people get offended or upset by the truth, then tough, people are offended by you because of a number of **real** reasons!

The older generation are the ones who seem to suffer the most with poor health care including: loneliness (due to family members working to take care of their own immediate family and thus lack of time to visit elderly relatives leading to isolation), insecurity (financial, failing sensory inputs, and shrinking social networks) and exclusion (from decent housing, public transport, local amenities, and common consumer goods) – yes folks unless something significantly changes in society these are the issues people who are fortunate enough to live a long life have to look forward to in old age. This growing social crunch is another big challenge the country (if not the world) has to face. In their infinite wisdom, successive governments have progressively cut from the budgets that pay for adult social care and piled on the pressure for earning a living wage for people who are at working age; leading to fewer older people receiving vital care services whilst concurrently the number of older people in need of care is rising.

The Western society on the whole prides itself on a civilised way in which people live and public services are a measure of the decency of our society; but at the same time the government due to economic pressures are peddling a different message: 'Once you are passed being useful in work, you become a burden to society. As a burden you are no longer a relevant priority as you add nothing positive to society. Therefore, to maintain civil calm you will be given a pension, which government will continue to tax, but concentration will be for social care for people who add benefit to the economic prosperity of the country.' The decisions government has made in recent times regarding the elderly can only be described as a method which the government can preserve the pension funds and redirect them to some other cause, i.e. increasing retirement age to the average age people survive ($\sim$ 75 year). This means the vast majority of people will not live long enough to enjoy retirement and government purses will not be overstretched by the burden of pensions. The question is what exactly does this say about government and society on the whole as to how human life is valued?

In addition, the manner which the elderly are treated by public services is also called into question in recent times. Most elderly homes are now in control of private contractors who are managing the business for profit. As with all business, cuts to services and quality are made to make profit; and now care for the most vulnerable people in society are being faced with care that is being traded-off with profit margins. This means even in care homes the elderly are treated as a burden with care executed in the most cost effective manner, which does not prioritise fair treatment or a respectable ethos of service. (The question of why more elderly people are 'conveniently' placed in care homes is discussed in a later chapter.)

Cancer treatment is of the utmost concern; as early diagnosis is critical. Government should increase public awareness through education programmes and media outlets about the symptoms of cancer and ensure there is adequate training, resources and support available for GPs to identify cancer in the early stages. There are issues here regarding paranoia among individuals. The strategy that works to get governments elected or in referendums, i.e. fear factor, works against reducing waiting time and reducing budgets; people always look at worse case scenarios for the symptoms they are suffering with causing hysteria and panic. Likewise, with GPs being concerned about legal action on wrong diagnosis they arrange unnecessary tests and scans to put the patients mind at rest. However, scans direct radiation into a human body and radiation, through radio waves, is likely one of the factors that can cause cancer; perhaps people need to consider this when they routinely walk through body scanners at airports. There needs to be a coherent process to prevent any unnecessary radiation given to patients and a degree of protection offered to GPs.

The cost and availability of cancer drugs are also of great concern and there has to be a 'grown-up' debate on this issue. I am no medical expert, but have some experience with chemotherapy and would not go through the process personally. Seeing the physical and mental effect of this type of treatment invariably means that individuals are trapped inside their own body and house with little energy to do anything whilst hoping the 'poison' kills the cancer cells before it permanently damages any other organs; the odds are other than minor forms of cancer they will have to take pills or go for regular treatments even if the cancer is 'cured'. Those who are diagnosed with cancer should first look to see if any lifestyle changes can help the reduction or annihilation of the disease; for instance, a strict paleo diet and / or broccoli has had some success as it speeds up and improves the body's ability to remove dead blood cells, and cancer is dead blood cells that the body does not recognise as being dead due to a mutation (Disclaimer: this is not medical advice and you should do your own research on the area).

Medical experts will only offer what they are told to within their own internal processes and what is available through the health service. The health service has accounting to consider; as a result, some of the latest cancer treatments will never be available in the NHS due to cost. In an attempt to resolve this inhumane decision making and to be competitive in the global economy the government should take control of medical research and produce cancer treatments under the umbrella of a public organisation. Here then treatments can be developed, the research can be operated on a non-profit standing and all medicine developed can be readily available for use within the NHS system. As soon as the medical research organisation is commissioned and producing treatments, the NHS can begin the arduous task or cancelling contracts with private suppliers; in this way cost of medicine can be more controlled and discussions about 'how much is a life worth' reduced.

There should be education and a firm understanding of our own mortality, prolonging the suffering of someone is something all people should think of as a cruel act if it was for a family pet, but, not for people. Humans do not want to face our own mortality so people strive to keep someone alive, even if that someone wants to be at peace. It also leads a very uncomfortable question that our species have to face, "If someone is diagnosed terminal, is it right and ethical to divert resources for palatable care when the resource can be used for someone who has a chance to live a long life (society have to remember that the NHS is resource limited)."

If you have a terminal illness (or similar i.e. brain dead to which certain organs maybe used to save one or more lives) then you have to face death before your time (in some cases people are in this position due to their own bad habits and their abuse of their own body, harsh but true), prolonging the stress, the worry, and in some circumstances the pain and suffering is not in your or others best interest. Yes, you have been dealt a bad hand, but the sad truth is we are all mortal and will eventually die; it is part of the circle of life. By reading this you may think that I have not experienced any loved one go through this type of scenario - you would be wrong. I have seen the degradation of the person I knew, the mind goes first and then the body. The feeling of being trapped and helpless sets in concurrently with pain and endless restlessness causing nausea and weakness.

After a few months, the feeling of wanting to be at peace at the same time of being scared to die enters thoughts. Eventually, the person just wants it to be over one way or another and regrets the treatment to prolong life, as it turns out that living in a prison full of discomfort and pain is like being in hell, but, the medicine, the chemo, keeps the person alive in pain and suffering, until eventually after the months, sometimes years of suffering, and being imprisoned inside their own body, they die and it is not a peaceful death. Leaving behind loved ones who took care of them for months, maybe years, and whose future has been drastically affected by being involved in all the circumstances that surrounds the treatment and life of the sick loved one. All you really want to do is blame someone for the suffering the person endured; but the thing is and it is something no one wants to admit to themselves, not even medical experts, all people involved added to the pain and suffering of the person who died without strength or dignity and without any resemblance of the person they were before the illness. This is my opinion is the worst outcome for everyone.

Euthanasia is a subject that needs to be discussed more in detail in relation for preventing people suffering as they do now. People need to have the knowledge that no matter what happens in the world, you are born, you live and then you die; with the goal being living as long and fruitful life as you can and whilst your alive take care of yourself and not abuse your own body as abuse could lead to an early exit.

A wise man once said, "I do not worry about death, as I did not worry about life until I was born; I was at peace before as I will be after; only in life do I worry and feel pain there is no fear otherwise so why should I fear death." The main point is, if there is a chance of a normal life, cost of treatment should not be a constraint, however, if the diagnosis is terminal there should be discussions about the cost of and whether palliative care is the best treatment or whether the treatment is 'go and enjoy yourself like you have never done before, a last hurrah; and say goodbye to your friends and loved ones so they can remember you as you are' so you can leave this world in dignity. I know which one I would choose, and it would be the one where resources that would have been diverted to me are available for others who have a chance of life. I would have the greatest time ever with the little time I had available and visit all those did me wrong in the world who are still around and say goodbye in a unique fashion. It is everyone's responsibility to ensure the longevity of the health service and ensure that resources are available to those who need it the most, those with a chance of a long life.

The NHS was founded to take care of people who through no fault of their own are in ill health or injured; it was never created to treat people who abuse themselves, especially on a long term basis. The NHS cannot survive; indeed, no state operated service can survive with people abusing the service because of ignorance, laziness and personal abuse. There is only one clear and concise conclusion that I can come up with: ***The public along with the politicians are working concurrently and coherent together to place as much strain on the NHS as possible to force privatisation of all services; one party is doing it without consideration of the eventual outcome (patients) and the other is either too incompetent or secretly willing it to fail to privatise the service for lobbyist interests (politicians).***

The US system of health care has to be resisted, as I write this chapter there is deep seated talks of an additional tax for health care within political circles and the worrying situation is people are considering it as a solution. Irrespective, the only solutions to the problem is for people to take a good honest look at themselves; for medical professionals to be frank and honest with patients even if it means upsetting them; to introduce KPT's for the NHS leadership and management to remove majority of the waste within the management structure; and drastically reduce the sway pharmaceutical companies have with GPs and doctors and work towards reducing the usage of medicine in favour of natural remedies to alleviate symptoms, even if it means the patient has to work through laziness and addiction to become healthy.

There needs to be a full-fledged drive towards the prevention of privatising health services to ensure the NHS services are not de-established by competition and fragmentation. The start of this drive is to ensure that no NHS patient is transferred to private clinics for care, but, to ensure that the NHS in the patient's local area can provide the care needed.

The problem is how to acquire or develop the type of people needed to make the NHS work internally and remove the waste caused by bad decisions. This means that incompetent and easily bribed (sorry influenced) politicians should keep their distance; the NHS requires protection from 'where there is blame there is a claim' culture; and the vast majority of managers and directors within the NHS are required to vacate or justify their abilities in their positions (given a short time period to achieve KPTs). A vital component is to gain a full understanding of the current NHS structure before any changes are formulated and actioned.

Competition between hospitals for additional budgets has to cease, instead the services should be concentrated around patient care and their needs. Thus, the Health and Social Care Act requires to be redrafted restoring some demographic accountability for the NHS (having the elderly or disabled travel long distances for care is outrageous and needs to be prevented); current issues lead to the elderly staying at home because of the logistics, this causes their health to deteriorate and they end up in hospital or worse. The current system, which has been costly to implement, is far too fragmented and not designed for the growth in population or for more people living with chronic conditions or numerous needs. It is incredibly difficult to manage patient care if medical specialists are separated by demographic issues.

There needs to be a combined and coherent healthcare for all ailments (e.g. physical, mental, and social care), whereas the current system provides three separate systems that are very loosely coupled and work independently. The education and qualifications of doctors and nurses requires to be amended to account for a whole person approach to ensure a single concurrent service can meet the needs of an individuals' health and care needs. That is not to say that one medical professional has to be an expert in all three areas but to ensure they are fully aware, in a generalised fashion, of the symptoms of all three besides have knowledge of how one can affect the other and once symptoms are spotted care can be undertaken by an expert in the respective field.

This leads to a discussion regarding mental health. Mental health is one of the most misunderstood ailments in the medical profession and not given the same priority as physical conditions. All people at one stage or another will suffer from mental health issues, it is a fact. Most people are completely ignorant of this or do not want to admit that our minds are susceptible to the occasional damage or diseases. It has to be noted something as simple as bacteria in your gut or numerous parasites (not to mention pressure on the brain caused by numerous things) or chemical changes in your body (mainly young adults) could influence thoughts, moods and decision making abilities. These are not a cause for concern, but, are sometimes difficult to diagnose differently to other major mental health issues; for instance, is losing your temper and lashing out an indication of a mental health issue or just what happens to all species of life on the planet when anger levels are raised beyond a threshold? The philosophy aside, mental health issues are difficult to diagnose early and sometimes mistakes happen that can lead to tragedy (i.e. murder); therefore, it is important to attempt to diagnose symptoms early.

There needs to be greater emphasis on mental health issues within the education system for early indications and self-diagnosis; for instance, to give people knowledge of their own indifferent behaviour e.g. addiction, anger, self-harm etc. Loved ones, friends and teachers would also carry with them the knowledge to help spot this indifferent behaviour and offer support; moreover, it will gradually become a non-taboo part of society. From this early 'warning system' (you could say) probable diagnosis from medical experts trained in all three areas can occur and support given before the individual deteriorates and need more costly intensive care.

Political incentives such as EU rules or the Transatlantic Trade and Investment Partnership treaty (TTIP) (if it goes through) and others, can dramatically affect public services including the approved suppliers to the NHS. This invariably means that without drastic legislation to ensure decisions of which supplier to use is driven by the medical professionals, the NHS could be facing another administration nightmare instigated by government. The NHS is a British institution that should be able to be self-governed without interference from government, well until both the NHS and government is more competent with management decisions. The suppliers to the NHS should involve other British companies without the need to import goods or services from foreign investors or suppliers. If the 'goods' are not available in the UK, the government's job is to ensure that it will be sooner rather than later, not sign trade deals at the expense of British jobs or future availability and pricing control. Thus, the NHS needs to be protected from treaties that are political in nature to ensure that budgets are brought together at a local level with integrated services.

Those patients, who have the ability to pay an additional premium for care or those who have abused their body on purpose, should be expected in the future to be charged for their health care. The only path to stabilise and protect the NHS from being privatised or from additional taxation which everyone will be accountable for is to ensure that the NHS is available 'free at the point of contact' for those who through no fault of their own need expert care. For those who lack the sense of responsibility for their own health and fitness should not be expected to receive free health care at the point of contact from a certain age. If individual patients are taking regular trips to hospitals due to injury (i.e. through extreme sports or YouTube videos) then their needs to be a set limit for providing free health care and once it is breached every attempt needs to be made to recuperate the cost of care from the patient. Additionally, foreign patients who need care should pay for care as soon as reasonably practical and this includes visits to GP surgeries; for too long foreign care debt has been a big issue with the NHS and accountants still struggle to chase the debt. Any profit made from the collection of debt should be ring fenced for use within the health care system.

For some time, the health care system has concentrated on 'fire-fighting' (a term I used when fixing a problem temporarily not preventing one) patient care with little emphasis on prevention. Without preventative action the NHS will not be sustainable due to reasons already given. There has to be a preventative maintenance programme aimed at keeping people out of hospital and more responsible for their own health and wellbeing.

The ambition of this programme should be to improve the uptake of physical, mental and social activity to prevent degenerative problems and diseases both individually and in society, i.e. to personally incentivise people to take more interest in health and more interest in social responsibility whilst taking care of those less fortunate than themselves. In essence, attempt to bring to the forefront a type of social justice were all people look out for one another. This could also assist in personal wellbeing and overcoming mental issues such as, lack in confidence, thinking where not worthy or good enough, loneliness, and bullying. (Ambitious I know! But if society continues to go down the path it is now, it is not going to be a bright future as people will be more stressed, more likely to self-harm or commit suicide, more elderly left alone to die and more social unrest). In the short term, this type of programme should have a separate budget associated with it until patient numbers drop, NHS budgets become under control and management structures become more professional with waste removed so people can understand how the NHS functions.

When the tipping point is reached i.e. patient numbers have dropped and the cost of operating the NHS falls, then the two budgets can be slowly integrated together until finally one budget for the NHS can be used, with the NHS services being two integrated groups: one for prevention, and one for diagnosis and treatment. I know that this type of programme will need a long life attached to it, perhaps over a decade, but what is the alternative further firefighting: - higher taxes, privatisation, and an increase in suffering and further ignorance for all. All people need to think about the future of care services and how decision made today will affect the future of those people who have yet to be conceived. At the end of the day, like all maintenance departments, if most money is being spent on prevention rather than treatment then the department and all those who interact with it are satisfying their own responsibility.

The message that needs to be sent is: the NHS is here to provide expert care if needed; and advice to help people stay healthy and outside hospital; but, it is not a service for people to abuse at will. Any abuse of the service will be met with the recuperation of costs from the patient.

Furthermore, major decisions involving the health care system has to occur at local level, centralised control does not work and part of the problem is the size and difference in population within boundary regions. The health system should to be shaped at the local level with patients and health care representatives sitting down at the same table whilst improvement plans are being drawn up. The current system of employing very expensive managers and directors working at the national (and local) level, all with private health care and living in luxury, will never work. Patients and some front line health workers know the real problems, not a person in an expensive suit; and knowing the problem is the first stage of trying to solve it. Currently, changes are being made at a local level being driven from the national level without an understanding of the problem; throwing money at the problem and make arbitrary change driven by lobbying will end in disaster. The health care system is larger than the government and needs to be co-managed by the people who use and need the services; they have a vested interest in making it work.

This leads nicely to factors that affect not only the reputation of the NHS, but also possible mixed messages sent to the people from government, i.e. dealing with the NHS outsourcing of services (to make money for the NHS), more specifically food, snacks and drinks available. The NHS should be a shining light of health services and I have to question why unhealthy products are predominantly available within NHS owned buildings. It is not the right message to be portraying. All unhealthy snacks, drinks, and food need to be removed from NHS establishments; for the reasons of reputation and the high cost to the patients and visitors (it has always surprised me why people continue to pay over the RRP for products in hospitals, clinics, etc.) and replaced by healthy foods at a reasonable price for visitors and freely available to patients and NHS workers. Another outsourcing strategy that is most uncivilised and quite disgusting is the high charges for car parking. Not too long ago people could visit their friends and loved ones at hospital without paying to park, now however, you need to save quite a bit of money just to go a visit someone. For those who do not have a lot of money or not fit enough to travel to hospital by any other means have no choice but to pay. This causes them to reduce visiting loved ones due to the high cost of parking, leaving the patient staring at dull walls alone; when the best medicine for patients is for friends and family to be beside them comforting them in their time of need. Thus, to assist in a speedy recovery it is important for friends and family to be near and to have little obstacles in coming to visit, hence, car parking needs to be free and fund raising strategies put in place in hospitals to raise additional funds on a volunteering basis.

There also needs to be a targeted approach to tackle the problems of high strength, low cost alcoholic drinks. Successive governments have merely increased tax on the drinks in the hope (the cross fingers tactic) that it will put people off purchasing alcoholic products. Unfortunately, what has happened is drinking habits have changed with the problem shifting from lager to cider, imports of drink from abroad (booze cruise), and competition from supermarkets keeping prices at an affordable level with the added benefit of greater tax revenues received by government. The only affect it has had is with bars and clubs shutting down leading to empty buildings and adding to the further degradation of towns and cities. To effectively stop people drinking using this method, prices would need to rise considerably, but, that would punish occasional drinkers who use drink for social occasions and the latest science reveals that some alcohol used in proportion is actually good for you. In summary, raising prices through taxation is good for government with added revenues, bad for all consumers.

Government needs to stop interfering in people's choices, therefore, if people want to drink, let them, it is the same with drugs (including cigarettes, E-cigs, and class ? drugs). The government needs to provide exceptional education from early years with respect to the impacts of drugs and alcohol on the human body and the costs to the user of health care because of it. Yes, if people wish to drink and take drugs that should be their choice, but they should not expect free health care at the point of contact. It is that simple; they should have the knowledge of the effects of taking too much and know where to get support before it becomes a major health problem; and if ailments or illness is caused by overuse, they should be charged extra for using the NHS services. This has to be a line that needs to be followed; if people are seriously ill because of their own abuse of their body do not expect free health care at the point of contact. If they cannot afford health care, because of unemployment or other reasons, then community service should be offered that is suitable for them to do in repayment of the treatment provided; in essence to ensure they are providing value to society. The NHS cannot afford to treat people who do not respect themselves enough to prevent illness by mistreating their bodies. This needs to be objectively controlled as the human instinct is to help, but people can only help someone who wants to help themselves; and there is a huge ethical and moral discussion about diverting resources away from people who need help through no fault of their own to help people who are purposely ill or injured through their own decisions.

This brings leads onto the problems of obesity. In the UK, this problem has been caused by government and predominantly US 'fast food' outlets being allowed to open up chains to profit from people who are too busy working or too lazy to cook good food at home. This problem is also encouraged by parents who throughout the generations have become softer with their children and lazier in how they want to parent and feed them. These are problems which are difficult to solve by themselves, but then added to it is the introduction and growth of multimedia technology e.g. computer, tablets, smart phones, games consoles, etc., which have various people hooked and allow parents to settle down and watch television whilst the technology does the babysitting; allowing adults/parents (mainly under the age of 40) to ignore children and their partner for hours. All these issues work together to create a problem that everyone should have seen coming from the US - an obesity epidemic, which is costing the NHS ~£20 billion a year to treat the symptoms caused by unhealthy eating.

As mammals, people are naturally drawn to eat salty and sugary food because of taste and perhaps this is why it is difficult to steer clear of these things as most healthy food does not taste as good and is more expensive to buy. Hence, the issue is again about responsibility and most problems people and the NHS face today are down to laziness or over stressed over worked people and profiteering driven from government lobbyists.

In an attempt to solve this problem, maximum permitted levels of salt, sugar and fat in foods per day needs to be finalised and knowledge given to parents, schools and other professionals. Government needs to put in place a system that makes operating fast food outlets extremely difficult, for instance, 100% tax on all unhealthy food sold followed by a 60% business tax; in hope that the number of outlets will reduce and turn people away from purchasing high fat burgers and high sugar drinks. This will unfortunately put jobs at risk and increase the possibility of legal action against government, but nonetheless hard choices have to be made to prevent the implosion of the health service. Concurrently, the cost of high sugar, salt and fatty foods available in supermarkets should increase with higher taxes; with the 'bad food' tax offsetting the cost of the healthier alternatives to entice people into eating more healthy choices.

Schools should provide lessons and exercise programmes every day for their students and encourage parents to partake in the activities to help generate a healthier household. Knowledge and skills should be offered by the NHS to help people make better choices with what they put into their bodies along with discounted memberships to health centres to promote physical activity. Local government should work more closely with community health centres to offer family health packages which are hoped will also improve social interaction within the local community. Unfortunately, those who are suffering from an illness caused by obesity should be offered further advice about health and fitness, but the immediate treatment should be given at additional cost.

Some of the proposed strategies to enable the efficient operation of the NHS are harsh! But knowledge of the human condition has taught me over the years that unless people suffer some sort of recompense it is unlikely that people will change their attitudes, behaviours or mind-sets (that they are entitled to whatever) when it comes to their own choices that has led them into trouble. In order to incur a positive change for everyone, it is unfortunate that a few who choose not to change or have the attitude that 'It is my choice what I decide to do to my body and government services are supposed to be there for me when I need it', will have to learn the hard way if the NHS and society is to heal itself from the 'pit' it is currently in; individual responsibility is needed.

There is no easy way to put it some will be 'lambs to the slaughter' due to their own stubbornness and stupidity and will incur more pressure and stress because of being chased for debt due to health treatment. It will take more than one of these stories before some people 'get the message'. It is unfortunate that some people from current generations lack responsibility for their own actions and government services have allowed abuse of the services for too long of a period that this abuse has become ingrained in society. It will be a difficult path to change mind-sets, but, to save the health care system from being fully privatised at high cost to everyone and yet another insurance 'scam', it is a path that has to be travelled together.

The strength of government and NHS management should be seen as 'riding the wave of tragedy' when the 'do-gooders' complain about uncivilized treatment of people, draconian health care system, emotional hard luck stories to invoke reaction, etc. But this is the thing; people need the ability to be responsible for taking care of their own health and not rely on the NHS to do it for them. To achieve this, the NHS has to prioritize people who are innocent in their illness or ailment, and those who are purposely in need due to abuses of their own body have to be charged and placed at the bottom of the priority list.

The messages of what the NHS is for and not for along with knowledge, via education, has to be given to people, i.e. 'the government is not your nanny or your babysitter or your parent (although it suits MPs of today for people to be over reliant on government to protect them, it means government can easily manipulate people for votes) and the NHS is not this unlimited resource that is yours to abuse when you so desire (require it)'. I know this is a cliché, but 'people are responsible for their own health and safety, no one else is'; it is time people travelled back through time, metaphorically speaking, and took back control of their own responsibility for themselves without the expectation that someone else will. The NHS will only survive if people use it only when needed, and not for their own convenience. Ultimately, for people who have abused themselves, the NHS should treat the underlying cause at a cost, but, the patient's health is their own responsibility not the NHS's or governments. However, if the patient is seen to have worked hard to improve their level of fitness and lifestyle (decision making) in regards to health then any debt that exists should be reduced or cancelled/annulled in faith. Perhaps commissions are needed to debate whether treatment agreements need stipulating that the patient at least maintains their level of personal responsibility for their health. (A debt caused by health care treatment could carry with it further stressors that might affect individual health; the US system has seen homelessness rise, family breakdowns, and suicides due to debt companies chasing for the cost of health care when insurance does not cover treatment or if patient does not have any.)

Care for the elderly is not only the public health care's responsibility but it is also the responsibility of family and friends; for too long now public services has been a convenient resource to use to take care of elderly relatives because of time and energy constraints of others. The care services should introduce a system of safety checks for people at a certain age and health status to identify risks facing them to ensure as practicable as possible that they have the support when needed. The system should be robust enough to allow medical professionals to discuss care with family members or close friends to reduce the feeling of insecurity and loneliness and give the elderly patients the feeling that others care. This type of preventative measure should enable early signs of possible problems, even as simple as needing grab rails, are actioned to reduce the chances of hospital visits.

As much as possible the reduction of elderly people placed in nursing homes should be the target, as unless it is their own idea the feeling of being 'dumped' because no one has the time or the will to visit them in their own home needs to be reduced and eventually distinguished. Carers working with the care services have a very difficult job, with most of the services being provided for by outsourcing to contractors. These are predominantly women who sometimes have to go above and beyond the call to take care of some of the most critical patients inside their own home and involve heavy lifting due to being assigned to an unsuitable patient. There are also issues revolving around the time available to spend with the patient(s) being driven by the contract companies' ability to make a profit, whilst at the same time paying minimal salaries to the nurses. Again, the solution to this problem is to remove the outsourcing issues and provide patient care in their own home directly through the NHS whilst being used in conjunction with persuading more family and friends to physically interact with the care service. More organisation with regards to assigning nurses to patients should assist in ensuring that the patient is not too much to handle if specialist care is required.

Everyone involved within operating of the NHS must have the ability to grow and learn lessons when something is wrong or a mistake occurs in order to improve quality of care and value for the tax payer. The present system of additional levels of review and expending NHS workers time to ensure paper work is completed correctly provides only the opposite of what is needed to be achieved for an efficient and cost effective NHS. There must be minimal monitoring agencies and paperwork to complete.

Digital technology, although most is used in detriment to the strengths of social cohesion and interaction, must be commissioned to streamline and make more efficient public health services. The idea of a centralised database for patients is at risk of incurring private data to be available in one place, especially with the incompetence of officials at this moment in time (people have all heard of news stories of memory sticks and laptop being left on trains); instead localised databases are needed. These databases will form a nationwide service oriented architecture to enable information stored on the databases to be accessed by a terminal in other areas as needed and there needs to be an in-house NHS IT department whose prime job is to maintain this infrastructure and provide adequate firewalls to protect against hackers. The IT department should also work with anti-virus specialists to ensure data integrity and security.

Hansard (House of Lords Debate) (2010-11) June 2010, vol. 719, col 623-4.

Office for National Statistics (2010b). 'NHS staff 1999-2009 Overview'. ONS website. Available at: www.ic.nhs.uk/statistics-and--data-collections/workforce/nhs-staff-numbers/nhs-staff-1999-2009-overview (accessed 5 May 2015).

Turnbull James K., (2011), Leadership in context: Lessons from new leadership theory and current leadership development practice [online]. Available at: www.kingsfund.org.uk/leadershipcommission.

(8)

EDUCATION FOR THE FUTURE

Education was and probably is still seen as vital to achieving personal achievement and economic prosperity. A healthy society rests upon an education system that can open minds to new knowledge and experiences to teach skills that people need to flourish in life. But the education system is failing to provide the necessary needs for the future and has been taken over by an over bureaucratic system that overcomplicates the teaching process and places undue pressure on teachers to satisfy the proverbial 'red tape'.

Successive governments have spent far too much money dealing with the symptoms of a failing education system instead of preventative action at the source of the problem. Each and every tax payer faces the burden of the cost of education from early years through to university but is rewarded by low educational achievement (with high pass rates), poor aspirations and external problems influenced by it, drink and drug misuse, criminality and social justice warriors. Over the past two and a half decades the solution to poor achievement has been to reduce passing grades, making exams easier, teaching to test, etc., and can be described as placing a 'sticky plaster' over the issues. It has unfortunately had the after effect of young people lacking the skills and knowledge they need to perform in the modern workplace and, more importantly, the critical thinking skills needed to become directly involved in evolving societal norms.

To add to the concerns, government, parents and all the support services, especially schools, have created a culture where children (and adults) of all ages are nanny-ed (so called child centred culture) to the extent that substantial risk, stress and pressure has been removed from daily life of children. Meaning life after school becomes a major shock to the system that has contributed to the growing mental health problems of young adults. Furthermore, it is clear from anyone who took GCSEs (and the US/European equivalent) that current examinations are far easier to revise for and do than in the past. For example, students had to take exams for all subjects within the same week with only a hint of what would be in it and this helped prepare students for life after school where hard work and perseverance was promoted above all else, where they experienced stress and pressure, which assisted them transition into adult life. It is clear that the stress and pressure experienced by current students is not comparable to what the elder generation felt when they were revising and sitting exams, as schools of the past taught a diverse range of subjects and rarely taught to test.

Schools are now more concerned with reputation and wanting to give students an enjoyable experience rather than preparing them for adult life. Additionally, most new parents are far less concerned with academic achievement of their children since they are too distracted with technology, social media, and other addictions because they too were nanny-ed as they grew up hence are used to not doing things they do not want to or disinterested in. Besides, looking after children is hard work and they have never been taught that hard work receives positive outcomes as a child, as they were cultivated in the first generation of the child-centred culture.

Lack of discipline in schools is a major factor for teachers and is also one of the reasons why teachers are being turned away from the profession. There has been a reverse in culture at schools were teachers are now apprehensive about disciplining those students who need it, concurrently, with the lack of discipline given to children in their home environment has created a culture where teachers are unable to discipline children and the children know it thus carry on with their disruptive behaviour. The change has been driven directly from government and strengthened by those non-job lawyers, solicitors and social workers who are making money by giving more powers to children rather than adults and parents thus spreading the message that discipline is a 'thing' of the past in this new legal world i.e. child-centred approach in PC terms, child worshipping in reality. It has led to many teachers being sacked from schools when they confront unruly students with their teaching career in tatters.

It is sad to realise that these teachers are exactly what is needed in schools to improve performance, but the legal system, government and some parents will not allow it as is goes against the nanny state. As a result, many teachers become disillusioned within schools and anxious of disciplining therefore angering students (of all ages) due to possible repercussions, via made up stories, many of which would be taken seriously and the teacher treated as guilty. This had led to schools being populated by teachers who run the very real risk of being bullied by very young children with them being powerless to stop it due to threats of a legal and reputational nature. It has also led to children realising the power they have over adults, including their parents, even though they are completely unaware of what life is or repercussions of their actions as they move into adulthood. If a teacher has the unfortunate circumstance of having unruly and disruptive students in their class no amount of qualifications or training will help the teacher impart learning to the entire class.

The education system is reliant upon the quality and the skills of teachers, but, the teachers can only be as good as curriculum limitations permit along with the schools own administration system. Government have been trying to oversee schools from a central base (via monitoring agencies); but this approach is not working. There is a continuing push by government to acquire more qualified teachers in all areas of education and with it greater emphasis on aligning teaching methods with areas of learning. In theory, both should raise teaching standards; however, both have led to a detrimental impact on the quality of teaching.

Teachers should be encouraged, if not expected, to update their own knowledge and skills as a condition of remaining in the profession, but, teaching is more about interacting with students rather than being dependent on qualifications. Government and think tanks have neglected the importance of this over the years and placed priority on qualifications not teaching interaction with which to base teacher assessments on. Consequently, to conform to raising standards additional paperwork has been created for teachers to complete that is largely based on academic work to satisfy monitoring requirements setup by the department of education (DfE). Denoting, that more teachers' time is diverted away from lesson planning to complete the necessary forms - the exact opposite of what is needed.

Teaching has become more about administration rather than teaching and requires substantial time at home with which to plan and set-up lessons. The system itself has also caused additional stress and pressures on teachers with little remuneration to go along with it. Furthermore, the system is turning away individuals from the profession due to lack of support, academic snobbery and too much administration activities distracting attention away from teaching. Most human systems created by academics to satisfy certain requirements neglect the overall problem the developed solution should be addressing. Monitoring systems are good if it takes little time to complete, but, becomes a major distraction if long fields require completing. With substantial government funding placed into employing monitoring staff to assess teaching lesson standards, teaching has now become a job sharing scheme between completing complex forms, lesson planning and actually teaching students with more time being spent completing the monitoring forms. Why are monitoring forms needed? – do qualifications alone not mean quality in teaching standards.

The answer is no! There is a significant amount of elitism and snobbery involved in teaching and academia on the whole, which has unfortunately infected industry. Teaching qualifications are a distraction for creating a poor education system to suit the nation's main industry (which currently is the service industry given that the West have moved most manufacturing opportunities abroad for economic and profit reasons. The outcome has been the need to employ skilled workers from abroad, which also helps to justify immigration numbers; however, overall the entire developed system has let generations of children down and government has been deceitful and complicit in this failure.); it gives the illusion that the best people are employed in the profession. There is clearly a distinct difference between what makes someone a good (or world class) teacher and someone who has teaching qualifications. The modifications to teaching practice and quality processes has been a way to justify employing academic specialists at universities to test new theories out which has only bastardised something that arguably worked well into something worse for all stakeholders concerned (e.g. students, parents, industry, economy, etc.).

The monitoring forms and agencies have been set-up because the mainstream people with teaching qualifications had degraded the quality of teaching in schools; and is seen as a method of preventing further degradation. Nevertheless, teaching qualifications does ascribe to completing planning and monitoring forms perfectly as the courses are developed by academics and not necessarily by those who know how to be a good teacher, i.e. there is no professional who works on the front line of teaching that produces real class achievement year-on-year involved in teaching qualification course specifics. It has become an embarrassment for the teaching system with people who are good teachers choosing to leave and those who could be fantastic teachers choosing not to go into the profession because of the cost of obtaining what are qualifications not directly useful for teaching practice besides all the administration issues. (Spending several years to acquire qualifications that will not help on the front line of people's chosen profession is a waste of money, time and effort, likewise people who could make great teachers might never enter the profession because of the financial implications of entering a teaching course and pointlessness of participating in it).

This notwithstanding, there is also another problem with human culture at present regarding the paranoia surrounding male professionals working with children, consequently males are being turned away from the profession. Sensationalising news reports concerning the minority of relationships that have occurred between male teachers and female students (or children) besides stories surrounding grooming incidents have caused males to consider teaching a high risk profession with little remuneration. It has become so easy for female students or children to communicate a story about a male teacher they do not like without any evidence and subsequently very little support or benefit of the doubt (innocent until proven guilty) given to the male teacher in such circumstance. When a story like this appears in local news broadcasts or papers a career, a personal life and a reputation is ruined irrespective of being innocent; it is becoming a profession solely dominated by women. Ironically, there are more female teachers having relationships with male students than the opposite way, yet most are not decided as being mainstream news stories and sometimes given a small segment in a paper every now thus are not seen as culturally repulsive if the subject was a male teacher.

To give the impression government is attempting to improve education standards, KPI's have gradually creeped into schools causing them to alter the manner with which they grade student's ability to obtain funding. The result is that good performing schools, in terms of grades, receive higher funding than those who do not; meaning that it is in the schools' best interest to obtain good performance from students and so marking schemes have been created to 'blur' actual student performance in relation to the required level of K&S acquired.

The pressures upon schools have created an ethos focussed on fiscal challenges that has had a detrimental impact of seeing educationally challenged students as a burden even though the schools have access to additional financial help for poorer students. (How the schools manage the funding is subjective and is often not allocated to students who need it the most thus has little effect at bridging the gap in educational achievement.) Therefore, it is in the best interests of the school to concentrate on higher achieving students as their dominant intake leading to a proportion of students, who arguably are ignored, entering adult life with no prospects of leading a fulfilling life.

Meanwhile, teaching to test and providing the students with mock exams (which frequently include the identical questions to the exam), providing multiple choice answers and creatively refashioning (marking criteria) how exams, coursework and test papers are graded (e.g. giving marks for keywords, correctly repeating of values given in the question, and other creative techniques, help schools massage actual achievement levels giving even the most academically challenged student the chance to pass *(I was once asked to give a Chinese higher education student some marks for spelling his own name correctly so he could scrape a pass, needless to say even though I refused; he was awarded a pass by someone else)*. This has led to schools advancing the A grade, which heretofore the highest grade possible, to A** (or 9 or other country's equivalent) to account for the drop in attainment levels and permit those who would otherwise fail to pass. This also gives the school the facility to ignore their responsibility to help academically challenged students in their studies, give less homework and make the task of teaching for performance levels easier (with detrimental impacts for society.

But, there is something damaging to the economy of the country if actual performance is being manipulated for the schools own financial benefit, as it places greater burden on further education responsibilities on businesses to account for the actual performance of people entering the workplace. There is also something very damaging to the reputation of the education system if this type of creative manipulation can occur to account for the degradation of attainment levels in children. If professionals and parents think it is a good idea to cheapen what was once a robust system, which could correctly identify those who failed to meet the grade as they continue through to higher levels then place interventions in place to help before it was too late, are either deluded or have been failed by the education system previously.

Homework, exams and course work should be more aligned with the original GSCE curriculum with more creative approaches to teaching where schools teach a wide variety of knowledge and skills with practical applications and not teach to test, as the 'teach to test' system is damaging the ability of young people to adapt to life outside schools. This invariably means that students will receive a diverse range of knowledge and skills they may or may not need within final assessments. Therefore, exams will inherently be more difficult to revise for and preparation should be seen as a method to harden students for adult life and work to prevent the growing mental health epidemic.

A scheme of grading from project, homework, coursework and exams should be used to assess individual students and some exams should be considered as open book, i.e. to match real world circumstances with allotted time to complete extended to suit. The marking scheme should account for students that may not have the ability to achieve within academic studies and might wrongly be identified as unintelligent when their strength is in problem solving and/or practical innovations using instinct to guide their solutions, as such will struggle in exams (most real engineers make design choices based on instinct not mathematics). Therefore, the curriculum should be developed with creativity and hands-on practical education at the core, thus, qualification outcomes should also be dependent on these core attributes.

Irrespective, the KPI's for schools' financial benefit needs to be abolished and replaced by funding per student capita basis, meaning that no school will have a financial advantage over others including private schools to abolish inequality and privilege. Those schools that benefit from large state subsidies and business rates relief worth millions are schools generally reserve for the richest in society, i.e. private schools. This type of elitism serves to promote inequality in society; however, these types of schools should contribute to raising standards across the board. Private schools should be strongly encouraged to work more closely with state funded schools in their respective geographical regions and create a partnership where the resource rich schools share resources if and when required with other schools. Moreover, it should be the task of government, including local government, to place as a condition of continued benefit that performance (and reputation) of state run schools improve year on year with certain key subjects being sponsored by these aforementioned private schools. Whilst this may not match the private schools' business plan the only other option should be to remove the subsidies and tax relief.

Modern grammar schools seem to be on par with the privatisation of schools in the USA, where schools are operated for profit. There is an argument that this new type of governing system will mean less accountability for school achievement levels and remedial actions will give the illusion of improvement, i.e. continuous improvement of the competency framework. Like the health service, this type of business model should be resisted and instead management of schools should be made accountable for the success or otherwise on both how the school is performing and budgets are managed, for example, schools that give away free IPads or tablets to every student and then suffer financial issues or school buildings that have fallen into disrepair and need to be replaced, have clearly been badly managed. Those responsible have be made accountable and decisions made about whether or not to place the people on a black-list to ensure they cannot be in a position of decision making until they have at least retrained and proven competence.

Management and school leaders should be encouraged to resist making schools an enjoyable place for all students and return to the 'old fashioned' viewpoint that schools are there to teach children knowledge, skills and discipline they need in their adult life. The nanny and child worship approach has only worked to create a world full of depressed people who are then prescribed antidepressants and/or people who have diminished common sense to take care of themselves.

There should be a proactive approach in education starting by building a common purpose between all stakeholders (government, governors, parents, and industry leaders) to not only advance the education system to provide relevant knowledge and skills for the future but also break down the cultural barriers that exist between faiths, children's home backgrounds and family values to adapt the schools' ethos that in some way maps to parents, industry and the students preconceived values.   This does mean that parents will need to be actively involved in evolving school ethos, thus, schools should be more open to voices from parents and accommodate parent's viewpoint in any change to school processes, which should champion the need of each student.   Governing boards should work towards ensuring performance in schools is continuously reviewed and processes amended to account for the gap in achievement levels, especially with disadvantaged students, by providing parents with bi-directional communication with respect to their own children's education needs.

Government needs to promote early-years interventions for those children who struggle with basic education as a social requirement. Additional support is needed for young children and their parents (there is a tight coupling between parents who are academically and economically challenged and their children who struggle in school); those parents who have been failed previously by the education system has to be offered support for family education i.e. to resolve a problem caused by historic failures in education.   Major problems with behaviour and educational achievement has to be dealt with before they get out of hand; the general practice of isolation and ignoring children who constantly struggle or be disruptive will never achieve an outcome that is positive for society; route causes need to be investigated and resolved.

Underperformance in schools should be dealt with on an individual basis with the schools themselves proceeding with preventative action before local government become involved. Greater transparency and partnerships with parents is needed to help those students who are struggling within an academic environment. A full open investigation has to occur before the student performance affects his/her life choices (between relevant stakeholders including parents) to find the underlying cause of why the student is struggling (even if it is found to be under nutrition) and an action plan delivered to help the student attainment levels. However, unlike current government propaganda there needs to be a firm realisation as to the extent schools can compensate for the differences in social background, family values, and parental support in assisting to improve achievement levels of children. The lack of discipline and interest given at home and the extent schools can compensate, due to the problems exasperated by the legal system, to 'reign in' unruly students to help them succeed in education is extremely limited and no amount of additional funding will help schools bridge the gap in these types of cases.

The new modern day parent has a bad habit of projecting their own flaws onto their children rather than ensuring they grow-up without suffering the same affliction. A prime example is a parent who has been identified as suffering from a learning 'disorder' who then misconstrues their children(s) lack of interest or laziness as the same 'disorder'. Thus, just accepts this as a reality and fails to push their children through their lack of interest leading to a child who does not try besides disseminates all of their education woes on the incorrect diagnosis driven by, generally lazy, parents who have forgotten how to parent in the best interests of their children – the 'I want to be your best friend or I want you to be happy because of the lack of a father figure, etc.' scenario(s). Schools cannot compensate for this type of parenting no matter how much funding they have or how much the teachers try. Unfortunately, types of scenarios such as this are quickly becoming an epidemic, which is spreading faster in the West than anywhere else on the planet due to nanny state mentality. This is leading to the East becoming more successful in knowledge and technological advancements, leaving the West behind with poorly educated people.

Regrettably, academics, psychologist and government have removed any sense of the reality of laziness of both parents and students from teaching specifics. Currently, every child or adult who struggles to comprehend or remember learning materials is quickly diagnosed, some by medical professionals some by what can only be described as 'guessing' based on incomplete knowledge, with a learning disorder or condition. The word laziness has all but been removed from any teacher training materials and courses – the West it would seem no longer suffers from laziness in academic studies. Unfortunately, the resources that are designed to help people who have real learning conditions or disorders succeed in education are now diluted and distributed to those who are merely lazy; and the likelihood is most who are diagnosed with a condition or disorder are just lazy and / or dis-interested. Laziness has to be one of the most misunderstood issues society has to deal with; it is possibly why the education system is gradually worsening because no problem can be solved when 'b#llsh%t' is part of the issue. The West cannot continue categorizing lazy children and adults as suffering from a disorder or condition. There needs to be greater emphasis on finding out the root causes of any learning issues schools identify; it has become all too easy to register children and adults as suffering from a mental condition/disorder.

The understanding that children's education, behaviour and discipline do not begin at school, but, commences shortly after birth is needed; schools acquire students who have already preconceived values and ways of behaving that may not be compatible with the school learning ethos. Parents are the principle barrier when it comes to children's educational requirements (now there is a controversial statement, but nevertheless true). There is a growing trend in two areas that makes parenting easier for parents but subjects children to being 'palmed off' with technology and becoming used to having their wants satisfied (meaning that birthdays and Christmas are no longer special for the children involved).

More than any other time in history both parents work, meaning that their children are looked after by other people. When it comes to the parent's spare time they would rather relax and de-stress, including the lazy parents, meaning their children are ignored and technology is allowed to do the babysitting (i.e. IPad). Concurrently, as the parents are tired or just lazy children are given what they want most of the time after they have a little temper tantrum, because parents do not want the hassle, leading to some children behaving in a spoilt and privileged manner and used to getting what they want as they enter school.

During this early period before the children enter school, their parents who have previously grown up in an ever increasing nanny state firmly believe that educating their children is the prime responsibility of schools and therefore they do not put much time into education of their children. These 'value' continues throughout the children's childhood life, furthermore, is completely contradictory to the schools' values and ethos. What society have then is parents who arguably 'love' their children, but, do not place value in educating from birth nor becoming engaged with school ethos for actively supporting schools in their task of educational achievement.

Hence, there are two major problems that have to be considered external to the school environment to help schools help children succeed within a teaching environment. Prospective parents have to be conditioned with the understanding that being a parent means that most of their spare time is to be used to further educate their new born through play; besides allowing other people or technology to 'look after' or babysit does not promote strong healthy family connections. It may mean the future of family responsibility is to defer to a permanent parental presence until the child or children enter schools. Once they enter school it is the parent's responsibility to ensure that their children's education levels in all subjects are on par with what is required – this does denote the school needs to continuously amend their own ethos to account for diverse student intakes and for parents to become actively involved in school policy and extra curricula activities, including homework. It also means allowing technology to babysit or completely ignoring their own children whilst doing something more enjoyable has to become a 'hobby' of the past – IPad and tablets have always been and will always be a bad distraction from responsibilities as a parent. Newsflash – if parenting is easy, has little stress and you have time to do your own thing during the day, you're doing it wrong and having a detrimental impact on your children wellbeing!

The second involves a reduction, no demolition, in child centred parenting, discipline and schooling (child worshipping). This system has been created as a means of distracting people from the real problems in the world and to create additional non-jobs in the legal and public sector. I would go as far as describing the system as continuing down a path of child worshipping where the children have control, power and with it an attitude of being untouchable no matter their behaviour. Parenting involves your children not liking you for large parts of their childhood, and 'hating' you in those teenage years; if you are their best friend something is wrong with how you are bringing them up. Children need discipline, constraints and punishment for bad behaviour; they do not need to be spoilt (this goes for those who cry poverty too), boys should not be treated as girls or vice-versa; and they need a decent night's sleep and a proper healthy diet to help their body and brain develop.

Many parents have such a perverted perception of what 'taking care of their children' means that they fail on all of these points. More young adults/teenagers now are so materialistic, have narcissistic characteristics, more confused about their gender, have an overwhelming need to be popular, fight for causes without possessing any facts around the area of their cause (i.e. are manipulated through hearsay and gossip), have become so used to sitting down most of the day wasting their lives away on video games, have a poor diet and little common sense, yet, possess educational qualifications such as GCSE's or higher but struggle to spell, need a calculator for simple mathematical problems and suffer more mental health problems than the generations before. These are but a few social issues that the child-centred approach with parenting and schooling has achieved and I genuinely cannot think of any positive outcomes. However, the outcome does give a population that is easier to control and manipulate with propaganda and incur the ability for government to point the finger of blame for social problems at many different areas.

Until the next generation of children flow through this perspective new education system, there should be a system of further family education for certain new parents to be because some ideas and parental techniques have much to be desired. In today's society, there is a strong argument for an IQ test for parenting before prospective parents are allowed to become pregnant, but, this will constrain freedom of choice and works against producing an advanced free society. Consequently, there needs to be checks in place, training courses and regular home checks not to 'spy' on parents, but, to ensure additional support can be offered, if needed. Moreover, parenting cannot continue being seen as a means for financial security or as part of a work prevention scheme. Having children should be seen as the most important choice that anyone can make in life, the current way people's mind-set are is becoming pregnant is seen as something they want and completely ignore the ramifications to their own life, i.e. they want the child or children but not the responsibilities to go with it.

Once the child is born, new parents realise that their freedom has been constrained with the new born being hard work thus looks for something to keep the child distracted so the parents can continue with their own interests or hobbies with little hassle. Recent technology advances have been a god send to those parents who have no time or energy to give their children. Parents too have become distracted with gadgets, social networking sites and TV to really take notice of what their children are doing, what their bedtime should be for adequate sleep and what food they eat for balanced healthy body and mind; for example, even brushing teeth correctly, especially in the UK, most parents have little interest in, their eyes and thought are elsewhere - usually on a gadget.

Education and with it discipline is far from the parent's main thought and that is the problem that schools are facing (I say parents, however, with men and fathers becoming passive to women and mothers and women becoming more controlling and wanting to be in charge all the time, it is mainly women whom prevent discipline by fathers; and with it nanny and spoil their children). Unless parents 'come on board' with their responsibilities from the day their child is born schools are fighting a losing battle. The current system of amending marking schemes to keep schools' performance high has been actioned along with grouping trouble makers together and to some degree ignoring their education needs through fear of the child or children causing the teachers some legal 'headaches'. This has produced a degraded education system to which only works to the benefit of social science and education academics who continue to justify their existence by using children to verify and validate their newly created theories.

The message needs to be given through schools and media outlets to children and adults that education success is not the governments or schools responsibility. These institutions provide the services to give education to people, but, children's education achievement is in the hands of the values, attributes and disciplines given by parents to their children. Schools and governing boards are there to provide support and interventions for those struggling to achieve; but, parents who choose not to be inclusive to the educational needs of their children from an early age are problematic to the tasks of academic success and is the prime reason for the cheapening of the education system on the whole and works to the detriment of society's best interests. Ultimately, if many children fail their courses in schools, the legal system will be used by parents (as with the blame culture due to the nanny state) to prosecute (financially) the school and place even greater financial burdens on them that will continue to effect the next generation of students that flow through. It is why the creative marking scheme and criteria is used within schools to misrepresent reality.

All people in society need to consider the multifaceted nature of the problem and all work towards the solution with relationships between all stakeholders and responsibilities understood and upheld because despite additional funding given to schools they are struggling to work in the best interests of the children with pressures from population numbers through to preconceived values given in the home environment. Only when schools, government, communities and especially parents acknowledge that placing the blame purely with schools is misguided can a professional learning environment be created where all stakeholders work collaboratively to achieve an agreed upon goal. Parents are the key and the ones that can drive their children to academic success or academic failure. Unfortunately, unless parents succeed with their responsibilities as a parent (which is hard work, stressful and being 'cruel to be kind') then government will continue to degrade the educational system to enable children to pass courses they would otherwise have failed.

However, it is clear that even if parents fulfil their responsibility to their children, some will struggle within a school environment due to the stagnant teaching methods used that do not inspire interest in children. Different learning styles has to take president with the alteration of the curriculum meaning that teachers will need to be able to provide different learning methods, perhaps to groups of students, if the default method of teaching is failing to produce positive results. Moreover, sitting in a classroom and delivering PowerPoint presentations (or similar) for long periods of time needs to be resisted and more investment made in the creative learning process to secure interest in students to learn (there is nothing worse than sitting in a classroom fighting to stay awake whilst a teacher continues to speak for what seems to be an eternity). This type of teaching relies on smaller class sizes to achieve results, thus, large class sizes should be restricted to improve teaching standards to all students.

Schools primary job is to help children develop self-awareness and emotional skills they need to be able to cope with modern day life. The development of social and emotional skills through the use of Mindfulness to build resilience is becoming the norm in schools across the West (even used for adults) and sold as the practice of being present in the moment and forgetting what worries or concerns you may have so you can concentrate on bettering yourself. It is portrayed as something to help prevent the thought of not being good enough and the brokenness people feel is our fault; and if people work hard, they can fix it. It does sound good in theory and could work to improve the mental health issues facing young people in this new world and according to academics, including psychologist, can work alongside other treatments for mental health problems such as depression and anxiety. This notwithstanding, it seems like another 'fad' to help people cope with the problems surrounding themselves and their local environment rather than working to resolve the prevailing problem. It is another example of the nanny state attempting to give the illusion that they are attempting to take care of people in the current climate without actually attempting to cure the problem, but, will make the new generation look towards the government to solve their ails more than any previous generation did.

Young adults are less capable of dealing with the difficulties of life now than previous generations, I cannot image how bad mental health conditions will be in future if children continue to be furnished with a soft approach that promotes looking towards others, including government institutions, to take care of their every need because they are emotionally and mentally weak to deal with the difficulties of life; and this is what mindfulness is promoting. Continuing down this path is producing children that are so used to getting what they want through continued whining and being stroked whenever there is something troubling them that when they become young adults they believe that protesting (i.e. whining) in groups will eventually get what they want and become confused and depressed when they fail.

Most young adults only listen to sound-bites and ignore the context of the full story for some ill-founded belief based on main stream media bias and propaganda to give their own boring life purpose and meaning by being involved in some sort of movement for change. Most young adults involved in protests do not possess the knowledge about the issues they are protesting about besides take part in demonstrations for change to match their personal belief system or mind-set, i.e. feminists or gender identity; and tend to be very aggressive with people who use facts and science to debate with them. They then play the victim and commence with demonization tactics to discredit the individuals who are intelligently debating the issues, i.e. name calling and labelling. The truth is these people are suffering delusional beliefs supported with no truths or facts and thus possess little hope or intelligence. The facts are erroneous to their cause thus will dismiss the truth if it contradicts their belief system; the US protests about Trump is a prime example of young adults embarrassing themselves and showing themselves up to be uneducated people who do not possess the critical thinking skills they should have. The most disconcerting circumstance is most of the protestors are at University or have been University educated; the only conclusion to be made is the West seems to be producing highly educated dumb people with high levels of knowledge, not competence, in very small areas who are crying out for change and protection of free speech whilst preventing truth and other people's thoughts and beliefs from being presented.

This is a sign of insanity and the human race loosing sense of belonging and what is really important in the world. But not just this, the people involved in these movements do some very strange activities, which only a short period of time ago would have involved a mandatory trip to a psychiatric ward for an evaluation, e.g. chanting, slut walks, rape culture, dancing in courtyards or streets, setting things on fire, etc.... (It is the snowflake or butterfly syndrome describing people who get triggered or offended / upset by, and let's be honest, pretty much everything that they believe goes against their current viewpoint without possessing true knowledge, the facts or details or the realities of the other side of the argument). It is becoming a demoralising trend in Western culture, as these are the people who are allowed to vote with the outcome influencing truly intelligent human life; it is no wonder why poor quality politicians are always voted into government and the freedoms people have degraded and removed

Admittedly, government will permit some leeway on things that are unimportant in daily life, but, these young adults find it difficult to cope with being refused, which sometimes ends in them lashing out like they did with temper tantrums when they were children. What society has are groups of young adults protesting about how they are not getting their own way and demanding that their voices be heard. And why not as children they have been taught that throwing temper tantrums generally gets them what they want due to the nanny-ing/mothering of them. Whilst concurrently, the same people who are fighting to be heard are calling for people who have contradictory views to theirs to be silenced in all media outlets and in public forums. It increases the risk of severe mental health conditions because they cannot understand why they are not getting their own way, as life lessons up to that point have shown them that they can.

There are other avenues to consider for dealing with building resilience without giving public money to mindfulness charities and projects along with wasting time and resources with training courses (how much is it costing for clinically training professionals to train and provide these courses?).

Real resilience and mental toughness is born out of parental discipline, good education system and most importantly not nanny-ing children (and adults) from birth. Both of these attributes can be given by good parenting (by both parents - a single parent or one subdued parent does not give children the discipline they need, it requires both to prevent any spoiling of them and reduce materialism later in life), strict education system that promotes respect for teachers, and a bullying policy that comes down hard on the bully and the bully's parents. Becoming involved in a martial arts programme teaches 'being the best that you can be' philosophy whereby competition is with yourself and not with others; it is a type of philosophy that achievement in schools should also be based on – improving their own academic achievements based on their current ability level rather than competing to reach a level set by government and feeling like a failure when the results are lower than what was expected. The priority should be given to hardening children from a young age to give the self-confidence to be who they want to be and stop being concerned about what others think about them

Currently, to accompany the new nanny courses in schools there is a continued push to introduce children to sex and relationship education at an early age, with concentration given to sex education. This is a system that has been copied by government from other countries to prevent social issues such as: young mothers, dealing with hormone changes, emotions, diseases, underage sex, etc. Unfortunately, the system has been copied from countries with a strong religious and family culture, and simply does not work in countries where the people do not practice strict religious beliefs or have strong family connections i.e. do not sit around the table at meal times. Therefore, can people really be surprised when the latest data shows a consistent rise in young pregnancies and single parents' year on year.

The lessons have also been introduced when children are given electronics with free access to the internet whose parents may not monitor the activity, where children have been sexualised through media outlets and clothing manufacturers, where being popular whether in the real world or online is of prime importance; and thus will only serve to escalate the problem the new system is attempting to prevent. Instead, relationship education need to be introduced to young children with the emphasis given to why relationships happen, the benefits and negative impacts of becoming emotionally involved with someone else, including respecting each other's space and knowledge about areas of the body off-limits to others including parents. Sex education needs to be contested at such a young age to avoid early experimentation, which unfortunately is happening. Sex education needs to be introduced to relationship education at a much older age, when or just before puberty occurs and given in the first year of high school.

Human society is living in a technology driven world and it is a natural transition to use technology for teaching. However, the philosophy is now looking for reasons to use different types of technology (including software) for teaching rather than concentrating on what the learning objectives of lessons or lectures are and what specific should be learned to acquire more knowledge and skills. Using technology for teaching in this way becomes a distraction to actually teaching the children; it may look awe inspiring but is it effective? (The current outcome of using technology in schools does not inspire confidence).

To some degree it gives the illusion that the school's curriculum is attempting to keep up to advancements in technology, but, only some subjects require the use of advanced technology for learning. In addition, planning and conducting lessons using technology, i.e. smart boards, adds more work for the teacher and the learning objectives or moreover the success of learning are questionable and subjective in nature. Planning lessons should consider the knowledge and skills acquisition of the children (or adults); automatically planning a lesson using advanced technology needs to be resisted if using no technology has the desired effect of reaching the learning objectives.

The questions should be asked 'what do we need the children to learn?' and 'does the use of technology make planning and delivering the lesson produce more efficient and effective learning?' The use of technology should not be a priority for teaching certain subjects; more effective teaching strategies permit 'learning by doing' and humans acquire knowledge best by repetition and practicing methods taught. Technology is most effective through learning by playing, nonetheless, in a school environment (high school and above) learning should be taken seriously by all stakeholders and students need not be distracted by technology. Using technology abundantly early on can affect the motivation to learn or do without the use of technology. Children and adults should be learning about theories, methods and patterns to help them develop complex problem solving and critical thinking skills that they should be able to complete without the use of software tools that does the work for them.

The whole problem with technology becomes abundantly clear at colleges and universities where academia is producing people who have high level qualifications, including PhDs, are promoted as experts in their respective fields, but, are incapable or at best inept at solving complex problems without the use of software tools. Many are fully experienced in how to use specific software tools and the methods used for statistical analysis, thus proficient in producing professional documents to a appear knowledgeable in the problem they are working on. Nevertheless, statistics are a manner to prove a hypothesis irrespective of the real data and the reality of the world; and a tool is 'dumb' and 'stupid' and only as useful as the person using it.

Higher Education System

With students now paying additional fees at the point of contact (other than those received from higher taxes (and NI contributions (in the UK)) throughout the students' career) for education they are seen as consumers of education consequently academics are now operating the universities and colleges as businesses and have now a process to give the students what they want in order to entice more students into these types of educational facilities. Students also have more of a voice in what they are taught, how they are taught, and what university policies are. In essence, universities are now setup to please students and to 'nanny' to their every whim rather than give them a quality education with quality degrees; thus, allow policies to change to please those that are easily offended by anything and everything to avoid anyone being upset, hence, sell themselves as being liberal.

Author Note: It was clear when I began working in industry in my chosen field (at that time) from obtaining a bachelor's degree that academia did not prepare me for life in industry. I incorrectly had confidence from my qualifications and I initially struggled to cope within an industrial environment; fortunately, I was and still am driven to succeed and eventually became proficient in my work from many initial mistakes but with it gained experience. Throughout my time in industry I interacted with many experts from academia, private consultants and people with high level qualifications and realised that I had fundamental differences in knowledge levels and common sense approaches to understanding and solving problems. I realised these people had/have similar issues I once had when I came to industry, but, they were completely ignorant/deficit of their own short comings. Obtaining high level academic qualifications did not even help incompetent managers overcome their inability to do their jobs in fact it made them more of a liability by making their incompetence worse by convincing them that mathematical manipulation of data helps their organisational, planning and project management skills.

What has been achieved is a pandemic of smooth talking 'b£llshi@@£r's' that uses professional presentations and charts to 'point the finger of blame' to others. Business solution to this type of incompetence is/was to continue to increase the management hierarchy ('too many Chiefs, not enough Indians') – I found this is the approach used throughout Western culture to 'solve' incompetence – do not solve the problem, just throw people at it and hope for the best. It is a philosophy that is making the West less competitive in a global market, products more expensive and tax rates (including shadow taxes) higher leading to increased poverty levels.

After several years of being inconvenienced by their mistakes, covering up and correcting them whilst realising that these people are highly paid compared to other more useful and intelligent people, I made the decision to return to academia to find out why this is happening. The outcome of eight years studying and observing academics and student alike, I have come to realise that there is substantial issues in academia that can be categorised as a complete waste of time and energy; where waffle is awarded higher than useful; and where there is an unnerving obsession with reference format in work. There is also substantial political nonsense throughout institutions, which are producing more 'experts' in nothing apart from theories based on mathematical and data manipulation not well founded in the real world, software tool usage, professionally prepared presentations and documents, and smooth talkers giving the illusion on diverse knowledge that diminishes the reputation of high level qualifications; aside from grouping those who have earned the qualification with all those who have not due to relationships between academics. There is also a problem with the lack of skills to complement the knowledge in academia and is driven by the lack of real world skills of the academics teaching the students. This section has taken years of drudgery and frustration to complete and is a summary of the findings made.

Some academic disciplines require essays, or large pieces of textual work, to be graded, which nicely leads to marking schemes used by academics to justify the knowledge acquisition of students. These types of work(s) are largely based on subjective marking techniques of the academic responsible for grading. In these circumstances, it is very difficult to obtain an unbiased grade for students as most subjective marking is largely based on the academic's view on the student who produced the work, not on the work itself. In essence, the work produced could obtain a low mark because of personality clashes between the student and the academic. I have experienced a number of significant differences in grading of these types of work between different academics and in some circumstances students have failed their course before secondary marking has been accomplished correctly.

Additionally, it is remarkable how some work produced by students is given low marks even though what has been produced is useful (especially from part time industrial students) and can be used for someone else to gain knowledge. Whilst, some work that can only be described as 'intellectual waffle' is given high marks because they have presented the work, especially the reference format, academically correct, yet, produced something of little use or value. This type of scenario occurs all too often in academic fields and people should question the usefulness of academia in furnishing people with knowledge and skills and awarding appropriately earned qualifications based on usefulness on what was produced as part of the learning outcome. It is the same argument with awarding students with PhDs (or other research degrees) following a thesis that is basically a literature review with some results from a standard format questionnaire presented in complex graphs and charts without any real work or new knowledge gained - it is just a survey!

Thus, when marking students work they specifically look for the academic marking specifics (academic methods and methodologies) rather than concerning themselves with the context of the work and thinking to themselves 'perhaps this is useful and deserves further interest', instead they critic and give low grades as being not academically appropriate. Thus academic work, which may be waffle or academic blah-blah and meaningless, obtains a high grade because it has been presented according to the academic elitism/snobbery processes.

The problems are abundantly clear whenever government or think tanks take advice or research findings from academia with which to base projects or decisions upon. Generally, in fact in the high 90% of cases, the problems they are trying to solve become worse. A prime example is how to deal with sex offenders - all Western countries after putting in processes, driven by research outcomes, with advice from academics, has generated more reoffending from the people partaking in the rehabilitation program than those who did not. The problems can be credited to academics spending substantial time critically analysing other academics work rather than experiencing the real world or do not have 'on-the-job' frontline experience with which to base decisions on (they also insist students analyse the papers they read). However, to critically analyse something you need the pre-requisite of knowledge in that specific area and preferably some real world frontline experience as without these analysis of theories cannot be done effectively or correctly. Furthermore, without any validation or proof that the theories being analysed are true or work, what is actually being accomplished by critically analysing it is producing words that are meaningless and without justification. Thus, most decisions made from research in academia have had a detrimental impact on society leading to degradation of services and social culture; the evidence is painfully apparent everywhere globally.

There is also another issue, concentrating on reading other academic's work and referencing it accordingly then analysing it seems to be valid for academia, however, academics do not accept placing real world experience in academic work to be assessed. Observation, which is the heart of science, is invalid and will achieve low marks if presented to academia without a valid reference to other academic's work; common sense is also just as invalid. It is why many people with high academic qualifications struggle to understand the complexities and workings of the real world even in their specialists' fields because their goal of obtaining a qualification means that they have been (and need to be) removed from it.

On return to the real world and having to deal with real world issues, they struggle or worst of all their work is used to amend legislation or societal rules. Most academics have a close minded view on what the reality of the real world is that they require evidence, tests, and sampling conducted and controlled in an academic manner in order to prove methods and theories. When time and time again the work academics produce is a waste of money thus gathers dust because they cannot in their own minds look further afield as they lack real world experience. Their only concern is mathematical provable theories that for the large part completely ignore the real world realities and human behaviour. Thus, actioning academic work in the real world comes at very high risk, especially any and all projects involving human behaviour. Questions should be asked about the academic process when research and teaching outcomes are not having a positive impact on society.

In the social science discipline, where the science in wishy-washy at best, most ideas are based on opinions besides most of the work is not based around real world events. What is being produced is lots of waffle that is irrelevant to anything and not justifiable in the real world yet can be validated using social science techniques – (oh and thank-you for those social science and psychologist academics who created and justified a child worshipping culture; well done for dismantling human society!). What is happening in academia is useful work is consistently marked low due to conjecture and opinions based on real world experience and sometimes academics will fail students who have produced arguably some brilliant pieces of work because the academics lack real world experience along with a draconian marking scheme that concentrates on presentation over usefulness. It is not the student's fault if they have experienced more than the academic who is marking the work. If something cannot be justifiable in academic terms, e.g. graphs, data, references, etc., the work is completely dismissed; thus, ideas that people have based on frontline real world experience are being totally dismissed and never progress to a level where people can make decisions based on the work produced. This is probably why some of the most basic and simplest solutions never come to fruition because they are stopped by academics that lack knowledge and experience in real world events.

It is further proof that academia is becoming factories to make profits for the university itself because for the large part they are not producing people that have enough knowledge and skills for the real world and not engendering the research benefits to society that they should. Indeed, most academic work is being wasted along with the degradation of the worth concerning qualifications. This is only strengthened by the disillusionment industrial student feel (along with a sour taste in their mouth) when coerced to take courses in academia that has little to do with real world issues they are dealing with on a daily basis. Some industrial students are told by academics that they are wrong and do not know what they are doing even though some of the methods used in industry are successful, robust and repeatable. It does not work toward building mutual respect and only creates further lack of reverence for academic knowledge and expertise.

This leads to whether academics should be automatically placed on a pedestal in society. It is clear that most academics are 'bluffing' their way through their career in academia whilst some academics realise some of their colleagues are not worthy of earning their salary nor should be involved in research projects due to their incompetence and lack of knowledge. But, these few academics will not make issue due to possible career suicide as academia is comparable to a tight-knit club where a 'clique' is in operation and any official backstabbing is frowned upon and will probably backfire due to smooth talking into higher management connections. Justification for existence is once again down to 'who you know' and not 'what you know' or 'how useful you are'.

Something needs to be changed to reverse this trend.

There are many academic presentations I have sat through featuring many simulations using software tools, but, the Q&A sessions lead only to consider that the presenter's knowledge in the field is only as good as the computer simulation allows them to be, i.e. the software tool uses algorithms to optimise a solution and the person then reverse engineers the solution to generate a theory or method and sells this as knowledge. This means that given a new problem to solve the person has little expertise with which to develop a solution without trial and error using a software tool. In essence, it becomes an enigma of having expertise in using technology but little expertise in understanding the problem and how to develop a solution because the software tool uses many iterations (sometimes millions) to calculate a solution that may or may not be valid for many different reasons. It would seem like there is an elitism/snobbery, internationally, for those academics that can produce complex mathematical simulations and present their results in graphical format, even though a large percentage of graphs produced have little indication of understanding the problem, how useful the solution is, or how the methodologies and methods can be duplicated for other problems. For the large part becoming a 'doctor' or obtaining a PhD generally involves producing graphs and discussing the shape of the plot, even if the graphs are meaningless (I have seen plenty of meaningless graphs and waffle to go along with them). And do not get me started on statistics and those experts in performing data analysis using statistical methods!

However, some disciplines, like physics, are not designed to produce immediate results, but, sometimes what is found has devastating consequences, i.e. the atomic bomb; yet most of physics is based on a "cheat" that mathematical propositions is created from after which funding is generated, justified by exaggerated research outcomes, to allow academics the freedom to continue to work free from pressure to prove their theorems. This type of system has been hijacked by the academic researchers involved in bio-technology that again could have more devastating consequences than any physics propositions proved true by stumbling upon it.

Exaggerating research outcomes to acquire funding seems to be part of normal everyday practice for academia to justify their existence even though research in academia produces little in terms of progress compared to industrial research; though the academic environment should far out perform industry in respective fields. This notwithstanding, academia are proficient in giving the impression that they are at the forefront in innovative research so much so that the research papers produced show promise, well that is until industry produce something that invalidates the results. In most research areas academia is now being left behind with outdated practices playing catch-up by knowledge grasp from any and all connections to industry without the experience of what to do with the information without advice from those without high academic qualification (however, they will not admit it and will present themselves as experts).

There is a term used in academia to justify research that has no real world application – Academic Research; and there is a lot of this type of research being pursued in academia. Substantial resources, including millions of tax payer research money, is spent doing purely academic work which produces nothing more than words, diagrams, graphs, and flows that then is stored to gather dust with the work used as a reference for other researchers to use to publish more papers. There is no payback or any possibility of real world application; therefore, what has been produced has been a complete waste of all the resources that has contributed. From the work, however, students can be awarded a PhD, academics can acquire further research funding for more purely academic research and the working people are blissfully unaware that their money is being wasted with the outcome being experts in, for loss of a better word, 'nothing' apart from mathematical and data manipulation with some presentation and software tool usage skills.

It is clear that most academics and most people with higher level academic qualifications are good at mathematical manipulation of data, good at producing paperwork, graphs and presentations but seem to mentally struggle in understanding holistic issues relating to the real world aspects of the problem they were/are working on. Industry is only now beginning to realise the problems with employing people with high academic qualifications. Many PhD's are extremely good at using technology (especially software) or justifying ideas using 'wishy-washy' science (that people with practical knowledge in the area would most likely discredit) but because they lack the ability to understand, think or solve complex problems using structured methods; some have become highly paid complications or liabilities. For this reason, industry is now becoming more motivated to look for employees with low level academic qualifications and then train them in the correct methods.

It is sad to say many people who have the title of 'doctor' (have a PhD) are not experts in their respective fields but are experts in using one or more software tools with statistical capabilities; and most are arrogant with it. This notwithstanding, there are some (a few) who have earned the title of 'doctor' and produced a thesis that is or can be useful, yet, most struggle to acquire the award due to frustration with academic snobbery but moreover examiner knowledge deficit; and become intertwined with the reputation of those majority who are experts in tool usage and/or smooth talking only. Unfortunately, this scenario has come about because of the management processes involved in awarding qualifications and due to political culture in academic institutions.

More PhD's than at any time in history are being awarded by examiners when what has been produce is a 90% thesis surrounding a literature review in their chosen research area followed by a 10% discussion concerning a methodology or methods to further knowledge in the area without any real justification where it fits in or whether it would be useful in the real world. What has been produced is a thesis that is a large literature review, basically produced as a summary from reading academic published papers, followed by 'diagrams or equivalent' and a discussion how the 'diagrams' works. These theses impart no new knowledge to anyone, yet, are awarded the highest academic qualification and the author is then marketed as an expert in their field in spite of not earning that reputation. It is the reason why most theses catch dust and cobwebs.

How and why this happens relate to how the independent research areas at academic institutions work. Examiners are supposed to be chosen based on their suitability to the research area being assessed, however, due to the networking prowess of workshops and conferences, academics strike a relationship with various other academics at other institutions as it is in all of their best interests to share knowledge and work to the benefit of each other. When the main research supervisor chooses an external examiner it is based on their relationship with each other and how much quid-pro-quo is between them; as there are financial gains for being an external examiner. This relationship also means the major critical evaluation of the thesis being assessed is not the prime concern as much as the continued quid-pro-quo relationship between the academics – a corruption of the examination process.

This notwithstanding, there are some students whom through the specialisation of the research area emerge with an external examiner who has little or no relationship with the prime supervisor or the internal examiner; these student's thesis is subjected to scrutiny more than the others. It is primarily these students who either fail or who have earned the academic qualification; these are far and few between and often become disillusioned with academia due to the inequitable examination process and/or the quality of academics chosen to oversee and grade their research. Most students in this category suffer at the hands of academics who give the illusion of knowledge and whom have never fully understood a problem in context or worked towards a practical solution to a real world problem. The reality is it is a large majority of these students whom industry need and who can drive innovation in the future.

As an example, due to complexity and multi-disciplinary nature of my PhD research project the choice of external examiner was difficult find and justify to the extent that 4 academics eventually made a choice of external examiner which unfortunately none of my supervisory staff had a relationship with. At the time the decision needed to be made I could not find details of her expertise as all of her research was protected; only her current career status was readily available. After being confidently informed that the choice of examiner was suitable, after 5 minutes within the viva-voce I realised that something was deeply concerning regarding her depth of knowledge. To be honest after all the issues I had to deal with from the industrial sponsor and the academic staff during the PhD, this turned the whole experience into a complete farce. There were no questions from the external relating to the work in the thesis, but, questions regarding approaches to the work, which are discussed regularly in workshops or conferences.

It was clear the external only had basic knowledge in these areas too as she only described views that are given in 'sales pitches' by various companies who are attempting to sell tools to universities and other research institutes at said conferences. She was also quite arrogant with it. Needless to say after the first five minutes I watched the time go by because there was literally no point me being there. The situation was almost comical with most of my effort taken to prevent me from saying, "you do not know what you are talking about' and not saying more than once in a sarcastic way, 'what has that got to do with the research project I am being assessed on' with most of the time taken up by looking at the internal examiner hoping he was thinking the same things.

Long story short, the thesis was temporarily referred but she did not want me to sit another viva-voce; she was so out of her depth that she did not even realise that what she referred the thesis for was a completely different research area unrelated to the research topic; she wanted additional research to be added that matched her new research interests. Many hours of researching and telephone calls later I found out the true reason why she appeared to be completely out of her depth and most definitely should not have been anywhere near assessing my research project. I also asked a professor colleague at another university who has some knowledge of the areas covered to assess the thesis and his feedback was only positive. After pointing out the obvious regarding the external and the fact that her new research interests has zero interest with me or my research project to my supervisory team, who appeared completely oblivious to her lack of suitable qualifications for the project, they pointed the finger of blame to other academics.

I was advised not to take issue higher as I would most likely be asked to rewrite the whole thesis. Therefore, I wrote and added a two page 'laymen' description of something that was blatantly obvious to someone with real knowledge in the area, where the boundary of the research is and where the possible link is for her research interests with a simple block diagram that a child could follow. The thesis passed without issue afterwards even though I purposely altered something that would have been easily identified if the thesis was reassessed correct as it should have been. I changed it back when I submitted the thesis to the repository. Overall, post graduate education has been a very interesting experience.

It is difficult to control the examination process to avoid any collusion between supervisors and examiners, however, current research degrees have little specific marking criteria and are based on subjective opinions of the examiners, moreover the external examiners. If the research is found to be original based on examiners knowledge of the research area, then it must be possible to produce a marking criteria for how the thesis is structured and presented. The choice of external examiner should be made by professionals not part of the supervisory team and be authorised via an examination board that will assess suitability of the examiner to the specifics of the research project. Moreover, government needs to work to remove the quid-pro-quo system currently operating at all universities globally to ensure that future 'doctors' earn the title rather than be given it due to relationships within the academic community.

For anyone who has the motivation to learn and has spent some time in higher academic institutions, they will question the knowledge and skill levels of the academics. They quickly realise that apart from basic knowledge in the area the academics are imparting and selling well through self-promotion and smooth talking, they have little to offer in detail with most of their knowledge detail being out of date; this is especially prevalent when the academics do not say anything that isn't already on a PowerPoint presentation. Academics are all too competent about talking about various areas of interest using buzz-words (smooth talking) but struggle to hold a conversation when quizzed about the details, nonetheless, can still divert attention away with their smooth talking and mathematical manipulation skills. The problem has become so apparent that most academics (I and many others have interacted with) have taken to using questionable sources for information, i.e. Wikipedia, and even uses the site for reference.

Sometimes academics misunderstand or become confused what the buzz-words mean, invariably, this embarrasses them when discussing technical issues with other academics, which unfortunately adds to the real problem of different vocabularies between academics from varied specialities (i.e. communication issues), or when a student has knowledge in the area; or worse, they pass on this misunderstanding to their students. (I remember a student who spent 4 years on a research area being supervised by an academic whom mistakenly misunderstood a buzz-word, all the research papers he read did not explain what the buzz-word really meant and has substantial gaps in understanding and description (they were produced by other academics). Subsequently, the student spent another 2.5 years correcting this mistake by changing their research topic).

This notwithstanding, these buzz-words do create new research avenues where government funding can be sought, even though nothing new has actually happened apart from creating the buzz-words themselves. Academics are so proficient at smooth talking and justifying their existence they give the illusion these new research areas is looking into something new when the reality is there is nothing new what-so-ever. People and government departments have to realise sometimes (arguably most of the time) academics are wasting large portions of public money to justify their existence and own career ambitions in obtaining further funding for universities. New research areas should be based on the reality of new research for the future not on the illusion of new research areas and money should not be allocated to justify buzz-word creation.

The problem is academics have a lot of knowledge by accomplishing a literature review in a very small area, but, their reputation and status relies on them expanding their knowledge to other fields. They do this by reading published papers, acquiring knowledge whilst grading student work, which they then sell as their own, and by networking at conferences. They have very little input from industry unless they are a principle investigator on an industry/government sponsored research project and then struggle with practical knowledge of how things actually work as most are career academics or whom have been sponsored by industry to be a professor because the company struggled to 'fire' them. Irrespective, academics are not subject matter experts in what they teach or what they are currently researching; most of their work is reliant on the students they supervise to keep them apprised of recent developments and new buzz-words.

There is also a problem with arrogance and ego at academia caused by the automatic respect given to them by society holding them as the intellectual elites in the world with some being paid six figure salaries. Their ego is prominent in their personality that when they are criticised by other academics/peers, industrial representatives or upstaged by a student (who possesses more updated knowledge than them) their behaviour changes to that of a spoilt child. This is one of those behaviours which struck me and others as bewildering considering they are placed on a pedestal in society.

It seems like if someone is an academic (possesses a PhD) or is a professor, most develop a closed vision or representation of reality with a precarious increase in ego and arrogance that their ego is easily bruised and 'battle lines' drawn because they have a false sense of their own importance and knowledge (and skill) levels. They interact with people in such a way to express their importance even if the expression is ill-founded. Most new academics struggle without the software tool they are experienced in, so much so that without the software tool at their disposal nothing is achieved. It is one of the reasons why when industry give academics the information needed for a research project (through NDA agreements) and attempt to work with them; the outcome fails to achieve expectation because academics are so self-involved and arrogant that they are unable to expand their minds and realise that perhaps they are not experts they think themselves to be. This is so apparent in most international standard documentation or guides that completely ignore the constraints of the real world and is deficit in real world justification of methodologies and methods used in the documentation that state theory in an ideological boundary; probably because most have not experienced industry or who have failed in their brief stint within it.

The distinct lack of understanding of where true knowledge lies is the prime reason why most research work coming from universities is squandered and transferrable skills low; most new discoveries have been made by sheer incompetence or by stumbling upon it accidentally (i.e. graphene discovery). It is hard to realise this reality as the cloak of misconception is consistently placed over the knowledge excellence at universities. The number of technical papers published is one of the cloaks that keep universities fully funded. Many academics can be described as 'one trick ponies' that continue to sell one method or methodology throughout their career and apply it to different problems through discussion points within papers. They can do this because most academic publications are produced and peer reviewed by other academics that the author(s) knows due to networking connections – it is the quid-pro-quo scenario. It is why many papers are published which have a distinct lack of research 'meat' but incorporates a literature review with either mathematical equations, graphs or block diagrams or a combination of all with substantial gaps in rationalisation (some of the recent papers I have read involve research outcomes that was done 20-30 years ago in the past and just repackaged as new methods or methodologies).

For someone who has intelligence or real knowledge in certain areas, academia has become somewhat of an embarrassment apart from those few times when something develops out of sheer coincidence or accident. Problems are apparent when academics or experts who are researching the same area publish disparate and contradictory results with the outcome being confusion about what is true or reality (especially when it relates to health issues). This scenario happens too frequently to take any of the research seriously and undermines the benefits of researching within an academic environment. The main reason being is statistical analysis permits contradictory results to be justified using the identical data sets; it is not that surprising that this type of scenario is occurring more often than in the past with the availability of statistical software tools with various types of analysis functions available.

For the large part most of what academics understand is placed in a format that is difficult for the average person to comprehend. The complex language, sentences and mathematical formulae used, unless you possess the knowledge to structure and decode, seems like a different language altogether. However, possessing the 'Rosetta-stone' for academic blah-blah invariably means that the most complex mathematical formulae or symbols are not complex to understand whatsoever. It is again the illusion that academics are working on complex problems and solutions because unless people go to university, the knowledge to understand the patterns and symbols used is absent; thus, appears to be complicated and encourages the consensus that academics are subject matter experts who should not be doubted. It does provide the facility for the most incompetent and disorganised academics the ability to hide at universities as long as they are proficient at smooth talking and repeating what is on PowerPoint presentations. They are so good at this task it becomes possible to hide from other academics, but, difficult to place a cloak over their lack of knowledge with people who have hands-on experience in industry.

I once was a superior to someone who caused me a number of managerial headaches - he was lazy, did not arrive on time and broke numerous terms of employment conditions. Yet, with the knowledge I have now regarding academics, I respect him a lot more than the vast majority of academic I have interacted with purely because, irrespective of his flaws, I know he was useful, possessed knowledge and skills in his field and I gained some value. Whereas, most academics, especially those who use smooth talking and buzz-words to justify their existence, there is no justifiable value from the tasks they do. In all honesty some of what they are teaching and placing in national and international standards is 'damn right criminal'. The truth being told, if I was the head of a university the first task would be to consider options open to me to remove some of the most highly paid academic staff members (some of which are on six figure salaries) and replace them instantly with people more experienced in respective fields, even people akin to that employee that caused me so many headaches, as it would place universities in a better position to provide students with better knowledge and skills for their future. At least then I would know value is being received for the money that is being paid.

What society have then is academics and students who have read and gained knowledge but possess no real practical hands on experience that fills the gap in knowledge and skills books are unable to provide and frequently ignore due to theory taking precedence over issues of reality. It should not be difficult to realise where the problem with academia is in relation to producing people with *relevant* knowledge and skills to drive the country forward.

This notwithstanding, there does come a point where academics have to become involved in academic politics to defend their position or research area from other academics. This type of politics is similar to industrial or office politics, but, less intelligently done and has more similarities to primary school child politics of blackmail, threats, and name calling – it really is uncomfortable seeing academics behave like primary school children in any disputes they have between them. It should be beneath people of this type of stature to behave in such a way, but then again most academics have not been in the real world of work or have failed in industry, therefore, handling disputes defaults to such primitive demeanours. The 'covering the back strategy' generally involves stabbing their own students in the back or pointing the 'finger of blame' elsewhere, but, due to their disorganisation and incompetence somehow it tends to backfire, especially when it is directed at someone used to playing adult office politics.

Nevertheless, a large majority of academics are in academia because of network connections of their previous supervisors, themselves being smooth talkers, the corruption the examination process and the realisation that there is no real accountability for their performance in universities and thus will struggle in industry for many different reasons. The number of projects that have failed or failed to produce useful outcomes and remained unfinished (though something, i.e. a method, that does not work is a useful outcome) is far too big and would be completely unacceptable in industry. Academics are inherently disorganised besides their arrogance and ego gets it their way of realising that they are unable to manage research projects in an efficient manner. They become too reliant on students and RAs to manage their projects for them and too set in their ways to change. Young academics are proficient at software tool usage only and the older generation tends to stay-away from software and slow to use ICT; although both have delusions of grandeur that they possess knowledge and abilities far beyond their own competence level that makes them believe they know what they are doing. It is amazing to think anything is actually achieved at universities apart from pieces of paper being passed around the complex. *N.B. Academics being managers is even worse than managers in industry, they are more disorganised, more arrogant, more lazy and highly paid for it; yet they have the good sense to surround themselves with administrators and other academics (who 'suck-up' for their future career prospects) to overcome identifiable weaknesses.*

The old adage of 'throw people at the problem and they will come up with a solution' still counts at colleges and universities. These are the choices open to academics when they become principle investigator of a project, they can surround themselves with people and divert student's attention away from what they should be doing to help the academic fulfil their own deliverables. The extent to which this happens means students actually do the work the academics should be doing then the academics assesses the work, makes their mark on it, and sells it as theirs; if anything goes wrong blame is directed at the students or the RAs, but, anything positive the academic will glow in the praise and feed their own ego. Hiding incompetence and lack of knowledge at colleges and universities is easy as long as you follow the same unwritten system that has been used for decades. It is this system that needs to change to ensure that the new generation of teachers and academics that are employed to impart knowledge to the next generation of children and adults are competent and have enough knowledge in the subjects they are involved in to furnish and drive innovation into the future.

To coincide with the type of elitism/snobbery at play in academia, if an existing academic is applying for a vacancy at a university, for example lecturer in an engineering subject, it should go without saying that the candidate should possess qualification, knowledge and skills, and some experience in the specific domain the vacancy is for. However, surprising as it may seem, having knowledge, skills or experience in the specific domain being advertised for is not a necessity to fill the position. Proof of publishing journal or conference (possibly workshop) articles is of paramount concern, which is easy for academics due to the networking scenario. More often than not universities will dismiss applicants who have more relevant qualifications, knowledge and skills, and experience in the domain and give the position to someone with a better journal publish rate, which may or may not be remotely similar to the domain in question, within the last year or so. Unfortunately, this means that when a student is being taught there is a high degree of probability that the lecturer might not possess any detailed knowledge (or any knowledge beyond basic or what is written on presentations) in the subject area.

In relation to the inept decisions made by senior academics and management levels (i.e. school Deans), you have to stand back in amazement and awe of departments and research groups that are populated by academics (the sheer audacity and arrogance of them) whose academic qualifications do not match their current employment title in any way. It would seem as though in real term these academics cannot acquire an academic position in their own speciality but somehow senior academic staff and management allow them to diversify into other specialist fields at the expense of other more qualified and experienced people. This problem is more prevalent in the department of engineering in all academic institutions, especially those who have a systems engineering department, but, does exist in most. There are academics that possess qualifications in either business, psychology, management, law, sports, textiles, art, and other such areas who seem to think, along with senior academics, that they have the necessary expertise to be engineers (no, just NO!). There is not attempt made to confine or constrain their activities, they firmly believe that 'yesterday they could not spell engineer, today they can be one'. Research funding for engineering projects is sometimes managed, overseen and accomplished by these people with the outcome being a complete and total failure in real terms, but, in academic terms is seen as being successful research exercises (totally dumbfounded!!! – the amount of tax payer money wasted is scandalous). Systems engineering, arguably all engineering, has been hijacked and infected by a disease (pretenders) who have damaged, possibly beyond repair, the reputation of real engineers.

These academics, due to lack of any knowledge what so ever regarding engineering, believe everything every 'sales man' says, but, they also become involved in developing international standards, legislation and guides that are used for manufacturing and defence companies worldwide. Not only this, they have the impudence of thinking they can correctly supervise and assess PhD student's theses that includes real technical engineering, design, mathematics, logic and physics. They also have the nerve to critique the work presented in theses; how dare they go anywhere near any real engineering research or project – students deserve to have their work assessed by real engineers who have experience in the related areas covered in their theses.

There is no attempt made to distinguish the lack of any real expertise with these people; they are treated on par with others who, rightly or wrongly, deserve the title of engineer. There are some who genuinely believe that they know what they are doing and it does not matter what problem they are looking at, e.g. developing jet aircraft or human interaction with technical systems or IT communication systems, these people without any real knowledge, skills or expertise in any of the specific areas believe they can do it all; and sell it using complex language / vocabulary and buzz-words to incompetent industrial management, research funders and government officials. These types of academics are so arrogant and have a huge ego they will not accept that they are wrong even if evidence is shown to them by real time served engineers; it is unsurprising that they tend not to interact with real engineers, only high level management.

This notwithstanding, I am extremely confident that all real engineers they interact with, even those who are extremely passive, use all their strength to stop themselves from punching them in the face within five minutes of meeting them. Their arrogance does nothing without knowledge and only serves to anger people who have spent years homing and developing their knowledge, skills and expertise. These academics do not even realise the standards and guides they produce, along with the questionable logic regarding family of systems or systems of systems, show the distinct lack of knowledge in the areas; they cannot understand that developing a system alone is predominantly far more complicated than integrating two independent systems together – a real experienced engineer would know this and does not need to be informed otherwise. They truly are an embarrassment to the Engineering community.

These types of academics are vexations, which are causing some very real issues for society and need to be removed from causing further problems with immediate effect. Perhaps they would be more use to society picking rubbish up from the street; oh wait probably not, they would sell themselves as environmental engineering management experts and possibly develop over complex international standards and guidelines that requires millions of pounds worth of investment, which might influence legislation, and leave every tax payer worse off and streets full of rubbish; never mind, it was a bad idea best just pay them to stay at home where they can do little harm.

The issue is there are some competent students who become entangled with these types of academics in various departments with their reputation being tarnished by the academics who have no justifiable claim to be involved in areas they are incompatible with, especially those who believe they are entitled to be identified in their job description as an (academic) Engineer. The term engineer seems to be the main focus to make people sound more important than they are and this practice needs to stop e.g. Software engineer is in reality a software programmer and cannot become an engineer just by learning code, project engineer is in reality a project manager who elicits basic technical knowledge from engineers, sales engineer is a 'posh' sales assistant that needs basic knowledge of engineering products not in engineering, etc.

A major concern in academia stems from the requirement of every lectureship in a particular department or school requiring the prerequisite of a candidate publishing papers within the last year in major journals or conferences. This means all the knowledge, skills, experience and expertise of all industrial people are automatically 'locked out' of most academic positions regarding teaching and research activities. The result can be summarised as 'What is in academia, stays in academia', leading to the problem of career academics with little or no experience of their speciality in the real world. Therefore, with the lack of industrial experts in academia to pass on real world knowledge, skills and experience, there is little chance of students gaining knowledge and skills they need know to help them in the future.

This notwithstanding, the problem does arise due to senior academics and management completely dismissing industrial experience from any and all applications into the profession.

Most have a deluded opinion that they are the experts in their own field, with most not possessing any real world industrial experience to justify their claim. It would seem as though any industrial experience is completely irrelevant in academic circles for academic positions. The UK is the world leader in this type of scenario and is the main reason why there are large skills gaps in the country and why industry complains about the lack of skills of graduates and continues to look internationally, more than any other time in history, to fill available positions.

The problem in academia is apparent by the fact post graduate student have to partake in mandatory courses designed to help them be more attractive to employers. The irony is these courses are written and developed by career academics who have either not being in industry or who have failed in their brief stint in it. It does not take a genius to realise what value will come from these courses. Having been through similar monitory courses at different academic institutions, I can honestly say what a complete waste of time these were; but, serve to divert attention away from the real problem of the lack of skills graduates possess. They do however justify the existence of additional academics and HR professional in academia, but, sadly does nothing to resolve the problem; which is mismanagement practices, the quality of academics, the teaching practice and material, and the deluded sense of expertise throughout most if not all departments.

There are a lot of people paying a lot of money, especially those struggling on the 'breadline', for academics who are producing little value to society; it is a practice that can only be described as criminal. Currently (July 2017) in the UK, universities are facing a pension fund deficit of £17.5billion to keep academics and senior management that do not deserve their current salary with high paid pensions. There is a strong possibility that the already poor education service received by students will degrade even more by funds being diverted away from frontline teaching and research activities, besides tuition fees increasing, in order to fill the pensions gap. It would seem that the same scenario which plays out in the public sector is widespread in academia – those who are inept / incompetent but possess smooth talking skills are paid the most and protected, whilst those who are useful pay the price for greed and poor decisions.

People should be in outrage of the management and employment processes used in academic institutions. With situations regarding job application, school processes, mismanagement, poor decision making, and the lack of real expertise in relevant domains to teach students the necessary knowledge and skills for the future to help fill the skills gap, (especially in the UK) academia in its current form has ceased to be fit for purpose. The problems with inept and incompetent smooth talking 'yes' people in management in industry seem relatively insignificant compared to the problems schools and academia in general is faced with.

It is not all doom and gloom though. Some academics do possess real knowledge in their area and do work hard to produce something useful, but, they are far and few in-between; therefore, are hard to find in a pool full of ill-founded arrogance and egos. These academics find it hard to advance their career or expand their research group because they are 'stone walled' or blocked by others who do not deserve their positions in academia. This type of scenario is a tragedy because the one thing academia needs more than anything else is useful and knowledgeable academics in high level positions. The sad realisation is producing something new and useful from research takes time meaning publishing research outcomes also takes time and these academics have integrity not to repeat the same thing in a different titled paper. Consequently, the number of published papers useful academics have in their name are generally low in comparison to those who mass produce what is essentially a literature review with a continuing repeat of the same method used in previous papers; therefore, will be blocked from advancing their career. Thus, the majority of academics who are not as useful produce many papers, which undeservedly are published and consequently have the 'goods' to acquire promotion into high level positions.

As long as industry remains obsessed with academic qualifications as a prerequisite for some positions, young people will have no choice but to attend academic institutions to acquire those important qualifications in order to compete on the job market. The irony is their education experience will most likely consist of being between 80-90% self-taught with what can seem like an enormous amount of debt at the start of their independent life with little real skills being transferred. This is a striking condemnation of how badly the education system has been mismanaged over the years. The realisation is the experts are still within the frontline of industry and the Doctors and Professors in academia are a long way behind and show no signs of reducing the gap.

Employing academics should be based on experience of real world problems related to their chosen speciality. Moreover, career academic, like career politicians, needs to be resisted. Having people at universities whom have succeeded in industry and have gained frontline experience and knowledge as to what works and what does not work need to be endorsed and be a stipulation and constraint of being employed as an academic and being a professor. (No sponsorship from industry should influence professorships at universities (the likelihood is this person is someone who they would like to remove from the company therefore should be seen as being unsuitable for a university environment)).

Universities more than any time in history are concerned with new academics having research experience and experience with using common academic software that they preclude people who do not possess these attributes. The problem is software can be taught as it is merely a tool and people who are experts in using tools are not best suited to be academics who impart learning or quality research for the benefit of society; hence the current problem. People who have succeeding in industry on the frontline have natural research experience in critical thinking, solving complex problems or managing projects and therefore there is a natural progression for the skills to be transferred to research in an academic environment. Moreover, if quality in universities is to improve academic elitism/snobbery has to be removed from the constraints of employment.

Job evaluation should be based on the success academics have with amending lectures to keep up with latest developments, achievement rates and research outcomes. Some lectures are still based on knowledge gained several decades ago without any amendment and most lectures along with academics fail to distinguish between pure theory and something that could work in the real world. The lectures fail to provide the correct learning outcomes for students who are looking to work in industry and concentrate in the correct methodology that is based on theoretical constructs that have little or no place in real world activities. It becomes a matter of educating the use of specific software tools, concentration upon theorists whose work may or may not be valid; and methodologies far removed from real world realities.

The reality of higher education for most students is to gain a qualification then forget most of what they learned, as what is learned in generally unsuitable for real world application except in those small niche areas university caters for. The other reality is higher education students are coerced into paying high tuition fees to progress through a course with little face time with lecturers. Most knowledge is gathered through self-taught principles of reading books and published papers with minor inputs from the academics. This is not surprising as there is little motivation for academics to place priority on updating lecture material or teaching, as it does not assist them in progressing their career goals. As such, students are seen as a necessary inconvenience as for academics to climb the salary grades they are required to acquire funding for the university with research grants, thus, the priority is to write research proposals.

Students are directed to the reading material they need to help them in their essays or project work, there is generally little other help or guidance from their academic lecturer. With the present state of procedure and culture at colleges and universities the only conclusion for prospective students is if they wish to acquire knowledge in certain areas it is more financially rewarding (no fees to pay) and just as difficult (self-taught) to read a book on the subject area and gain experience with 'on the job' training to gain the necessary skills to go with the knowledge gained. For industry leaders it is more efficient and less costly to train new employees straight from school rather than employ someone who is indoctrinated in academic culture, as it is extremely difficult for these types of people to transition into fast paced, high pressure environments.

However, for many students who have stayed in academia since school it is easy to become indoctrinated in the methods and theories taught or researched in academia due to the lack of real world experience of both the students and the academics. This works in detriment of society as most guidance and advice acquired from government originates from highly academic qualified people, generally academics at universities, who have been sheltered from real world experience in their chosen field. This precedes to a misunderstanding of problems and a presented complex solution written in convoluted language with graphs, tables, charts and diagrams to give the illusion of being an expert when logic dictates if a problem is complicated to understand the solution should be simple to comprehend and implement, i.e. the reverse of what has and is happening to the health service.

Academics must possess the ability to alter the lectures accordingly and work with the international community to change standards and guides to account for real world application of theoretical constructs, moreover, the information provided must identify theoretical constructs in the narrative. Research outcomes should be based on innovations not on the number of published papers; and funding for universities should be equitable with this change. In essence, there needs to be real value coming from teaching and research activities; publishing papers due to networking connections have failed to achieve quality in research activities and teaching outcomes. The government and research funding agencies are also complicit in this problem as the system is set up to keep the class system at universities stagnant and to keep universities fully funded irrespective of the quality of teaching and research arising from the institutions – it has become a club that has detrimental effect on every tax payer who are not receiving quality for the money given. There need to be some meat to add to the complex mathematical formulae and graphs, furthermore, university innovation should surpass that of industry as universities are allowed to fully concentrate on the research areas without additional pressures industry has to face. Investigations need to occur if industry is still leading in cutting edge research.

These combined should help develop an appraisal scheme that should eventually filter out those academics whom deserve their place at universities from those majority who are merely hiding their own lack of knowledge and competence through smooth talking, promotion of their own self-importance, network connections, and buzz-words. The system should also permit new high quality academics to be employed at universities to help prepare young adults for their future using a combination of theoretical constructs and practical applications with in-depth discussion on the similarities and differences to best suit future innovations in all fields.

Additionally, academics should be considered subject matter experts in identifying the problems between theory and practical applications of theoretical constructs; currently, there are very little academics who can do this remotely effectively. A stronger bond between industry and academia should allow for academics to 'prove their worth' and the level of knowledge and skills they possess by succeeding in bridging the gap between theory and practice concurrently with academia and industry.

Most students will find their way into industry and it is important that universities and new theories drive the progression to enable the future generations follow their dreams and their career choices; having good quality academics is the only approach to achieve this. Additionally, courses should become more aligned with the knowledge and skills needed by industry on the whole for innovation. At present, most courses are purely academic in nature as such of little value or use to students who career path ventures outside of an academic environment or those few catered for industries that use the same software tools.

There is a need to provide students with a route to career and personal success through education by providing an integrated curriculum to further integrate academic studies to practical real world applications. The new curriculum should achieve the rise in standards that is needed; the lack of this type of integrated curriculum has been a major issue in all education areas for the past three decades. There needs to be close partnerships with industry and science institutions with additional qualifications available to students being accredited and proper work placements available that is hoped will benefit all parties involved.

Careers advice has been on offer for many university students and young adults for many years, but the standards and working practices have faltered with the default being an exercise of completing a 'Career Aptitude Test' questionnaire (which is based on very loose science) with little else being offered. Experience for many young adults/students is the careers advice service is not helpful and does not take into account additional guidance based on personal circumstances. Hence, there needs to be a rejuvenated focus on face-to-face guidance on routes to further education, careers and apprentices based on personal preferences along with current knowledge and skill levels in various areas individuals possess. Moreover, careers advice should be concerned with what path an individual would be happy to take rather than what default path they should. This will hopefully resolve the problems of students being assigned onto a course and failing due to disinterest and completing apprenticeships just to gain a qualification and some work experience thus ending up in an unsatisfying career. Furthermore, the new careers advice system should be flexible and adaptable to account for new industries, be able to cope with giving advice and support for those whose skills, knowledge and experience have been earned from a non-transferrable job; and evolve quickly to account for the needs of new technology insertion into the country's business model.

Most important of all, universities should be centres of knowledge and skills excellence and nothing on campus should dictate otherwise. It is for this reason alone why any building or activity involving the belief in mythological Gods or political ideologies should be removed from all campuses; colleges and universities are places to learn facts and truths thus are no place for advocating mystical beliefs or ideologies. These beliefs and ideologies should be thought of as getting in the way of evolving one's mind to a higher plane of thought besides knowledge acquisition requires people's minds to be open to new possibilities. Religion and ideological beliefs (caused by confusion, indoctrination and being lost) closes people's minds to teachings in a biblical book or scripture as such cannot be shaped or developed even if what is found to be fact and true contradicts the person's religious or ideological beliefs. Higher education institutions should be intolerant to religion, other ideologies and political movements for this reason. Thus, all places of worship and prayer rooms need to be removed from college and university campuses; likewise, these institutions should cease promoting liberal ideologies based on beliefs, i.e. gender identity. Concurrently, they should promote freedom of speech and stop giving way to people who are offended by other people's free speech.

The second most important issue in modern times is the call for more schools, colleges and universities to have safe spaces within the campus to allow people to go so that they can be safe from others. Who ever thought of this idea should be dismissed from their position immediately and university managers and chancellors who have allowed safe spaces at campus should also be relieved of their positions with immediate effect. Concurrently, all adult students who use these facilities or who are actively involved in protesting or other such activity to acquire one should be expelled from their courses and be unregistered from the college or university and told to mature before reapplying. Safe spaces are an example of the nanny state wanting adults not to be mature enough to cope with life's problems without looking towards public institutions, thus government, for help. As for the removal of separate toilets for individual sex/genders – trust me this will increase the number of complaints of sexual assault and rape, especially from hard core feminists and those who are just confused about who and what they are.

People at higher education institutions should be capable of standing their ground, arguing their intent and 'sticking up for themselves' on any and all issues within the local environment using civilised means to resolve any disputes. People who want to bury their 'heads in the ground' or shy away from disagreements or controversy have no place in these institutions. It is about discussion and debate even though other people might have completely different mind-sets, viewpoints, beliefs or controversial opinions; it is not about protesting, hiding, or preventing other voices being heard. People who are involved in these activities need to be removed from campus as they do not possess the mental strength or maturity to be at university in the first place. It is why children in schools should be hardened by all those around them to prepare them for what is predominantly a ruthless and hard world to live in full of diverse views with incompatible opinions to your own.

$$\boxed{9}$$

CAREERS FOR THE FUTURE

The story of the past three decades has been the dismantling of national industry and has been the largest change in the economy in the post-war era, unfortunately, it is a continuing saga. It caused major changes to the way people of the country lived and the decimation of the industrial heartlands in the northern base has in effect made the UK become two different countries: the prosperous south with its banking and technology centres decoupled from the struggling north. The facts are the manufacturing share of the economy has almost halved since labour came into power in 1997; with the North-West shedding ~212,000 manufacturing jobs with the pay gap between north and south continuing the rise. As the manufacturing base declined, the financial sector grew at a staggering rate as it did in the US. Indeed, one of the critical elements in the 2016 presidential race concerned blue-collar anger and resentment; but America is different as it still remains a formidable manufacturing power with a strong industrial background, unlike the UK and some of Europe. Here in the UK, there is a habitual balance of deficit and an economy heavily reliant on debt driven growth that is a 'big bang' waiting to happen, which will be substantially worse than the 2008 recession.

Successive governments kept the consequences of the change to a financial economy hidden from the people by massaging the figures and overselling the jobless figures with 'spin' - a method that has and continues to work very effectively. It works so well the past exercise of transferring people from long term unemployment to long-term sick is only now becoming an issue which the government of today is dealing with by another form of creative accounting, namely changing the names of the benefits given to people and how employment statistics are recorded.

The reality now is a situation where well-paid jobs in factories (or mines: re: miners strikes in 1980s) have been replaced by low-paid jobs in call centres and distribution warehouses with most manufacturing jobs outsourced to other countries were cheap labour is available. There is a lack of effective demand, and cutting welfare payments will, unfortunately, make the situation worse, not better. The cost to the tax payer because of a decision made 30 years ago is still abundantly clear: a higher number of people on incapacity-related benefits; and due to low paid and part time work there is a greater reliance on tax credits and other top-up payments with higher levels of people not in work for a number of different reasons - cost are a staggering est. ~£20-30 billion per year (Report from Sheffield Hallam University). This signifies that the crash of 2008 is most definitely not the main cause of the budget deficit, the cause lies in the destruction of the UK industrial base and all that has flowed from it (obviously, I am talking specifically about job related budget issues and not about funding for wars, health care, etc.), This story resonates throughout Western countries where business leaders have taken advantage of cheap labour and tax rates in Eastern, African and third world countries with which to manufacture their products.

People from the north of UK has realised that this is one of the major issues for the financial troubles of the country and with distrust of politicians at an all-time high only now has the ruling government of the country realised that reviving the struggling parts could obtain those crucial votes, well at least in rhetoric. The culture of the affected areas has been badly damaged and local areas are in need of rejuvenating, sadly even those that have recently gone through a multi-million-pound upgrade. It is depressing to see lots of empty new industrial units and people reliant of benefits pay-outs with no intention of being productive in society, but, understanding the root causes of why, leads to the decisions made by successive governments since the 1970s. To place the problem in context, since the early 1980s and the late 2000s, the number of people working in industry has fallen from 8.9 million to 2.9 million, which makes the UK have the highest decline than in other advanced economy. The higher welfare spending is a product of inadequate work incentives and successive governments blaming individuals for their own predicament, whereas the societal issues surrounding welfare is rooted in job destruction extending back at least three decades.

Even today, the UK continues to have a shrinking manufacturing sector. In November 2016, industrial output fell by 0.4%, with resource industry (oil, coal and gas) dropping by 3.8%. This notwithstanding, the UK economy in the same period grew by 0.5%, but manufacturing output fell 0.9% meaning that the UK economy driving factor was due to consumer spending and with over 71 million people in the country it is hard not to fathom why. The outcome denotes the overall decline in industrial output continues to show long-term trends with industrial output adding little to the overall UK growth. Globalisation, a Western creation, has had a detrimental effect on the labour market, social wellbeing, and potential industrial applications that could help the environment and people prosper.

However, the government and business leaders are not to fully blame for this development, all people in the all-Western countries are the main contributors to these declines directed by clever marketing and government. People live their lives in complete contradiction to the problems they are facing in daily life; it is the main human condition that has puzzled me for years. There are few decent interesting well paid jobs in the country, but, it does not stop people promoting foreign products or services nor thinking twice about the impacts of being educated to fill professional (non-jobs) in the country that has detrimental consequences to society, i.e. legal professionals and/or banks / traders. People live in complete ignorance about the holistic outcomes of purchasing foreign made products or the repercussions to human attributes in society of promoting high-paid non-jobs in the country.

People do not care about the working conditions people and children in other countries endure making the gadget, clothes or technology bought on a regular basis as it does not affect their own life directly; and this is a very important fact the people should realise. Governments and business leaders are aware of the problems associated with making products (e.g. waste, pollution, workers' rights and pay, etc.) and to conceal the problem that would present financial and social issues if the product or service was provided in the home country, they knowingly take advantage of other more desperate people in other countries. Conscious it would appear is the least of their concerns in modern day capitalism.

The problem is due to costs, whether people like it or not the economy (or inflation) has a dramatic result of making everything more expensive for everyone in the country, including businesses. Paying for wars, overinflated government and public sector, government created non-jobs (including H&S), benefit pay-outs, and increases in population all have a detrimental consequence of increasing inflation and thus cost of living that dominos the wage rate upward to compensate. These are the main reasons why making things in Western countries has become so expensive both for the producer and consumer of products and services.

Less developed countries (I use the term loosely) have reduced real estate and plant costs, fewer regulations, access to a large pool of workers queueing up just to earn little, and are less concerned about the health and safety implications of pollution and working with poisonous chemicals; in essence, it is all about convenience and cost effectiveness. Whereas in Western countries costs have increased substantially due to non-job creation and with it more regulation, more companies needing to employ people to govern the paperwork, more emphasis (bordering on obsession) on qualifications (snobbery/elitism), more pressure to be diverse in the workplace meaning more migrants fill positions native people would have filled, and employing the right people for available positions appears to be problematic, hence, the increase in management hierarchy to compensate for incompetence. It all means that some Western countries, inconveniently ones with high levels of immigration have become less competitive and therefore the manufacturing base continues to shrink as a result.

Unfortunately, the path taken by Western countries are now being adopted by the countries that have benefitted from the manufacturing base being moved their and are now experiencing similar issues regarding inflation and increases in cost due to additional regulation – China is as prime example of a country that has taken full advantage of Western business leaders greed and now experiencing similar fiscal issues as the West.

What has just been described is not a secret for most people, however, why do people accept acquiring a boring unappealing paid job whilst at the same time ensuring that businesses continue to manufacture goods in foreign lands by buying products made not in their own country? Government has made it difficult to do anything fun for free and people cannot afford to pay over the odds for entertainment, technology or transportation; so people look on the market for the cheapest products that satisfy their wants (not needs, the only need is for food and shelter (e.g. farming and building industry)) and government regulation has made it very challenging for companies to make anything in the country that is competitive to foreign made goods. Yes, government has provided incentives for some companies to remain to do business in the country, but, at tax payers expense – in essence, if people in the country buy homemade 'things', not only have people paid more than the foreign made equivalent, but, the likelihood is the tax they have paid out of their salary has helped the company make the product for profit in the first place. This type of scenario is only available to people above the higher middle class and generally working in jobs that can be classed as non-jobs that are detrimental to society. Thus, most other people will be forced to purchase cheaper made foreign products and as life has been made quite dull and tedious, entertainment products (televisions, tablets, phones, etc.) are used to fill in the time leading to unhealthy effects on societal interactions.

For smaller countries whom have allowed a substantial population growth such as the UK, a globalised system works well, but, a service, legal and education industry born from non-job creation leads to an all-out nanny state where people spend most of their time complaining about their life, suffering from depression and where the highest paid jobs either should not exist in the first place or works against the best interests of the majority of people in society. There needs to be a shift in thinking about the future of industry and about the worth of people in society to provide them with decent quality interesting daily opportunities to earn a living and give a sense of worth in society. The non-job creations have to be phased out and regulation reduced significantly to rely on peoples own common sense, ethical and moral standing about pollution and contract negotiations, based on a new formed curriculum within the education system that promotes responsibility above economic concerns.

However, the growth of management, the legal system, the financial sector and think tanks (which might as well be called simpleminded institutes who really struggle to fulfil the prime role of thinking and rely on people to conduct statistical analysis on real data to provide recommendations generally based on best guess hypotheses) have taken the main roles in the job market behind general service staff and unfortunately the sectors are far too big to cut down immediately. There are many people employed in these non-job roles most of whom are highly academically qualified smooth talkers in expensive suits but incompetent and inept in their positions and most cannot solve practical problems, thus, the possibility and practicality of retraining them to do something useful in society is low. This is the biggest challenge facing Western industry today; it is framework based on academic snobbery with the ability to talk about something to give the impression of knowledge without possessing the ability, intelligence or competence to fulfil their deception of knowledge; and this deception is equally applicable in academia too.

The lack of opportunities, poor education system, not experiencing life as a child due to mothering (over-protection and spoiling from parents with nanny state culture), technology, and non-job social service people preventing proper parenting, have made the youth of today less resilient to life, easily stressed out and more susceptible to depression meaning that their productive levels are considerably lower than migrants who have a working mentality. Industry has realised this and favour employing migrants or people from migrant backgrounds more than native people for this reason. But, as already mentioned more migrants, equals more population, equals more pressures on public finances and services which lead to unsustainable levels for the country to manage effectively and creates a poorer standard of life for everyone.

If all was equal and the country managed to account for the majority of people, there would be no skill shortage and very little need to employ migrant workers in skilled positons whilst native people struggle to find opportunities. This situation exists because young adults in society have been <u>failed</u> by the education system, government and most importantly their parents. Thus, the problem with industry is closely related to the disassembling of the education system to account for the movement of the manufacturing base abroad and to fill the service and non-job roles the government created.

If a country and the people in it are to prosper both socially and economically, the right people should be employed in roles within their current competency level, but, not necessarily within their current knowledge and skill levels as these can be trained fairly quickly with someone who is competent and willing to learn. Unfortunately, the situation is completely blurred as the new politically correct culture has caused real skill descriptions to be confused, i.e. the word engineer has lost all relevance in the job market and thus degraded the value of real engineers in the community - A software engineer is not an engineer, they are software programmers and to confuse them as being engineers is dangerous and costly. Even academia is guilty of defrauding the value of real engineers and does explain why engineering projects involving CAD design has caused considerable embarrassment for businesses, especially the defence industry, with considerable problems (e.g. Eurofighter, and the disaster of a fighter jet the F-35, which has been design on a computer by software programmers taught by academia how to use parametric software and manipulate mathematical formulae, i.e. not engineers). Real engineers would not have made the same rookie mistakes thus would have identified functional issues considering interaction with the environment before the jet went into production.

Consequently, the current culture is not viable or compatible for the change to match the right people with the correct competency levels, however, if a country could prosper with industry based on smooth talking, deceit, lies, 'stab in the back' attitudes, employing more people to cover for incompetence, greed, arrogance and ego, the West would be a collection of the richest nations on the planet without any debt to pay to anyone. But, this is not the case as the financial economy for the majority of Western based countries is economically bankrupt with the debt ceiling consistently being raised by governments to account for mismanagement.

The government need to persuade industry towards making slow changes to the industrial framework based on natural waste. Denoting companies need to begin to use employment justification not based on academic qualifications but based on practical problem solving abilities and competence; (qualifications and competence are uniquely separated due to how schools and academia currently operate and not necessarily related, although they should be). Concurrently, government needs to set the schooling system based on learning to structure problems and solutions by developing a curriculum that ensures children will use their hands as much as their heads to ready them for life after school. (There is a consensus that concentration in schools should be towards software and technology and the strategy is to amend the curriculum as such and bring more technology into the classroom; however, I would argue technology is a distraction to what should be taught. It relates to a few simple questions that I have asked many 'experts': How is software and digital technology going to show the next generation how to build something, how to do agriculture, take care of children (family planning), how to cook a healthy meal, how to keep oneself healthy, how to survive without energy and how to think things through thoroughly; which people should all agree is amiss.

Yet, society introduces technology to young children when they are too immature and inexperienced to understand the ramifications of its use; for example, people live in a world where online bullying is something that is causing children lots of issues. Here is a thought - remove children from online networking sites and switch the 'bloody' thing off until they are mature enough to fully comprehend and emotionally deal with all the surrounding issues – if you want to talk to someone or someone wants to talk to you, use a phone or call round to their house).

Now more than any time in history, due to the forthcoming automation, the country needs to be innovative. The only way to do this is to invest in the future of industry and with this investment there requires to be a pool of people who are capable and competent to learn new knowledge and skills efficiently and be fit enough to cope with a challenging environment. But, the path society is proceeding down works against this as children are not experiencing life with spending too much time on video games and being mothered/nanny-ed, they grow-up not having the stamina or interest in doing something useful unless it involves high gains. It is one of the main issues why young people are pacified by working in a job that requires little thought or hard work. This notwithstanding, parenting and schools have to change to give young adults a sense of accomplishment and usefulness in society and with it confidence to innovate and work towards doing something useful in society, i.e. turn back the time when there was honour and pride in working for society's benefit.

Simultaneously, academia (schools, colleges and universities) have to be returned into being non-profit and operated as educational institutions only and free at the point of contact. The culture surrounding academia should change from being about obtaining a degree to succeed in the workplace to institutions that provide qualification for people who wish to challenge their mental capability (in looking at real world problems and providing a methodology that may lead to solution development) or because people are interested in research without having to deal with the time pressures in industry. Moreover, industry should be less concerned about employing people with high levels of academic or training qualifications and more interested in who the applicant is and the willingness shown to learn new and useful things. Furthermore, there needs to be a process to filter out smooth talkers to prevent the problems the West is facing at present in industry and academia with high levels of incompetence and corruption in management positions.

Despite all the problems with the financial economy, increasing population and the forthcoming automation, industry has to become more environmentally friendly and people need to accept that some of their daily habits work in the worst interests of their own social life and health interests; and the consumerist lifestyle damages all life on earth. Industry has to lead by example and driven by government incentives to motivate change in habits. New industry needs to have its foundation in social equity and allow people to have freedom with flexible working controlled by deliverable timescales.

At some point, especially with the forthcoming automation, pollution concerns and cost of oil and gas, people will have to realise that our freedom of choice as to work location and what to do for work is going to have to be compromised. One of the provisions that should transpire is a rule that states 'people should only be allowed to obtain a working position within a certain square mile radius of where they live' to reduce pollution and travelling stressors. Concurrently, to enable a more efficient transition for the future the government should create a system that allows people to move house more quickly. What this type of system will do is not only minimise the travelling distance to and from work, but, it will also encourage using different greener forms of transport; to reduce the numbers of vehicles on the road and to improve the quality of air people breathe.

The government should to look into infrastructure development/investments to allow people with greener forms of transport to get to their destination in a safe manner, i.e. cycling tunnels, so people can leave their home and enter these cycling tunnels to remain dry and warm, and with work not being far from home can ride without becoming too 'sweaty'. This will have the added advantage of keeping people healthier which will reduce the pressures on the health care system and improve the quality of people's lives as they will live a healthier lifestyle. If the plan is restricted to a cycling time of 30mins., it would reduce the stressors of having to travel in a car Xhrs to get to work and Xhr to get back home. It is this sort of freedom constraints that people should consider as the right path to take and be happy to choose this direction as long as there is decent paid interesting work in the area because otherwise it is another scheme government invests in that people do not want to do.

People need to be educated to a level to understand that future resources are extremely limited thus running out and ideas like this would mean a better life for everyone. Nevertheless, decisions as drastic as these cannot be left for the government to decide, it should to be voted for by the people using digital government. If people choose to accept the rising cost of transport and the worsening health conditions caused by the amount of polluting traffic on the roads, then government should accept this decision as long as people understand the full ramifications of not choosing a system that improves lives at a small cost of inconvenience.

Most office type work can be accomplished at home without the need to take up valuable office space thus this can release the pressures with the morning and evening commute and the costs of building office blocks. This will allow people who choose the path of office or administration work to work flexible hours to suit their home life and give them freedom to choose when and how long to work as long as deliverables are met. Some opportunities should also account for parents, hence, be reserved to coincide with school term times to avoid unnecessary use of expensive childcare placements, but, also to reduce the stress and pressure on parents to accommodate their children's needs with work schedules. More flexible working hours can be offered to fit around family life and with it offer more freedom within the working environment. Furthermore, meetings can be performed online with the latest conferencing communication software, which will reduce the costs to the business of logistics and reduce the number of aeroplane trips to other countries. There can also be a reduction in the number of office blocks built with some land returned to nature to help purify air and reduce issues of flooding.

It is hoped with a new knowledge based agenda driven by government more young people will become involved in science based disciplines and this is where investment is needed to allow the sector to grow faster than at present. Closer partnerships with academia can reap rewards with the advantage of more industrial experienced people becoming part-time academics to drive forward innovation to solve present and future problems. Investments in shared education complexes is needed that can accommodate diverse learning environments accompanied by areas where industry can invent new technology and be competitive in the global market. This will also work towards resolving the gap between academic practices and industry requirements for skilled people besides accounting for servicing, maintenance and advancing the forthcoming automation revolution that will put most non-skilled and non-job positions in control of mathematical algorithms and robotics.

For those people who are interested in pursuing their interests but find it difficult to locate professional opportunities close to home there needs to be a system in place to allow them to pursue it by themselves. This is where local government can provide access to resources and training courses and with it promotion of home work to reduce pollution in all forms and offer substantial freedoms in life. It is envisaged once government is changed to an administration department only, with greed and corruption prevented by legislation, and a more critically thinking population it will give people the freedom to pursue their interests with a stipulation that their interests should work towards benefitting society in some way. This is envisaged as the main area of growth to account for automation and herald in the post-work (or post-slavery) era. It does sound scary for everyone involved to allow people to have true freedom of choice for how they contribute to society. Imagine what society can achieve when people live a more interesting and fulfilling life that is their choice thus not coerced into seeking employment due to pressures of a financial nature. Then comes the problem of how to financially account for how people are contributing to society – a similar system currently used for research institutions and universities can be evolved to permit people to publish regular updates on their personal research or innovations that then can be assessed by suitable experienced people who have chosen to pursue a career in professional office work.

For those whom are failed by parents and the education system the important point to realise is government needs to assist, as much as reasonably practicable, in overcoming the problems that have occurred for this situation to be prevented and provide these non-skilled workers with opportunities to grow. This growth needs partnerships with industry to provide interesting opportunities along with on-the-job training prospects that should be optional in most cases, but, for those in need of help (and motivation for people struggling with laziness) should be part of the terms and conditions of the position and continued financial support. The most important aspect of this is these positions are to be part time (and hopefully flexible to accommodate people's family life) to allow freedom for people to express an interest in something that can expand their knowledge base and help them succeed in life.

The system will require people give details on how their out of work interests could benefit society moreover it should prevent the onset of laziness (or bone idleness) where people just sit at home watching television or playing video games for long periods of time and ignoring their potential in life. Moreover, there should be concentration not on the financial aspects of business but on the human attributes and the drive for people to not only enjoy freedom but also the work they choose to do on a daily basis.

For the post-work era, the country needs to slow down and reduce the pressure to produce things and continuously purchase products to feed the emptiness in people's lives. People need to realise consumerism does not provide happiness but exasperates the problem with lack of choice in life; and as a result reduce gathering 'things' to concentrate of living life for true happiness.

"The more people have, the more they think they need and the more miserable, controlling, self-centred, self-involved, unhappy, socially isolated and grumpy they become. People cannot see the relationship between collecting 'things' they do not need and what they truly need to be happy and live fulfilling lives." – Author.

Only when people cease to collect 'things' to feed an addiction will this new system become feasible as there are far too many people buying 'things' on a regular basis for the pressure to reduce production to begin declining. It becomes a balance of additional real freedom of choice against gluttony and addiction. If people cannot control their negative attributes of being human (i.e. materialistic) gathered from this current capitalist society run by greed, then any change in the system will be open to abuse and eventual failure. As with anything, it is not just the government that is to blame for how things are right now, all people contribute to the problems with the majority feeding the corporatocracy that continue to interfere with education, health care and politics for their own benefit; and whom are directly responsible for continued human suffering globally.

It is a matter of personal responsibility and becoming actively involved in the evolution of society that can make the post-work era a success. There is also a choice, make it work or face poverty and with it all the human suffering people have seen in third world countries for decades. People's current behaviour of feeding the greed and government structure in its current form will never make the post-work era a success; it simply does not work in their best interests of protecting the wealth. Simple logic states that having a country that works for the majority is substantially better for all than a society that only works for the few minorities with wealth. So let all society work to change it, before societal problems become too vast, too complex, for people to resolve without human suffering or bloodshed.

10

WHAT IS BEING SUCCESSFUL IN LIFE

The definition of success is an accomplishment of an aim or purpose. However, success in human terms is more related to making (or having) money and the connection between success and being an honourable kind human being with integrity, ethics and morality has been completely lost. The relationship between being successful and happy has also taken a detrimental path, for example there is no point in being rich if you are harried, stressed and miserable. The irony is when people talk about a successful person there talking about people who have large bank accounts, yachts and expensive cars or someone who in charge of nations; religion is irrelevant. There is an automatic perception that people within these boundaries are happy, but, this simply is not true. Indeed, most heroes or idols that people are told to aspire and look up to, due to some of their actions, are able to do various things because of their wealth status not because they have been successful in life, there is a distinct difference.

The real truth is, because they have the ability to surround themselves with expensive holidays, houses, cars, aircraft and 'bling' they become bored with their life and seeks to be praised by people and one of the most successful ways to achieve this is to set-up and run charities or gives money to them. It has contributed to the problem of celebrity worshipping and praising those that have inherited their wealth, been lucky with a gamble or committed fraudulent acts to acquire wealth (search Bill gates and his university roommate on the creation of the first windows operating system as an example). However, no one can justify being successful after being born into wealth (it is an accident of birth) nor can success be related to those who steal from others or by deceitful means.

This notwithstanding, many multimillionaires and billionaires say the definition of success has nothing to do with money or fame, but, contradict their rhetoric by the growing greed to maintain or expand their own wealth by various means, moreover, by exploiting those who work in life or those who are desperate. Others, especially celebrities, measure success by how many people worship and adore them. The trouble is the majority of people have listened to messages like these over the generations and live their lives in the constant pursuit of money, status and fame at various levels of achievement. This drive contributes to the bullying problem in schools (related to fashion, technology and economic status) and instils in people the implication that money is uniquely correlated to success and that without money people cannot be successful in life. Consequently, many people live life with this in the 'back of their minds' thus causes them to purchase things on a regular basis for their five minutes of fame and to make themselves feel batter, and prevents them from fulfilling their ambitions and life goals.

The 'poor quality' leaders of the world falsely give hope to all by spreading the phrase 'Money can't buy you success', the proverbial – success leads to money; 'Money rarely leads to success', when clearly there is a certain privilege with being from a wealthy background in both schooling and career opportunities. People in the world see the wealthy do better at education (intelligence is questionable though), obtain the better positions in academia, industry and government; the wealthy have the corner of the market related to the best positions, better life prospects and better lifestyles. However, taking advantage of a biased capitalist system that is rigged even before they were born is not the definition of being successful in life. If attaining the highest career opportunity or the highest paid job to acquire wealth is your definition of success, then it is to the detriment of positive human attributes. Irrespective of academic achievement, motivation to work hard or willingness to learn new knowledge and skills, unless you are willing to compete with others in the most dirtiest of games government has architected in the name of competition, the likelihood is you will never realise it as a goal and the people who do have used underhanded means to achieve it.

Wealth is superficial and human made as a means of controlling people, which leads to a never ending spiral of 'the more you have, the more you want; the more you spend, the more you need'. (It is the reason why the elites do not mind if poor people win the lottery, as poor people generally do not possess good money management skills and will spend lots quickly, thus, good for the economy). With wealth arises the detrimental effect of a person's ethics, morals and the convenient forgetting of one's own conscience in order to continue the trend of greed and gluttony. Evidence of this is not hard to find (look at all the wars in the Middle East, exploration for resources, devastation of rain forests and with it tribal culture, environmental pollution, etc.; evidence is available if people just showed the willingness to look for it); look at the devastation and destruction the wealthiest people in the world have caused in all the countries of the world. They use government resources to influence people's thoughts and feelings from primary school through to retirement to ensure people are pacified with what is on offer in life with that little offer of hope for 'social mobility', whilst they plunder globally and nobody seems to notice, nobody seems to care.

Do not misunderstand the message being presented here in this section, all the people who have become wealthy from having little money in their family have been laser-focussed on their work plus their only concern was their finances and how they would be received by their peers. There is nothing wrong with that, or is there? If their prime focus is on their bank balance, when have they given consideration to working on improving who they are as a person?

People need to remember that striving to have lots of money or being famous in some way leads to complacency in succeeding as a human being; and the odds are striving for a goal of wealth will inevitably end in failure for 99% of people. The only message people can acquire from failure to achieve a wealth standard is that they are unsuccessful in life and will have to live a life devout of wealth knowing that other people are just plain better than them in life and therefore achieved a greater level of success.

If wealth and status is a mark of success then ~99% of people living on earth are completely unsuccessful in life and are therefore miserable, depressed plebs who deserve to be ruled over and manipulated by those who, by an accident at birth or by hook or by crook (or lucky from a gamble), are more financially successful than them in a rigged system that works by keeping the majority working hard for little gain. It does not take too much philosophy to realise there is no relationship between wealth or fame and being a success as a human being; wealth is just something people strive to acquire a better life in a system controlled by the people who control the money – and not necessarily the government.

Success is:

Liking yourself - People now have the ability to change who they are if they do not like themselves via plastic surgery. The problem is this does not alter who they are as a person and only offers a short term fix from the mental health issue of personal deprivation due to difficulty of life and life chances. Life is easier if people worked on improving what makes them unique and be less concerned about what other people are saying or think. People need to turn away from social media and go and meet people who have similar mind-sets, they will probably find that it is not them people do not like it is the fact that people like mindless human drones not people who are different to them or their beliefs.

Liking what you do - The majority of people are in jobs during the day that are mind numbingly boring and unchallenging or people do things in life that they instantly regret. These people feel the need to counteract the effects by taking drink or drugs to cope with the misery of daily life - if your miserable make a life change that makes you happy, it is difficult with all the constraints set by government, but, make a change and prevent the downward spiral into depression because it is hard to recover and there is a chance you will end up being a shadow of the person you were once as a child.

Liking how you do it – a competitive world means people do what is needed to gain an advantage over others, including their friends; this tends to lead to dirty strategies. Or, it may be that you need to do something in a job that you fundamentally disagree with but need to do it to keep the position or it may be something else that poses questions on you own morals and ethics that has a detrimental effect on mental state in the long term. People need to ensure no matter what life throws at you, you execute daily life in a manner that suits your own 'positive' ethics and morals; if something you are asked to do or something you yourself are doing questions these, you need to have the courage to stop and argue your case with yourself and/or others.

People need and should achieve the progressive realization of worthy goals; the key word is worthy, i.e. saving lives. Success is nothing to do with status in society but a lot with what you do when nobody else in looking, those personal achievements that may go overlooked by others and have zero financial implications. Moreover, it is about happiness and wealth does not buy happiness, if it did there would be no wealthy person overdosing on drugs, committing suicide or suffering depression.

Furthermore, acquiring wealth and status (no matter to what degree) involves embracing the darker attributes of humanity and it is after all what all governments in the world require from their citizens – to be consistently fighting amongst themselves in a competitive world where only a few succeed because only a few places are available to give the illusion of hope for all. It adds to the strength of diverting people's attention away from the real issues in the world and who is responsible for them; and why there is considerable emphasis on differences between people in mainstream media rather than a celebration of what makes all people different yet the same.

So be successful as a human being, work to achieve your personal goals - the things you want to do in life that people before you have been unable to do due to life constraints put in place by successive governments. Furthermore, to do this means you need to become actively involved in politics to change government from the establishment being in power to an administration department that helps govern in the name and voice of the people.

Being successful means having the freedom to achieve what you want to achieve in life and therefore success, happiness and freedom are highly related besides an impact on one will affect the others: less freedom means more unhappiness and less likelihood of being successful as a human being. However, success means being masters of our own destiny and as long as the majority are subservient to the rules and laws set forth by the minority in government, 99% of people will be unsuccessful in life no matter what wealth is possessed or status in society people have.

The only conclusion is the generations before have lived relatively unhappy unsuccessful lives from childhood till retirement as the majority have been coerced into jobs they did not like but were happy to be pacified by due to the financial constraints set for them by government and being presented with soaps that depicted families in worse conditions than them; these constraints also contribute to people not knowing how to live a happy successful life. To be successful as a species, all people need to 'turn our backs' on what is sold as 'our way of life' because this only benefits a few in society; as a result, it should not be defended from any attack on its very foundations. People need to let it go and for it to become part of history all people should not be proud of. A line needs to be drawn on 'our way of life' with freedom for people in daily life given more priority by a vast reduction of constraints in society; with the number of people in the world today it should be possible to continue progressing technology and providing essentials for all at the same time as giving people time to achieve their own personal goals. The irony is people who are allowed to succeed will inevitably benefit the nation's economy positively more than any other time is history; as happy people are more productive people. Just image the problems that could be solved and new discoveries made if people succeeded in life rather than just persevered in rigged societal norms people know them today.

I am personally enervated of seeing people struggling in life and living in stressful environments with little happiness throughout the years. Freedom is important to fight for and people need to ability to live a life they want to live and not be met by constraints that forces their actions into something different that does not make them truly happy. People need to embrace the possibility of fulfilling dreams thus becoming successful as people and it does mean breaking the connection between wealth and success. People's drive should be concerned with what made ourselves dream when we were children and people need the ability to carry that process through into adulthood. Constraints in life should not prevent people from succeeding in personal goals, but, it does and will continue to do so as long as established politics, politicians and the corporatocracy are permitted to create legislation on society's behalf; thus, giving people have no choice but to follow their laws and rules.

It might mean turning our backs on the financial economy as a means of controlling people and resources and a new equitable system being developed that benefits all equally. It would mean prospects are not rigged to benefit those with larger bank balances but be available to those whose goals complement the positions in society that are needed. Everyone in society would play the game of life without the arrogance or ego of attaining a higher status and thus contribute equally to the growth of humanity. It would be a scary change in societal norms, something that has not been seen since people could lay claim to their own plot of land. The only choice in life would be simple and be based on a simple question – what do you want to work at to succeed in and how will it benefit society? Satisfying this question would all be what is needed to move forward in life. People would be able to follow their own interests and work to their own strengths in their own way.

It would take a lot of growth as a species and I think the current system would be unlikely to change in this generation, but, securing a government that administers only and legislation put in place to avoid lobbying or other potential perversion of democracy is the first step to that growth. The problem is giving up power and power of influence will be difficult for the establishment and the oligarchs, they will not give it away out of the goodness of their hearts; nonetheless, people need strength to fight and resist manipulation through mass media outlets to achieve this objective. Otherwise, more people than ever before will end up living in poverty followed by civil wars once the money becomes scarce due to the downfall of the financial economy, which is inevitable in the next 30-40 years. The majority of people should force change for a better way of life and leave the draconian societal norms behind as part of history to give the future generations a better chance of fulfilling their dreams; and preventing some of the tragedies and devastations that has occurred since the conception of the banking system and the addiction to fossil fuels.

Let us humans finally grow as a species and succeed by allowing true freedom to prosper. I have faith all people can contribute in society and do what they want to do in life as long as all the constraints are removed that prevents our culture growing into an intelligent environmentally safe advanced society worthy of the title 'the most intelligent and responsible species on the planet'.

In summary of this section: the degree of success is highly related and coupled to societal constraints brought forward by governments. To change this, constraints need to be removed and government power reduced significantly to effectively govern with zero power, but, high accountability. The influence of wealth needs to be removed and freedom of choice for people significantly improved so that saturation in certain disciplines is part of history. As long as people can prove they are contributing to society in some way people should be allowed to continue in their own personal efforts for happiness by succeeding in their own personal goals. Societal norms should be adjusted to account for this change. The impact on the lifestyles of the wealthy should be dismissed as an equal society is a happy one and the time of this type of separation and inequality needs to come to an end.

Human growth has been held back by the pursuit of wealth and with it more wealth and with that more wealth. It contributes to the devastation and pollution in the world and the instigation of poor education policies to prevent people from acquiring critical thinking skills to enable the wealthy people to get away with certain questionable acts. The choices are fight for change or accept the outcome of possible extinction due to climate change, wars, or famine or……. Basically, a change is needed and one that will send shockwaves through the 1% of society that has most of the wealth and is responsible for the most of the continued suffering in the world. It is time for the majority to be successful and understand success is highly related to human characteristics and attributes. It is these that need to be worked on and freedom fought for to gain improvements in the level of success individuals achieve in life.

11

A CHALLENGE FOR HYPOCRACY

The world is full of hypocrisy and contradiction. Governments and banks talking about the economy with regard to decisions people are told have to be made to save the economy. When society comprehends later the government and the banks themselves do the exact opposite of what they have said and the majority end up being forced to pay more than twice to clear up their mistakes ('Where is our &*%$£% money, you filthy robbing %**%$&*'). Society encompasses people who call themselves religious who do not follow the religious text or complain when people do, whilst most of people cherry pick from the religious text and ignore the passages that are deemed uncivilised, unbelievable or barbaric in modern society. In essence, being religious for the whole is a contradiction in terms.

There are many examples of hypocrisy throughout daily life and too much to discuss within this book thus concentration is given to politics and the outcomes of election promises. Throughout my entire adult life I have never experienced a political party who wins an election follow through neither on their election promises nor on their own manifestos. This seems to be a reoccurring pattern in every democratic country; the situation has become a matter of the abandonment of principles that democracy was built on and unfortunately this abandonment of principles has swept throughout society and at all levels. There are numerous examples of hypocrisy in recent years regarding politicians, law enforcement, liberal idealists, religious people and those social justice warriors whom always need a cause to fight.

A prime example of hypocrisy concerns people with different opinions to mainstream, which have been invited onto debate shows on TV, tend to spark an outcry from various people. For instance, if the interview is with a 'far-left' or 'far-right' (whatever these are, labels are there to demonise and vilify) political party member especially those who have views about nationalism over migration or religion or culture, there is a problem. What is the outcry about? Are people worried about intelligent debates or concerned that knowledge could counteract a belief system. This sort of outcry and how the media production companies handle these type of issues, means that free speech seems to only be available to those who might not offend (or upset) any certain minority groups of the audience or will refuse to answer any of the questions asked of them (political spin or divert attention to something else). The irony is these very same people who are offended by various comments are the same people who promote freedom of speech and use labels to demonise others; in essence, they are attempting to quell the voices of people whom have a different ideology or mind-set from themselves.

The promise of truth, honesty, and real social justice principles has become utterly irrelevant and replaced with the quest for power with a control agenda the leaders continuously push for; and the majority of people just complain and accept the ever worsening conditions, wanting change but afraid of choosing it. Politicians have now become people who push forward on the ideologies of the few wealthy in society and have become partisan ideologues (advocates of an ideology) that are dishonest by nature. The situation has perpetuated to the extent that some politicians have switched off to their dishonest nature and become self-involved in the story they are marketing or presenting to the majority for their own continued survival as a politician. Political survival is reliant on the selling of hypocrisy and is a most important trait when it comes to high level positions in government. When a politician delivers a public statement they are required to appear genuine and then after a short period of time the statements given are contradicted by either their private words or their actions, which are then defended by feeble excuses mapped onto real world events that people who cannot critically analyse the situation all but buys into.

In many democracies, the political party who wins the election boasts about the victory and declares it the will of the people when in the majority of cases the election has been legally rigged. For example: votes from people not worth the same as others (majority states), first passed the post systems, or the previous government has changed election boundaries to ensure advantage in elections (gerrymandering) or like in the UK for many years the government has been soft with many non-working people in society to acquire votes. (Gerrymandering is the redrawing of boundary lines for election votes and has mainly been used in the US for a number of decades but is becoming popular throughout the West. Such that politicians (those in government) have the ability to choose their voters (partisan boundaries) not the voters choosing their government representatives - so called packing and cracking. Thus, allowing certain votes to count for more than others in other boundary areas). In any case, given voter turnout no successful candidate can honestly suggest that the result reflected 'the will of the majority' and this is not to mention the issue of voter fraud. In the US, if the presidency were decided by the popular vote rather than the Electoral College, voter turnout and voting behaviour would probably be vastly different.

The reality is, if successive governments fail to fulfil their election promises people are less inclined to continue to vote in elections with the feeling that the result does not matter as the winning political party will just do what they want anyway. It is the reason why most people cannot be bothered to read a manifesto because it takes time to analyse the promises and is completely meaningless once the party acquires government (just like the conservative's manifesto was ripped apart by the deal with the DUP in the 2017 snap UK election; meaning that the party is in government without a manifesto voted for by the people and they can just 'make it up' as time goes by). Instead, people who do vote base it on historic family voting patterns or sales pitches given by electoral leaflets or the fear of change. With Trump being victorious there are many critics coming forward about the US election system, I wonder if the same would happen if Hilary won. It would seem as though a system that has been used since the conception of the USA, upon a major political swing, makes even the 'smartest (I use the term loosely)' of people wilfully stupid and hypocritical – Trump must be stopped he is an evil misogynistic racist president (siting his travel ban), even though they were quiet when Obama put a similar ban in place in 2008.

The truth is these crocodile tears and manufactured outrage of these liberal professionals and Western politicians pretending to care about other less fortunate people vexes me considerably. They have the resources to actually make a difference but they choose not to, instead none of them cried outrage when Western drones strikes slaughtered thousands of innocent civilians; refuted or prevented their own or other coalition governments turning Libya, Syria, Afghanistan, Iraq, Yemen, into killing zones, etc.

How many of them are transparent about the truth with these invasions into foreign resource rich lands or why Saudi Arabia is still friends when they have a worse human rights record than ISIS. How many of them did more than tweet from their gated communities or mansions when people from the Muslim faith sought revenge attacks throughout Europe for what Western governments and the corporatocracy have done in their home lands for decades. (Don't get me wrong I am not a sympathiser, I just understand route cause and effect through critical thinking and analysis).

People, even poorly educated people, in society have the ability to find out the truth but people have lost the energy to because the charge of hypocrisy has lost all rhetorical power; instead, people just except the situation(s) and carry on with life whatever government or third parties throws at them. Society does not expect any sort of integrity anymore in any situation; this does signify societal breakdown - credibility has lost all meaning. The problem being that modern Western society is now built on pretence of the idea of good ideas until a convenient excuse comes along to replacing those ideas with principles of hypocrisy where the most unscrupulous and amoral benefit at the expense of others.

All political debate has been reduced to a black and white argument (my party good, their gang/party/government bad) when the reality is far from good versus evil because in modern politics the boundary between the two is completely blurred. Nevertheless, it does not stop governments from using primitive/draconian forms of crowd control to restrain those pesky protesters who cause governments and oil/gas companies' problems.

Mainstream politicians cannot serve without being partisan ideologues and thus hypocrites because they require being self-serving (take care of themselves at the expense of others). It is why people are all indoctrinated into the ideology of a parliamentary democracy where the need for a nation to provide order and organisation was the moral fact in society. Unfortunately, soon after a nation recovered from WW2 order and organisation in a free democracy was mutated into governments must act, citizens must obey; and the fact of this distinct separation meant that the few could act without the majority approval and the citizens of the nation must obey the rule of law or face the force of government and the authorities (e.g. police, courts, debt collectors, etc.).

If mainstream political parties placed in their manifesto the truth, for example: continue to interfere in foreign lands both militarily and politically and as a country people should expect retaliatory action; or the government shall continue to allow migration into the country because it gives us and business leaders an excuse to keep salaries low and those on the breadline distracted so that people fight amongst themselves; or the government will continue to add additional funding at everyone's expense for the NHS even though the service will continue to be worse due to uncontrolled immigration, poor education, privatisation, mismanagement, etc.; or the government will continue to amend the education system to enable schools, colleges and universities to be operated as a business at everyone's expense and continue to fail in producing well educated people capable of critical thinking to ensure people are easily manipulated into continuing to vote for established political parties. The problem with established political parties funded by private wealth can be summarised as follows: We, the government, will continue to work in the interests of the economy (for the benefit of a few). We will ensure wealth is directed and flows to the oligarchs besides continuing with a system that ensures the majority of people have little to look forward to in life apart from working a boring, uninteresting job and hopefully never collect their pension while, concurrently, not having the ability to realise how much their being 'screwed' and manipulated by a class hierarchical system that has already been rigged to ensure more for the few and less for the majority.

The recent wars on terrorism are a prime example of politicians and defence contractors hiding the real truth behind various actions and not being held accountable for their own terrorist acts in foreign lands. Like in both of the world wars, occupations in foreign countries are the order of the day for Western countries in the Middle East, Africa, and some eastern European countries. Some of these occupations are enforced without the agreement/permission of the current government in said country and some are instigated by interference and manipulation of political events in the countries. Once bases are setup, NATO forces (with the UN's knowledge) bomb the country's armed forces whenever they come too close to the occupied areas and sell the situation as aggression. It is like the occupation is the good guys fighting the forces of evil and therefore will unlawfully occupy a region of another country and if the legitimate residence of said country fight back or attempt to push the invading forces out of the country peacefully or otherwise, the Western backed army will purposely kill any aggressor thus take ownership of the area. The international community in partnership with the UN 'sits back' and allows them to do it with the Western backed media selling it as defending themselves against evil aggressors. When clearly, the good guys are not what is being 'sold on the can'; it is an unlawful occupation of aggression and the aggressors are killing native people for attempting to remove an invading fleet – just as some of Europe did with the NAZI occupation of Europe.

It is critical thinking about the situation independent of listening to mainstream media reports and politicians that make you question foreign policy actions in foreign lands and realise things are not what they appear to be. Hypocrisy is one of the most damaging tools used by leaders of business and governments globally and often used in conjunction with the official secrets act and excuses of national security. It has the outcome of Western powers accomplishing deviant and often immoral, unethical and fatal acts in foreign lands in the name of protecting the economy or national interests. Eventually, all people living in Western countries will feel the after effects of allowing their government to exercise their powers in such a manner. People whose family members have died or suffered by the hand of Western backed forces will not forget or forgive and in circumstances such as these ignorance and dis-interest will not guard from the repercussion of sitting back and allowing a democratically elected government using the country's armed forces and intelligence agencies (CIA, MI5, GCHQ, etc.) to do such acts. In a democracy, people have a chance to change and hold to account the people who have the position to make foreign policy decisions, but, people choose not to vote for change and it is primarily led by fear of voting for politically inexperienced people who might fail to keep ourselves safe. Fear, because the 'poor quality' leaders of the world say people should be consistently living in fear and fear change from the natural world order.

The question for everyone to ask themselves becomes a case of 'what kind of hypocrites should people vote for in the next election?' because that is what people are doing consistently and consecutively since greed replaced social responsibility. Whilst the question posed seems cynical it is far more cynical to believe that mainstream political parties, those who rely on lobbying and sponsorship from the wealthy to drive their parties' interests and campaigns, can ever be completely sincere and credible as a party who will work in the interests of the people. Governments and the oligarchs believe the majority with little wealth and influence ought not to think and it is the main reason why education is gradually worsening with younger people more than any time in history suffering mental illness because of it. Indeed, political sincerity, unless people demand change, will always lose over deception, corruption and double-dealing.

Deep in our subconscious all people know the truth behind how elections and governments work; and modern governments do not make much of an effort to cover their underhanded deals or decisions because who can make them accountable. Many protests have attempted to force the governments hand in various decisions that are in opposition to their election promises, but, with a large pool of people working in the armed forces and the police whom are at the government's beck and call, the protesters are soon dealt with using draconian measures. The protestors are then vilified within the media who are in bed with the ruling government besides the majority of people are too busy working to pay for their livelihood, houses, cars, family, etc. to risk losing their jobs to bring to account a government who are behaving irresponsibly and enforcing an ideology onto others.

This notwithstanding, people need to have the ability to punish hypocrisy and preserve what is left of credibility. People need to strengthen the meaning of honour and principles in life because it is the only way society can bring ideas into reality rather that the ideas of personalities (e.g. celebrity culture, political celebrities, selling empty promises, etc.). People need to have the courage to turn away from career politicians and mainstream parties and ensure millionaires are all but locked-out from being part of a government political party. Moreover, people need to have the capability to remove any politician and even the elected political party who has been found to be dishonest about their manifesto promises easily at any point in time; and people need to demand this system be put in place with immediate effect. Concurrently, government should not have the facility or power to make decisions that affect the majority of people; these decisions need to be given to the electorate in the form of a digital referendum using digital government. N.B. For digital government, each person will need to be identifiable by a government registered number, e.g. national insurance number, passport number, migrant ID, etc.; in order to partake in democratic elections or decisions made by local councils/states.

The national election should be about who the majority would like to administer the country on their behalf based on manifesto promises, which should form a legal contract between the political party and the people. Electoral systems that rig this type of outcome should be removed from the country's election practice, which means all Western democracies should amend the process from its very foundations to ensure every vote is worth the same and that the majority's voice in each representative's area is used as the basis for election results, i.e. systems such as first passed the post and the electoral college should be banned. Practices such as gerrymandering are required to be monitored by a political neutral monitoring agency to ensure fair play within the electoral process.

To go along with these changes and to ensure no political party has advantages over others, even independents, allowing lobbying and private donors to interfere in fair elections and government decisions should be made an illegal practice for all political parties. No longer should government and its resources be used as wealthy play grounds to acquire further wealth for themselves.

But, as long as people continue working and paying their taxes like good citizens; and continue to vote for the same established parties, hypocrisy and all the repercussions will be delivered onto the majority whilst gaps in inequality will continue to rise and less freedoms given. The majority of people need to revolt, stop paying ever increasing taxes and stand-up to the people in charge for positive changes to freedom to happen. (*'Let them march all they want, so long as they continue to pay their taxes'.* – Alexander Haig 59th United States Secretary of State, 1982).

Should People Be Interested in Political Events?

If people refuse to be interested in politics, then change is hard to achieve and voting decisions will be based on a 'fancy' leaflet and mainstream media biases. But, why does society have this problem mainly with native people, as people who are from migrant families have a great deal of interest in politics and political events. The problem spans from the time when responsible capitalism was changed to irresponsible greed and thus diminished returns on people's investment into politics. The problem is people's interest has been reduced to a few easy to remember issues:

Who is causing wars and where? – Usually the 'answer' is gathered from propaganda and politician spin;
What is the latest crime gossip? – does it affect my behaviour in the activities I do, or can I have a conversation about this either online or at work;
Are there any changes in the law that could get me in trouble? – Motoring offences, tax changes, etc.;
Any faux-pas politicians have done which are funny;
What are the latest scandals that 'creams my corn'?

Either way, people do not seem to be interested in the 'bigger picture' and how not being interested means politicians and the events caused by their decisions could and more than likely will come back and 'bite them badly'. The biggest problem is in todays' society people do not have much spare time; from working to looking after children (when they are not distracted by technology) and ensuring their online social networking posts are up to date, time and effort to take a keen interest in political events is diminished to a 30minutes news broadcast or gossip on sites such as Facebook. The counter argument is there is always time to spend investigating issues that could affect the future of their own life, but people prioritise what is happening in their own small bubble right here, right now and energy is spent taking care of this rather than looking further afield.

Politics affects how people feel and phycologist would agree things that make you feel bad, you probably should make a change and discard it. For most people, it is exactly what they do with politics – give little attention to it, apart from a brief thought at election time. Other people obsess over politics, so much so that they spend 24hours a day worrying about it and it becomes a distraction from everyday events that depression is a very real after affect. The problem with this obsession is answers and the truth is further away than those who spend little time reflecting on political events. Either way, what do people receive in return, nothing – there was a popular US bumper sticker in the 1960s that read *'If voting changed anything, they'd make it illegal'*, it is why the election system is strictly controlled and works only for those with vast amounts of money to spend on electioneering. Not being interested in political events or being too interested that people become lost in confusion has the same impact: it keeps the majority locked inside a government created system and servicing it.

The drawback is generational in nature and is highly coupled to diminished returns, it is why people do not want to risk their current way of life to bring to account government, because there is a firm belief that politics does not change. The message government and people who control the counterfeit money are receiving is the population are reassured and compliant and thus they are being successful in achieving their own selfish goals without too much disobedience.

This notwithstanding, any type of politics, political event or foreign policy cannot exist without either the threat of force or coercion into an ideology. Politics and violence are intrinsically linked without the people in politics ever getting their hands dirty, but, investigations reveal a relationship between all violence in the world and some political ideology; no matter what spin or colour politicians portray their actions the indications of some sort of threat with vehemence underpins it all. The relationship between money, wealth, power and government is based on one and the same philosophy – taking money / wealth from people against their will; all other government action will fall apart without this type of control over the people. Although, government has done an excellent job in indoctrinating people into believing that the system society operates with is justified, i.e. people give money for the benefit of all.

People who are forced to do something and given no choice about it, generally, have ill feeling towards the person, group or people who benefit from their own hard work, but, government is a propaganda powerbase and a force that is too big to fight and resist with a bad education, thus, people accept it and carry on with their lives. The problem is if people firmly believed that society or our way of life is worth preserving, no government would take money that they did not earn by one type of coercion or another, and people would give money voluntarily knowing the money would go to good causes that would personally benefit themselves and whole of society. But, deep down everyone knows this is not the case, which is why government forces taxation on the majority to continue with its and the oligarchs' violent enterprises globally for the benefit of the few whilst believing that the majority are a resource worthy of exploiting for their own selfish interests. The benefit of the few is where the problem arises and where it is laid to rest.

There are many different ways to live, but, government has seen it fit to enforce a way of life and ensure that alternative ways of living are 'few a far between'. Humans as a species have gained the skills and knowledge to evolve from primitive ways of living (i.e. living in a cave) to inventing technology to progress to the stars, yet, politics remains the same – the few in control of the many. The government and the people who control the counterfeit money ensure people who wish to leave the game of 'our way of life' are forbidden to do so by constraints on land, resources, and waterways – people are forbidden to leave the game. In some circumstances, people who try have their assets and any money frozen from the bank it was entrusted to. Concurrently, government will ensure the mainstream media will sell these people as someone who is untrustworthy and vilify them (and threaten the ones they love) with the same strategy. The messages are 'no exit is permitted', 'freedom is a state of mind – people have to work to give back to society, real physical freedom will never be reached and if it is attempted violence or 'squeeze' tactics are used to 'drag' people back in'.

The war on drugs, terrorism, and 'travellers' can be seen as prime examples of people attempting to separate themselves from government control yet survive in society ruled by money and subsequently met by violence and vilification in some parts of the world, whilst in others a connection between the ruling government and drug empires exist for mutual benefit. Yet, possibly one of the most striking examples in recent history of people struggling to be self-determinate is in Catalonia's referendum in Spain (2017). The ruling government in Spain ordered the country's police, and some armed soldiers, to do whatever is necessary to prevent the referendum taking place. Naturally, people in the region who were highly motivated to vote for independence was met with violence from their own police force and major civil unrest endured. The region at this time can only be compared to Nazi intervention in Europe where people's voices were quietened by threats of violence or worse. The government and the regions own police force were behaving like an occupying force trying to prevent real freedom and self-determination from occurring to keep control of the region, and the people in it, firmly with central government. 100,000s of people voted in the referendum and in some areas it made no difference to the tactics used to prevent the referendum from taking place, they did however fail. The police force was certainly not there to ensure peace or protect the innocent; the sad realisation is the money used by taxes to provide tools to the country's police and armed forces was now being used to control and threaten Spain's own people from a peaceful referendum. People need to think that if a government uses these types of tactics against their own people, what actions would national government use against people, regimes or governments in foreign countries.

The majority keep working, paying their taxes and other bills and either live in complete ignorance of where the money is being directed to or just accepting the outcome. The outcome of which is to invest in more technology used to control the majority, to invade foreign countries and bomb, thus kill, innocent people reduce their freedoms and enable the exploitation of the poorest people in the world. While the people in government who order such things walk away with healthy bank accounts and substantial connections in corporations.

The problem with this way of living is by not resisting unethical and immoral government decisions it opens all to retaliatory actions by those whose family and friends have been victims of a national government allocating funds to enable armed forces to use technology for such acts. People should be far more concerned, fearful and disturbed by what their own government is doing both at home and abroad because whether people admit it to themselves or not, all in society will be the ones (at mercy) on the receiving end of any revenge attack or any reduction in freedoms set forth by government. By sitting back and accepting societal norms set by central government people are both implicit and complicit in actions leading to reduction in freedoms and an increase in suffering both at the national and international level. Ignorance, laziness, fear of loss and 'can't be bothered' attitude is no excuse for allowing a government to commit acts in Western people's names for the sake of 'national' best interests (the interests of the few wealthy more like); put yourself in the place of those people who have suffered or whose loved ones have been 'collateral damage', would you be able to forgive and forget the people of a country whose national armed forces have committed such crimes?

So here society is, not taking an interest in political events means that people will continue to be slaves to societal norms set by government and the oligarchs thus freedom will continue to remain a 'state of mind' rather than in reality. Furthermore, people should be concerned with freedom and about being potentially at risk of retaliatory actions from 'terrorists', moreover, all in society should take a keen interest to why people are forced to hand over money to government without having a voice or a chance of bartering on the amount based on current quality of life each person is experiencing. It is true just accepting the way things are and removing completely any interest in political events will lead to being less stressed, being more productive and completely ignorant of the truth. Like the slaves of the past who eventually ceased fighting for their freedom and just accepted their masters' commands; they lived a quiet life far removed from having any real choice in life but still faced the repercussions of their masters' immoral decisions. Temporary as this might have been, it was a blissful existence until do-gooders decided to take on their cause which happened to benefit the slave owners more, i.e. no more providing housing, health care, food, guards, or entertainment; work was offered in repayment for money and all other concerns was the workers. Is it any wonder why governments abolished slavery, having employees rather than slaves is in the best interests of the economy and business owners.

Life has not really changed much since then. People still have masters (government) who coerces and manipulates their actions and takes more than their fair share of hard earned money and uses it to further the interests of the wealthiest in society at the expense of all others. People still are coerced (forced) to work in low-paid jobs they do not like to survive in society governed by money, which is worthless counterfeit pieces of paper and metal, whilst the real wealth is controlled and protected by the governments. Government (masters) still employ an army (police and armed forces) to expand their control and punish those who contest the rule of law or wish to escape their control for a chance of real freedom.

People need to wise up, slavery has not been abolished; it has merely evolved for the benefit of the wealthiest in society. If people believe they have freedom in society today, then try and follow your dreams, try not doing something you do not want to do to live in the modern society. It works for a minor few, but for the majority constraints of modern life will coerce them into something not part of their life plan or dream. Modern society has been set-up and evolved over the centuries to ensure the majority work for the benefit of the few, set tough and unfair competition for highest paid jobs and let the majority of people fail to succeed due to limited opportunities (is it any wonder why we have people with PhDs working at fast food outlets).

'Leaders' will not change society like they did in the past (slavery to working people) because no other system will benefit more those at the top of the rich list; any changes will swing more freedom, rights and power back to the people. As the financial economy continues to drift into disrepair (with 100s of trillions of pounds debt for the world's richest countries – a statement that would make even the poorest educated among us say, huh or WTF!) and implodes on itself due to the corruption, fraud and the magical creation of money without any physical properties, who do people think will suffer the most from the inevitable outcome of such a crash? Do people think the crash will 'hurt' those at the top or is it possible that there is a reason why over a long period of time the wealthiest in collusion with governments have removed anything of real value from circulation (i.e. gold and silver) and produced worthless paper and virtual money to give to the majority?

Politics is about change, it is about control and not being interested in it means the people who control the money supply control the actions of each and every single individual in society without most realising it due to indoctrination activities in schools, media outlets, propaganda, and parents (who have previously been indoctrinated into the same system). Is not being actively interested in politics or political events any different than just accepting being under the control and manipulation of a wealthy powerful master, just as people were in the past. The truth is the overwhelming majority are just as subservient as slaves once were because they sit-back and accept decisions that affect their lives from a central government.

Political events, whether or not the majority are informed, agree or not will always affect innocent lives, just as the terror attacks in the last decade (2010's) all over Europe have affected many innocent lives. Being interested in political events is one avenue to instigate action that will benefit the majority and bring accountability to government decisions. People need to realise that merely complaining without action is the same as sitting on the couch doing nothing. People should demand freedom, people do not need to be controlled by other people; government and those who control the money are not Gods, they are just human like everyone else, but, appears to have the delusion that they have the power to control and coerce millions. What makes them question this belief? – Nothing! It is the millions upon millions of people who carry on with their daily activities in complete ignorance of the reality of life.

People need to have the courage to stand and present the message to government and those who control the money: 'We are human beings, we deserve to be free and live the life we want to live without being controlled by government. We deserve to follow our interests and dreams wherever it takes us without being constrained by societal norms put in place by the people who control the money. We can be responsible and do not need threats of violence or intimidation to make us behave in a civilised way, but, most of all we all deserve freedom from oppression and exploitation to enjoy life for the brief time we have on this planet'.

Being interested in political events should wake people up from the blissful sleep they are living now. Yes, it will cause more concern over world events and give rise to being more stressful and less productive in daily work, but this may be a good thing. It might cause a sense of patriotism and influence actions to join the group of protesters against government decisions. But not only this, it might compel people to spend less time on social networking sites or online gaming and spend more time investigating the actions of their government to find out the truth about what is happening in the world and work to prevent further chaos and destruction in the name of the national economy, i.e. become less ignorant. Only when people's voices become loud enough to drown out that of the government (and its employees) and the oligarch, will people then have a sense of self-control, self-determination and with it freedom. This is why people, even those who are completely disillusioned with government, should take interest in political events and then take a more active role in the community to oppose government wrong-doings in an attempt to lead a more fuller, freer life liberated from central control. It will be difficult to do but if enough people within the country joined in action, it might be possible to break the relationship between government and violence; then create a government that merely administers the country without power of control.

Why do the Political Elite Always Have Enemy to Fight?

In the past, people firmly knew who the enemy was that required to be fought against. The government could be seen as the obvious and only response from internal and external threats with the existence of these threats was the clearest possible justification for governments to command and for subjects to obey. However, in the advent of economic based politics an 'enemy' is possibly the most subjective term in the entire world. The complexities of politics mean an enemy appears to be one that needs to be fought against at the same time as supported, as both are good for the national economy (or so people are uniformed). The complexities surrounding this can be summarised by the people who funded terror attacks such as 9/11. Saudi Arabia has been proven to have strong connections to the terror groups responsible, yet, still considered friends of the West. According to politicians and mainstream media, the West are at war with Middle Eastern terrorist groups, whilst at the same time the terrorist groups continue to be armed with weapons and ammunitions made by Western defence contractors. The word enemy is a paradox; the economy and government needs an adversary to fight and paradoxically needs a friend to purchase arms, whom might be one and the same group or country.

Government is seen as a central control for people otherwise it is presented, mainly influenced by religion, that people would be an enemy to every other, i.e. people have to be controlled otherwise chaos will reign. Government spends substantial resources and energy giving graphical accounts of possible 'enemies' and the threats they pose; their relationship to main stream media sells this to people as the government is working to keep all safe. The current architecture of society is based on the need for something to protect people not only from themselves, but, also from all other national and international threats as without these threats there would be no need or justification for government. This statement might be true for a minority of people, but, government places considerable emphasis on enhancing the threat giving firmer grounds for the case of the continued existence of government and the greater justification for calling for and enforcing loyal obedience. The greater description of the threat, the grander the case for unity, the better case against criticism and rebellion, and the greater case for more government power over people. It can be described as simple mathematical logic to instil control over people and has proved very effective since the conception of ruling leaders thousands of years ago.

Democracies need enemies to fight every second of every day. Without these enemies, societies have no need for a group of people in government to issue laws to govern or to justify the need for continued funding by taking money from people's hard earned salary. Thus, if there is not a real enemy to fight, it is the governments (and economies) best interest to indicate or exaggerate the existence of an enemy or create one to fight (NATO have been looking for justification of their existence since the end of the cold war – the war that never was!). Governments can be described as a societally accepted protection racket that uses stories about enemies, creates an enemy or arms an enemy (using public money) just to gain support or cooperation for those whom inform people of the story, i.e. the government, - it is a self-justifying mechanism.

The consensus among people is war or conflict should be resisted, but, leaders of the world who determine policy know that without war the nation's economy would stagnate; as a result, government (whether it is a democracy, dictatorship or communist) is needed to 'drag' people along with a story into supporting the government's decision for conflict. To achieve 'buy-in' all that is needed is to inform people that they are under attack, denounce protestors for lack of patriotism and expose the country to danger - the strategy is very effective. In modern times, with information available via the internet, government has had to do more than tell a story, they might even choose to subject the people to the very threat they are telling a story about (even the most 'educational challenged' among us should suspect that something is amiss with the terrorist attacks in Europe – how can people who are on the watch list be allowed to commit terrorist acts and how can someone be allowed the roam freely knowing they are affiliated with terrorist groups?).

Protecting 'our way of life' is a good example of something that needs substantial improvement and thus not be protected, but, a campaign that portrays an enemy challenging dominant national values work to unite people against the existence, real or imaginary, of foreign threats. The power to unite people using an enemy leads to subservience and obedience to government. This is to ensure governments control over people as without an enemy the likelihood is people would divide and weaken the powerbase of the country thus power would dissipate to the people, i.e. supporting government is reinforcing protection for all; and the scenario can be described as 'you are either with us or with the terrorists'. When something is presented in this way people would naturally abide by governments decisions not wanting to be labelled as a terrorist sympathiser or something else.

The inherent skill of speech writers and legal experts is to justify acts the government do in the best interests of protecting the people in the country. Once justification for government has been declared as protecting the people there comes an idea of a nation; and people that work against government ideology takes on a more 'sinister role' and subsequent potential punishment i.e. whistle-blowers (these really are not liked by government – if Hillary Clinton had her way the WikiLeaks founder would be assassinated by now).

It does not matter who the enemy is, just like it does not matter who the nation's friends are; it is merely about the economy and what would make the best investment for the main shareholders (oligarchs). It is quite possible if there were no governments in the world and everyone concentrated on their closest environment, there would be no wars i.e. the majority would not be coerced or forced to fight for a group of power hungry people who was themselves protected from the devastation of war; there would probably just be localised conflict about land just as there has always been. But there is and government is in control of all the nations land, finances, police, and armed forces besides directly influencing what people think and do by a number of indoctrination systems in place – for decades the government's enemy has been sold as living in or originating from foreign lands or is it.

The issue government now has is people have become so malleable to being indoctrinated into a narrative that when government decides to create an enemy with stories that unite against an assailant, with migration being what it is, mainly due to the West destabilising foreign countries, the 'enemy' is now not located in foreign lands. It is a significant shift in human political behaviour that, due to poor quality politicians, they have not accounted for and to some degree has created some uniformity and intolerance. This is major 'backfire' that the all-Western governments are 'firefighting' and has led not to unity but to countries which are divided. A system which governments have used for centuries to control the population, due to mass migration and globalisation, has now begun to fail.

People are living in interesting times where the usual call to arms by the 'poor quality' leaders is leading to segregation and internal conflict within nations. Leaders are unable to fathom why or come up with a justifiable plan to reverse this unique trend, consequently, they are amending legislation, arming police with military spec equipment to protect areas of economic prosperity, politicians and VIPs not against the 'enemy' but to protect the avenues of power from the people of the nation and to enforce subservience (just like times of old).

Now more than ever the term 'enemy' takes on a whole new meaning for government; who the enemy is and how they are portrayed requires a greater deal of significance for governments to maintain control not only of the country but of their power-base. The lack of critical thinking attributes given to people by the education system has uniquely back fired against the 'poor quality' leaders in government. The new enemy is both within the nation's borders and outside it with no significant way of separating the 'enemy' or an effective manner to control or manipulate people's minds as the proverbial 'train has left the station' with this government threat story. Every strategy government has used to unite the nation has failed and seen more people turn against the establishment. Good quality politicians and business leaders should realise a story is only as good as the background environment it is set in and over the past 20-30 years the background environment in all Western countries has changed significantly and so should have the stories about 'enemies'.

It is unlikely any country will unite against a 'common' human enemy ever again (unless mass deportation materialises) and the stories from established government will have to be more intelligently thought out if it is to remain part of a relevant power in society. Nevertheless, I do hope government(s) evolve into an administration department only and gives people back their freedom and choices thus give strength and incentive to cease all occupations and wars in foreign lands. It does not excuse actions that have been done in the name of all people in the country, but, it would start the path to a 'steadfast' peace between different part of the world and the realisation that different cultures based on diverse religions will always be inherently incompatible with current Western philosophy.

The Media Influence

For an open debate regarding national and world events, the free flow of information and alternative viewpoints is crucial for open debate and countering propaganda that is selling one message (that may not necessarily be the 'whole' truth). For too long, mainstream media has concentrated power into too few hands, including the BBC, and it is damaging society's chance of true democracy by not presenting the real truth to the public. The media plays on the emotions of people for a selfish purpose to influence opinion and policy makers. To a certain extent media has a unique role in deciding outcomes of elections or new legislation and it is for that reason why the only involvement with government should be to ensure, even if it will damage the reputation of politicians, undiluted news is given to the public.

If a national media company is posting coverage selling one viewpoint, whilst another national or international foreign new organisation is covering the same story but with a different message being presented, then various excuses are often used such as propaganda or fake news. However, it is clear both countries (or more) are guilty of spreading, not the truth, but a version of it to the public. Disproportionate coverage of news stories is driven by economic bias rather than political bias, but economics and government are uniquely interrelated. Pre-existing fame and the ability to generate controversy also holds the media attention, for example, if Trump was not so controversial news networks would closely follow Hillary Clinton's election campaign more, as is happened only CNN concentrated their efforts here.

Business opportunities also drive news coverage by attracting partisan audiences, which reflects political biases so instead of straight talking news bulletins there is context and analysis featuring statistics and possible truths with interviews with so called 'experts'. Phycology also plays a role in news coverage. Government realise that indoctrination is important to ensure people will tend to seek out news reports that do not challenge what people believe about the world, thus, creates an ideological bias which news networks perpetuate views on. Photos are important to present to the viewer, a photo can speak a thousand words, but, a photo accompanied by uniquely edited bulletins can convey emotions, realism and credibility to propaganda news. The images are for a lasting impression in the mind of the viewing public, i.e. images of North Korea testing missiles with bulletins vilifying the leader has made people believe they are a threat to peace without any evidence to support the claims, even though Western countries test missiles (even nuclear) in various parts of the world on a regular basis and is completely unreported in mainstream media outlets.

One of the most noticeable developments in news is fact-checking and has been made famous by the US election of 2016. Many new software companies have jumped on the proverbial 'band-wagon' and developed their own algorithms and tools to not only make predictions about election outcomes but also to check numbers given by politicians with real data and generate polls that can influence voter perceptions. The whole problem with tools like this is fact checking statistics is a bit like saying statistics tells a true story of real events; statistics prime job, despite what all mathematicians say, is to manipulate real data into selling a story that satisfies a hypothesis someone wants to be true irrespective to what the real data shows. In which case, fact checking tools and polling data can influence opinion based on a set of hypothesis that media moguls wants to present to the public; and media moguls are usually donors to political parties. This can add more coverage to news stories and possible election candidates to produce an incessant cycle of coverage topics to manipulate people's opinions and obtain 'buy-in' to the message being presented.

To add to the problem, news media, especially journalist, are presented as those who are watchdogs of democracy and finders of the truth. There needs to be some agency whose prime directive is to monitor the workings of power and deliver the truth to the public, but, I seriously doubt any national news network is capable of delivering this directive; it would work against their business model. The business model relies of keeping partners and customers happy and government is one of the largest partners and customers' media moguls have to retain to keep their business profiting and lighten their tax burdens; therefore, it is in their best interests to work with government when presenting news stories to the public. Occasionally, some news networks present news that does not shine a bright light on politicians, i.e. expenses scandal; so occasionally real journalism does slip through the cracks. This notwithstanding, in the UK, the outcome of the expense scandal footage saw one of the most popular newspaper outlets close and cause a delay in Rupert Murdock's takeover of Sky – a punishment for releasing the truth, perhaps? If anything, it was a warning from government that there will be possible retaliation on any news media outlet who publishes truth about the shady dealings of government officials.

However, the relationship between mainstream media and government has to work for mutual benefit. Despite the wealth of the media moguls, the government has considerable influence over their operational processes; it is why the same news report in one national news network sells one viewpoint and in another country a different network sells a different viewpoint on the same story. These viewpoints are driven by the country's government's national interests to ensure, as much as reasonably practical, people are influenced to believe their own government's viewpoint. News coverage is also the most influential interface to spread fear among the majority and to induce the public to look towards the government for protection and security. How is democracy or truth supposed to work if the public is being presented with opposing views and absent of full context?

Elections are most certainly won or lost by the power of news coverage and there is a possibility that outcome of wars also rely on the power of news 'buy-in'. Either way, the national news can be and most certainly is used as a powerful propaganda machine for supporting certain political parties and unsavoury government decisions whilst spreading the message of justification to the public. Media, especially news media, has to be separated from the control of wealthy moguls and government with regulation insisting on reporting the truth, the whole truth, and nothing but the truth. Maybe then, government and its affiliates can be held accountable for decisions that do not work in the best interests of the public or respect for human life.

Moreover, the public should not be expected to pay for a media outlet without having a say in how it is run, and how much presenters, executives or stars are being paid. Likewise, it would not be fair if everyone at the BBC (or other government funded network) had their salary published when other people's salary are not. Therefore, the government should abolish any and all TV licences and inform the managers of the news networks that, like other TV channels, they have to gain funding via advertising.

There also needs to be legislation preventing any government representative from initiating a relationship with any news network manager and work towards removing one large network organisation owning several channels. Thus, by separating the media from wealthy moguls and government, news networks have more of a chance of being an independent free reporting news media channel and would put more money back into the purses of the public.

(12)

TIME FOR CHANGE

Regrettably, people are gradually evolving into an over sensitive, easily offended, quite dumb, greedy and stupid species, just like the human race depicted in the film Idiocracy, which procreates at will without thought of the consequences. Who wants or only shows the will to follow but at the same time whinges and protests about little issues based on gossip or social tweets without any substantiating evidence. It is really depressing and disappointing, not to mention all human-kind should be ashamed, to see this happen in real time.

Fortunately, the human race has now reached a level of intelligence that it should be possible to align knowledge with our consciousness to enable a change in the way people live so people can benefit from the many diverse ways we see ourselves and the global world. So much so people should be capable of thinking and behaving in a manner to achieve higher levels of awareness. If people try, all in society can genuinely shake ourselves awake from the blistering sleep we currently live in now and evolve into a more conscious species and a more powerful force for good. Thus, stop worrying about outcomes of football matches, balance sheets, stock markets, celebrities and soap-operas and instead re-evaluate who we are and where we want to go as a species (you know! Stop to ask ourselves what the truly important questions in life should be that have been too dangerous to ask previously through fear or indoctrination).

It is clear, as a people we have to put to rest ancient traditions in all the sense of the word and 'grow-up' as a species before it is too late. Among those 'things' should include ceasing to worship non existing mythological Gods and come to the realisation that due to an accident of nature, call it evolution or something else, we have been born on this world and have only one life and this life should be filled with enjoyment and happiness with the drive to learn as much as we can before the inevitable end of our mortal lives. We should strive to learn from mistakes our own species have made throughout history and endeavour not to make them again. We should also strive to respect other forms of life and learn as much as we can about how and why they exist without interfering in the natural habitat of other creatures.

Many lives are wasted by merely living to exist and this not only explains those who choose not to work for a living and not to work on improving themselves, but, also those people who do work hard for a living in a job that does not challenge them and would not hesitate in leaving if they have the resources to do so. Think about it, what kind of life is it – doing a job you do not like wanting to retire just so you can escape the dullness of working life; this is the essence of wasting a life away – and most of us, due to indoctrination from birth, live a life like this. Let us face facts, you go to school where you grow up with the continued message of 'what job do you want to do when you are older?' and come out a young adult just smart enough to work the machines and fill out the paperwork; to then work your entire life and give most of what you earn to others; to then retire with your body too damaged or weak to really enjoy some freedom with little hobbies or interests.

Throughout this working life the odds are you will have had several relationships that have not worked out (and had to deal with the repercussions) and sometimes involving children, which you help indoctrinate into the same type of life as the one you are/have lived even though there has been little real enjoyment throughout the years. Only to end up sitting on a couch watching television wondering what your own life was really about waiting for the inevitable whilst seeing your pension pot raided and the cost of living forever increasing with poorer health care than you experienced as a child. This is, unfortunately, the very essence of a wasted life when it should have been filled with more good times than bad; whilst being filled with the sense of fulfilment knowing that you have succeeding in life as an intelligent, knowledgeable and free human being having lived a life full of choices that were your own not based on a foundation of society driven by the elites (oligarchs).

All people have one life on this planet and everyone should make the best of it and enjoy all that planet earth has to offer (I think the wealthy among us has a more fulfilling life than the vast majority). The majority of people are comfortable following direction from those above, i.e. government, but, as a people we can no longer afford to be followers. For thousands of years the majority have been followers, some through fear and slavery, other through the lack of drive, and others due to laziness – this only benefits those at the top of the financial pyramid and/or tyrants. These people use their status and contacts to subvert democracy for their own benefit at the cost of everyone else and people continuously just carry on with life accepting this as 'just the way it is'. There has been little change in how society works since medieval times – those with money have the ability to get resources in order to keep the majority under control and with the ability to manipulate poorer people's actions for self-gain.

The point is, ever since the birth of civilisation there has always been the established elite in society and it really does not matter what era or year in history is examined the 'status-quo' has always been in existence, along with the unwavering and harsh crackdown on those who disobey the law set by the elites in society. Leading to the majority who are fearful of retaliation or not having the guts to stand-up to the small, but resource rich people of the elites; and so throughout the generations people have become unhappy followers who just accept ever worsening conditions. It is time for people to use their own minds and individuality to stop being obedient, subservient followers of politicians who proclaim themselves to be rulers of the country even though a democracy is about the people being in control of their own destinies.

People should no longer accept governments, the corporatocracy or banks being a law unto themselves nor accept or be manipulated by what the established elites want us to do. People in society should have the right to make their own rules with which to live by and be highly motivated in becoming involved in decisions that affect their own lives; and thus prevent those at the very top of the pyramid (the 1%) being allowed to control the quality of people's lives. This is the message this book is attempting to portray – be leaders in your own right, do not be followers; have the gall to stand-up and be counted to make sure your own life is filled with fulfilment and enjoyment, not regret or depression; do not live your life in the pursuit of money as money is created by man is controlled by man and is what enslaves us all and holds back the progress of humanity.

Secondly, people must learn the futility and the suffering that comes with poisoning ourselves. There is an unnerving pattern of people, to get through the misery of present daily life, to use chemicals to poison our bodies and minds just to cope with society's fallacies. Another reality check is if people feel the need to take something to make them feel better in their life, there is something wrong with the way they are living and their thought processes; and the underlying problem has to be solved not made worse. This problem is even at school level where children behave not as themselves in order to be in a group whose leader is more confident and gives other children a false sense of belonging. As a species, we have to educate our children and ourselves to not behave as someone we are not just to 'fit-in'; as a society, we have to reject pretending to behave as someone we are not just to be popular, and promote being confident in who we are as an individual. Society should de-emphasise the pressure to be academically gifted and place emphasis on what makes someone special, in this way the burden on children to succeed can be lifted and concentration can then be diverted to the acquisition of knowledge and thus learning more about the world around them and growing skills best suited to their own interests.

As a civilisation, people should not forget about how our action, our population needs and greed affect nature. There is a distinct lack of concern about nature and great emphasis on greed and money; the attitude at the moment is 'whatever is cheaper and can achieve more profits with little or no concern about the environment'. There should be fresh emphasis in giving knowledge to young children about respecting nature and how our actions are destroying some of the natural wonders of the world in the hope this will help change bad habits in the future. The understanding that without other life on this planet our own survival is at risk is something that should be continuously taught throughout childhood along with the critical aspects of the balance of nature, the bees, bugs, microscopic life that are needed to keep our existence going; thus, giving the correct and factual message that poisoning habitats will eventually lead to us poisoning ourselves. Lessons learned from human complacency and greed with respect to nature is easy to be found, but, is not talked about nearly enough as it should and the curriculum should be open to subjects more related to protecting other species of life, from plants to mammals.

Since WW2, there has been a drive from all governments and military leaders to develop more devastating weapons to use on the battlefront because of paranoia and distrust of other countries. We surely do not learn from our mistakes in history! Society should not stand-by and let military technology be developed for the express purpose of killing. There are enough weapons in the world today that causes so much human suffering all seemingly for the purposes of greed and profit. In the past, if a leader wished to take control of land and resource, the solders would have to invade the land and fight hand-to-hand, but not anymore. With most people being obedient, subservient followers, the leaders (oligarchs) of the country use the capability of the modern armed forces along with soldiers who mindlessly follow orders without question to cease control of that resource, especially when there is little resistance – it could be said this is a coward's way, unlike that of the past. The bottom line is, at this moment the human race has become a greedy unconscious (showing no will to analyse our own actions) species and we are forever trying to feed our greed, and to hell with the consequences. As a species, we cannot do this anymore; there are too many people on this planet and dangerously dwindling resource availability.

Eventually, once the 'lights do go out', people might find the vast majority of us have no knowledge or skills with which to survive and as a species will default back to a time in history when we fought amongst ourselves for those precious resources that we are presently using irresponsibly. Currently, we are at a tipping point, there are enough resources on this planet to feed us, clothe us, and keep us warm and to provide food for us to consume. But, if people continue with greed and the current level of breeding habits, the planet will no longer be able to cope with all aspects of life. The current system of genetically modifying crops or spraying crops besides using chemicals to improve yields is only a temporary solution and is working towards poisoning ourselves with the very chemicals used to help feed all of us; the chemicals are a contributor toward cancer (the richest among us do not have this affliction). Do we really want this as a species? Not only this, the pressure to produce enough food for all has the emergent property of over farming the land, thus, destroying the lands natural ability to sustain life; once this happens no amount of genetic manipulation could grow crops on the land for some time.

Any intelligent lifeform would not want to purposely poison themselves just so they could carry on feeding themselves. People need to be responsible in our actions and sacrifice what we want for the greater good of society. We need to think of the future, four generations into the future, and attempt to imagine what life will be for them if population numbers continues to increase and the numbers of wars subsequently increase to cease control of those ever more important resources. One thing is for sure, if the majority continue to follow and breed at high rates, all that will be left is war, famine, disease and pestilence; and this will be the reality for human life in the future. It is now time for us, in this critical point in human history, to lead by example and show ourselves that we are indeed an intelligent species worthy of existing and can make a change in our habits, attitudes and beliefs.

As for our current 'poor quality' leaders and oligarchs, the current system society have today suits their purposes, but is so short sighted; people have to firmly believe that eventually once life becomes too hard for the poor, the 'peasants will revolt' and they will come after what the wealthiest possess. They will have no choice, no option and therefore no fear and once this happens the rules will change and a new game starts; I really do not think all the money in the world will make much difference at that stage. The established elites in society have to change their habits, reduce greed and compromise on lifestyle choices to be all in it together to share in societies benefits. Unless, the elites do things in the best interests of the majority of people, the people will go after them and the chances are they will show as much conscious, caring, and morals as the elites have shown the majority of people throughout the years; and everyone knows the lack of compassion shown by the elites when they are looking to make money and profits, i.e. wars, civilian deaths, mass murder, mass poisoning, promotion of poverty, etc.

The manner in which the majority is governed has to completely change and needs to be as drastic as rewriting the societal foundations of government, otherwise the majority of people without much wealth will eventually fall well below the poverty line and the systems in place will abandon them to homelessness and ill health before any uprising begins. It will not be an instant decline but a gradual decline year on year and it will be a planned decline to ensure the wealth of the richest in society.

Many years ago the established elites realised on the conception of the modern banking system that people will not accept changes on a dramatic fashion (quick, overnight change). The elites realise it takes many decades to make the majority 'buy' into new techniques and governing strategies, i.e. it took over three decades of clever marketing for people to trust banks enough to place money into them and to change from real solid physical gold and silver into counterfeit notes; change to people's habits comes with time and clever marketing strategies. What has happened now is the richest people in the world, since the end of WW2, have made gradual changes to the systems that benefit them at the expense of the majority. This has led to the increase in inequality and the pursuit of money at any cost leading to poorer health care, poorer standards of living and a massive migration movement to keep salaries low. Throughout these changes, massive marketing campaigns have been assumed to present to people that immigrants are good for the country and that capitalism is good for the economy and everyone.

In recent times, there has been a 'blame game' between politicians and corporate businesses due to the fall in safety, security and wellbeing in the country. The reality is the majority of people are forced to give more to pay for bills or to bailout banks or other companies; what is happening is a planned movement of money up the pyramid from the poor to the rich (there will always be a cyclic boom/bust economy with the fractional reserve system - a system based on fraud).

To protect our health and security the system has to fall before the majority do. No longer can the majority keep on voting in elections for the 'same all thing' because of the media demonization of other smaller parties. The way in which the world is progressing there is not going to be much freedom left for our future descendants if the majority keep standing idle and accept changes to the detriment to the quality of life. Society is now being separated from the rich in towns and cities all over Westernised countries with raising taxes and new taxation leaving larger housing for those more 'better off'. Government needs to have the guts, gall, honour and commitment to work for the majority of people in the country rather than working for their own selfish interests (financial) with the corporatocracy. People are seeing a gradual fall in freedoms and financial security that is accelerating because of the realisation the banking system, set in place in the 1800's, is now over inflating and failing, thus, the elites are doing their best to ensure they have enough resources to survive the next great depression. People need to realise the current capitalist economy is nothing more than a Ponzi scheme that will/is imploding on itself and is unsustainable.

There is desperation in regions where natural resources are to be found in the fight for control and to acquire profits; in foreign countries this has led to civil wars and instability. These wars are the last attempt by Western powers to control resources after pressure on foreign governments has not created a 'puppet' government; and forced leadership change or assassination has failed to produce results. The people in these countries are oppressed and slaughtered (purposely or by collateral damage) one way or the other using people in the armed forces whom follow orders without question or remorse and/or some torture other human beings for their own entertainment (the irony is the mass media has indoctrinated Western people praise these soldiers as heroes), and has caused the rise of 'terrorist' cells that hate Westerners.

How much longer will of the majority of people in Western countries 'stand idly by' while the oligarchs cause so much chaos and devastation in the world. The truth is society have to let the current system of ruling government 'burn, die, fold in on itself, lay to rest, etc.' in order for a chance of peace in the world. The new world deserves a new system to rise using the strengths of capitalism, the strengths of socialism, and the strengths of communism to create a social governing system that actually listens to people, respects people and ensures concentration to the prime directive of government – to ensure the safety, security and wellbeing of people in the country. Moreover, large corporate interests should be relegated and placed into the 'nice to have' category when government decisions have to be made; otherwise, continuing with the current system of governing will severely affect the lives of people who have not even been born yet.

People come across 'forks in the road' in life that require a decision to be made, most decisions are based on financial considerations or from information received from mainstream media, so much so that we ignore our own doubts and questions within our subconscious and defer, just as society for centuries have deferred, to the common message/narrative given by governments. These doubts, or headlines, hint at the association between governments, banks, and big corporations (the oligarchs). We all feel as though the wars in the Middle East are more about resource control than the 'war on terrorism'. People turn a blind eye whilst Western engineering and construction firms clean up the mess made by Western bombs all paid for by tax payers to rebuild countries in the Western image among native people who in all likelihood do not wish to have no choice but to live in that image (data shows that bombing cities and then rebuilding them demonstrates a spike in economic growth). We fight our own conscious belief that there is an elite band of people behind the politicians who are 'pulling the strings' causing the chaos in the world, abusing their privileges and perverting true democracy because it denotes that to fix the system these people need to be removed from interference. It also hard to look at one's self and realise that we are all responsible for the rise and continued support of these people due to our consumerist ways and changing means drastic action is required that will affect our way of life (each individual will be required to change their ways).

Our subconscious feeds into conspiracy theories and we all like 'thing' in our lives to forget about the misery of daily life and thereby provides a convenient opportunity to switch on the TV, message people on social networking sites or play games on consoles to forget all about what the voice inside our heads is trying to tell us. Thus, being pacified in our indoctrinated view of history, which continues the narrative of waiting until the next general election to vote for change, whilst concurrently continue to vote for the same old thing and 'cross our fingers and hope for the best'.

The true story of the modern economic global powerhouse is a mere continuation of the old slave trade, but, this time exploitation of people, sometimes desperate people, to feed a most brutal, self-serving and ultimately self-destructive search for resource to make profit for the few at the top. The truth is barely told in main stream media outlets and what we are told is that greed and consumerism is good as it provides jobs and prosperity for all, and for decades we have all believed it more than we have taken notice of our subconscious. The problems in the world has little to do with politics but has a lot to do with each and every individual in society who sits back and allows this destructive behaviour to continue. I suppose this is why people have such a difficult time listening to themselves and the real story behind the ever increasing resource grab (for luxuries) at any cost that ultimately gives us the gift of distraction from real life events. We have convinced ourselves that economic growth (i.e. GDP figures) benefits all of human kind; that the greater the figure the better the benefits; and politicians actions are morally justified although at the same time ethical reprehensible. The real account of modern day acceptance (the fact that we are all living a lie); denotes people have created a virtual reality that hides a devastating cancer beneath the surface that is slowly eating away at our ethics, morals and intelligence; but, we pass it off as just a conspiracy in our own heads driven by indoctrination from a young age.

Yet, we cry out for change without having a coherent plan or knowledge of how to achieve this change we so desperately need as a species, whilst staying quiet and unheard. We consistently moan and complain about real issues though keep feeding the problem by voting for the same old thing, keep being bamboozled by fear mongering and demonization, accepting more taxation, ever growing costs at the same time as poorer services, worsening infrastructure and a growing sense of cultural indifferences that we are all waiting till it explodes into violence and unrest. The oligarchs depend on the fraud and corruption of big banks, corporations and governments; the oligarchs are not a conspiracy, the data and common sense logic shows this is not the case; the corporatocracy (the largest partner) is not just big business it is ourselves who feed it. People make it happen by purchasing things they do not need or want on a regular basis to make them feel better about themselves. Most of us work for the corporatocracy and depend on it for goods and services they provide; and is why most of us find it difficult to stand up and oppose it. We cannot attack or bite the hand that we firmly believe feeds us.

The systems in place provide homes, jobs, food, health care, fuel, clothes, and utilities for Western civilisation and concurrently in the shadows within foreign lands create a world that for many is a fight for life and death and with it an increasing hatred for the West and its values. How can anyone defend a system that necessitates such suffering for the advantages of others? That is the question we should all ask ourselves and then, hopefully, manifest the courage to 'step out of line' and challenge the concepts, procedures and legislation that through indoctrination we have accepted as civilised society, which we know deep down inside is driven by government propaganda describing democracy and capitalism that in actuality is deceit, greed and eventually, if not checked, self-destruction.

People base the way we vote on our easy to access media, which is part of the corporatocracy – is it any wonder why society does improve for the majority? The media, schools (including colleges and universities) and law enforcement know their place, they are taught to immortalize, reinforce and inflate the system they have inherited through the threat of losing their jobs and with it all they have gained; and they are efficient at spreading the message. If the authorities are opposed they can be ruthless as in the Western world ink on paper if far more powerful and influential than a 'gun to the head'.

People need to take a chance and vote for something new after accomplishing a thorough investigation into what the people who represent the party stand for and stop falling for the ease in which the established elites can demonize through media outlets. Suggestions in this book raise some important and ethical considerations when voting for new government in a democracy, i.e. more power to the people and removing the advantages of the wealthiest in society to pervert democracy. As for the banks and corporations, there is nothing inherently wrong with them they just need to be managed not only by a unbiased government for the people through regulation (or deregulation), but, also by each and every single one of us. People can no longer take a blind eye or look the other way when various methods are used to maximise profits for stakeholders. We must listen to our subconscious and not ignore it by pacifying ourselves with other distractions; if your life is miserable, change it; do not take a drug to cope with it. Trust in established politics has to be removed and changing of the 'old guard' actioned. In essence, we must give in to wisdom, open our hearts and minds and become conscious about the world around us and how our actions, and the actions of governments and businesses, affect others throughout the world, and then take action to cease wars, famine, and economic slavery globally.

People should not concern ourselves about reaching higher in the financial pyramid and thus stature, we should be working to demolish it and with it greed, the need to exploit desperate people and the pillaging of the planet to feed our 'comfort' addictions.

We need to stop being slaves to a system we know is unfair, unequal and unbalanced and put pressure on those who make decisions to break away from politics as usual and concentrate on 'things' that really matter and give power back to people by providing a better education with which to handle life's issues. Real change has become a 'battlefield' not with weapons but with minds and people need to have the strength to fulfil the conviction to make the future a better place for all. The self-proclaimed leaders of the world will not change their habits; they know which way their 'bread is buttered'. Moreover, it is time to take control of our own destiny rather than be puppets of all who represent the oligarchs; it is time to ask the important questions of ourselves of how to move forward and alter the cycle of doom and gloom.

However, power is not where you think it is; people all over the world have just accepted the status quo not willing to be involved or stand-up to those who are. Ask yourself – "with all the destructive weapons in the world, with nations feeling free to invade other countries without justification, with leaders walking away from unlawful and illegal acts around the world; starvation, mass killings, ritual deaths, wars in countries throughout the world with corporations profiting from all these actions and people who feed the corporations suffering the consequences" - is this a world we really want to perpetuate or ignore. If this is the way in which people want to accept life, then you are subjecting the future and other forms of life to further suffering that will eventually lead to human-kinds self-destruction.

It is time to change, stop being manipulated by clever marketing and have the strength and motivation to connect with 'real' reality. People need to take a risk, fight on the battlefront to be counted and respected; and most of all be free so you are the only person who can affect your own life – take power back from the oligarchs and use it to do some good for yourself and others. Then maybe, just maybe, the problems of the world will not seem to be unsurmountable once everybody has a choice in the real issues that affect society and life in general. Forget about small issues and inconveniences, take action on the larger ones and most of all do not let the wealthiest in society walk away from their responsibilities and unethical actions.

It is time to change all our ways!!! Or give up and wait for the inevitable to happen.

Religion

To help us 'grow' as a species we need to turn our backs on religious mythology and ideology (including gender identification) for one very good reason – it distracts ourselves from living our lives. People who are very religious and thus follow the religious texts and doctrine to the best interpretation of the texts are sometimes labelled as terrorists or extremists. The two main religious books were created from the work started from step-brothers, one brother from wedlock and one created from an affair. The religion created from the son born from the wife became Christianity and the other became Islam; hence, they are very similar books with the same God – one could assume these brothers spent a lot of time together with one altering the works of the other slightly to produce a marginally different message to distinguish between the faiths.

Unlike the Quran, the Christian book has been altered since its conception to spread a different message to the Old Testament. The disciples realised that people after many conflicts and suffering were not accepting what was the cruel God described within the Old Testament, so they decided to bring some elders together and rewrite the book to describe a more forgiving God (a book that was written from the word of God (allegedly), was now being rewritten by human prophets?). Whereas, the message of the book of Islam remains almost identical to the original with the exception that the passages are more from word of the prophet Mohammed than the word of Allah (i.e. Mohammed-ism). Thus, the people who follow the texts completely have a main goal of wiping out people who worship other Gods or people who have turned their backs on Gods completely – the infidels (although there are many different interpretations of the texts). Whereas, the New Testament has replaced a brutal unforgiving God for a caring and forgiving one. The message any person can conclude is although God is perfect in every way, God completely changed who it was to something with a completely different world view. It is not very likely an omnipotent being would change personality so quickly because of a species it itself had created; and is now far too busy or self-important to become involved in human matters even if its creation is heading to a path of self-destruction.

As a species, we have to forget about this utter rubbish; religion is nothing more than an obscene, manmade fairy tale just like every other God our species has worshiped since the dawn of time. The truth is humans have always worshiped Gods because we are attempting to make sense of our own existence and look towards a higher power due to not knowing how we came into being. People need to accept that our existence is nothing more than an accident of nature and is due to many coincidental astrometric incidents that occurred many years before any life existed on this rock we call earth. The mixture of proteins and other chemicals created basic cellular life, which then evolved over millions of years into more complex life forms; hence the theory of evolution.

The irony is most people who label themselves as religious, do not follow the teachings of the religious doctrines; with most forgetting or ignoring all the barbaric, unbelievable (talking burning bush, flying snake, Noah's ark, etc.) and cruel passages and cherry pick the moral and ethical passages, which then get interpreted to suit people's own mind-sets. Meaning these people are not actually religious, they just believe some passages in the books are heinous and/or make-believe and thus dismiss them without a second thought. Hence, as a people most of us are not religious, we just like to think ourselves as such (well except those who think they're going to receive 24 virgins for killing people) for ethical and moral standing and to believe there is something else (a better existence) other than this one life.

Religion has been the cause and a reason used to instil control onto vast groups of people throughout history; it is time we all stopped being hypocrites and realised there is no higher power and start to find out who we are as people rather than living a life completely lost and confused by our existence. People have to come to the realisation that this what we have right here and now is us, call it an accident if you like, and we have to make the most of it and stop wasting our life thinking there is something better in what we have been told is the afterlife. People need to live this short life, make it count and stop being distracted by thinking we have to suffer and be tested in this life to live another in eternal happiness.

It is unsurprising that in the most religious parts of the world the people are either the most oppressed (incur the most suffering) or the most likely to commit acts of terror. Religious people just need to 'wake-up' and take control of their own destiny and lives; and start believing in themselves rather than a mystical entity and a doctrine written in a far distant past by primitive people.

Religious (and democratic) states are always in conflict, but, what if we had a state or society that turned it back on theocracy and religion instead adopted the teachings and philosophy of Titus Lucretius Carus, Democritus, Galilleo Galilei, Herbert Spenser, Charles Darwin, Bertrand Russel and Thomas Paine and other scientific philosophers and logisticians. Make the work and what these people stood for be the foundation for knowledge acquisition and echo the motivation for learning how our world works for our children and we make that scientific and rational humanism our teachings and see if that state and country falls into tyranny, slavery, famine and torture. Humans, as a species, would then see that the idea of worship, credulity, servility, slavery to religion, our indoctrination into how society works and how our present democracy is set-up (a few people setting rules and laws in society) where bad ideas to begin with in the first place. (Adapted from the philosophy of Mr. Hitchens)

Climate Change

There is something happening to the world's global temperatures, but, we are not the cause of it. Humans are contributors to what is a cyclical astronomical event that the earth and sun has gone through many times before in its history. The impacts of climate change are seen by everyone via severe flooding, droughts, unpredictable weather, temperatures, etc., and is a principal concern when it relates to our own security. There is clearly little we humans can do to prevent the inevitable change the earth is going through, but, there are ways in which we can slow the process down and educate the future generations on how to cope with the impacts.

Reducing our global emissions is the main goal, but due to our current way of life, it is going to be very difficult to achieve. Society have already received so many contradictory advices from academic research on how to improve air quality and reduce pollution (re: fiasco regarding diesel engines), and the government has begun with renewables (for the benefit of rich land owners and the royal family). The probability of reaching zero emissions by the second half of the century is an impossible task due to our addiction to power and with it fossil fuels. Nuclear energy has been declared one of the cleanest energies to use, however, more nuclear means more waste which cannot be easily disposed of and would most likely cause more of a catastrophic problem in the future. The other issue is climate change is 'hitting' the poorest people the hardest with price increases to reduce usage of certain fuels causing premature deaths and increase in poverty. Clearly, the draconian art of increasing prices to reduce usage, although affective, is only placing the burden on the people who need it the most. The rise of third world countries into coal power (china has used coal to rise to the largest economic country of our time) has only increased the problem of global warming and air pollution; and the problem is only growing.

The Government cannot and should not restrict the growth of another country using the same method as the British did many years ago during the industrial revolution, nor can people be arrogant enough to declare that if as a country we can reach zero-emissions (impossible) then problem solved. More technologically developed countries need to work with other countries to help them build an infrastructure that is not reliant on fossil fuels, but, is built upon the foundation of renewables and persuade them to leave the resources in the land and create a more sustainable living. In order for us to do this we need to emphasise research in our universities to concentrate on zero-emission zero-waste generation of power like never before. Currently, universities are profit related research driven and this focus has to change to general research for zero emissions power generation for non-profit outcome. What this means is the 'can we make any money from this research' mentality has to be left behind like a bad memory and universities and government has to look towards the future for our new knowledge based economy.

It is clearly easier to physically test the outcomes of research projects in new towns and cities that are being built and this is where the 'quid-pro-quo' relationship comes to fruition. Our knowledge base should be used for our economic advantage to assist growing societies with technology and education to create a sustainable future, whilst be a proving ground for ground breaking research that can be integrated into our own infrastructure once the proof of concept has been fully validated.

Defence and the Armed Forces

'I wonder what sort of world we might have if the money used for wars were diverted to eradicating world hunger or to make basic health care available to all; whilst concurrently working to alleviate the sources of slavery (even economic slavery) and protecting nature to ensure clean air, water and all the natural things life needed to thrive.' - Author.

The prime duty of any government is the defence of the nation, but, attached to this clause is: '… and its interests'. This attachment has been used to justify certain acts by successive governments in the use of armed forces in foreign lands and this cannot and should not be allowed to continue. Thus, the prime duty of government should be in relation to its own borders and any clause should include this as a stipulation. Without this further government officials, like Blair, can abuse the armed forces and command an (illegal) invasion without discourse leading to an outcome of spreading hatred for Western people and our values (and who can argue that the victims of this act have the right to seek justice and/or vengeance, as we would seek the same in similar circumstances). Hence, government has to be obligated to act in a reasonable and responsible manner with our armed forces defending and protecting our borders and only with substantiating evidence allow for exception of this rule to prevent any further issues with false reporting from government heads on WMDs, for instance. The armed forces should not be used so government officials and leaders of governments can 'play with the big boys' and be part of a gang of bullies (the similarities between students who want to be part of school gangs and resort to bullying of others to fit in, is quite remarkable).

Military is over reliant on technology and this could be one reason why whenever the Western coalition forces take part in any military action anywhere in the world there is always many innocent civilian deaths. Advanced sensor technology could also cause real human skill to fall short of standards and allow complacency to creep into operations. People should question why other military powers, i.e. Russia, can stop, detain or kill Isis fighters or retake ownership of previously owned countries, i.e.

Crimea, without the loss of civilian life. But, the Western coalition operations consistently cause devastation and loss of innocents besides being completely incompetent and ignorant with their actions. Are people directed to believe this is just a coincidence or is it because the Western forces soldiers lack skills due to technology taking centre stage in military acquisition or is it because Western politicians and armed forces do not care about civilian deaths in foreign countries? Irrespective, one thing is perfectly clear, ethics and skills training of Western armed forces are now at a poor standard and needs to improve considerably to rejuvenate the reputation of the West globally.

However, the government should be committed to ensuring the country has a responsive high-tech armed forces with the capacity to respond to emerging threats; this needs to be managed in a controlled manner. Society cannot rely on partnerships with private companies or with international manufacturers to supply software, hardware and expertise to build the technology needed. Indeed, some of the worst project management problems have occurred through red-tape and dodgy business transactions due to people with little expertise and knowledge but a high degree of incompetence in this industry re: Nimrod, F-35, and Flight Simulator Technology.

The turnover is thought to be about £22billion a year of public money being used to purchase technology from private companies in the UK, thus many jobs are at risk to any change in procurement procedures. But, there needs to be a complete rethink on the rules and procedures that govern the training and procurement of technology to remove any abuse of public funds for greed of private contractors. All equipment should be supplied by publically own technology firms whose only business is to supply the country's armed forces with the latest innovation in technology to keep our armed forces ready and safe with concentration being upon integration, interoperability and sustainability; with it the accountability of the public for technology procurement. This should remove profiteering from buying and selling defence equipment and emerge with strict laws preventing any technology from being sold to foreign interests. No longer can the reputation of country be tarnished by supplying weapons to others who use them to kill innocent people and oppress entire nations. Society must turn our backs on these types of business deals even if it means our economy takes a short term 'hit'.

There has been an unnerving shift in how the armed forces are training and has become too over reliant on technology and software, which consistently requires updating and renewing; even the current training technology requires to have the maps updated on a regular basis at a cost of £millions with no justifiable reasons given (defence contractors spend million upon million lobbying government officials ever year). Training should keep to the basics and train human conditions (train to control natural human reactions to shock events) and cease the over reliance on technology to provide the answers, i.e. knowledge and skills before ICT.

The armed forces should not be made to purchase equipment designed purely on a computer without seeing results of prototype testing; (currently the F-35 is the most expensive warplane ever designed (on computer) and is being built even though a large number of faults both in software and hardware exist (2017); European countries are being forced, by US and NATO, to buy them for continued support against possible aggressors.) These issues have to stop and a more stringent training needs analysis has to be conducted that concentrates on technology usefulness for training and for combat, developed and managed by people with expertise and experience in the field not by academics or bureaucrats with little practical knowledge on such things as: maintenance, environmental effects, software glitches, EMF faults, etc. to prevent the government from wasting money on another F-35 or Nimrod disaster.

Thus, the heart of the country's defence strategy should focus on the men and women who have volunteered to risk their lives to defend the realm and this is where money should be concentrated upon. There needs to be a veteran's register to ensure people who have fought for the country receive proper support on leaving the service to reduce the possibility of homelessness, mental health conditions and increase their employability.

Concurrently, there needs to be more emphasis on the quality of people allowed to join the armed forces; presently, the force is full of people who follow without question, it is why personnel invaded the Middle-East and did and saw many inhumane things. There needs to be people of conscious, people who inquire about the orders given if the orders seam vague of justification and these people require support of superiors if it comes to questioning orders from above. It should lead to an armed force that is free from political manipulation for corporate gains, moreover, a more professional force that will resist innocent deaths (collateral damage) in operations. This new more professional humane force should improve the reputation of our armed forces in any overseas operation with a character for committing to peaceful resolution of conflicts between warring factions.

One of the major technical issues regarding defence and security is the vulnerability to cyber-attacks. A cyber security charter is needed that should be continually updated in line with technology refresh. It is hoped that this will reduce the likelihood of security threats and hackers breaking into vital systems and causing a catastrophic systems failure or stealing private information. In defence technology, there should be a programme of risk assessment to determine whether a system (touch screen, operating system, software architecture, etc.) is adding further risk of possible systems failure within an operational environment and if a less technological based solution is perceived to be better than the current one, then the system or sub-system(s) should be exchanged to favour a more hardened solution than something that looks 'pretty' but comes with various risks, i.e. screen cracks and touch screen operability being compromised. For security information, the data should no longer be allowed to be downloaded onto a memory stick or portable hard drive to prevent issue such as, being left on the seat of a train. Instead, the information needs to remain in secured facilities being accessed by appropriate security measures through a service oriented architecture type solution with strong encryption associated with service calls and data retrieval.

The nuclear deterrent is an expensive show piece which if used would surely be the end of the current way of life, thus the nuclear deterrent should be completely decommissioned. Along with this all foreign nuclear weapons must be removed from our country. It is time we as a species 'grew-up' about the real risks of playing poker with nuclear weapons and realised the government is willing to accept the reduced quality of healthcare, poor infrastructure and bad state of housing, just to be classed as a world super-power by having our own nuclear system. There needs to an active and increased momentum to work with world leaders on the unilateral disarmament efforts to reduce (nah eliminate) the world's stockpile of weapons – the reality is if one nation used them the likelihood is the entire world air/oceans will become polluted and it is in essence a suicidal strike that will affect all.

International Development

Throughout my years I have been impressed when the public show a consistency of – giving to charities. The strength of the public to transform the lives of people in poor countries has been the main factor for keeping faith in people. It is just a shame most charities redirect the money given to places other than that on the front-line and successive governments are redirecting public funds to areas of strategic and economic advantage for friends in private sectors. Whilst in some small scale this does help ease the problem of poverty, lack of human rights and starvation; the big picture is consistently ignored and generally the overall problem not only remains but continues to increase incurring further suffering for more people. For the government to authorise any transfer of public money from national issues into international development, there has to be a full investigation of where and how money is to be spent along with the long term projections into solving (not maintaining) the problem not which corporate business can make money from it. If projections show the money can help some people with the overall problem increasing, due to population size or civil wars, for example, then further thought is needed before any authorisation is given. As a society, we should not be in a position to help the minority at the expense of the majority – a better solution is required that works towards eradicating the problem.

The process of deciding where the funds should be allocated requires a complete re-think; no longer should the public accept vital public money to be directed towards a country that has expensive nice-to-have projects, i.e. Space Programmes and/or to countries knowingly supporting 'terrorist' groups. Money needs to go to countries that desperately need it to tackle real human issues, but, not at the expense of further suffering of people in our own country. That is to say if as a country we still have a homeless problem, people living in abject poverty and a health care system that is on its knees; then government has to be forced to reallocate money to these areas at the expense of the international development. There needs to be no standing on the international stage boasting about how much money we have given to third world countries whilst problems are still prevalent at home.

The government have to 'crack down' on corruption and ensure good governance with the groups responsible for distribution of money within international development. The government can no longer sit back and hand money over without any consideration as to how the money is to be used. For too long, a large portion of money given has been used to buy arms for rebel groups, for nice-to-have projects and to assist the World Bank in executing projects that has an economic benefit for business rather than native people. There needs to be checks and balances that accompany any financial help to give transparency to the tax payer that money is being used for the correct ethical and moral purpose. In essence, the 'party is over' for those responsible for the irresponsible financial exchanges between the country and international partners; it is time to tighten up the procedures and give accountability for cost of international development projects.

Economic Responsibility

Since the Brexit vote in 2016 the UK is on course to take an unprecedented est. £66 billion toll (perhaps more) on public finances according to the Institute for Fiscal Studies (IFS) with a weaker gross domestic product (GDP) will knock a further £31 billion from tax revenues by 2019/20. But that is not all; to account for this extra borrowing almost £15 billion is required to maintain government and its services; which will increase the nation's deficit significantly. Exactly how these 'think tanks' come up with these figures is beyond my understanding, but one thing is perfectly clear, there does not appear to be anyone in a responsible position (government, think-tank, banks, etc.) who truly knows how the economy works or how to resolve the deficit; and if you ask me I am not responsible for the countries debt problems, neither are >99% of the people living in the UK. The politicians in government and banks are responsible and whom have made substantial wealth for business owners from the decision made (i.e. lobbyists). They are the ones who set budgets, they are the ones who have authorised a drastic increase in population numbers and all the issues it brings, they are the ones who orchestrate wars in other countries to the betterment of arms dealers (sorry, defence contractors) and large corporate businesses (e.g. oil, gas, mineral, technology firms and construction industries). Why should the people in the country suffer cuts to services and increased pressure with taxes and shadow taxes?

Once I asked using the 'freedom of information' rules for information regarding who the UK owes all the money. I received a 325-page report full of numbers in tabular form, which told me nothing about where the money goes, who it goes to, or who we owe the debt too; so I asked in simple terms for a list of names, countries or banks; after 13 attempts to obtain an answer I gave up. It became clear to me this type of information is not to be fully transparent to the public. I can only assume it is a virtual debt with banks and other countries in the form of I.O.U's that are promises to pay back. All I can say is there are plenty of billionaires and multimillionaires who live in the UK, who do business in the UK, let them pay it off.

It is time people took time to care about the decisions government is making and send the message to politicians and the wealthiest in society - 'this is your problem of your own making, you sort it – stop making our lives harder. If you want to grandstand on the world stage, rage wars internationally for your corporate partners, do it on your back not ours'.

Either people can carry on in economic ignorance and hope that it might work for the majority as well as the capital cities, banks and the corporatocracy. But, the truth is people now live in an era where we are worse off than our parents or grand-parents in real terms with the health service under huge strain and faces a real threat of having all the services privatised for the financial benefit of a few, thus, incurring a further financial burden on all of society / the majority.

To turn the situation around in the health service, education, government, the banking system and every area that makes society function, society needs the right kind of people in the right positions. The problem is people who possesses honour, integrity and the correct work ethic will never be able to acquire a position where they can make a difference because they will be seen as a threat to all those in high management level positions of a company, institution, organisation, and government. This is the problem people have to cope with today. There is a desperate need to dismiss substantial amounts of people in all management levels throughout all areas and replace them with competent people, who may or may not possess or suit the current levels of qualifications of experience on their CV, just to remove the problem. The issue is it is extremely difficult to remove the problem as the wrong type of person might have a glittering CV perfectly matched to a position, but, in reality in all the experience shown on the CV there is a possibility that they have failed in each and every single position they have held (it is bad experience); a CV does not illuminate this issue nor will a reference.

Only by choosing the right people in all important areas can society change direction together. There are no promises that the problems can be solved quickly or that life will improve over night, but people can ensure the country's finances and priorities are governed and managed correctly to reduce our dependence on borrowing off others. Everyone who works for a living wants a country and an economy that works for them and not for the few (already well-off). Families require decent schools that teach more than how to pass a test and all people deserve good health care. The majority feel lock-out of major decisions that affect their lives and want a say into the decisions made by all government levels, and suggestions in this book will help. A sense of belonging and safety comes from taking control and being responsible for factors that affect our own lives, not by being followers of people in the capital who can make our lives better or worse at a drop of a hat.

People deserve a country where everyone plays by the same rules, including those with money and at the top of the capitalist pyramid we all are trapped in at the moment. A country where everyone works together to tackle the scourge of greed and misery and where the quality of life gap is eliminated for those willing to contribute to a new knowledge based economy. This requires everyone to take a stand to inform those who make decisions that the current manner in which society is managed is not the way forward. It does mean taking a risk and placing trust is each other and it will denote both public and private sectors working hand in hand to force change because those in charge do not want the avenues of power to be dispersed. But, for the sake of future generations the government has to become nothing more than a centralised administration department with negligible power of influence over people's life choices.

The time of the oligarchs and economic slavery for most must come to an end to cease further human suffering, environmental decay and to protect other forms of life. The people need to demand a good quality of life and that decisions cannot be made without the approval of people both nationally and in relevant communities. People need to have the right to live a fulfilling life, not a life cycle of school, work and death where only the rich and deceitful can enjoy life. It is time for change, but as history has taught those at the top do not want change and will not give it freely. It is up to all of society to make them relinquish their power of influence and produce a fairer, freer society and the only way to do it is to 'hit them where it hurts the most' financially. Yes, it will sting us all for a short period of time but most of us have little to lose and if communities stick together the authorities will not be able to claim it. Whereas, the people at the top have lots to lose and with it will come a large 'hit' on their ego but with it clarity and maybe, just maybe, compassion and an epiphany that a fairer freer society will prosper them as much as it will everyone else.

Fixing the World's Problems

The 'stumbling block' and every solution to the worlds' problems always focusses around money. Money is created from printing presses, it is created from chopping trees down, it is created from 'monkey' metal with various different coatings; it is not worth much physically but is expensive to create. Money has not been created by the planet; it is not created by a mythological God; it has been created by humans to make sure the people who control the money have the most of it, whilst the people who do not use their time being productive in order to make more money for the people who are highly connected to the people who control the flow of money. This system has been the same since the old kings and queens of England; and strengthened by the abolition of slavery and conception of the banking system in the 1800s whose prime responsibility is to keep money flowing upwards to the elites in society.

As money is manmade and created to maintain control of the majority in society, we as a species are delusional if we think money is going to solve problems such as climate change, resource usage, and reducing pollution levels. When investigating what money has done and what it has caused, money is on par with religion as it has caused so much human and wildlife suffering on the planet. The world's problems concern the lack of courage and will shown by everyone to make a difference and with this lack of will we have the potential of making extinct many forms of life, which includes our own at some point in the future unless we all have the courage to change.

It may not be of interest for the wealthy and the oligarchs of the world, in this generation or the next, to change their habits and consider as a priority tackling the main problems in the world that concerns the growing irresponsible nature of greed. But, those that are born after 2030 will have to live through the ramifications of a world that has been damaged by human greed. Once this happens, no amount of money will be able to bribe the planet or the climate or the non-existent mythological God that many people believe in. Therefore, the lack of will or misinformed/delusional belief in a higher power means that as a species we are accepting 'the writing on the wall' not just for ourselves but for other species of life. It is this sort of attitude that disturbs me and it should disturb everyone else because whether we want to admit it ourselves we do have the resources, the technology and knowledge to fix all the world's problems right here right now, but, lack (or have no) will.

Situations that can be solved should be solved and should not be withheld due to some manmade system. Sitting back and hoping the people in the right places in society will be able to fix the world's problems is a delusional standpoint. History has taught us there is no one in government, no one in any corporate business has any interest in solving problems unless the solution means that someone is able to make money from it. The global problems require us as a species to forget about our man made greed and use our knowledge and resources for the best interests of all life on the planet; sadly, there will be no profit to be made with these solutions.

Human civilisation have to come to terms that we as a species have abused our position and most of us have been subservient financial slaves of the people who control the money since the conception of kings thousands of years ago. Aligning with this, humans have also created Gods to believe in to pacify and indoctrinate the majority into believing that this life is only the start and we have to be tested and suffer in this life for a better afterlife. For the elites, religion is a perfect tool for control of the majority and money comes a very close second to manipulating the lives of people. We need to put all this inequality and our delusional existence under God behind us and to work together to keep our species and others alive. Yes, it will cost money if we continue to keep the current financial system in place, but, money is manmade and as such manipulated and controlled by man, therefore, money is not a factor if and when the resources and the will of the people are available to solve world problems.

Let us just get it done and worry about the accounts later.

So here concludes the book! I hope the reader admits with themselves that within the current structure and architecture of society, self-determination is indeed an enigma, a paradox if you will. Each individual's characteristics, personality and other attributes, even what individuals do their entire life is driven from decisions made by others, especially those in and behind government (i.e. the oligarchs and/or lobbyists).

After reading this book, you should conclude that it is time this scenario changed for the betterment of society and freedom.

FINAL REMARKS

Some people would disagree with some of the discussion or rationale in the book, however, research in these areas proves the information to be correct. Indeed, some may say I might become the most hated person in the world in some cultures, religions and those worshipping ideological beliefs, similar to author Salman Rushdie was on the release of the Satanic Verses, because the brief discussions in the book relate to the realities of religion (and other beliefs), who humans are and have become as a species and the veracities of government. Those who have become upset, offended or argue that the details within have set the human race back generations, I say this – the book is based on real life events, experience, official data and documents; there is nothing in the book that is not based on facts and truths. Furthermore, it is not my intention to upset or offend anyone, but, I realised this was a distinct possibility.

The human race has buried its head in the ground for generations not wanting to deal with the real problems in the world because they seem so insurmountable; instead, problems have become exponentially worse as the population increases and new technology is developed. This book, which is what I hope, will be first of a series of books, only touches (barely scratches the surface) on the problems the world faces today. Undeniably, some areas covered (e.g. banking, law, religion, military, taxes, homes, environment, addiction, parenting, and human characteristics and attributes, etc.) needs to be discussed in greater detail and I hope that I get the opportunity to delve deeper into these areas in follow-on books to give people the information they need to help critical thinking responsibilities about the real problems facing everyone so all people can work together on possible solutions.

The purpose of this book is to make people more aware of the surrounding environment and what impacts their own personal decisions - it is longer than what was intended. I hope the reader takes some of the lesson in the book and becomes driven to make a change, more so, takes the time to become actively involved in not only government but monitoring and bringing to account decisions made by 'leaders' in public and business establishments. Moreover, the book's aim is to give knowledge to the reader that there are people behind government who do indeed pull the strings; overwhelmingly, politicians are not intelligent, knowledgeable or bright enough to govern the country for the majority and definitely not for the economy. They are useful celebrities who are trained to talk and use hand gestures to sway public opinion. It is a system that has worked effectively for 100s of years and my objective with the book is to make people aware that life does not have to be influenced, driven, and manipulated by the elites 'lobbying' government for their own selfish benefit. People can now no longer afford or accept this type of governing system or the enigma of freedom.

Furthermore, I hope a lesson learned from the book is individuals are responsible for themselves and they should not be indoctrinated into ill-founded beliefs or societal systems that have been / are in place well before they were born. Likewise, true freedom and self-determination is most definitely worth fighting for, even if the battle is with ourselves.